Dynamics of Virtual Work

Series Editors

Ursula Huws
University of Hertfordshire, UK

Rosalind Gill
University of London, UK

Technological change has transformed where people work, when and how. Digitisation of information has altered labour processes out of all recognition whilst telecommunications have enabled jobs to be relocated globally. ICTs have also enabled the creation of entirely new types of 'digital' or 'virtual' labour, both paid and unpaid, shifting the borderline between 'play' and 'work' and creating new types of unpaid labour connected with the consumption and co-creation of goods and services. This affects private life as well as transforming the nature of work and people experience the impacts differently depending on their gender, their age, where they live and what work they do. Aspects of these changes have been studied separately by many different academic experts however up till now a cohesive overarching analytical framework has been lacking. Drawing on a major, high-profile COST Action (European Cooperation in Science and Technology) Dynamics of Virtual Work, this series will bring together leading international experts from a wide range of disciplines including political economy, labour sociology, economic geography, communications studies, technology, gender studies, social psychology, organisation studies, industrial relations and development studies to explore the transformation of work and labour in the Internet Age. The series will allow researchers to speak across disciplinary boundaries, national borders, theoretical and political vocabularies, and different languages to understand and make sense of contemporary transformations in work and social life more broadly. The book series will build on and extend this, offering a new, important and intellectually exciting intervention into debates about work and labour, social theory, digital culture, gender, class, globalisation and economic, social and political change.

More information about this series at
http://www.springer.com/series/14954

Ana Sofia Elias • Rosalind Gill • Christina Scharff
Editors

Aesthetic Labour

Rethinking Beauty Politics in Neoliberalism

Editors
Ana Sofia Elias
King's College London
London, UK

Rosalind Gill
City, University of London
London, UK

Christina Scharff
King's College London
London, UK

Dynamics of Virtual Work
ISBN 978-1-349-69331-3 ISBN 978-1-137-47765-1 (eBook)
DOI 10.1057/978-1-137-47765-1

Library of Congress Control Number: 2016962713

Printed on acid-free paper

This Palgrave Macmillan imprint is published by Springer Nature
The registered company is Macmillan Publishers Ltd.
The registered company address is: The Campus, 4 Crinan Street, London, N1 9XW, United Kingdom

“This highly engaging, smart, and wide-ranging collection analyzes how, under the self-governing mandates of neo liberalism, the demands that girls and women regulate and control their bodies and appearances have escalated to new, unforgiving levels.”

—Susan J. Douglas, University of Michigan, USA

“In this inspiring collection, the labor involved in creating a viable self receives detailed analysis, with each contributor showing how expectations of beauty serve to elevate or condemn.”

—Melissa Gregg, Intel Corporation, USA

“This book incisively conceptualizes how neo liberalist and postfeminist tendencies are ramping up pressures for glamor, aesthetic, fashion, and body work in the general public […] ‘Aesthetic entrepreneurship’ is bound to become a go-to concept for anyone seeking to understand the profound shifts shaping labor and life in the twenty-first century.”

—Elizabeth Wissinger, City University of New York, USA

Foreword: The Making of the Body

Bodies are made. They are made in historical time with respect to class, gender, geography, economy and aspiration. Bodies are given to us within the family where the first body emerges. How the body is seen, treated and handled will form the basis of the individual's sense of their body. There is no such thing as a body, only a body made in relationship to another and other bodies.

The body, like the psyche, is an outcome of intersubjective engagement. In late modernity, as global capitalism gathers the world into one, the making of a body takes on a form that flattens differences (although not entirely), and the making of femininity is marked by a concealment of the work of body making. This work is so integrated into the take up of femininity that we may be ignorant of the processes we engage in. In so far as we are aware of them, we are encouraged to translate the work of doing so into the categories of 'fun', of being 'healthy' and of 'looking after ourselves'. These categories are not interrogated—except by body activists—and owe much to the industries that profit from these practices. As long as the work is slipped inside of these carapaces, the commercialisation of the body gives great riches to the style, beauty, fashion, cosmetic and surgery industry. As urbanisation continues its gallop, entry into modernity is marked by the uptake of beauty practices, a shared aesthetic and the gloss of glamour.

The chapters in this collection unpick these categories and reveal the ways in which subjectivity and agency have been rethreaded to weave new narratives. The girls Anne Becker interviewed in Fiji in the 1990s who started purging after watching US TV shows on the newly established TV so as to better approximate the bodies they viewed there showed us how local cultures were being effaced. At first we saw this as the export of body hatred to the emerging economies entering global culture and of course it is, but just as women are not passive consumers but agents in their own engagement with what late capitalist consumer culture offers as a way of belonging, we listened to the Fijian girls' explanations. They wanted to be part of the new world. They didn't believe themselves to be passive consumers. Neither can it be said that countries are passive consumers. African, Asian and Latin women have their own interpretation of the neoliberal 'femininity' project and mark their own idioms on the global conversation through influencing aspects of global imagery. Meanwhile young women across the world are employed in industries that sell glamour while working in abject conditions themselves whether in the nail bars of New York or the beauty salons in Shanghai. Women's bodies have become an updated version of Fanon's Black Skins, White Masks.

But let's complicate the matter further. Let's look at another level of the construction of the body. Let's consider how bodies have come to be so available for constant transformation. What is it about the way our bodies are constituted? How have the influences of the style industries become transmuted to inside desire? How is it that the body as is, is found to be so unsatisfying that it is in need of constant attention and work?

My clinical perspective of engaging and observing bodies, bodies that are ever younger and ever older (as age compression demands that 6-year-olds look like 12-year-olds and 70-year-olds like 40-year-olds), shows that the body is unstably constituted. In order for its owner to keep it going—and I describe the body in this way intentionally as this is how my patients do—the body requires constant attention. It needs to be critically assessed, to be available for modification, for fixing and fussing with, in short to be produced. Through these actions, an unstable body is reassured that it exists. The constant attention keeps it going. A sense of needing to be done to and then doing provides a form of ongoingness to a body that feels desperately unstable. Instability is the prompt to action.

But why is it so unstable? As preoccupation with beauty has become central in the lives of women, not just for the short period, it concerned our grandmothers and their mothers, so body instability has undermined the bodies of those who mother. As celebrities display bodies with no outward sign of having giving birth within a month post partum, as even a French Minister needed to look like birth had never touched her four days after she delivered as she walked out of the Elysee Palais in high heels, as women in Brazil have a tummy tuck following a caesarean section, so we see the management of birth and post partum as simply a punctuation point on the journey of lifelong body surveillance. The body is always to be regulated according to the dictates of visual culture, not the prompts from a baby's need for the breast and for succour or the mother's need to nurture and rest.

This situation puts a new and disturbing shape to the mother-daughter structure or perhaps I should say, the mothering person. It means that the baby—who acquires her or his sense of its body through the body of those who mother—is imbibing a body that is caught in regulation and preoccupation. This regulation and preoccupation informs the mother's relating to her own body, and it also informs her relationship to her baby's body, her baby's appetites, her baby's bodily explorations and the ways in which she takes up space. The baby enters into corporeality with the bodily sense that she must be watchful. She mimics what she sees. Her body is not simply unfolding; it develops with reference to prescriptive practices and with the internalisation of criticism and self-surveillance. By the time that girl is in the playground, she will be playing with plastic surgery apps that let her transform herself as she wishes in preparation for the time when aesthetic labour will form part of her daily routine.

As the instructive chapters in this collection show, adult women live with irresolvable pressures and contradictions when it comes to the body. We must affect to look young yet appear to know about the world while seeming innocent. We must decorate and transform ourselves but look as though this is neither a time, money or labour cost. We are to appear 'natural' and 'professional' and 'sexy' and 'nonchalant' and 'available' and 'desirable' and 'cute' and 'fun' and 'capable' and 'healthy' all at the same time.

Aesthetic labour has colonised our bodies, and like all forms of labour, the meanings we make of it and of our bodies are, as these chapters demonstrate, complex. We are managing the struggle for agency and self-expression in a time of ever-increasing commercialisation of the body. This is not an easy call whether in Newcastle, Lagos, Lima, Karachi or Melbourne.

Susie Orbach

Acknowledgements

First and foremost, Yvonne Ehrstein and Rachel O'Neill have contributed hugely to this book through the careful labour of editing. We are very grateful to them both for all their work. Thank you! We couldn't have done it without you!

It was an absolute pleasure and privilege to collaborate with all of the contributors, who have not only submitted excellent chapters, but have also been really great to work with. This book would not exist without your thoughtful contributions. Thank you for writing such stimulating, insightful and original chapters.

We would also like to thank Sharla Plant and Amelia Derkatsch at Palgrave for their support and good-humoured professionalism throughout. Vinodh Kumar's editorial work was also invaluable in bringing the project to a close.

Ana Elias would like to gratefully acknowledge her doctoral studentship funded by Fundação para a Ciência e a Tecnologia (FCT) (SFRH/BD/63854/2009) and would also like to thank her friends and family for all their love and encouragement.

Rosalind Gill would like to express her appreciation to City, University of London, for a period of sabbatical leave in 2016 that helped to facilitate completion of this project. She would also like to thank Jude Willetts for her generosity and all the many ways in which she supported this book.

Christina Scharff would like to thank the Economic and Social Research Council (grant reference ES/K008765/1). The Future Research Leaders grant provided her with valuable time to focus on this project. She would also like to thank her friends and family for their love and support, particularly Charles Jandreau and Penelope Scharff Jandreau.

Finally, we would all like to express our appreciation to many feminist friends and colleagues for ongoing conversations, debates, inspirations and provocations.

Contents

List of Contributors

Maria Adamson is Lecturer in Organisation Studies at Middlesex University, UK. Her research interests include gender inequality in professional work, gendered workplace identities, business discourses, particularly self-help, and the application of feminist theories within the field of organisation studies. Her work has been published in journals like *Sociology*; *Gender, Work & Organization*; and *European Journal of Women's Studies*. Her current project explores constructions of femininity in popular business celebrity autobiographies and business self-help. She is currently a principal investigator on the ESRC-funded research seminar series *Gendered Inclusion in Contemporary Organisations*.

Sarah Banet-Weiser is Professor of Communication at the Annenberg School for Communication and Journalism at the University of Southern California. She is the author of *The Most Beautiful Girl in the World: Beauty Pageants and National Identity*; *Kids Rule! Nickelodeon and Consumer Citizenship*; and *Authentic™: The Politics of Ambivalence in a Brand Culture*. She is the co-editor of *Cable Visions: Television Beyond Broadcasting* and *Commodity Activism: Cultural Resistance in Neoliberal Times*.

Virginia Braun is Associate Professor in the School of Psychology at the The University of Auckland. She is a feminist and critical psychologist, and her research explores gender, (gendered) bodies, sex/sexuality, and health—with an interest in the ways social, scientific, and individual meanings play out. She is also interested in the *doing* of qualitative research. She is the author (with Victoria Clarke, University of the West of England) of *Successful Qualitative*

Research and numerous works around qualitative researching, including thematic analysis.

Scarlett Brown is a PhD student in the School of Management and Business at King's College London, where she is undertaking an Economic and Social Research Council (ESRC)-funded research project into how non-executive directors are appointed onto corporate boards. Her thesis examines how the concept of the 'ideal' board member is socially constructed and gendered; how aspirant directors' networking practices are influenced by gender; and how gender structures the way that they make sense of their success and failure. She is currently Senior Governance Researcher at Grant Thornton UK LLP, and a regular speaker and panellist on gender and diversity issues in the workplace.

Sara De Benedictis recently completed her PhD in Cultural Studies in the Department of Culture, Media and Creative Industries at King's College London. Her thesis explored representations and reactions to birth on British reality television. She has worked as a research assistant for Dr Shani Orgad at the London School of Economics on a project about middle-class stay-at-home mothers. De Benedictis is currently a research fellow at the University of Nottingham working on a Wellcome Trust funded project entitled Televising Childbirth. De Benedictis' research interests include birth, motherhood, class, reality television, and austerity.

Amy Shields Dobson holds a University of Queensland Postdoctoral Research Fellowship in the Institute for Advanced Studies in the Humanities, where her work focuses on youth, gender politics, and social media. Dobson's projects include research into gender and cyber-safety education, sexting in schools, and female genital cosmetic surgery. She is the author of *Postfeminist Digital Cultures* (2015), published by Palgrave Macmillan.

Ngaire Donaghue is adjunct Associate Professor in the School of Humanities at the University of Tasmania, Australia. Her research centres on ideological aspects of gendered embodiment, with a particular focus on critical feminist understandings of body dissatisfaction and beauty practices.

Simidele Dosekun is a lecturer in media and cultural studies at the University of Sussex. She has a PhD in gender and cultural studies from King's College London. A transnational feminist cultural scholar, her research centres black African women to explore questions of gender, subjectivity, power and inequality, in relation to global consumer and media cultures especially. She is currently working on a book manuscript on new styles of feminine dress and subjectivity among class-privileged, young women in Lagos, Nigeria.

Adrienne Evans is Principal Lecturer in Media and Communications at Coventry University, UK. Her main research interests lie in the area of postfeminist sentiment in the media and how these are taken up and made to feel our own. Past research has explored this in relation to sexiness and contemporary precarious feelings of being sexy; current work develops these accounts through digital culture, postfeminist masculinity, and healthism discourses. Her co-authored books include *Technologies of Sexiness: Sex, Identity and Consumer Culture* (2014) and *Postfeminism and Health* (forthcoming).

Breanne Fahs is Associate Professor of Women and Gender Studies at Arizona State University, where she specialises in studying women's sexuality, critical embodiment studies, radical feminism, and political activism. She has written widely in feminist, social science, and humanities journals and has authored three books: *Performing Sex*, *The Moral Panics of Sexuality* (ed.), and *Valerie Solanas*. She also works as a practising clinical psychologist specialising in sexuality issues.

Jane Fisher is Jean Hailes Professor of Women's Health and the Director of the Jean Hailes Research Unit in the School of Public Health and Preventive Medicine at Monash University. She is an academic clinical and health psychologist interested in public health perspectives on the links between women's reproductive health and mental health from adolescence to mid-life.

Laura Favaro is a PhD candidate in the Department of Sociology at City, University of London. Her thesis examines discursive constructions of gender, sexuality, and intimate relationships in UK- and Spain-based women's online magazines, integrating analyses of the editorial content, user forum discussions and interviews with producers. García-Favaro has forthcoming publications in the edited collection *Pornographies: Critical Positions* and in *Australian Feminist Studies* on 'postfeminist biologism'.

Dana Kaplan is a cultural sociologist, specialising in critical heterosexualities, middle-class culture, and neoliberal subjectification. She holds a PhD from the Department of Sociology and Anthropology at The Hebrew University of Jerusalem. In her dissertation, she analysed the waning of the middle class in Israel from a cultural perspective, specifically focusing on culinary, spiritual, and sexual practices of the creative class. Her current research projects focus on beauty and class, and sexy atmospheres as urban branding tools.

Maggie Kirkman, a psychologist whose research is conducted in multi-disciplinary environments, is a senior research fellow at the Jean Hailes Research Unit in the School of Public Health and Preventive Medicine, Monash University. She is the lead investigator on the research project 'Elucidating the increasing demand for genital cosmetic surgery among girls and women in Australia'. She investigates the ways in which people understand and explain the vicissitudes of life, such as infertility, donor-assisted conception, abortion, and breast cancer during the reproductive years.

Michelle M. Lazar is Associate Professor in the Department of English Language and Literature and the Academic Convenor of the Gender Studies Minor Programme at the National University of Singapore. Her research focuses on feminist/critical discourse analysis; language, gender, and sexuality; and media and political discourses. She is the editor of the series *Routledge Critical Studies in Discourse* and is currently the president of the International Gender and Language Association.

Karalyn McDonald is a psychologist and research fellow at the Jean Hailes Research Unit and the Department of Infectious Diseases at Monash University. McDonald's research has predominantly concerned understanding the increasing demand for female genital cosmetic surgery and the psychosocial aspects of living with HIV, including women's reproductive decision-making and gendered experiences of living with HIV.

Rachel O'Neill is a Postdoctoral Research Fellow in Sociology at the University of York. Her research is concerned with dynamics of gender, subjectivity, intimacy and sexual politics. Her most recent project explored these themes through an ethnographic study of the 'seduction community' in London, UK. A monograph based on this research, entitled *The Work of Seduction*, is forthcoming from Polity.

Shani Orgad is Associate Professor at the Department of Media and Communications, LSE. She writes and teaches on media and cultural representation, gender, globalisation, suffering and humanitarianism. Her books include *Storytelling Online: Talking Breast Cancer on the Internet* (2005) and *Media Representation and the Global Imagination* (2012). Her current research examines the media constructions and lived experiences of middle-class stay-at-home mothers.

Laurie Ouellette is Associate Professor of Communication and Cultural Studies and Comparative Literature at the University of Minnesota. She writes about social theory, gender, labour, neoliberalism, and media culture and is the editor and author of six books, most recently *A Companion to Reality Television* (2014) and *Lifestyle TV* (2016). Her work has appeared in a range of journals including *European Journal of Cultural Studies*, *Cinema Journal*, *Television & New Media*, and *Cultural Studies*.

Sarah Riley is a reader in Psychology at Aberystwyth University, UK. Her research is informed by a poststructuralist approach to identity, with a particular interest in gender, sexuality, embodiment, and youth cultures. Her methodological interests are in discourse analysis, co-operative inquiry, and visual methods. Her main publications include the following collaborative works: *Critical Bodies: Representations, Identities and Practices of Weight and Body Management* (Palgrave Macmillan, 2008), *Doing Your Qualitative Psychology Project* (2012), *Technologies of Sexiness: Sex, Identity and Consumer Culture* (2014), and *Postfeminism and Health* (forthcoming).

Suvi Salmenniemi is Associate Professor of Sociology at the University of Turku, Finland. Her fields of interest include political sociology, cultural studies, feminist theory, and the sociology of class and inequality. Her ongoing research investigates therapeutic technologies of happiness and self-improvement as a lens to understanding how contradictions of capitalism are lived and experienced at the level of subjectivity. She is the author of *Democratization and Gender in Contemporary Russia* (2008) and the editor of *Rethinking Class in Russia* (2012). Her work has also appeared in *The British Journal of Sociology*, *Sociology*, and *International Sociology*.

Monika Sengul-Jones is a doctoral candidate at the University of California, San Diego in the Department of Communication and Science Studies Program. She is currently a visiting graduate researcher at the University of Washington in the Department of Communication. She holds an MA in Gender Studies at Central European University in Budapest. Her contribution to this collection is drawn from her dissertation work on the gendered, socio-technical achievement of the English-language 'freelance writer' online.

Kay Souter is Associate Dean, Learning and Teaching, in the Faculty of Law and Business at Australian Catholic University. Previous roles include Director, Learning Environments, Research and Evaluation at Deakin University and Associate Dean, Academic, in the Faculty of Humanities and Social sciences at

La Trobe University. Her academic background includes 30 years of teaching English and cultural studies at La Trobe and RMIT Universities, and she is widely published in these areas. She has a special interest in the representation of the female body, post-Kleinian psychoanalysis, and organisational psychodynamics.

Shirley Anne Tate is Associate Professor of Race and Culture and Director of the Centre for Ethnicity and Racism Studies in the School of Sociology and Social Policy, University of Leeds, UK, and Visiting Professor in the Institute for Reconciliation and Social Justice, University of the Free State, South Africa. Her research interests are 'race' performativity, Black women's bodies, beauty, critical mixed race, and institutional racism.

Rachel Wood is a research associate at Sheffield Hallam University. Her forthcoming book, *Consumer Sexualities: Women and Sex Shopping*, will be published with Routledge in 2017 and explores women's everyday experiences of sexual consumption.

Jie Yang is Associate Professor of Anthropology at Simon Fraser University. She was trained in linguistic anthropology, and her current research centres on psychological anthropology. She has done research on language, privatisation, happiness, mental health, psychotherapy, and the politics of gender and class in China. Her research focuses on the aesthetic, therapeutic, and neoliberal governance in China. She is the author of *Unknotting the Heart: Unemployment and Therapeutic Governance in China* and the editor of *The Political Economy of Affect and Emotion in East Asia*.

Part I

Aesthetic Labouring

1

Aesthetic Labour: Beauty Politics in Neoliberalism

Ana Elias, Rosalind Gill, and Christina Scharff

Introduction

In 2015 the Australian teenager Essena O'Neill quit Instagram and became headline news around the world. O'Neill, who had more than 600,000 followers on Instagram, earned 'thousands of dollars' from marketers for each post, she said, but could no longer tolerate the shameless manipulation of her images and the painful costs of 'self-promotion'. 'Resigning' from the site, she deleted 2000 posts and 're-captioned' the remaining 96 to draw attention to the artifice involved in their production—not just the (notorious) use of filters and 'retouching', much discussed in relation to magazine and advertising imagery, but also the poses, the happy and carefree attitude, and the fake intimacy involved.

Ana Elias • Christina Scharff (✉)
Department of Culture, Media and Creative Industries, King's College London, London, UK

Rosalind Gill (✉)
Department of Sociology, City, University of London, London, UK

A.S. Elias et al. (eds.), *Aesthetic Labour*,
DOI 10.1057/978-1-137-47765-1_1

Of one image she wrote: 'see how relatable my captions were - stomach sucked in, strategic pose, pushed up boobs. I just want younger girls to know this isn't candid life, or cool or inspirational. It's contrived perfection made to get attention'.

Much could be written about O'Neill's decision, her micro-celebrity status, the alternate trolling and celebration she received, and the way she became propelled from a teen Instagram fan base to an international news actor whose decision went viral. Her story highlights the breakdown of stable distinctions between private and public as well as trends towards 'authentic' forms of celebrity in which the commodification of youthful beauty nevertheless still plays a huge part. We open with her experience because it foregrounds many of the questions discussed in this book, including the perennial emphasis upon female attractiveness, and with it the pressures to live up to particular appearance norms at whatever cost to the self—whether that involves merely 'stomach sucked in' and 'pushed up boobs' or surgical procedures. It also points to the increasing entanglements of forms of visual appearing with rapidly changing digital technologies and social media—in a world in which increasing numbers of images of women are digitally altered in various ways. Alongside this, it demonstrates the proliferating experiences of surveillance to which many women feel subject when 'managing the body is…the means by which women acquire and display their cultural capital' (Winch 2015, p. 233). Above all, it highlights the multiple labours involved in 'looking good'—labours that are simultaneously physical, cultural, technological and also psychological. As O'Neill made clear, the marketability of her posts was not only about her 'perfect' body but also the appeal of her captioned opinions, signalling as they did a warm and accessible level of cool, and a 'beautiful on the inside' philosophy. This was put to work very successfully by O'Neill as her own personal brand and capitalised upon by many different companies whose clothes or products she promoted in the familiar post/anti/native advertising style of contemporary marketing. O'Neill's story, then, pulls together themes of beauty, authenticity, labour and entrepreneurial endeavour in a way that resonates with many of the concerns of this book.

The aim of this collection is to mark out a new intellectual terrain in beauty studies by examining the intersections between postfeminism, neoliberalism and subjectivity, through a sustained focus on what we are calling 'aesthetic entrepreneurship'. We argue that the politics of beauty remains a key set of issues and debates for feminism but one that frequently seems to be stuck in an impasse between polarised positions, stressing—for example—oppression by beauty norms versus pleasure and playfulness, female agency versus cultural domination, entrenched suspicion of the beauty-industrial complex versus hopefulness about women's capacity to resist. There has been a resurgence of interest in beauty among feminists in the last decade, and we want to build on this important work to open up new questions and theoretical avenues. Our contributions are three-fold: first, we situate the continuing focus on appearance within a distinctive cultural moment, characterised by *neoliberalism*, with its relentless exhortation to be active, entrepreneurial, self-optimising subjects. The force of neoliberalism in shaping experiences and practices related to beauty needs urgently to be understood. Secondly, we want to push at questions concerned with embodied beauty and to link them in a novel way with a growing literature focused on *work or labour*. The 'turn to labour' in sociology and cultural studies, we argue, has much to offer contemporary feminist engagements with beauty, highlighting the different forms of work that are involved in presenting the self. We engage with notions of 'affective labour' and 'emotional labour', and also with the newer ideas of 'glamour labour' (Wissinger 2015). We want to develop these ideas beyond their application to particular kinds of aestheticised cultural work and instead argue that they are wider-scale processes that have relevance across social life. Neoliberalism makes us *all* 'aesthetic entrepreneurs'—not simply those who are models or working in fashion or design. Finally, our collection points up the importance of subjectivity and the need to think about the 'psychic life' of neoliberalism and postfeminism. This means that we pursue a *psychosocial perspective* in relation to beauty, that is interested in the relationship between culture and subjectivity, in complicated and ambivalent subjective experiences, and also in the way that contemporary injunctions to look good require not only physical labours and transformations but also the makeover of psychic life to embrace qualities such as confidence, happiness and authenticity.

This introductory chapter is designed to offer a guide and a map to the ideas discussed in the collection as a whole, contextualising them in wider debates. The chapter is divided into two broad parts, each containing sub-sections. The first part—titled *Beauty is a feminist issue*—looks briefly at the feminist history of debates about beauty, before turning to the key contributions of current research which we see as including: the turn to affect within feminist beauty studies; the growing body of work on decolonising beauty; feminist research on surveillance of women's appearance; and the affirmative turn in beauty studies. The second part introduces aspects of our perspective, notably our critique of neoliberalism and postfeminism, the need to think about labour and our psychosocial approach. We argue that the current moment has seen an intensification of beauty pressures on women, consonant with Angela McRobbie's (2015) notion of 'the perfect'; that these pressures have also extensified leaving few spaces 'outside' their force field; and that there has been a quasi-feminist transformation such that subjectivity and interiority are now also subject to requirements for (self)transformation.

Beauty Is a Feminist Issue

Questions about beauty have always been central to feminism. Indeed, the politics of appearance might be said to be foundational to the feminisms that emerged in the West in the 1960s and after, with beauty taking its place alongside reproductive rights, violence against women, workplace and pay equality, and sexual freedom as a key issue of feminist concern. 'Origin stories' of the women's liberation movement often date its inception to a protest against the Miss World beauty pageant in 1970 in which activists railed against female objectification and the evaluation of women only in terms of their physical attractiveness. Since then, decades of research, writing and activism by feminists have largely centred on beauty as a tool of patriarchal domination, seen to entrap women in narrow and restrictive norms of femininity, contribute to their subjugation and make them ill with 'disorders' such as depression and anorexia. There are many different perspectives on beauty among feminists- by no means can we speak of a singular perspective. Radical feminism, Marxist feminism, black and anti-racist feminisms, and postcolonial scholarship all offer contrasting accounts. There are many summaries of beauty studies and some attempts to periodise the 'lifespan' of feminist debates on beauty (Chancer 1998; Craig 2006; Jha 2016). Here, we will simply highlight briefly three broad orientations that have been central to feminist research, before moving on to consider the new and emerging concerns of contemporary feminist beauty scholarship.

Much feminist work on beauty has been influenced by psychology. Psychology as a discipline has long dominated research on body image, with experimental studies examining how cultural constructions of the body impact self-perception and self-esteem (see Grogan 2007, for a useful discussion). More than this, though, psychology's understanding of 'media effects' has become a kind of widely circulated common sense and implicitly informs many understandings of beauty pressures even today. As we write, for example, the Women's Equality Party in the UK has just called for a ban on Size Zero models in London Fashion Week. Such a campaign rests on the assumption that seeing such thin models will have negative effects on women's self-esteem, leading to eating disorders and mental health problems. These kinds of ideas are widespread and taken for granted in journalism and policy discourses, even though they have been roundly critiqued in academic literatures for their individualistic, 'linear' and 'hypodermic' model of influence. They accord little space to resistance or even negotiation among people viewing negative images and essentially present appearance-related mental health problems in reductive terms as 'reading disorders' (see Wykes and Gunter 2004).

Another approach that has been prominent in beauty studies—though less mainstream than body image perspectives—is a feminist Foucaultian account, exemplified by the work of scholars Susan Bordo (1993), Sandra Lee Bartky (1990) and Jana Sawicki (1991). Broadly speaking, this perspective regards beauty as a disciplinary technology. It argues that women's appearance is subject to profound discipline and regulation—even when beauty practices are seemingly freely chosen. For example, Sandra Lee Bartky (1990, p. 75) has argued that women are 'not marched off to electrolysis at the end of a rifle' and nor are they passive but display extraordinary 'ingenuity' in beauty rituals, yet 'insofar as the disciplinary practices of femininity produce a "subjected and practiced", an inferiorized, body, they must be understood as aspects of far larger discipline, an oppressive and inegalitarian system of sexual subordination'.

For us this work has been formative in offering a non-institutionalised and non-individualistic understanding of beauty as a form of disciplinary power, though it is not without problems—most notably its lack of an account of the precise mechanisms that mediate between the 'beauty myth' and women's embodied practices (e.g. repeated dieting) or feelings of failure or shame. It does not have a theory of affect or a psychosocial understanding of how it is that ideals 'out there' get 'inside' to shape our desires, deepest feelings and what we find beautiful. It has been criticised for its cultural determinism and inattention to women's agency—though this has been contested as we discuss in the second part of this chapter. The body corporeal—fleshy, feeling, embodied –is not prominent in these accounts; it is rather figured as a cultural 'site' in which power and discourses of femininity play out, leaving some to argue that the body itself 'disappears' in these accounts.

A third established position theorises the ramping up of beauty pressures over recent decades in terms of backlashes against feminism. Susan Faludi (1991) and Naomi Wolf (1990) are the most prominent exponents of this view. Faludi characterises beauty as part of a wider backlash against second-wave feminism which she understands as nothing less than an 'undeclared war', which uses diverse means to frighten, cajole and bully women into abandoning feminist projects. This is aided by a 'media echo chamber' in which journalistic 'trend stories' with little credibility are amplified and recirculated so that they take on the status of self-evident truths. Wolf's target is more explicitly the beauty industry itself. She argued (1990, p. 2) 'we are in the midst of a violent backlash against feminism that uses images of female beauty as a political weapon against women's advancement: the beauty myth'. She contends that 'the more legal and material hindrances women have broken through, the more strictly and heavily and cruelly images of female beauty have come to weigh upon us' (1990, p. 1). This is not because feminism makes women unhappy, Wolf argued, but because feminist successes are met with ever more intensifying and unrealistic beauty ideals that then cause in women 'a secret "underlife" poisoning our freedom…a dark vein of self-hatred, physical obsessions, terror of aging, and dread of lost control' (1990,

p. 2). As Yvonne Tasker and Diane Negra argue (2007), backlashes are multiple rather than singular as feminism is characterised by complicated ongoing gains and losses. This historical contingency is evident in Faludi and Wolf's analyses which link key moments in US feminist history (e.g. achieving suffrage, the development of the contraceptive pill, the rise of the women's liberation movement) with intensifying pressures in fashion and beauty—including images of female desirability that became thinner and thinner the more advances women made in public life. Whilst at times such a view can seem almost to resemble a conspiracy theory—and may therefore be problematic—its strength overall is in highlighting that beauty pressures do not exist in a social and cultural vacuum but are connected to broader social trends in complicated ways.

The (Re)turn to Beauty

One of the things that is striking about feminist debates about beauty is the extent to which they polarise along well-worn fault lines—for example, those relating to pain/harm versus pleasure, or those concerned with female agency versus cultural influence. They also coalesce around broad theoretical divisions within feminist social theory more generally in which those concerned with representations are pitted against the new materialists, or those stressing bodily discipline stand counterposed to those interested in affect. Although feminism has not had 'beauty wars'—in the same way as the 'sex wars'—many of the discussions are similarly polarised and seemed at one point to have reached an impasse.

However, the first two decades of the twenty-first century have seen a significant resurgence of interest in beauty and some novel lines of enquiry which promise to interrupt the usual debates. As Ashley Mears (2014, p. 1330) has put it, 'beauty is having a moment in the social sciences'. The politics of beauty remains an intractable and politically pressing set of problems for feminism, but there is a new energy to the debates, and new theoretical vocabularies are developing. This is evidenced in the launch of new academic journals in the field, by new thematic sections of professional associations, by journal special issues and by novel empirical research programmes that look at a multiplicity of topics—for example dress, bridal beauty, fat beauty, queer beauty—and are increasingly focused upon everyday and mundane beauty practices in ways that foreground women's lived and embodied experiences. Perhaps most significantly, we have seen in the last few years the emergence of new (inter)disciplinary formations and new perspectives, influenced by wider debates in feminist theory. Rebecca Coleman and Monica Moreno Figueroa (2010) argue that this feminist 'turn to beauty' in social theory has re-centred agency and pleasure, embodiment, and intersectionality. To their account we would add the new interest in surveillance, and the 'affirmative turn' within feminist theory, as well as the prominence of 'third wave' feminisms, which are more positive about beauty and stress the pleasures and playfulness involved in styling the self. We consider these themes below, showing how they inform the ideas presented in this book.

Intersectional and Transnational Beauty Studies

A long-standing and important feature of feminist research on beauty has been its appreciation that the politics of appearance is not simply related to gender but also constituted by ideologies of race, class and nation. There has been extensive research on beauty pageants examining their role as nation-building projects and considerable analysis of the global/globalising nature of the beauty industry and its role in valorising particular racialised femininities over others (Banet-Weiser, 1999; Leeds Craig, 2002). Meeta Rani Jha (2016, p. 3) argues that 'physical attractiveness, whiteness and youthfulness have accrued capital just as darker skin color, hair texture, disability and aging have devalued feminine currency'. Margaret Hunter (2011, p. 145) understands this in relation to 'racial capital'—a 'resource drawn from the body that can be related to skin tone, facial features, body shape, etc'.

Skin lightening, hair straightening and particular types of cosmetic surgery—for example double eyelid surgery—have been extensively discussed as practices that are a consequence of racism and with it the privileging of Caucasian appearance. However, some scholars argue that to read participation in such practices in terms of internalised racism is to oversimplify, and, perhaps paradoxically, potentially to reinforce a racist and imperialist imaginary. It is notable that some new research complicates understandings of surgical, skin or hair practices as being about white hegemony or compliance with white beauty norms. JongMi Kim's (2012) conversations with young Korean women talking about nose and eyelid reshaping, for example, demonstrated that these surgeries were resolutely not understood as attempts to fashion a Caucasian look. Instead her young female participants were invested in a novel but distinctively Korean appearance. To suggest this is Western mimicry, Kim argues, is to see through an Orientalist gaze or through 'western eyes'—as Chandra Mohanty (1984) expresses it.

Jie Yang's (2011) research on Chinese beauty culture recognises the extraordinary power of Euro-American beauty ideals, now widely dispersed as a result of global media flows, but again cautions against reading Chinese women's uptake of cosmetic surgery only through this lens. She argues that the meanings of various reconfigurations of the face and body are intimately related to feminism, to neoliberalism and to the opportunities opened up by market capitalism to 'invest in one's body aesthetically' (2011, pp. 341–342). Gary Xu and Susan Feiner (2007) also locate the production and consumption of 'female beauty' at the centre of the Chinese economy, connected to both feminist and nationalist projects. Much other research highlights aesthetic self-making in terms of class distinctions or assertions of an urban metropolitan identity rather than as a racial and colonial project in a simple sense. Hua Wen's (2013) ethnographic research in Beijing situates women's decision to undergo cosmetic surgery as an attempt to take control over their lives but within 'structures of history and power and gender subjugation over which they have no control' (2013, p. 236). She understands their decisions in terms of an 'investment for personal gains' because 'the more physical capital a woman can hold, the more ability she may have to reshape the social, cultural and economic fields around her'.

All this research, then, cautions against reductive readings. On the one hand, it would be naive to ignore the vast power of the beauty-industrial complex in promoting and selling particular looks, and the products, labour or services to achieve them—for example, skin lightening creams, make-up, surgery, and so on. On the other, it is problematic to assume that researchers can simply 'read off' the particular meanings that engaging with such products or practices will have. Increasingly writers argue for the need to 'complicate' established positions on beauty (e.g. Figueroa and Moore 2013) and, above all, to examine everyday cultural practices of beauty and women's experiences of them.

Maxine Leeds Craig's (2002) research about black women's experiences of beauty parlours in the 1960s in the USA is an excellent example of a study that takes this more 'complicated stance' embracing a thoroughgoing intersectional approach. Craig argued that experiences of beauty were formed through a complex amalgam of reactions to white beauty standards, social expectations of black middle class respectability, notions of black power and black pride in the context of the civil rights movement, and discourses of black as beautiful, emerging black female entrepreneurship, and ideas of leisure and female bonding. Craig's work highlights the intersections of class, race and gender, arguing that hair straightening and other beauty practices were part of a strategy for class mobility and were also deployed to counter class-inflected racism and sexism by 'looking like a lady'. At the same time trips to the beauty parlour were experienced as opportunities to be 'pampered' and treated with respect in a way that was quite distinct from many other experiences for women of colour at the time.

Craig's work poses a challenge to accounts that see hair relaxing or straightening as reducible to racialised self-hatred or 'assimilation', questioning the notion that it is necessarily about 'mimicking whiteness'. Shirley Tate's work also complicates such readings of black women's hair, showing how it has become inserted into debates about natural versus unnatural, good versus bad, and authentic versus inauthentic identity. She explores how black women negotiate a context shaped *both* by a 'dominant white aesthetic' *and* an 'anti-racist aesthetic' that contrastingly values dark skin and 'natural' hair (Tate 2007; Tate, this volume, Chap. 11). Jha in turn argues that ideologies of 'racial uplift' in which appearance is entangled with notions of class and race and gender have also been visible in the Obama era, centred around precisely which black people were entitled to be the 'bearers of black culture' (2016, p. 42; see also Kobena Mercer's (1990) work on the 'burden of representation').

One productive way of theorising beauty in intersectional terms that also pays attention to local specificities is through the insights of biopolitical theory. Many have argued that beauty functions as a technology of biopower. Brenda Weber (2009) discusses 'appearance-based citizenship'. Jie Yang (2011) develops the concept of 'aesthetic governance' for thinking about post-communist Chinese femininities. Avaro Jarrin (2015) deploys the notion of biopolitics to think about how beauty functions in the reproduction of racial inequalities in Brazil. More radically, Mimi Nguyen (2011) and Minh-Ha Pham (2011) interrogate the 'biopower of beauty and fashion' and their entanglement with 'humanitarian imperialisms' in the period since the attacks on the World Trade Centre on 11 September 2001. In their powerful and important essays they show how notions such as the 'right to fashion' are intimately entangled in what some would characterise as a 'femo-nationalist' politics (Farris 2012). Going beyond the familiar observation that feminist discourses were deployed in authorising and legitimating the so-called 'war on terror' and particularly US bombing of Afghanistan, they explore the 'troubling histories of beauty's relation to morality, humanity and security'. Nguyen examines the Kabul Beauty School, which was set up by an NGO (Beauty Without Borders) largely sponsored by the US fashion and beauty industries, showing how its programmes of 'empowerment' were inseparable from the geopolitical aims of US military deployment. As Pham (2011, p. 392) puts it, fashion and beauty became 'a metaphor for the correction and transformation of veiled Afghan women into modern liberal subjects who desire appropriate aesthetic and political ideals'.

In sum, it is clear that much of the most exciting new work on beauty has an attentiveness to questions of race, class, nation, region, and to colonial and imperial dynamics, with an interest not simply in challenging the sexism of beauty norms but also in decolonising and transnationalising beauty studies. This emphasis is evident in this collection too. Not only does it seek to displace the familiar focus on Anglo-America by considering a variety of national contexts (e.g. China, India, Russia, Singapore, Nigeria and Israel), but, more fundamentally, the collection uses the concept of transnationality to understand aesthetic labour not as a uniform cultural or subjective formation but rather as a 'mobile technology' (Ong 2006) which is produced within 'scattered hegemonies' (Grewal and Kaplan 1994). It begins from a recognition of 'a transnational field as structured by radically uneven power relations, differences and perhaps even incommensurabilities' (Imre et al. 2009; see also Hegde 2011). To put it succinctly, we seek to contribute to critical thinking about aesthetic entrepreneurs as intersectional subjects who come into being in a transnational field.

Surveillance

Another emergent theme in contemporary studies of beauty is surveillance. Digital technologies have radically expanded what counts as surveillance and we are seeing the proliferation of new terms such as 'dataveillance' and notions of 'data bodies' and 'neoliberal optics' (Hayward 2013) as well as new modes of surveillance that depart from the dominant image of the Panopticon, used by Foucault as his metaphor for disciplinary power. Writers on surveillance now speak of synoptic surveillance (Mathiesen 1997), omnoptic surveillance (Boyne 2000) and gynaeoptic surveillance (Winch 2015) and self-surveillance (Lupton 2016; Gill in press-a). Surveillance studies has not traditionally 'placed difference, gender and sexuality at the forefront of their enquiries' (Walby and Anais 2015), but the emerging field of feminist surveillance studies (Dubrofsky and Magnet 2015) has a commitment to critical projects that are intersectional, interventionist and activist in their orientation—drawing as much from queer theory and critical race studies as from gender studies. It includes an engagement with pleasurable as well as coercive forms of surveillance—and of course the two are not mutually exclusive—identifying media surveillance of celebrity bodies and appearance as a potential invitation to 'scopophilic surveillance' in which women pore over images of female actors and pop stars, with a range of surveillant gazes: desiring, envious, anxious, hostile, and so on. In contemporary media culture we are relentlessly incited to surveil other women's bodies, a project that is enhanced by textual features such as magazine close ups, magnification, red circles and highlighted areas (e.g. to draw attention to cellulite or an un-depilated hair or other aesthetic 'transgressions'). Indeed, the 'surveillance of women's bodies … constitutes perhaps the largest type of media content across all genres and media forms' (Gill 2007, p. 255). This forms part of a broader 'surveillant imaginary' that is 'expanding vertiginously' (Andrejevic 2015).

Within forums such as women's magazines and cosmetics advertising a surveillant gaze is becoming more and more intense—operating at ever finer-grained levels and with a proliferating range of lenses that do not necessarily regard the outer membrane of the body—the skin—as their boundary—for example, that call for scrutiny of veins and capillaries or exhort that a fuller health and beauty profile can be determined by hair analysis or DNA testing. This intensified and forensic surveillance is seen repeatedly in contemporary beauty culture—with the recurrent emphasis upon microscopes, telescopic gunsights, peep holes, alarm clocks, calipers and set squares. Images of cameras and of perfect 'photo beauty' or of 'HD-ready' skin also proliferate. Most common of all are the motifs of the tape measure (often around the upper thigh)—an image that is becoming ubiquitous in beauty salons—and the magnifying glass, used to scrutinise pores or to highlight blemish-free skin, but—more importantly at a meta-level—underscoring the idea of women's appearance as under constant (magnified) surveillance.

Another area of interest in surveillance can be seen in the growing attention to 'horizontal surveillance' and 'peer surveillance'. Alison Winch's (2013) work has been important in theorising this in terms of the 'girlfriend gaze'—a modality of looking in which women and girls police each other's looks and behaviours. Winch (2015) calls this 'gynaeoptic surveillance'—a homosocial gaze characterised simultaneously by both affection and 'normative cruelties' (Ringrose and Renold 2010). Peer surveillance has been discussed in relation to social media (Dobson 2015; Ringrose and Harvey 2015), young people's image-sharing practices in relation to 'sexy pictures' (Ringrose et al. 2013) and as an embodied experience of being subject to a 'checklist gaze' in which young women describe being 'checked out' by others (Elias 2016). An emerging area of study is relational surveillance more generally—such as mothers' monitoring of their daughters' diets and clothing (the so-called 'tiger mom') and—we might add anecdotally from our own and others experiences—daughters reciprocal judging gaze on mothers: 'mum, you are not going out dressed like <u>that</u>?!'

The study of 'filters' and 'beauty apps' represents another area of increased interest in surveillance (Rettberg 2014; Wendt 2014). Located in a wider concern with self-monitoring and self-tracking and the 'quantified self' movement (see Lupton 2016; Neff and Nafus 2016), beauty apps might be understood as encouraging women to see and surveil themselves within a 'pedagogy of defect' (Bordo 1997) whilst also promising consumer solutions. They range across filters and selfie-modification apps; pedagogic apps offering tutelage over beauty ('your own personal beauty advisor on your phone'); surgery 'try-out' apps that offer you the opportunity to 'visualize a whole new you' after surgical enhancement, teeth whitening, eyebag removal, and so on; aesthetic benchmarking apps that give the—algorithmic—answer to questions such as 'how hot am I?' or 'how old do I look?'; and apps which use the camera functions of smartphones to scan the body for flaws and problems, for example moles, sun damage, the effects of smoking, and so on. As we have argued elsewhere (Elias and Gill in press), beauty apps 'increase the extent to which the female body and face are rendered visible as a site of crisis and commodification'. Increasingly they also produce feedback loops in which cosmetics (e.g. foundation, tightening serum) are claimed to reproduce on actual embodied faces the filter/surgical effects produced by these apps: a definite case of life being forced to imitate art/ifice. This collection contributes to this growing interest in surveillance through its theorisation of postfeminism and neoliberalism (see below) and through attentiveness to the ways in which beauty culture incites surveillance of the self and others—a surveillance we suggest that is not limited to the body but also extends to subjectivity and psychic life, such as having the correct set of affective dispositions or feeling confident.

The Affective Turn

The third broad development in beauty studies we want to foreground is the turn to affect in beauty studies—and in feminist theory more broadly. Contemporary research on the body and beauty displaces the overly rational unified subject with an appreciation of the importance of emotion and affect that is seen variously in conceptualisations of 'homo sentimentalis', 'emotional capitalism', of the affective body and the body without image (Illouz 2007; Massumi 2002; Featherstone 2010). (Over)simplifying for the purpose of providing a 'map' to a large and rapidly developing field, we would suggest that there are (at least) two *broad* perspectives on affect put to work in contemporary beauty research: a Foucaultian and a Deleuzian approach. Foucaultian—or more broadly discursive—approaches to affect and beauty develop from the perspectives of writers such as Susan Bordo, Sandra Lee Bartky and Jana Sawicki, discussed briefly earlier in this chapter. Foucault's work acknowledged the centrality of affect in power and technologies of self-hood—arguing that 'what makes power hold good' is that it does not 'weigh on us like a force that says no' but it 'produces things, induces pleasure' (1980, p. 119) —but did not explore this comprehensively. Contemporary writers seek to understand how passions like desire, rage, love or shame are bound up with subjecthood and how power operates through and mobilises affect (Isin 2014). Imogen Tyler's work (2008) explores how affects like disgust and contempt are mobilised through specific aestheticised constructions—for example of the 'chav mum'—showing that these reactions are partly animated by a particular construction of this figure's *appearance*—weight, hair, clothes, and so on. Shirley Tate (2013) has explored the force of shame in black British women's subjecthood and also the way that this is resisted 'through using alternative beauty discourses from Jamaica to produce new beauty subjectivities'. L. Ayu Saraswati in turn explores the naturalisation of hierarchies of skin colour in Indonesia, through the feelings of rasa and malu, arguing that women's engagement with skin lightening practices is shaped by the 'gendered management of affect' (2013, p. 12). More broadly, the discursive tradition is showing an increased interest in the work done by feelings and affective practices—whether these are 'ugly feelings' (Ngai 2005) or 'neoliberal feeling rules' (Kanai 2016).

A Deleuzian or non-representational approach, by contrast, is often less interested in the way that affects work to enmesh or animate power than in looking for 'lines of flight' or ruptures that disrupt the smooth operation of power relations. Rather than starting from bodily discipline—as some discursive theorists do—they start from the body itself and from 'embodied affective processes' (Coleman and Figueroa 2010). There is 'no single generalizable theory of affect' (Gregg and Seigworth 2010, p. 3) but interest in affect can be traced from Spinoza, Bergson to Deleuze and Guattari and offers a conceptualisation of what Patricia Clough (2007, p. 2) dubs 'bodily capacities to affect and be affected' in a way that 'is linked to the self-feeling of being alive - that is, "aliveness" or "vitality"'. The body here is not singular but multiple, and it 'experiences and gives off intensities' which do not cohere, but highlight the body's indeterminacy (Featherstone 2010, p. 195). Affective flows show the potential of things to be otherwise. A significant feature of this perspective is its rejection of the traditional notion of 'body image'. Riffing on the Deleuzian notion of a 'body without organs', Brian Massumi (2002) suggests a 'body without image'. Rebecca Coleman (2009) discusses this in relation to the 'becoming of bodies', arguing that 'bodies and images are not separable entities but rather that images make possible particular knowledges and experiences of bodies' (Coleman and Figueroa 2010). Indeed, in this volume (Chap. 21), Dana Kaplan explores modes of 'being' and 'becoming' in representations of the labour of beauty in popular culture.

Deleuzian-inflected accounts are radically reconfiguring the kinds of questions that are asked about beauty. For example, Claire Colebrook (2006, p. 132) argues that the new 'question of beauty for feminist politics … is not so much moral—is beauty good or bad for women—but pragmatic: how is beauty defined, deployed, defended, subordinated, marked or manipulated, and how do these tactics intersect with gender and value?' There is a new interest too in questions of temporality, influenced by the important work of Coleman and Figueroa (2010). They depart from traditional accounts of beauty practices and instead investigate 'bodily inclinations' (toward the beautiful) offering a more dynamic and temporally agile account. Drawing on research with white British girls and mestizo Mexican women they suggest that 'beauty is an inclination towards a perfected temporal state which involves processes of displacement to the past and of deferral to the future.' (Coleman and Figueroa 2010, p. 357).

The Deleuzian and autonomist approach to affect with its idea of 'biopower from below' (Hardt 2005) posits affects as evading, resisting and exceeding control. Affect is seemingly ontologically 'prior'—'the skin is faster than the word', as Massumi has famously put it. Whilst this idea has an instant recognition factor—most people can think of times when they felt something before they were able to put it into words—this view has been much criticised for its dependence upon problematic scientific (brain) research and for its implication that affect is somehow a-social or even pre-social. Margaret Wetherell (2012) has developed a rigorous constructionist and discursive re-reading of affect theory which has been taken up in feminist beauty studies by Jean McAvoy (2015) and Ana Elias (2016). This new body of work on affect offers productive directions for scholars wanting to take affect seriously yet troubled by the tendency of writing about it to treat it as somehow outside of culture and the social.

We argue that moods, fashions and feelings rarely completely surprise, and their cultural origins can be traced. There are patterns and regularities that are well documented and upon which the fashion and beauty industry survives: indeed it can tell us already what the key colour will be in three or four seasons' time and what kinds of clothes we will be wearing. This is more than forecasting; it is planning. A historical lens challenges the ideas of randomness, affective excess and unpredictability even further: when we look back, we see clear patterns relating to beauty, fashion, hairstyle, and so on, which may not be so evident in the contemporary everyday. Whilst individuals may be invested in seeing their own look as entirely personal and idiosyncratic, appearance is, we suggest, thoroughly social and cultural, and however quirkily they self-style, few people live outside the fashion-beauty complex entirely. Even rejections of it are patterned.

The Affirmative Turn

Closely connected to the 'turn to affect' is another 'turn' in feminist theory: the affirmative turn. As Clare Hemmings has argued in an important critique, affect 'often emerges as a rhetorical device whose ultimate goal is to persuade "paranoid theorists" into a more productive frame of mind' (2005, p. 551). This may be seen in the more optimistic and affirmative readings that emerge in some contemporary writing. There is in some contemporary work a palpable move away from a hermeneutics of 'suspicion' and 'scepticism' towards greater hopefulness and optimism which manifests not only substantively—an interest in happiness (Colebrook 2003) or passion (Davis 2015)—but also as a theoretical commitment to the affirmative, that is an interest in exploring life as something other than 'mystified false consciousness requiring the illumination of theory' (Colebrook 2003, p. 133).

Entangled in this are several different ideas: a desire to focus on 'positive or empowering emotions' (Davis 2015); a belief that even oppressive practices leave space for an affective 'excess' that can break free from singular meanings; a commitment to putting experiences before/above politics; a critique of other (feminist) scholars for their lack of 'respect'—what Lauren Berlant characterises as being 'aghast at the ease with which intellectuals shit on people who hold a dream' (2006, p. 23); a rejection of a 'feminist killjoy ethics'; and, at times, seemingly an embrace of a 'politically incorrect' 'bad girl' image (Lumby 1997; Davis 2015). These emphases reanimate long-standing points of tension in feminist theory around questions of agency and the role of the feminist intellectual (see e.g. Sumi Madhok et al.'s (2013) collection on agency and coercion).

It is important, as Maureen McNeil (2010) notes, that we do not lose feminism's 'critical edge' in the rush to theorising affirmatively. It is also worth problematising the somewhat caricatured version of feminism that emerges from some of this work: one would never imagine from reading it that feminists have written passionately of sex, desire, dancing and woman-centred pornography—let alone partaken in any of these activities. Instead feminists are presented as somewhat joyless, censorious characters, relentlessly imposing their political perspective on other women and in doing so sucking all the pleasure out of life. The resemblance to some representations of feminists in popular culture hardly needs underlining. Responding to Kathy Davis's provocation 'Should a Feminist Dance Tango?' Monica Moreno Figueroa (2015, p. 24) asks 'I wonder who is the feminist she visualises when thinking about this?… How would all the feminists dancing salsa, cumbia, bachata or whatever else respond to the idea that "they are out of character" or being a bit naughty?'

Rather than seeing Kathy Davis as a 'politically incorrect' outsider to feminism, we see her work as absolutely central to feminist scholarship on beauty. Her book *Our Bodies, Ourselves* won huge acclaim and several prizes; her research on cosmetic surgery remains a key text in gender studies—required reading for all our undergraduates—and her work on Tango also looks set to become a feminist classic. Thus, instead of revivifying old feminist battle lines characterised in terms of a marginalised voice speaking out against a feminist orthodoxy, we see it as both more accurate and more productive to regard this as a debate *within feminism*, an indication of the energy and vitality of the field of beauty studies—a field that increasingly involves positive evaluations of femininity as well as critiques of it. Debra Ferreday (2007, p. 5), for example, asks us to 'think through the questions of whether femininity can be adapted and what challenges such adaptations might pose, not only for mainstream culture, but also for feminist theory'. In turn Rita Felski asks:

> 'Is every experience of beauty also a source of harm? Is beauty intrinsically and inevitably wrong? If not, what might feminists say about such counter-instances? Can feminism only remain true to itself by insisting on the primacy of female suffering? Or is there a place in feminist thought for what we might call a positive aesthetic, an affirmation, however conditional, of the value of beauty and aesthetic pleasure?' (Felski 2006, p. 273)

Much popular third wave feminism also calls on feminism to engage with beauty and fashion in terms of playfulness and pleasure rather than coercion—directing its attacks less against a patriarchal beauty-industrial complex than against a particular construction of second-wave feminism. Arguing along these lines Debbie Stoller for example states that 'painting one's nails is a feminist act because it expands the notions of what a feminist is allowed to do or how she may look' (Stoller, quoted in Baumgardner and Richards 2000). This assertion might seem troubling—resting as it does on a critique of an imagined orthodox and punitive feminism, its construction of other feminists as 'killjoys' and its insistence on what Sara Ahmed (2010) has dubbed 'happy talk'. What we value about the affirmative turn, however, is its force as a catalyst to think more ambivalently about beauty politics, retaining an openness to multiple possible readings. This involves three things: first, an attentiveness to the possibility of *change*—seen, for example, in the increased positive visibility given to plus-size models, challenging what Bartky (1990) called the 'tyranny of slenderness', and the stretching of fashion and beauty to include more diverse queer/non-binary/androgynous looks. Second, the importance of holding onto—rather than denying—'ambivalences and contradictions' (Figueroa 2015, p. 23). And third, the need to slow down the 'rush to judgment'. As Rita Felski puts it:

> ‘The challenge for feminism is to rein back its compulsion to immediately translate aesthetic surfaces into political depths; or rather, to keep both surface and depth in the mind’s eye, teasing apart the multifarious sociopolitical meanings of texts whilst also crafting richer and thicker descriptions of aesthetic experience’. (2006, p. 281)

Lisa Henderson (2008) asks feminist and queer scholars to ‘slow down’, that is to be slow to condemn and ‘slow to discover meanings’. This resonates with Hemmings’ (2005) call to attend to affective dissonance and it involves taking particular care with practices that ‘seem to be at odds with our own values, preferences and politics’ (Dobson 2015, p. 8). Henderson calls this ‘slow love’, and it rests upon what Amy Shields Dobson (2015, p. 8) calls ‘an open, ambivalent disposition marked less by judgment than by curiosity’. Discussing female genital cosmetic surgery in this volume (Chap. 20), Amy Shields Dobson, Karalyn McDonald, Maggie Kirkman, Kay Souter and Jane Fisher aim to move beyond dominant binary logics of autonomy, choice and rational self-benefit versus victimhood and cultural determination. Also writing about vulval modificatory practices, Virginia Brown (this volume, Chap. 3) engages in a thought experiment which invites us on an imaginary journey between past and present by re-telling the non-consummation and annulment of the nineteenth century marriage of UK art historian John Ruskin and socialite Effie Gray in the contemporary climate. In this vein, this volume contributes to scholarship that is interested in exploring ambivalence, ambiguity and dissonance, and which is open to pursuing these interests in novel ways.

Aesthetic Labour: Beauty Politics in Neoliberalism

In recent years, there has been a flurry of writings on neoliberalism (e.g. Brown 2015; Crouch 2011; Dardot and Laval 2013; Gilbert 2013; Mirowski 2014; Mirowski and Phlewe 2009; Springer et al. 2016; Stedman Jones 2012). And yet, neoliberalism continues to be a contested concept, in part because it is contingent, slippery and sometimes remains undefined. The contested nature of the term neoliberalism has led some to map its meanings and interpretations (e.g. Hardin 2014; Larner 2000), whilst others have argued that the concept is no longer useful (Garland and Harper 2012; Clarke 2008). Crucially, however, most scholars tend to agree that neoliberalism involves the extension of market principles into all areas of life (e.g. Brown 2015; Dardot and Laval 2013; Mudge 2008; Shamir 2008; Springer et al. 2016), including subjectivity. Foucaultian scholars in particular have traced how neoliberalism extends to the reconstitution of subjectivities (Brown 2003; Foucault 2008; Lemke 2001; Rose 1992). As Michel Foucault (2008, p. 226) has famously argued, 'the stake in all neoliberal analyses is the replacement every time of *homo oeconomicus* as partner of exchange with a *homo oeconomicus* as entrepreneur of himself [...]'. Under neoliberalism, the enterprise form is extended 'to *all* forms of conduct' (Burchell 1993, p. 275) and encompasses subjectivity itself (McNay 2009). Conducting its life as enterprise, the enterprising self is bound by specific rules that emphasise ambition, calculation and personal responsibility (Rose 1992). It is this Foucaultian approach to neoliberalism which informs our perspective.

Crucially, the resources to become an entrepreneurial subject are unevenly distributed. As Jessica Ringrose and Valerie Walkerdine (2008) have argued, the subject of self-invention is predominantly middle class (see also Allen 2014; O'Flynn and Petersen 2007). And while discourses of entrepreneurial self-help have appealed to members of black and migrant communities (Gilroy 2013), the constitution of entrepreneurial subjectivities also produces its "others" (Scharff 2011; Williams 2014). In relation to gender, recent feminist research has argued that women, and young women in particular, are increasingly positioned as ideal neoliberal subjects (Gill and Scharff 2011; McRobbie 2009; Ringrose and Walkerdine 2008). As McRobbie (2009, p. 15) has shown, young women have become "privileged subjects of social change" who capably maximise newly won opportunities such as access to the labour market and control over reproduction. According to Bronwyn Davies (2005), the neoliberal self is defined by its capacity to consume, which further privileges the feminine through the long-standing association between women and consumption. The neoliberal incitement to self-transformation is also associated with femininity (Ringrose and Walkerdine 2008). It is mainly women who are called on to transform themselves, which becomes particularly visible with regard to the management of the body and sexuality (Gill and Scharff 2011). As we will explore further when introducing the notion of 'aesthetic entrepreneurship', the link between femininity, self-transformation and the body is key to understanding the interplay between gender and subjectivity in the neoliberal era.

Over the last decade postfeminism has also become a key term that speaks to distinctive gendered features of the current cultural conjuncture. In some formulations, postfeminism is defined by its relationship to feminism—its assumed 'pastness' whether that pastness is 'merely noted, mourned or celebrated' (Tasker and Negra 2007, p. 3) This relationship has long been understood as complicated involving incorporation, repudiation, commodification and featuring what Angela McRobbie (2009) dubbed a 'double entanglement' in which feminism is both 'taken into account' yet attacked. Increasingly, however, postfeminism seems to have 'cut loose' from a particular relationship to feminism and can be understood as a semi-autonomous 'mood', 'structure of feeling' or 'sensibility' whose primary relationships are less to feminism than to global consumer capitalism and neoliberalism (Gill 2016). Simidele Dosekun's (2015) writing about postfeminism in Nigeria exemplifies this argument. She sees postfeminism as a transnationally circulating sensibility which has the capacity to take hold even in contexts which have not experienced western-style feminist politics. A feminist movement is not a pre-condition for the emergence and cultural hold of postfeminism, she argues, showing how her Lagosian participants spoke about beauty practices in ways not dissimilar from (though absolutely not reducible to) their counterparts in London or Los Angeles. Also framing postfeminism transnationally, Adrienne Evans and Sarah Riley (this volume, Chap. 7) explore the aesthetic labour of Anastasiya Shpagina (aka Anime Girl) in the context of the 'living dolls movement', arguing that her aesthetics are an example of a transnational postfeminist subjectivity.

Postfeminism, some have argued, might be conceptualised as 'gendered neoliberalism' (Gill in press-b; Henderson and Taylor in press). Like neoliberalism, it should be used as a critical term, locating postfeminism as an object of study (rather than a perspective or historical period). That is, rather than *being* postfeminists we identify ourselves as *critical analysts of postfeminist culture*, interested in interrogating the ideas and discourses that comprise contemporary common sense. This understanding highlights the patterned nature of the postfeminist sensibility—a sensibility that is simultaneously discursive, ideological, affective and psychosocial.

A number of relatively stable and patterned features of this sensibility have been identified recurrently across studies and contexts. These stress the significance of the body in postfeminist culture; the emergence of 'new femininities' (Gill and Scharff 2011) that break with earlier significations in important ways the emergence of novel kinds of 'enlightened sexism' (Douglas 2010); the prominence given to notions of choice, agency, autonomy and empowerment as part of a shift towards entrepreneurial modes of self-hood (Banet-Weiser 2012); the importance of makeover and self-transformation, linked to the 'psychic life of neoliberalism and postfeminism (Scharff 2015; Gill 2016); the distinctive affective tone of postfeminism, particularly its emphasis upon the upbeat and the positive, with the repudiation of pain, injury, insecurity and anger (Scharff 2016; Kanai 2015; Gill and Orgad 2015) and finally—as we have discussed already—the importance of surveillance to neoliberal and postfeminist cultures.

One widely noted feature is the prominence accorded to the body in postfeminist culture—less for what it can do than for how it appears, which is figured both as the locus of womanhood and the key site of women's value—displacing earlier constructions of femininity which highlighted particular roles or characteristics (such as motherhood or caring). These were of course highly problematic, but today—and no less so—the body is to the fore:

> 'In the hypervisible landscape of popular culture the body is recognised as the object of women's labour: it is her asset, her product, her brand and her gateway to freedom and empowerment in a neoliberal market economy.' (Winch 2015)

With this shift, we argue, the 'beauty imperative' has gained ever more traction with arguments that (hetero)sexual attractiveness is the ultimate measure of a success for a woman—whatever else she is, she must also be beautiful and normatively strive for perfection (McRobbie 2015). In a Deleuzian frame, McRobbie (2009) argues that patriarchy has been 're-territorialised' in the fashion-beauty complex, creating unliveable pressures that produce a particular kind of melancholia and also 'illegible rage' expressed through 'postfeminist disorders' that include bulimia, anxiety, depression, drinking and forms of addiction. Our argument is that in this distinctively postfeminist and neoliberal moment, beauty pressures have intensified, extensified and also moved into the realm of subjectivity in new and pernicious ways, facilitated by new technologies and by aggressive consumer capitalism that is colonising women's bodies—and increasingly men's too, though with nothing like equivalent force.

The Intensification of Beauty Pressures

One instance of this new intensity can be seen in cosmetic brands' capitalisation on women's sophisticated visual literacies—facilitated in part by the affordances of smart phone cameras, the ubiquity of image posting and the utter routineness—particularly among young women—of practices of magnification and scrutiny when looking at images of the self and others. We argue that new ways of looking are developing that are without historical precedent: we have never before been able to subject ourselves and others to this degree of forensic surveillance. But this is the new normal. These novel 'ways of seeing' (Berger 1972) have yet to receive sufficient attention, but Terri Senft's notion of 'the grab' (2015) has been influential, as has Malcolm Gladwell's notion of 'the blink' (2005) (to capture the intensified speed of our engagement with images) and Sarah Riley's, Adrienne Evans' and Alison Mackiewicz's (2016) 'postfeminist gaze' (see also Gill in press-a). Beauty companies tap into this high degree of self-surveillance by dramatically expanding traditional make-up sets, which now include more products and more routines—for example Mac now has an eight-step routine for colouring the lips alone.

In Ana Elias's (2016) study of young women's embodied experiences of beauty, she was struck by the degree of forensic self-surveillance women practised—dubbing it 'nano-surveillance' because of the fineness and intensity of the scrutiny involved. Indeed, women's self-examination was the antithesis of the 'quick glance to check that I'm looking alright'. It could routinely involve intense scrutiny of eyebrows, magnification of pores and measurement of facial symmetry through the assessment of selfies. Elias's young female participants based in the UK and Portugal also felt themselves subject to constant evaluation from other people, particularly women. One woman vividly described her feeling that there was a routine 'checklist gaze' which involved a quick but sweeping scrutiny of the entire body. Similarly, the link between women's sophisticated visual literacy and the consumption of non-invasive cosmetic surgery can be seen in Katharine Morton's (2015) study of the geography of bodily discipline around ageing. She notes

> '…everyone is talking about the face. All of the respondents, both consumers and practitioners, also referred in fragmentary terms to particular features, for instance the neck, eyes and jawline, as specific 'sites' in which the ageing process was most visibly materialised. With regard to the face, almost all of the respondents went into significant detail about the manifestation of 'signs' of ageing upon their own, and others', faces.' (Morton 2015, p. 1047)

What was striking in her research was the level of detail and specificity evident in women's accounts of their own appearance. Such responses included reference to fine lines, wrinkles, pigmentation, lack of elasticity, dehydration and dullness as visible and material markers of the ageing process. She comments on the way in which they enact a 'clinical gaze' on their own faces—aided by new technologies.

Finally the intensity of beauty norms can also be seen by looking at their constitutive outside—by what, in this case, is defined as opposition to these norms. The costs of this are felt disproportionately by some groups of women more than others—for example, trans rather than cis women, disabled rather than able-bodied women, fat rather than slim women. Breanne Fahs' (2014) work has been powerful in showing how small the deviations from 'normative femininity' must be in order to be read as 'transgressions'. Her participatory action research, in which she encouraged her students not to remove body hair for the duration of the semester in which they studied her course, vividly illustrates the punitive force of ideals of female hairlessness—captured in students' accounts of others' reactions—and also offers significant insights into their affective and psychic experiences of 'acting out'—what she calls in this volume 'the regulatory politics of disgust' (Chap. 4). Shilpa Phadke (this volume, Chap. 14) also explores the tensions that arise from managing body hair, looking in particular at how feminist mothers in urban India discuss body hair removal, and other beauty practices, with their daughters. More broadly, there seems to be some kind of 'inflationary' process going on in which the most minor acts of resistance to expectations of female appearance are heralded as 'radical' and 'revolutionary' acts, perhaps part of the 'vernacular defiance' of popular and celebrity feminism (Gill 2016). In this context the most minor acts—for example going without mascara or having a visible panty line when wearing leggings—get treated as if they are revolutionary gestures that threaten to bring down patriarchal capitalism as we know it. Whilst writing this chapter, we read a magazine article about *Hunger Games* actress Jena Malone (Marie Claire, December 2015) which captures the flavour of this tendency. It characterises her as a 'fierce', 'sassy', 'badass' spokeswoman for 'girl power'. The act that garnered this judgment? 'Jena Malone ditches bra while running errands in Los Angeles'. Yes, that's it. Watch out world! We highlight this not to criticise Malone—her choice of underwear is entirely her business—but rather to draw attention to the hysterical ramping up of beauty norms to an extent that such an act could be considered 'rad' and 'badass'. To be sure, Malone is a Hollywood celebrity and therefore subject to more scrutiny than most women, but it is indicative, we contend, of a more general intensification of beauty standards that is widely dispersed. More hopefully, it is also indicative of the continuing power of small acts of resistance.

The Extensification of Beauty Pressures

Beauty pressure is not just intensifying but also extensifying in at least two significant ways. First it can be noted that the requirement to 'look good' is extending to new temporalities or moments in a woman's life.

It has shifted deeper into childhood, as media, cosmetics and fashion companies have moved in on younger age groups with magazines like Teen Vogue and product ranges, such as 'Good for you Girls': The Natural Start to Healthy Skin 'where girls are treated with respect and their skin is pampered and protected the way mother nature intended' (www.goodforyougirls.com). The other end of life is also comprehensively colonised, and strategic-commercial mobilisations of fear and anxiety about ageing are the beating heart of the beauty-industrial complex, as shown by Michelle Lazar's analysis of cosmetics advertising where the fixation on youth corresponds with the denigration of ageing (see Lazar, this volume, Chap. 2). If at one point, pregnancy represented, for some women, an escape from or relaxation of the demands of beauty (Tyler 2011), this is no longer the case, at least in the West. Analysing the visibility of the maternal in contemporary culture, Sara de Benedictis and Shani Orgad show how aesthetic labour has become a central feature demanded of the good 'stay-at-home' mother (this volume, Chap. 5). As McRobbie (2013) has noted 'vigilant attention being paid to heteronormative desirability on the part of the wife and mother' has been 'both expanded and more intensely visualized in the age of online communications: Instagram, Facebook, and the Daily Mail's Femail section which reproduces and in many ways replaces the traditional format of the women's magazines now available as a constant feed of images, updated hourly, and in recent times, concentrating almost exclusively on showing pictures of glamorous and famous young women's "toned" "post-baby" bodies.' (2013, p. 132). This is represented as a far greater achievement than giving birth or parenting—highlighting the value accorded to appearance. Meredith Nash's (2014) research on experiences of pregnancy notes a correlate in terms of fear of fat and pregnancy weight gain among women. Moreover, Rachel O'Neill's research undertaken with and among men who participate in the London seduction community shows how sexual desires of heterosexual men are shaped in relation to and through relations with normative feminine beauty ideals (this volume, Chap. 19).

A second form of extension of beauty pressure is to be found in the expansion of areas of the body requiring product-service solutions. Over a 20-year period we have tracked the quest of the beauty industry to find ever more areas in need of work and—crucially—consumption.

'Upper arm definition' became a big thing in the late 1990s; armpits were the new target in the mid-2000s. Female UK commuters, well used to hanging by a strap whilst standing on the train or tube, were systematically body-shamed about the appearance of their 'pits' (see e.g. Dove's video An Open Letter to the Armpit). These campaigns were closely followed by new regimes for dealing with the soles of one's feet—yes, seriously: you couldn't make it up!—leading to the foot spa being one of the top Christmas gifts in 2014 (and notoriously one of the most unused/regifted). And let's not forget the invention of the 'thigh gap' as a new standard of bodily perfection, alongside persistent narrowing and redefinition of the desirable appearance of female genitalia, as also discussed in this volume. Just when you thought there simply could not be any area of the body left for beauty companies to exploit, they invent new conditions, for example 'tech neck': wrinkles and 'slackness' on the skin of the neck as a result of bad postures adopted when using laptops, smart phones, and so on; and new 'lenses' with which to surveil the self: vascular, trichological, glandular and so on. The beauty industry has also increasingly moved 'inside' the body with a range of products—starting with vitamins and minerals and now extending to heavily promoted daily 'drinks' that promote collagen, anti-oxidant defences, and so on. Beauty/anti-ageing is increasingly something you swallow. Developments in genetics represent another new frontier for cosmetics companies—promised to female consumers as scientific interventions that work with your personalised DNA profile (see e.g. Geneu.com). The increasing relations between beauty and a range of other domains—pharmacology, surgery, genetic science, digital technology (e.g. phones that can be used to 'scan' the body) and even food (e.g. 'clean eating' that gives you the 'glow') are striking and have barely received attention from scholars.

Fashioning Subjectivity: The Psychic Life of Neoliberal Beauty Culture

Another 'twist' in neoliberal and postfeminist beauty culture is the way that it increasingly focuses on women's psychic life rather than simply their appearance.- exhorting women to get 'comfortable in their own skin', to 'feel good and you'll look good' and to 'be beautiful at any size'. The beauty industry's increasing interest in self-esteem and confidence has become known in shorthand as 'love your body' (LYB) or 'femvertizing'. In this volume (Chap. 16), Laura Favaro explores the gendered turn to confidence through a study of popular UK-based women's magazines and dubs it 'confidence chic'. LYB discourses are in part a response to feminist anger at what were seen by many as unrealistic and harmful images of female beauty. Dove's advertising campaigns—along with its Campaign for Real Beauty—led the pack and other advertisers quickly followed suit, notably those targeting a market dominated by women—for example, diet and sanpro companies. Today there is a steady stream of commercially motivated virally circulated messages and promotional videos, which target 'unhealthy' body image messages and call on women to believe in their own beauty. This is amplified by magazines and makeover shows with other ostensibly body-positive messages, including distinctively racialised ones (e.g. Love your curls, love your skin). As Rachel Wood demonstrates in this volume (Chap. 18), 'looking good' and 'feeling good' are also conflated in sex advice to heterosexual women in the UK. In Russia too, self-help literature calls upon women to work on and manage not only their body but also their psychic and emotional dispositions (Maria Adamson and Suvi Salmenniemi, this volume, Chap. 17).

As we have argued elsewhere (Gill and Elias 2014) LYB discourses are important and powerful because of the way they appear to interrupt the almost entirely normalised hostile judgment and surveillance of women's bodies in contemporary media culture. As such, they may have a profound affective force for women more accustomed to being invited to relate to their own and other women's bodies in terms of 'flaws' (spots, cellulite, dry skin) and 'battles', (with eating disorders, fat, self-esteem). Online discussions testify to many women's relief and joy at the positive message of LYB discourses, and the emotional power of being encouraged—for once—to feel okay about themselves (e.g. Lynch 2011).

However, the move to LYB should not be celebrated uncritically. A growing literature interrogates its impact and questions the supposedly 'benign' ideas upon which it rests (see Rodrigues 2012; Murphy 2013; Murphy and Jackson 2011; Banet-Weiser 2014). Critics have pointed to a number of problematic features of confidence chic. These include the 'fakeness' of the LYB visual regime. Many of the companies adopting the iconography of 'natural', 'real' women and passing it off as 'authentic' use precisely the techniques that they claim to reject: make-up and Photoshop. For instance, there has been discussion of the realness of/'visual fraud' of Dove Pro-Age texts (Murray 2013, p. 85). There has also been scepticism of the apparent diversity and democratisation of beauty on offer—what has been referred to as the 'diversity paradox' (Rodrigues 2012) or 'a mediated ritual of rebellion' (Kadir and Tidy 2011). As we noted elsewhere, Dove was exposed placing an advert in *Craigslist* searching for 'flawless' non-models for the next commercial. The ad stated: 'Beautiful arms and legs and face… naturally fit, not too curvy or athletic… Beautiful hair and skin is a must'. An article in *The Week*, commenting upon this, noted acerbically that Dove's 'come as you are' campaign has an 'if you're flawless, that is' clause attached.

It is also striking to note the fact that many of the companies involved in avidly championing an LYB ethic have been precisely those implicated in selling body *dis*-satisfaction over many years (e.g. Weightwatchers, diet brand Special K). Moreover, the adverts frequently rely upon making prominent 'hate your body' messages in the service of selling us their 'love your body' idea (and the product) (see Gill and Elias 2014 for discussion of Special K's Ssshh Let's Shut Down Fat Talk—which did just this). In this way they tend to reinforce the cultural intelligibility of the female body as inherently 'difficult to love' (see, e.g. Lynch 2011; Murphy 2013). In doing so they 're-cite' (Butler 1997) hateful discourse about the female body that depends upon its normalised cultural pathologisation (McRobbie 2009). Analysing 'empowerment' discourses targeting girls and young women that focus on beauty and the body as a source of empowerment, as well as practices of 'aesthetic entrepreneurship' on social media sites, Sarah Banet-Weister (this volume, Chap. 15) argues that these two forms of media production are intimately interrelated and together produce a gendered logic which centres the 'empowered' feminine body as a source of aesthetic labour.

In addition to all these critiques, we highlight the way in which current anti-beauty beauty discourses *blame* women for their own unhappiness or discontent—suggesting that female body dissatisfaction is women's own fault—women 'do this to themselves'. Feeling fat, feeling ugly, feeling flat-chested or too large-breasted, feeling that you don't look right and can't fit in or pass—all these are constructed as women's own problems—rather than being products of living in a culture that so emphasises and fetishises women's appearance and desirability. Women's (sometimes) difficult relationships to their own embodied selves are both dislocated from their structural constraints in patriarchal capitalism and shorn of their psychosocial complexity (see also Lynch 2011; Murphy 2013). All that is needed is to get over it—something these discourses suggest is a relatively easy thing to do: 'all you need is a pen and a piece of paper' asserts 'Operation Beautiful', whilst other texts suggest a digital upgrade—'selfie esteem' or a 'camo confession' (Dermablend).

Above all LYB discourses are implicated in a wider 'confidence cult' which operates as a new 'cultural scaffolding' (Gavey 2005) for the regulation of women:

> 'No longer is it enough to work on and discipline the body, but in today's society the beautiful body must be accompanied by a beautiful mind, with suitably upgraded and modernised postfeminist attitudes to the self. Women must makeover not simply their bodies but now—thanks to LYB discourse—their subjectivity as well, embracing an affirmative confident disposition, no matter how they actually feel.' (Gill and Elias 2014, p. 185)

In this way, beauty is recast as 'a state of mind', but we do not see a loosening of the grip of punishing appearance standards for women, but rather a move of beauty into the arena of subjectivity, an extension of its force into psychic life as well. It represents what Irene Neverla (personal communication) calls 'soft hatred'—a corollary of 'soft power'. This highlights the complexity of contemporary beauty discourses, entangled as they are with exhortations to self-love, confidence, gratitude and anti-beauty messages (in the service of selling beauty products) in a context of neoliberal and postfeminist governmentality and capitalism's move to colonise all of life—including our deepest feelings about ourselves. By drawing on the theoretical frameworks of neoliberalism and postfeminism, amongst others, and examining 'confidence chic' in a range of contexts, this book contributes to our understanding of the 'psychic life' of beauty.

The Turn to Labour

The final set of ideas that we want to bring to bear on beauty politics is the study of work and labour. At first glance this might seem an odd addition, but the new 'turn' to labour has given rise to a proliferation of different terms for thinking about work and we believe that this vocabulary is productive for engaging with appearance politics. This literature speaks to the need to unpack the different forms of 'labouring' that go into any particular kind of work—be this the 'emotional labour' of the flight attendant (Hochschild 1983), the 'aesthetic labour' of the barista (Warhurst and Nickson 2009) or the 'creative labour' of the media worker (Hesmondhalgh and Baker 2011). The very multiplication of terms—in addition to the above there are 'immaterial labour', 'affective labour', 'venture labour' and others—suggests a new interest in opening up understandings of the diversity of practices that constitute work, as seemingly 'simple' roles—for example serving coffee—are revealed to be complex accomplishments involving attentiveness to skin, hair, make-up, fashion, voice, body language, friendliness, managing emotions, dealing with conflict, and so on—as well as the more 'obvious' requirements of using coffee equipment quickly and hygienically and dealing with financial transactions. A growing body of research is concerned with aesthetic labour in the workplace. Irene Grugulis et al. (2004, p. 7) argue that 'there is an increasing tendency for organisations to manage the way their employees feel and look as well as the way they behave, so that work is emotional and aesthetic as well as (or instead of) productive' (see Hochschild 1983; Warhust and Nickson 2001). This development is seen particularly in interactive service industries, such as retailing, where recruitment and training focus on the emotions and appearance of the labour force deployed to deliver the service (Thompson et al. 2001). In the 'style' labour market, the looks, deportment, accents and general stylishness of the bartender, waitress or retail assistant are part of what gives the service being offered value—for example makes it cool or upmarket (Nickson et al. 2001). In Richard Lloyd's (2006) study of Wicker Park in Chicago, he discussed how businesses moving into the area sought to hire artists not simply because they represented cheap labour but crucially because they could lend their 'hipness' (e.g. stylish anti-style appearance, body piercings, etc.) to cafes and restaurants, and thus became implicated in what Lloyd calls the 'industrialization of Bohemia'. Increasingly, sociologists of work and labour tell us, employees have to 'look good and sound right' (Warhust and Nickson 2001) in many contemporary workplaces. What 'right' is varies by place, by employer, by branding strategies but is profoundly classed, aged, gendered and racialised—also inflected by sexuality.

Aesthetics, in this case, refers not only to appearance but also to voice, posture, demeanour, body language, self-presentation on social media, and so on. For example women's voices were historically deemed 'wrong' for broadcasting, and in the UK, news presentation, right up to the mid-1970s, was exclusively done by men. It was often said that if a woman were to read the news 'no one would take it seriously' (Holland 1987). Whilst this seems absurd to contemporary observers, it is a clear example of the entanglement of gender, aesthetics and authority. In the workplace today, this continues to be an issue, with a feminine self-presentation both being culturally demanded for women yet associated with lower status and with not being taken seriously. Much research highlights the difficulties for women—especially those in senior positions—negotiating these conflicting demands, and a plethora of advice exists on how to perform the 'right kind' of feminine self-presentation, whilst eschewing presentations of femininity that are 'trashy' (a code word for lower class) or too sexualised (see Entwistle 2000, on the fashioned body). Ngaire Donaghue (this volume, Chap. 13) looks at these issues in relation to academic dressing via an analysis of discussion on two 'academic fashion' blogs. One of the key issues in these discussions concerns the rights of young women to reclaim a normatively feminine aesthetic without having it undermine their claims to scholarly seriousness. Adopting an auto-ethnographic approach, Scarlett Brown (this volume, Chap. 8) also looks at women's aesthetic labour in academia, exploring her experiences of achieving the 'right' professional demeanour.

As we have noted, class is also central to aesthetic labour and also affects men. A report published in 2016 by the Social Mobility Commission in the UK found that as well as private schooling, a first class degree from a 'top' University and several periods of unpaid internships, graduates entering the financial sector have to have 'polish' and the right 'aura'—concepts that were broken down to include dress, confidence and comportment. One interviewee said it was easy to spot candidates who did not have appropriate 'polish' (read: class privilege) by their bad haircut and 'their suit's always too big…they don't know which tie to wear' (Social Mobility Commission 2016, p. 88). Advice on how to achieve 'polish' is—like confidence—at the heart of a rapidly expanding self-help literature and YouTube micro-blogging industry, and an ever-growing number of companies is moving into this terrain to offer tutelage in these classed, racialised and gendered 'qualities'. Smartworks, for example, claims great success for its 'two hour core dressing and interview preparation service' (http://smartworks.org.uk/what-we-do/).

In recent years there have been a number of discrimination lawsuits against this kind of employer behaviour. Clothing retailer Abercrombie and Fitch, for example, has been subject to suits from employees regarding disability, weight and the wearing of a headscarf—and has been widely critiqued for what some see as its extraordinarily narrow 'lookist' hiring strategy. Whilst it is good to see these kinds of challenges, mostly they represent small and isolated acts of individual resistance that pose little threat to the wider way in which companies and organisations operate—namely hiring people who they perceive as fitting with their 'brand' and attempting to shape the appearance of their employees to reflect and promote brand values. To counter the age, gender, class, transphobic and homophobic, disability, weight and appearance discrimination in organisations requires not simply some legal contestation but a profound cultural shift.

In her valuable article on aesthetic labour, Ashley Mears (2014) examines a family of terms connected to these practices. Body work, she argues, might be thought of as the unpaid work people do on their own bodies—beauty work is a subset of this. Display work is that performed in jobs that require a high level of bodily display—for example, modelling or stripping. Bodily labour, by contrast, is paid work on the bodies of others. Tracing the rising visibility of salon work in media culture, Laurie Oulette (this volume, Chap. 10) shows how this previously devalued beauty service labour is now glamorised and its risky and exploitative dimensions disregarded. Also focusing on beauty care workers, Jie

Yang (this volume, Chap. 6) demonstrates how Chinese workers provide holistic services, which focus on physical *and* psychological aspects, thus exercising a particular form of governance of life.

Aesthetic Entrepreneurship

The notion of aesthetic labour has further developed during the period we have been working on this collection. Elizabeth Wissinger (2015) published an important study of the modelling industry that resonates powerfully with our aims here. Based on interviews with and ethnographic observation of models in New York City, Wissinger's work foregrounds the ongoing and relentless requirement to work on and construct the body, style and reputation. It is similar to the kinds of activities dubbed 'display work' by Mears (2014), but extends this concept. Wissinger calls it 'glamour labour':

> 'Glamour labour works on both body and image—the bodywork to manage appearance in person and image work to create and maintain one's "cool" quotient—how hooked up, tuned in, and "in the know" one is. Glamour labour involves all aspects of one's image, from physical presentation, to personal connections, to friendships and fun.' (2015, p. 3)

In our reading 'glamour labour' brings three significant ideas to contemporary understandings of beauty work. First, it highlights the proliferation of different domains across which 'glamour' is practiced. Importantly it is not limited to the physical body but also involves personality, relationships, lifestyle and—crucially—social media use. It is hard to underestimate the significance of this—at the time of writing model Gigi Hadid has been crowned the world's most influential beauty ambassador—displacing Fashion Week front row tastemakers such as Anna Wintour who has held the position for decades. This is not because of Hadid's catwalk appearances but because of her 23 million followers on Instagram—her digital presence both complements and far exceeds her role as a jobbing model—and Wissinger's analysis captures this. Second, glamour labour is a development from notions of aesthetic labour because it 'fuses' different aspects of bodywork, showing how they have 'bled together' and become inseparable. Conceptually this is an important development of notions that relate aesthetic labour only to particular workplaces. With glamour labour there is no outside of (beauty) work. Finally, the notion is important because of its emphasis upon dynamism—glamour labour is never done. It is always unfinished and in a state of becoming. As Wissinger (2015, p. 26) explains

> '[I]n recent decades modeling work has come to require embodying the ideal of a malleable body…modeling work became the work to always be ready for, or in the process of, transformation, and in so doing glamorized this process for the general public'.

We want to build on these interventions. First we want to argue that 'glamour labour' is not just the labour of models or others in the beauty business but is increasingly a labour in which we are *all* expected to participate (whether we do so or not). It is, of course, clear in fashion design, in clothes and beauty retail, in many sections of media and entertainment, among people who make their living in part from their own or others' appearance, in the growing numbers of people who post pictures of their daily outfit online, in the booming 'industry' of beauty vlogging—and in many other kinds of 'work'. But, more than this, we believe that some form of aesthetic labour is increasingly demanded of all women (and increasing numbers of men), as we live in societies that become ever more dominated by new forms of visibility, appearance and looking, and in which more and more of us partake in the endless labour of 'curating a visible self' on and offline (Dobson 2015). As Monika Sengul-Jones (this volume, Chap. 12) argues, gendered and racialised aesthetic labour also takes place on online freelance marketplaces where female freelance writers engage in different forms of 'body work' to manage their self-presentation online. Just as the concept of aesthetic labour is too important to refer only to employment, so the notion of glamour labour has an analytical value that goes far beyond modelling. Today—at least in the West—we are all living in the image factory.

Second, we would like to develop the notion of glamour labour by extending it to *subjectivity* to highlight the way in which aesthetic practices increasingly constitute aspects of psychic life. Part of the malleability Wissinger discusses, and the ethic of self-transformation and self-reinvention that characterises many contemporary beauty narratives, involves making over the whole self rather than just the surface appearance. We call this aesthetic entrepreneurship so as to draw links with existing work that explores and critiques neoliberalism as a social, cultural and psychic project—not simply as an economic and political one. The notion is also important in explicitly refuting accounts of beauty work in terms of 'docile bodies' or 'passivity'. 'Entrepreneurship' captures not only the labour involved but also the agency and creativity with which people go about styling, adorning and transforming themselves.

Finally, by using the notion of 'aesthetic entrepreneurship', we seek to highlight the links between contemporary beauty politics and neoliberalism. The new centrality of notions of labour in thinking about contemporary subjectivities is connected to neoliberalism and its attempt to construct the person as 'enterprising': 'a calculating, self-reflexive, "economic" subject; one that calculates about itself and works upon itself in order to better itself" (du Gay 1996, p. 124)—and this includes appearance. Like the neoliberal subject more broadly, the aesthetic entrepreneur is autonomous, self-inventing and self-regulating in the pursuit of beauty practices. Preoccupations with appearance, beauty and the body are turned into yet another project to be planned, managed and regulated in a way that is calculative and seemingly self-directed. As Dosekun (this volume, Chap. 9) has shown, the psychological and physical risks of beauty are managed and borne by the aesthetic entrepreneur, paralleling wider trends in neoliberalism where risk is individualised. Based on our research on the psychic life of postfeminism and neoliberalism (Gill in press-b; Scharff 2016), aesthetic entrepreneurs may repudiate injuries (see also Scharff 2016) as well as affects that are more difficult to reconcile with the quest to be entrepreneurial, such as anger and insecurity. Certainly, the structures of feeling of aesthetic entrepreneurs are complex and merit closer analysis. What we hope to have outlined in this introductory chapter, however, is an approach to contemporary beauty politics, which allows us to analyse the interplay of affect and surveillance in the context of beauty politics, whilst not losing sight of ambivalence, dissonance and, importantly, the ways in which subjectivity not only intersects but also breaks with wider structuring forces such as neoliberalism and postfeminism. We believe that the notion of aesthetic entrepreneurship allows us to grasp some of these complexities through its link with neoliberalism, the way it draws on and is embedded in wider research and debates on different forms of labour, and the emphasis it places on questions of the material, social and psychic life of beauty.

References

Ahmed, S. (2010). *The Promise of Happiness*. Durham: Duke University Press.

Allen, K. (2014). 'Blair's Children': Young Women as 'Aspirational Subjects' in the Psychic Landscape of Class. *Sociological Review, 62*(4), 760–779.

Andrejevic, M. (2015). Foreword. In R. E. Dubrofsky & S. A. Magnet (Eds.), *Feminist Surveillance Studies* (pp. ix–xviii). Durham: Duke University Press.

Banet-Weiser, S. (1999). *The Most Beeautiful Girl in the World: Beauty Pageants and National Identity*. Los Angeles: University of California Press.

Banet-Weiser, S. (2012). *Authentic™: The Politics of Ambivalence in a Brand Culture*. New York: New York University Press.

Banet-Weiser, S. (2014). Am I Pretty or Ugly? Girls and the Market for Self-Esteem. *Girlhood Studies, 7*(1), 83–101.

Bartky, S. L. (1990). *Femininity and Domination: Studies in the Phenomenology of Oppression*. London/New York: Routledge.

Baumgardner, J., & Richards, A. (2000). *Manifesta: Young Women, Feminism and the Future*. New York: Farrar, Straus and Giroux.

Berger, J. (1972). *Ways of Seeing*. London: Penguin.

Berlant, L. (2006). Cruel Optimism. *Differences: A Journal of Feminist Cultural Studies, 17*(3), 20–36.

Bordo, S. (1993). *Unbearable Weight: Feminism, Western Culture, and the Body*. Berkeley: University of California Press.

Bordo, S. (1997). *Twilight Zones: The Hidden Life of Cultural Images from Plato to O.J.* Berkeley: University of California Press.

Boyne, R. (2000). Post-panopticism. *Economy and Society, 29*(2), 285–307.

Brown, W. (2003). Neoliberalism and the End of Liberal Democracy. *Theory & Event, 7*(1). Retrieved October 10, 2016, from e.jhu.edu/article/48659

Brown, W. (2015). *Undoing the Demos: Neoliberalism's Stealth Revolution*. New York: Zone Books.

Burchell, G. (1993). Liberal Government and Techniques of the Self. *Economy and Society, 22*(3), 267–282.

Butler, J. (1997). *Excitable Speech: A Politics of the Performative*. New York: Routledge.
Chancer, L. S. (1998). *Reconcilable Differences: Confronting Beauty, Pornography and the Future of Feminism*. Berkeley: University of California Press.
Clarke, J. (2008). Living with/in and Without Neo-Liberalism. *Focaal, 51*, 135–147.
Clough, P. T. (2007). Introduction. In P. T. Clough & J. Hailey (Eds.), *The Affective Turn: Theorizing the Social* (pp. 1–33). Durham: Duke University Press.
Colebrook, C. (2003). Happiness, Theoria, and Everyday Life. *Symploke, 11*(1–2), 132–151.
Colebrook, C. (2006). Introduction. *Feminist Theory, 7*(2), 131–142.
Coleman, R. (2009). *The Becoming of Bodies: Girls, Images, Experience*. Manchester: Manchester University Press.
Coleman, R., & Figueroa, M. G. M. (2010). Past and Future Perfect? Beauty, Affect and Hope. *Journal for Cultural Research, 14*(4), 357–373.
Craig, M. L. (2002). *Ain't I A Beauty Queen? Black Women, Beauty and the Politics of Race*. Oxford: Oxford University Press.
Craig, M. L. (2006). Race, Beauty and the Tangled Knot of a Guilty Pleasure. *Feminist Theory, 7*(2), 159–177.
Crouch, C. (2011). *The Strange Non-Death of Neo-Liberalism*. Cambridge: Polity.
Dardot, P., & Laval, C. (2013). *The New Way of the World: On Neoliberal Society*. London: Verso.
Davies, B. (2005). The (Im)possibility of Intellectual Work in Neoliberal Regimes. *Discourse: Studies in the Cultural Politics of Education, 26*(1), 1–14.
Davis, K. (2015). Should a Feminist Dance Tango? Some Reflections on the Experience and Politics of Passion. *Feminist Theory, 16*(1), 3–21.
Dobson, A. S. (2015). *Postfeminist Digital Cultures: Femininity, Social Media, and Self-Representation*. New York: Palgrave Macmillan.
Dosekun, S. (2015). For Western Girls Only? Postfeminism as Transnational Culture. *Feminist Media Studies, 15*(6), 960–975.
Douglas, S. J. (2010). *Enlightened sexism: The seductive message that feminism's work is done*. Macmillan.
Dubrofsky, R. E., & Magnet, S. A. (2015). Feminist Surveillance Studies: Critical Interventions. In R. E. Dubrofsky & S. A. Magnet (Eds.), *Feminist Surveillance Studies* (pp. 1–20). Durham: Duke University Press.
Elias, A. (2016). *Beautiful Body, Confident Soul: Young Women and the Beauty Labour of Neoliberalism*. Unpublished PhD thesis, submitted to King's College London.

Elias, A., & Gill, R. (in press). Beauty Surveillance: The Digital Self-Monitoring Cultures of Neoliberalism. *European Journal of Cultural Studies.*

Entwistle, J. (2000). *The Fashioned Body: Fashion, Dress and Modern Social Theory*. Cambridge: Polity Press.

Fahs, B. (2014). Perilous Patches and Pitstaches: Imagined Versus Lived Experiences of Women's Body Hair Growth. *Psychology of Women Quarterly, 38*, 167–180.

Faludi, S. (1991). *Backlash: The Undeclared War Against American Women.* New York: Crown.

Farris, S. R. (2012). Femonationalism and the "Regular" Army of Labor Called Migrant Women. *History of the Present, 2*(2), 184–199.

Featherstone, M. (2010). Body, Image and Affect in Consumer Culture. *Body & Society, 16*(1), 193–221.

Felski, R. (2006). Because It Is Beautiful: New Feminist Perspectives on Beauty. *Feminist Theory, 7*(2), 273–282.

Ferreday, D. (2007). Adapting Femininities: The New Burlesque. *M/C Journal,* 10(2) [online]. Retrieved October 13, 2016, from http://journal.media-culture.org.au/0705/12-ferreday.php

Figueroa, M. G. M. (2015). On Dancing, Lipstick and Feminism: A Response to Kathy Davis. *Feminist Theory, 16*(1), 23–25.

Figueroa, M. G. M., & Moore, M. R. (2013). Beauty, Race and Feminist Theory in Latin America and the Caribbean. *Feminist Theory, 14*(2), 131–136.

Foucault, M. (1980). Power/Knowledge: Selected Interviews and Other Writings, 1972–1977 (C. Gordon, ed; C. Gordon, L. Marshall, J. Mepham and K. Soper, Trans.). New York: Pantheon.

Foucault, M. (2008). *The Birth of Biopolitics*. Basingstoke: Palgrave.

Garland, C., & Harper, S. (2012). Did Somebody Say Neoliberalism? On the Uses and Limitations of a Critical Concept in Media and Communication Studies. *TripleC, 10*(2), 413–424.

Gavey, N. (2005). *Just Sex? The Cultural Scaffolding of Rape.* London: Routledge.

du Gay, P. (1996). *Consumption and Identity at Work.* London: Sage.

Gilbert, J. (ed). (2013). Special Issue: Neoliberal Culture. *New Formations: A Journal of Culture/Theory/Politics,* 80/81.

Gill, R. (2007). *Gender and the Media*. Cambridge: Polity.

Gill, R. (2016). Post-postfeminism? New Feminist Visibilities in Postfeminist Times. *Feminist Media Studies, 16*(4), 610–630.

Gill, R. (in press-a). Surveillance Is a Feminist Issue. In T. Oren & A. Press (Eds.), *Handbook of Contemporary Feminism*. New York: Routledge.

Gill, R. (in press-b). The Affective, Cultural and Psychic Life of Postfeminism. *European Journal of Cultural Studies.*

Gill, R., & Elias, A. (2014). 'Awaken your Incredible': Love Your Body Discourses and Postfeminist Contradictions. *International Journal of Media and Cultural Politics, 10*(2), 179–188.

Gill, R., & Orgad, S. (2015). The Confidence Culture. *Australian Feminist Studies, 30*(86), 324–344.

Gill, R., & Scharff, C. (Eds.). (2011). *New Femininities: Postfeminism, Neoliberalism and Subjectivity*. Basingstoke: Palgrave Macmillan.

Gilroy, P. (2013). '… We Got to Get Over Before We Go Under …' Fragments for a History of Black Vernacular Neoliberalism. *New Formations, 80–81*, 23–38.

Gladwell, M. (2005). *Blink: The Power of Thinking Without Thinking*. London: Penguin.

Gregg, M., & Seigworth, G. J. (2010). An Inventory of Shimmers. In M. Gregg & G. J. Seigworth (Eds.), *The Affect Theory Reader* (pp. 1–25). Durham: Duke University Press.

Grewal, I., & Kaplan, C. (1994). *Scattered Hegemonies: Postmodernity and Transnational Feminist Practices*. Minneapolis: University of Minnesota Press.

Grogan, S. (2007). *Body Image: Understanding Body Dissatisfaction in Men, Women and Children*. London: Routledge.

Grugulis, I., Warhurst, C., & Keep, E. (2004). What's Happening to 'Skill'? In C. Warhurst, I. Grugulis, & E. Keep (Eds.), *The Skills That Matter* (pp. 1–18). Basingstoke: Palgrave Macmillan.

Hardin, C. (2014). Finding the 'Neo' in Neoliberalism. *Cultural Studies, 28*(2), 199–221.

Hardt, M. (2005). Into the Factory: Negri's Lennin and the Subjective Caesura (1968–1973). In T. S. Murphy & A.-K. Mustapha (Eds.), *Resistance in Practice: The Philosophy of Antonio Negri* (pp. 7–37). London and Ann Arbor, MI: Pluto Press.

Hayward, M. (2013). Atms, Teleprompters and Photobooths: A Short History of Neoliberal Optics. *New Formations, 80*(1), 194–208.

Hegde, R. S. (2011). *Circuits of Visibility: Gender and Transnational Media Cultures*. New York: New York University Press.

Hemmings, C. (2005). Invoking Affect: Cultural Theory and the Ontological Turn. *Cultural Studies, 19*(5), 548–567.

Henderson, L. (2008). Slow Love. *The Communication Review, 11*(3), 219–224.

Henderson, M., & Taylor, A. (in press). *Postfeminism Down Under: The Australian Postfeminist Mystique*. Abingdon/New York: Routledge.

Hesmondhalgh, D., & Baker, S. (2011). *Creative Labour: Media Work in Three Cultural Industries*. Abingdon/New York: Routledge.

Hochschild, A. (1983). *The Managed Heart: Commercialization of Human Feeling*. Berkeley/London: University of California Press.

Holland, P. (1987). When a Woman Reads the News. In H. Baehr & G. Dyer (Eds.), *Boxed-in: Women and Television* (pp. 133–150). London: Pandora.

Hunter, M. (2011). Buying Racial Capital: Skin-Bleaching and Cosmetic Surgery in a Globalized World. *Journal of Pan African Studies, 4*(4), 142–164.

Illouz, E. (2007). *Cold Intimacies: The Making of Emotional Capitalism*. Cambridge: Polity.

Imre, A., Marciniak, K., & O'Healy, A. (2009). Transcultural Mediations and Transnational Politics of Difference. *Feminist Media Studies, 9*(4), 385–390.

Isin, E. (2014). Acts, Affects, Calls. *OpenDemocracy* [online]. Retrieved October 13, 2016, from https://www.opendemocracy.net/can-europe-make-it/engin-isin/acts-affects-calls

Jarrin, A. (2015). Towards a Biopolitics of Beauty: Eugenics, Aesthetic Hierarchies and Plastic Surgery in Brazil. *Journal of Latin American Cultural Studies, 24*(4), 535–552.

Jha, M. R. (2016). *The Global Beauty Industry: Colorism, Racism, and the National Body*. London/New York: Routledge.

Kadir, S., & Tidy, J. (2011). Gays, Gaze and Aunty Gok: The Disciplining of Gender and Sexuality in 'How to Look Good Naked'. *Feminist Media Studies, 13*(2), 177–191.

Kanai, A. (2015). WhatShouldWeCallMe? Self-Branding, Individuality and Belonging in Youthful Femininities on Tumblr. *M/C Journal, 18*(1). Retrieved October 10, 2016, from http://journal.media-culture.org.au/index.php/mcjournal/article/view/936

Kanai, A. (2016). Laughing Through the Discomfort: Navigating Neoliberal Feeling Rules in a Tumblr Attention Economy. In T. Petray & A. Stephens (Eds.), *Proceedings of The Australian Sociological Association Conference, Cairns, 23–26 November 2015*.

Kim, J. M. (2012). *Women in South Korea: New Femininities and Consumption*. London/New York: Routledge.

Larner, W. (2000). Neo-liberalism: Policy, Ideology, Governmentality. *Studies in Political Economy, 63*, 5–25.

Lemke, T. (2001). 'The Birth of Bio-Politics': Michel Foucault's Lecture at the Collège de France on Neo-Liberal Governmentality. *Economy and Society, 30*(2), 190–207.

Lloyd, R. D. (2006). *Neo-Bohemia: Art and Commerce in the Postindustrial City*. London/New York: Routledge.

Lumby, C. (1997). *Bad Girls: The Media, Sex and Feminism in the 90s*. Sidney: Allen & Unwin.

Lupton, D. (2016). *The Quantified Self*. Cambridge: Polity.

Lynch, M. (2011). Blogging for Beauty? A Critical Analysis of Operation Beautiful. *Women's Studies International Forum, 34*(6), 582–592.

Madhok, S., Phillips, A., & Wilson, K. (2013). *Gender, Agency, and Coercion*. Basingstoke: Palgrave Macmillan.

Massumi, B. (2002). *Parables for the Virtual: Movement, Affect, Sensation*. Durham: Duke University Press.

McAvoy, J. (2015). From Ideology to Feeling: Discourse, Emotion, and an Analytic Synthesis. *Qualitative Research in Psychology, 12*(1), 22–33.

McNay, L. (2009). Self as Enterprise: Dilemmas of Control and Resistance in Foucault's The Birth of Biopolitics. *Theory, Culture & Society, 26*(6), 55–77.

McNeil, M. (2010). Postmillennial Feminist Theory: Encounters with Humanism, Materialism, Critique, Nature, Biology and Darwin. *Journal for Cultural Research, 14*(4), 427–437.

Mathiesen, T. (1997). The Viewer Society: Michel Foucault's Panopticon Revisited. *Theoretical Criminology, 1*(2), 215–234.

McRobbie, A. (2009). *The Aftermath of Feminism: Gender, Culture and Social Change*. London: Sage.

McRobbie, A. (2013). Feminism, the Family and the New Mediated Maternalism. *New Formations, 80–81*, 119–137.

McRobbie, A. (2015). Notes on the Perfect: Competitive Femininity in Neoliberal Times. *Australian Feminist Studies, 30*(83), 3–20.

Mears, A. (2014). Aesthetic Labor for the Sociologies of Work, Gender and Beauty. *Sociology Compass, 8*(12), 1330–1343.

Mercer, K. (1990). Black Art and the Burden of Representation. *Third Text, 4*(10), 61–78.

Mirowski, P. (2014). *Never Let a Serious Crisis Go to Waste: How Neoliberalism Survived the Financial Meltdown*. London: Verso.

Mirowski, P., & Phlewe, D. (2009). *The Road from Mont Pelerin: The Making of the Neoliberal Thought Cllective*. Cambridge, MA: Harvard University Press.

Mohanty, C. (1984). Under Western Eyes: Feminist Scholarship and Colonial Discourses. *Boundary, 2*(12/13), 333–358.

Morton, K. (2015). Emerging Geographies of Disciplining the Ageing Body: Practising Cosmetic Technologies in the Aesthetic Clinic. *Gender, Place & Culture, 22*(7), 1041–1057.

Mudge, S. L. (2008). What Is Neo-Liberalism? *Socio-Economic Review, 6*(4), 703–731.

Murphy, R. (2013). *(De)Constructing "Body Love" Discourses in Young Women's Magazines*'. Unpublished PhD thesis, University of Wellington, Victoria.

Murphy, R., & Jackson, S. (2011). Bodies-as-image? The Body Made Visible in Magazine Love Your Body Content. *Women's Studies Journal, 25*(1), 17–30.

Murray, D. P. (2013). Branding 'Real' Social Change in Dove's Campaign for Real Beauty. *Feminist Media Studies, 13*(1), 83–101.

Nash, M. (2014). Picturing Mothers: A Photovoice Study of Body Image in Pregnancy. *Health Sociology Review, 23*(3), 242–253.

Neff, G., & Nafus, D. (2016). *Self Tracking*. Cambridge, MA: MIT Press.

Ngai, S. (2005). *Ugly Feelings*. Cambridge, MA: Harvard University Press.

Nguyen, M. T. (2011). The Biopower of Beauty: Humanitarian Imperialisms and Global Feminisms in the War on Terror. *Signs, 36*(2), 359–383.

Nickson, D. P., Warhurst, C., Witz, A., & Cullen, A. M. (2001). The Importance of Being Aesthetic: Work, Employment and Service Organization. In I. Grugulis & H. Willmott (Eds.), *A Sturdy* (pp. 170–190). Customer Service: Empowerment and Entrapment.

O'Flynn, G., & Petersen, E. B. (2007). The 'Good Life' and the 'Rich Portfolio': Young Women, Schooling and Neoliberal Subjectification. *British Journal of Sociology of Education, 28*(4), 459–472.

Ong, A. (2006). *Neoliberalism as Exception: Mutations in Citizenship and Sovereignty*. Durham: Duke University Press.

Pham, M.-H. (2011). The Right to Fashion in the Age of Terrorism. *Signs, 36*(2), 385–410.

Rettberg, J. W. (2014). *Seeing Ourselves Through Technology: How We Use Selfies, Blogs and Wearable Devices to See and Shape Ourselves*. Basingstoke: Palgrave Macmillan.

Riley, S., Evans, A., & Mackiewicz, A. (2016). It's Just Between Girls: Negotiating the Postfeminist Gaze in Women's 'Looking Talk'. *Feminism & Psychology, 26*(1), 94–103.

Ringrose, J., & Harvey, L. (2015). BBM Is Like match.com: Social Networking and the Digital Mediation of Teen's Sexual Cultures. In J. Bailey & V. Steeves (Eds.), *Egirls, Ecitizens* (pp. 199–226). Ottawa: University of Ottawa Press.

Ringrose, J., Harvey, L., Gill, R., & Livingstone, S. (2013). Teen Girls, Sexual Double Standards and 'Sexting': Gendered Value in Digital Image Exchange. *Feminist Theory, 14*(3), 305–323.

Ringrose, J., & Renold, E. (2010). Normative Cruelties and Gender Deviants: The performative Effects of Bully Discourses for Girls and Boys in School. *British Educational Research Journal, 36*(4), 573–596.

Ringrose, J., & Walkerdine, V. (2008). Regulating the Abject: The TV Make-over as Site of Neo-Liberal Reinvention Toward Bourgeois Femininity. *Feminist Media Studies, 8*(3), 227–246.

Rodrigues, S. (2012). Undressing Homogeneity: Prescribing Femininity and the Transformation of Self-Esteem in 'How to Look Good Naked'. *Journal of Popular Film and Television, 40*(1), 42–51.

Rose, N. (1992). Governing the Enterprising Self. In P. Heelas & P. Morris (Eds.), *The Values of the Enterprise Culture: The Moral Debate* (pp. 141–164). London: Routledge.

Saraswati, L. A. (2013). *Seeing Beauty, Sensing Race in Transnational Indonesia*. Honolulu: University of Hawaii Press.

Sawicki, J. (1991). *Disciplining Foucault: Feminism, Power and the Body*. London/ New York: Routledge.

Scharff, C. (2011). Disarticulating Feminism: Idividualization, Neoliberalism and the Othering of 'Muslim Women'. *European Journal of Women's Studies, 18*(2), 119–134.

Scharff, C. (2015). The Psychic Life of Neoliberalism: Mapping the Contours of Entrepreneurial Subjectivity. *Theory, Culture & Society*, 0(0) 1–16 (published online ahead of print).

Scharff, C. (2016). Gender and Neoliberalism: Young Women as Ideal Neoliberal Subjects. In S. Springer, K. Birch, & J. Macleavy (Eds.), *The Handbook of Neoliberalism* (pp. 217–226). London: Routledge.

Senft, T. M. (2015). The Skin of the Selfie. In A. Bieber (Ed.), *Ego Update: The Future of Digital Identity*. Dusseldorf, Germany: NRW Forum Publications.

Shamir, R. (2008). The Age of Responsibilization: On Market-embedded Morality. *Economy and Society, 37*(1), 1–19.

Social Mobility Commission. (2016). *Socio-economic Diversity in Life Sciences and Investment Banking*. London: Social Mobility Commission.

Springer, S., Birch, K., & MacLeavy, J. (Eds.). (2016). *The Handbook of Neoliberalism*. New York: Routledge.

Stedman Jones, D. (2012). *Masters of the Universe: Hayek, Friedman, and the Birth of Neoliberal Politics*. Princeton, Woodstock: Princeton University Press.

Tasker, Y., & Negra, D. (Eds.). (2007). *Interrogating Postfeminism: Gender and the Politics of Popular Culture*. Durham: Duke University Press.

Tate, S. (2007). Black Beauty: Shade, Hair and Anti-Racist Aesthetics. *Ethnic and Racial Studies, 30*(2), 300–319.

Tate, S. (2013). The Performativity of Black Beauty Shame in Jamaica and its Diaspora: Problematising and Transforming Beauty Iconicities. *Feminist Theory, 14*(2), 219–235.

Thompson, P., Warhurst, C., & Callaghan, G. (2001). Ignorant Theory and Knowledgeable Workers: Interrogating the Connections Between Knowledge, Skills and Services. *Journal of Management Studies, 38*(7), 923–942.

Tyler, I. (2008). 'Chav Mum Chav Scum': Class Disgust in Contemporary Britain. *Feminist Media Studies, 8*(1), 17–34.

Tyler, I. (2011). Pregnant Beauty: Maternal Femininities Under Neoliberalism. In R. Gill & C. Scharff (Eds.), *New Femininities: Postfeminism, Neoliberalism and Subjectivity* (pp. 21–36). Palgrave Macmillan: Basingstoke.

Walby, K., & Anais, S. (2015). Research Methods, Institutional Ethnography and Feminist Surveillance Studies. In R. E. Dubrofsky & S. A. Magnet (Eds.), *Feminist Surveillance Studies* (pp. 208–220). Durham: Duke University Press.

Warhurst, C., & Nickson, D. (2009). Who's Got the Look?' From Emotional to Aesthetic and Sexualised Labour in Interactive Services. *Gender, Work and Organisation, 16*(3), 385–404.

Warhust, C., & Nickson, D. (2001). *Looking Good, Sounding Right: Style Counselling in the New Economy*. London: Industrial Society.

Weber, B. R. (2009). *Makeover TV: Selfhood, Citizenship, and Celebrity*. Durham: Duke University Press.

Wen, H. (2013). *Buying Beauty: Cosmetic Surgery in China*. Hong Kong: Hong Kong University Press.

Wendt, B. (2014). *The Allure of the Selfie: Instagram and the New Self-portrait*. Amsterdam: Institute of Network Cultures.

Wetherell, M. S. (2012). *Affect and Emotion: A New Social Science Understanding*. London: Sage.

Williams, R. (2014). "Eat, Pray, Love": Producing the Female Neoliberal Spiritual Subject. *Journal of Popular Culture, 47*(3), 613–633.

Winch, A. (2013). *Girlfriends and Postfeminist Sisterhood*. Basingstoke: Palgrave Macmillan.

Winch, A. (2015). Brand Intimacy, Female Friendship and Digital Surveillance Networks. *New Formations, 84*, 228–245.

Wissinger, E. (2015). *This Year's Model: Fashion, Media, and the Making of Glamour*. New York: NYU Press.

Wolf, N. (1990). *The Beauty Myth: How Images of Beauty Are Used Against Women*. London: Chatto & Windus.

Wykes, M., & Gunter, B. (2004). *If Looks Could Kill: Media and Body Image*. London: Sage.

Xu, G., & Feiner, S. (2007). Meinü Jingji: China's Beauty Economy. Buying Looks, Shifting Value, and Changing Place. *Feminist Economics, 13*(3–4), 307–323.

Yang, J. (2011). Nennu and Shunu: Gender, Body Politics, and the Beauty Economy in China. *Signs, 36*(2), 333–357.

2

'Seriously Girly Fun!': Recontextualising Aesthetic Labour as Fun and Play in Cosmetics Advertising

Michelle M. Lazar

Introduction

Femininity is work. Theoretical notions of 'doing' and 'performing' femininity have pointed to the actual labour involved in constituting identity. An integral aspect of heterosexual feminine identity labour in many cultures is beautification or the doing of beauty work. Women, as part of doing heterosexual femininity, are expected to undertake seriously aesthetic labour upon their bodies, which involves time, money, skill, effort, physical discomfort and sometimes even health risks. Beauty as labour is not a novel idea in itself; however, it is taken up within a neoliberal postfeminist culture (Gill and Scharff 2011) in newer ways. Postfeminist culture has intensified the personal aesthetic regime of women, by increasing the scope and scale of working on and perfecting the female body (Negra 2009). Allied with a consumerist ethic, greater diversity and specialisa-

M.M. Lazar (✉)
Department of English Language and Literature, National University of Singapore, Singapore, Singapore

A.S. Elias et al. (eds.), *Aesthetic Labour*,
DOI 10.1057/978-1-137-47765-1_2

tion of personal grooming services have spiralled, demanding ever-intense consumption by women. An intensification of personal grooming has entailed greater self-surveillance and discipline, as no part of the body may escape scrutiny and work. In all this, the neoliberal postfeminist subject, far from being a helpless victim, is positioned as a willing participant, whose pursuit of beauty is unrelenting and self-generated and is actively entrepreneurial in achieving her desires.

Aesthetic labour in postfeminist culture, then, can be described as what women want and can achieve. The latter implies the moral character of the postfeminist subject as determined, proactive and confident, taking pride in her groomed appearance because it 'speaks for' the woman she ostensibly is. Although aesthetic labour indexes the postfeminist subject, paradoxically, the labour involved is sometimes also elided. Yet, this only further accentuates how clever and skilled the postfeminist subject is in grooming herself, without the appearance of doing so. Negra (2009, p. 126) comments:

> in conforming to contemporary beauty norms, women are under particular obligation to efface the signs of their own labour; they are expected to know how to use makeup in such a way that they do not appear to be made-up. This entails a greater emphasis on brow grooming and depilatory functions and a far greater emphasis on moisturising and sunscreen products to retain the health of the skin and guard against the signs of aging.

This chapter focuses on the erasure of aesthetic labour of a different kind, namely, by recontextualising labour as play in cosmetics advertising. Here, the serious time, skill and effort invested in beautification get re-framed as easy, enjoyable girlish fun. The postfeminist girlishness is not based on a naïve, passive and inexperienced subject position, but one that is active, knowing and purposeful even in play. A girlish subjectivity, in fact, is presented as every woman's entitlement to playful pleasures (Lazar 2009). A feel-good femininity, it counters an imaginary feminism that is censorious, uptight and 'so old school'. Beauty products and practices, therefore, are represented as sources of fun and pleasure entitled to all girls and women.

Targeting teens to young professionals, the data for the study comprise cosmetics advertising in Singapore for brands from Japan, the UK and the USA. This suggests that the 'postfeminist sensibilities' (Gill 2007) evident in the adverts, in other words, are not simply or solely Western, but constitute a mix of Western and Asian elements, and more accurately represent a transnational cosmopolitanism. The analysis of postfeminist aesthetic play is presented in three sections below,[1] using a feminist critical discourse analytic approach that seeks to analyse contextualised semiotic features of discourse (e.g. language, visual images, typeface), as invested in social meanings of power and ideology (Lazar 2005).

Make-up as Fun, Easy and Playful

Make-up is construed as light hearted and fun. In the examples below, a youthful fun-loving feminine subjectivity is produced for whom both make-up and femininity are signified as fun—*seriously girly fun*!:

1. Come over to our swanky new counter for some *seriously girly fun*! (Robinson's Beauty Hall, ST 3 July 2008)[2]
2. *Edgy, fun and of the moment*—that's what the Bobbi Brights Collection is all about. Beautiful bolts of colour designed by Bobbi Brown to be worn one at a time, when the mood strikes. (Bobbi Brown, ST 19 March 2009)
3. Bring home the pop mode look book for *makeup DIY fun* and a polaroid of your new look. (Tangs Beauty Hall, ST 6 March 2003)

Enjoyment and pleasure in the make-up experience, moreover, is linked to the ease of applying cosmetics. In example (3), aesthetic labour is at once indexed and effaced by the phrase 'DIY fun'; 'DIY' based on a 'look

[1] Some examples in this chapter were previously discussed in Lazar (2009), which had dealt more widely with various aspects of an 'entitled femininity', that is, entitled to pampering and pleasuring the self, celebrating normative femininity and participating in the 'girlification' of women.

[2] The data include conventional print advertisements, advertorials and mailers. Notation of the data cited in the chapter includes, in the following order, (1) the brand name, outlet or advertorial title; (2) if the adverts were from Singapore's main English daily, then the abbreviation 'ST' or 'ST Urban' to refer to *The Straits Times* or its lifestyle supplement, respectively, is used; and (3) the date/year of publication.

book' implies work which one is obliged to undertake, but it is represented as an activity that is easy and enjoyable.

Further, the elision of work due to ease and self-gratification is promoted through the marketing of time-saving cosmetics. A preoccupation with time is considered a characteristic trait of adult females in a postfeminist era, where women are represented as super-busy and time-starved (Tasker and Negra 2007). Beauty labour, therefore, is presented in cosmetic adverts as quick and undemanding which, while emphasising the economy on time, preserves the unquestioned reliance on cosmetics in the doing of femininity.

4. *Instant* Beauty Solutions. Who says makeup has to be serious to be good? Benefit is famous for delivering *quick fixes* for every gal's peskiest beauty dilemmas with a 'double' dose of wackiness mixed with know-how. Tired eyes? Want a rosy glow? Lash envy? Want red carpet radiance? Unshapely brows? Want a flawless complexion? Benefit will make you go from Now to WOW *in an instant!* … Come on over and get your *instant* sexy flush, radiance and cover-ups! We'll solve all your beauty dilemmas *in a jiffy*. Looking gorgeous is a piece of cake at Benefit! (Benefit, ST Urban 16 October 2009)
5. Take the ettusais pore cleansing challenge! Experience the effectiveness of ettusais' triple sebum off mask! see *instant* results as this mask removes whiteheads and blackheads, unclogs pores and gives you clearer, smoother skin. (ST, 25 March 2005)
6. *Speed* brow. Tint, tame & set your brows *in record time* with this brush-on gel that dries to a natural-looking finish. One shade dresses up all brows! Lessons included. (Benefit mailer 2008, p. 8)
7. *Instant* brow pencil. Turn your sparse, skimpy brows into perfectly natural, polished brows with our new *instant* brow pencil. The creamy powder-like texture glides in easily and comes with a special blending tip … Step-by-step lesson included. (Benefit mailer 2008, p. 9)[3]

A semantic field comprising related lexical items on time is evident in the adverts either as an adjective ('instant', 'quick', 'speed') or as a time

[3] This was a multi-page mailer, in a booklet form, from the brand Benefit.

adverbial ('in an instant', 'in a jiffy', 'in record time'). In (6) and (7), in fact, time is incorporated in the product name itself—'speed brows' and 'instant brow pencil'. Speed does not compromise the beauty effects achieved; instead, the end quality is always 'good' (4), better than pre-application ('clearer, smoother') (5), 'gorgeous' (4) and 'polished' (7). At the same time, the brand or product is also effective in promising multiple deliverables: in (5) 'this mask removes whiteheads and blackheads, unclogs pores and gives you clearer, smoother skin'; in (6) the gel tints, tames and sets the brows; and in (4) everything from eyes, lashes, brows and complexion are included. Examples (6) and (7) mention that lessons will be included with the product to guide the consumer, thus revealing that effort and skilled know-how are needed in the execution of aesthetic labour. Yet, the reassurance of speediness provided in the copy (and also highlighted in the product names) makes the effort seem almost effortless. The latter is described in (4) as 'a piece of cake', plus it is fun ('with a double dose of wackiness').

In some instances, the labour involved in beautification is completely effaced through an expressed re-signification of play. In the following examples, a semantic field involving 'play', along with related notions of experimenting, 'creativity' and 'dress up', is established.

8. *Dress up your eyes with vibrant colors and faux lashes* and *reveal a different side of you!* (Dior, ST 24 May 2007)
9. It inspires customers *to play with the colors to create their own looks* instead of sticking to what the brand prescribes. (Girl Power, ST Urban 2 January 2009)
10. Get *creative* and enhance your makeup skills in this hands-on makeup workshop conducted by a Dior Makeup Artist. *Play* with colors and learn how you can *create looks* with hues in greens, pinks and blues to compliment your eye shape! (Dior mailer, no date)

The emphasis on play achieves a number of effects. Firstly, the actual feminine labour involved in beauty practices gets recontextualised as non-work, as a pleasurable feminine activity. Even in those instances (see 10) where learning make-up skills at a workshop indexes serious labour involved, it is couched in enjoyable play terms. Women are invited to participate actively in the play and to experience make-up in these terms. Secondly, a sense of nostalgia is hinted at when, as little girls, playfully experimenting with make-up (and dressing up in grownup clothes) was an ostensibly amusing activity. It not only naturalises the experience of make-up as an intrinsically 'girl thing', but also prolongs that experience into female adulthood. In other words, one is never too old to keep experimenting and having fun with cosmetics. Finally, playing with make-up is integrally tied to a 'play' with one's identity. As the examples show, using make-up entails an unconstrained, creative presentation of the self as new, unique and different, and entirely of one's choosing. Identity, in other words, becomes the performance of a particular 'look' or style. As Hollows (2000) reminds us, consumer culture has been vital in offering plentiful opportunities to 'play' with identity through the use of commodities, so that a woman's sense of who she is increasingly comes from what and how she consumes.

Make-up in a Play World of Dolls and Toys

Aesthetic play in cosmetics advertising is also taken up quite literally and specifically in terms of entering the play world of dolls and toys, which is the focus of this section. US cosmetics brand Benefit, in particular, characteristically uses doll images in its advertising. In an announcement of the brand's opening in a shopping mall in Singapore, for example, Benefit's iconic life size plastic doll is pictured sitting triumphantly on a motorcycle with her arms raised, while steered from behind by a human male. Carried on one raised arm are Benefit shopping bags (ST Urban, 3 July 2008). Other ads show close-ups of doll faces drawn next to cosmetic products (Benefit mailer 2008). The dolls are not merely to be looked at and admired; instead, they 'come alive' and interact with the viewer in a number of ways, blurring distinctions between dolls and humans.

For instance, through attribution of human consciousness to the doll images, viewers are given access to the dolls' thoughts and words. Through representation of a thought bubble, the iconic Benefit doll is attributed a volitional thought process, jubilantly announcing the doll's (metonymic of the brand's) arrival: 'Robinsons Raffles City, here I come!' Similarly, via a thought bubble, another doll donning sunglasses extends an invitation to the target consumer to visit a different outlet: 'Pop by our new home for uber-licious offers!' (ST 16 October 2009). In yet another ad, a different doll is given a speaking voice, signified through use of double quotation marks: 'Hi. I'm Hollie Wood … Benefit's resident celebutant!' Hollie Wood directly addresses the consumer, introducing herself as the brand's representative celebrity debutante. In all these examples, the use of exclamation points lends an emphatic and energetic tone to their expressions as animated individuals.

Sometimes, the dolls have individualised names, which personalise them. Besides, Hollie Wood, other named dolls in Benefit adverts include Lana, Gabbi and Betty. The latter three dolls, in fact, are featured together on a single page, each emblematic of a different physical type. Based on slightly variant skin tones and different hair colour (blonde, auburn and brunette), alongside each doll image, a lipstick and shadow/liner colour chart is provided, with the following captions:

11. • lana's lovely light neutrals
    • gabbi's gotta-have medium neutrals
    • betty's beautiful deep neutrals

These doll images do not simply serve as cute illustrations. Rather, an overarching caption in the same, but enlarged, font type used in (11) directly addresses the viewer to 'love your look', which invites target consumers to identify with one of three archetypal categorisations of white western women represented by the dolls. However, in the context of a Singaporean audience, the (white) Western-ness, arguably, may be construed as indexical of a 'global' cosmopolitanism (Lazar 2006).

Some ads forge an even closer relationship between women and dolls by drawing women into the doll world, and vice versa:

12. 'I'm already a perfect 10 but I'm adding 10, so this makes me a 20! You do the math. I bronze and highlight in one sexy sweep with this powder duo for my goddess-like glow. Try it. If you're lucky, you'll look almost as good as I do!' (Benefit mailer 2008, p. 22).

13. 'I used to be a little envious of gabbi (she's so popular) so I made her my new best friend! Now, I take her everywhere I go & we're both seen in all the right places. Love ya, gabby!'

    [Accompanying the copy is an image of a cosmetics bag with Gabbi's face on it and the caption: 'Gabbi Glickman gets grabbed by Glitzy n'Shine … Go Gabbi. Go!'] (Benefit mailer 2008, p. 23).

The dolls, in both cases are 'persons' to be admired and envied. In (12), Hollie Wood is a super-beauty (not just a 'perfect 10' but a 20!) with a 'goddess-like glow', achieved through the application of a certain face powder. Ironically, dolls, too, have to engage in aesthetic labour to achieve super-perfection, which the human consumer is invited to aspire towards and, as we are told, might only barely approximate. Example (13) is about Gabbi Glickman, a doll which exemplifies a certain 'look' (see 11), and which has a cosmetics bag with her name and face printed on it. From the point of view of a girlish subjectivity within a play world, Gabbi (the bag and the doll) is personified and envied for her popularity ('she's so popular'). She is tactically made into 'my new best friend' in order to accrue some of Gabbi's fame by virtue of association: 'Now, I take her everywhere I go & we're both seen in all the right places'.

In the two examples, the distinction between doll and human is erased. On the one hand, in urging young women to try Hollie's beauty regimen with the conditional possibility of achieving her ultra-perfect plastic appearance, the female consumer is ironically rendered non-human. Yet, on the other hand, Gabbi Glickman, a doll image, is drawn into the human world and made to participate in human activities ('made her my new best friend' and 'I take her everywhere I go & we're both seen in all the right places'.) The erasure makes sense only through the adoption of a girlish subjectivity, in which treading the line between fantasy and the 'real' constitutes a form of identity play. From a girlish subject position, aesthetic labour, in fact, get naturalised as even dolls do it, and feminine insecurity, envy and desire to achieve doll-likeness get normalized. The idea of a human doll may well be a purely representational gimmick, but it is not uncommon in reality, and with very real implications (see Evans and Riley, this volume).

Dolling of women is also found, in the metaphorical language of one of the ads:

14. To all ladies, it's time you get the recognition you deserve at Northpoint! In celebration of International Women's Day, we have lined up exclusive privileges and rewards just for you...

I WANT TO DOLL UP!
Get dolled up with the latest red earth cosmetics...
I WANT TO INDULGE!
Every $50 you spend entitles you to a stamp...
I WANT TO CELEBRATE LADIES' DAY!
Enjoy pampering treats and rewards on this special day...
(Northpoint, ST, 8 March 2007)

'To doll up', in this case, is not literal but describes the act of titivation. As a metaphor, it involves the mapping of one domain (the child's world of dolls) on to another domain (the adult feminine activity of beautification). Although 'to doll up' has become a common form of expression, it is revealing how feminine aestheticisation has been popularly conceptualised in terms of achieving a doll-like appearance. In the ad copy, the 'I want' clauses foreground the perspective of the desiring feminine subject (Brundson 1986; Gill 2009); an image of a smiling, directly gazing model further suggests that the desires are attributed to the feminine self. Moreover, the use of exclamation points in this case, along with the use of upper case, lends an emphatic, even demanding tone of voice. The advertiser (and the red earth cosmetics), in turn, are represented in the service of meeting women's self-generated desires, by providing opportunities for their self-gratification. Self-gratification, fundamentally, rests on the ability to afford 'the latest red earth cosmetics', enjoy a minimum expenditure threshold ('every $50 spent') and earn 'pampering treats'. Although it may seem incongruous that beautification and/through material consumption are explicitly linked to the celebration of International Women's Day, from the point of view of postfeminist femininity which is emblematic of contradictions, this is hardly surprising. Within a postfeminist consumerist discourse, in fact, the day designated by the United

Nations to recognise, globally, women's actual contributions and achievements in society gets recontextualised in rather exclusionary middle-class terms ('exclusive privileges and rewards just for you'). The blending of the serious (social contribution and recognition) with fun (indulgent consumption) produces the notion of the 'seriously fun', which underscores, in this case, aesthetic labour as a middle-class pursuit.

Besides dolls, the world of play in cosmetics ads also includes cute cartoon characters. Although not conventionally associated with the beauty industry, below is an ad depicting an iconic feline cartoon character called 'Hello Kitty'. Hello Kitty is a caricature that belonged to a general cutesy Japanese popular culture since the 1980s. It quickly gained a fan base among girls and young women across Asia, for whom Hello Kitty collectibles have become a popular craze.

15. The ultra-luxe way to be pampered and playful! Announcing our limited-edition, glittering Swarovski crystal compacts, the collection privé of Kitty Kouture world. The ultimate in exclusivity, a sophisticated client's social status is all but assured!

    Kitty Showcase at Tangs Orchard.

- Photo ops with Kitty Mild and Kitty Wild!
- Choose a look for your purr-fect makeover!
- Fall in love with our hot bods in kitty getups!
- Purr over our kitty tattoos and balloons!

Not only is the 'Hello Kitty' caricature used recognisably as a decorative design on cosmetic cases, the ad invites consumers to participate in a wider commercial world of Hello Kitty paraphernalia: 'Kitty Mild and Kitty Wild', 'kitty getups', 'kitty tattoos and balloons'—all of which are reminiscent of Hello Kitty collectibles for girls. The target of the ad, however, is not children but women who can afford to indulge in a Swarovski crystal-studded Hello Kitty compact case. A girlish pleasure in Hello Kitty collectibles is here re-signified in terms of exclusivity, sophistication and social distinction. Like example (14), middle-class women with disposable incomes can afford to be little girls at heart and indulge in frivolous luxurious pleasures.

Playful Register

Another dimension of aesthetic play is performed through a fun, youthful register. In line with an entrepreneurial modality characteristic of neoliberal postfeminism (Gill and Scharff 2011; see also Elias, Gill and Scharff, this volume), this fun register can be read as a form of symbolic entrepreneurship, associated with a girlish postfeminist subjectivity. By symbolic entrepreneurship, I mean a purposeful linguistic/semiotic creativity and innovativeness, which here includes wordplay, flouting linguistic conventions and the use of irony to index a popular, light-hearted postfeminist identity. For example, alliteration (based on repetition of similar sounds) is evident in some cases. 'Majolica Majorca' is a Japanese cosmetics line, whose playful name sounds like a magic incantation (like 'abracadabra') (Girl Power, ST Urban, 2 January 2009). Alliterative word play also consciously draws attention to itself as in the following Benefit ad: 'Say super, shiny, sheer, sexy lips five times fast!' (2008, p. 12). A copy for lip gloss, the multi-adjectival product description is presented in the form of an amusing tongue-twisting word game, in which the reader is invited to actively participate ('Say…'). Vocalising the list repeatedly in quick succession achieves the dual purpose of making it a fun activity while aiding memorability for the product's qualities.

Not only sounds, but letters, too, are creatively exploited. In the Hello Kitty example discussed above (example 15), the word 'couture' is deliberately misspelt with 'k' to achieve graphological similarity with 'kitty'—'Kitty Kouture'. Similarly, the word 'purr-fect' is creatively misspelt, alluding to the purring sound of a cat. A different type of graphological play involves a whimsical typeface. A Japanese brand, Fasio, draws 'eyelashes' on to its caption 'S*T*AND *U*P*!* G*I*R*LS*'. To those letters which I have marked in italic, small spidery black lines are added to the top to resemble eyelashes. This lends a tongue-in-cheek effect to the directive, which suggests that women can stand up (and stand out) by stereotypically batting their eyelashes with the help of Fasio mascara.

Semantics or word meanings are also exploited artfully. 'Cute as Hell' is a Japanese brand whose packaging is inspired by a 'gothic-Lolita cutesy' (Pretty Baby, ST Urban, 10 July 2008). The brand name plays on semantic incongruity, with the unexpected collocation of 'cuteness' with 'hell'.

In the Hello Kitty ad discussed above, target consumers are themselves transformed into cats metaphorically, by establishing semantic similarity between animal characteristics ('purr' and 'paws') and female consumers:

16. Purr over our kitty tattoos and balloons!... Get your paws on MAC Hello Kitty Complete Makeover at [venue details].

As part of a fun register, a playful language style which is upbeat, chatty and colloquial is construed, too. It is a manner of speaking which simulates 'girl talk'. Below are three such examples:

17. Justine case. mini beautifier kit ... 'just in case'. 'I'm always prepared for the unexpected ... just in case. Justine case is my indispensable instant makeover just in case of a beauty emergency. I keep one in every fabulous handbag I own, just in case. And just in case, my best friend steals my handbag, I keep several of these crafty kits on hand in my car, in my gym and at home ... just in case'. (Benefit mailer 2008, p. 22)
18. Rush hour. 'Whew! I'm a go, go, goin'! Betcha didn't know I could multi-task—I can chew gum & gossip at the same time. One better is rush hour, my all over face color. It's Beverly Hill bliss in a stick! A few quick strokes and I'm ready for lunch at The Ivy'. (Benefit mailer 2008, p. 23)
19. High brow. 'I'm not an ageist, but seriously, sisters, droopy brows are a bummer. I always keep my brows perky & so should you. High brow makes it a snap. Just draw the linen-pink cream-in-a-stick evenly under your brow and blend. You'll look 10 years younger. Promise'. (Benefit mailer 2008, p. 23)

The 'girl talk' above constitutes elements of knowingness, humour and irony blended together and in the process normalises make-up as a necessary part of 'doing' femininity. Produced from the first-person point of view, the utterances index a discourse of intimate female friendships (McRobbie 1997; Talbot 1995), based on informal and colloquial language—contracted forms ('I'm', 'didn't', 'betcha', 'goin'), slang ('bummer', 'a snap') and expressive punctuation ('Whew!' and 'It's Beverly Hill bliss in a stick!'). Plus there is candid, sisterly advice-giving ('seriously, sisters, droopy brows are a bummer'; 'Just draw the linen-pink cream-in-a-stick evenly under your brow and blend'.) and personal assurance ('Promise').

Embedded in the discourse of intimate friendship is a certain knowingness and/or self-humour. In (19), the disclaimer 'I'm not an ageist, but…' represents a knowing female voice, someone who is socially aware and does not want to appear politically incorrect. The disclaimer, nevertheless, allows the speaker to perpetuate the status quo from a 'safe' distance (van Dijk 1998). In fact, following the disclaimer is advice on how to achieve 'perky' brows and a promise of looking a decade younger. The socially progressive voice against ageism, therefore, gets subverted from a position of knowing about ageism, yet upholding the ideology of perpetual youthfulness, achieved through make-up.

The girl talk also offers a facetious yet ironic uptake on feminine experiences. In (18), multi-tasking which is conventionally regarded as a feminine attribute is given a facile re-interpretation ('I can chew gum and gossip at the same time'), and instead of describing the peak-hour workday, the product name 'rush hour', ironically, refers to women who would be headed to a West end celebrity haunt (The Ivy) for lunch. The reference to busy women juggling many social responsibilities gets re-signified as women with the luxury of time on their hands and money to spend. The light-hearted, rhythmic beat of the clauses ('I can chew *gum* & gossip at the same *time*. One better is rush *hour*, my all over face *color*'), moreover, suggests not taking oneself too seriously.

The glamorous yet superficial lifestyle of postfeminist femininity is rehearsed in (17) as well—someone who is acquisitive ('every fabulous handbag I own') and neurotically obsessed with her appearance. The commendable virtue of foresight and planning for 'the unexpected' and 'emergency' are confined narrowly to the activity of beautification, even while beautification is depicted exaggeratedly, in metaphoric medical terms (as 'emergency', 'kits'). The repetition of the phrase 'just in case' (six times) and keeping the beauty kit everywhere ('in every fabulous handbag', 'in my car, in my gym and at home') signal an inordinate preoccupation with one physical appearance which is, at the same time, rendered playful. Facetious as this represented lifestyle is, it is presupposed as an entitlement of modern day femininity, which is available to middle-class women, who may not be represented as actually working a job (see 18).

Conclusion

In this chapter, I aimed to show how through recontextualisation—the shift, representationally, from one kind of context to another—feminine aesthetic labour gets conceptualised as play in cosmetics advertising. One way of understanding the effects of recontextualisation is that it allows the labour dimension of beauty practices to be suppressed, elided or overlooked, in favour of experiencing it as fun and play. Another way of understanding what is going on is that through recontextualisation the distinction between work and play itself gets dissolved, that is, when beauty practice is so enjoyable and easy to do, it ceases to be 'labour' in the conventional sense. Either way, what gets foregrounded in these adverts is the enjoyment and pleasure brought about by make-up, which induces the voluntary and wholehearted participation in the aesthetic project of the feminine self. In other words, beauty work is not about what women should do; rather, it becomes what women want to do. It is constitutive of the structuring of desire: why engage in beauty work? Because it's fun. It's a girl thing! Gaining young women's consent and participation, as McRobbie (2009) has argued, is fundamental to the maintenance of a postfeminist consumer culture. Active participation, moreover, naturalises beauty work and averts confronting uncomfortable ideological questions relating to beauty ideals, 'compulsory beautification' and the coupling of beauty with femininity.

The girlish postfeminist subjectivity entailed by aesthetic play construes femininity as pleasurable, fun and carefree. More than that, girlishness comes to index self-confidence in women's gender identity. In response to an imagined austere feminism that would keep women from celebrating their femininity in playful and pleasurable terms, postfeminist culture allows women to be free and forever young at heart. However, with a premium placed on youthful femininity, postfeminist representations are acutely age conscious. From promoting the ideal of a youthful appearance, beauty advertising now requires women, no matter what their age, to imbibe a youthful disposition as well. The flip side of what Negra (2007, p. 75) describes as 'a new age flexibility', which blurs traditional distinctions between youthfulness and mature adulthood, is the heightening of age anxiety among adult women. Indeed, youthism and ageism could be viewed as two sides of a coin, where the fixation on youth corresponds with the denigration of ageing. Girlishness, furthermore, as evident in the luxury consumption and lifestyle shown in this chapter, is a distinctly middle-class identity. Only women of means can partake of prolonged girlhood and have *seriously girly fun*!

References

Brundson, C. (Ed.). (1986). *Films for Women*. London: British Film Institute.

Gill, R. (2007). Postfeminist Media Culture: Elements of a Sensibility. *European Journal of Cultural Studies, 10*(2), 147–166.

Gill, R. (2009). Mediated Intimacy and Postfeminism: A Discourse Analytical Examination of Sex and Relationships Advice in a Women's Magazine. *Discourse and Communication, 3*(4), 345–369.

Gill, R., & Scharff, C. (Eds.). (2011). *New Femininities: Postfeminism, Neoliberalism and Subjectivity*. Basingstoke: Palgrave.

Hollows, J. (2000). *Feminism, Femininity and Popular Culture*. Manchester: Manchester University Press.

Lazar, M. M. (2005). *Feminist Critical Discourse Analysis: Gender, Power and Ideology in Discourse*. Basingstoke: Palgrave.

Lazar, M. M. (2006). Discover the Power of Femininity!: Analysing Global 'Power Femininity' in Local Advertising. *Feminist Media Studies, 6*(4), 505–517.

Lazar, M. M. (2009). Entitled to Consume: Postfeminist Femininity and a Culture of Post-critique. *Discourse and Communication, 3*(4), 371–400.

McRobbie, A. (1997). 'More': New Sexualities in Girls' and Women's Magazines. In A. McRobbie (Ed.), *Back to Reality?: Social Experiences and Cultural Studies* (pp. 190–209). Manchester: Manchester University Press.

McRobbie, A. (2009). *The Aftermath of Feminism: Gender, Culture and Social Change*. London: Sage.

Negra, D. (2009). *What a Girl Wants? Fantasizing the Reclamation of Self in Postfeminism*. London: Routledge.
Talbot, M. (1995). Synthetic Sisterhood: False Friends in a Teenage Magazine. In K. Hall & M. Bucholtz (Eds.), *Gender Articulated: Language and the Socially Constructed Self* (pp. 143–165). New York: Routledge.
Tasker, Y., & Negra, D. (Eds.). (2007). *Interrogating Postfeminism: Gender and the Politics of Popular Culture*. Durham, NC: Duke University Press.
van Dijk, T. A. (1998). *Ideology: A Multidisciplinary Approach*. London: Sage.

3

Rethinking Ruskin's Wife's Vulva

Virginia Braun

Introduction

We look at the past through contemporary eyes, understand it from our present, and can use the familiarities and *unfamiliarities* in what we see as a tool for critical insight—to render strange what has come to be taken for granted. Here I take a particular historical event—the non-consummation and eventual annulment of the marriage of UK art historian John Ruskin and socialite Effie Gray—as the starting point for a thought experiment intended to denormalise and reframe contemporary vulval modificatory practices. I have written about the vulval aesthetics, representation and practice for over 15 years (Braun 2004, 2005a, 2009a, 2009b, 2010; Braun and Kitzinger 2001; Braun et al. 2013; Braun and Wilkinson 2001, 2003, 2005); I now invite you to join my imaginative journey between the past and present, to (re)make sense of contemporary

V. Braun (✉)
School of Psychology, The University of Auckland, Auckland, New Zealand

A.S. Elias et al. (eds.), *Aesthetic Labour*,
DOI 10.1057/978-1-137-47765-1_3

aesthetic female genital labour *as* genital labour, rather than (just) personal aesthetics and choice.

Setting the Scene: 10 April 1848, Scotland

It is the wedding night of nineteenth-century Britain's 'greatest critic and social thinker' (Prodger 2013), the art writer John Ruskin. John, 29, has just married Euphemia 'Effie' Gray, 19. Presumed virginal, they will tonight consummate their union with coitus—and will go on procreate and live happily ever after. Except this does not happen. Six years later, Effie files for marital annulment, based on non-consummation. Speculation runs rife—is it Ruskin's 'aversion to children, his religious scruples, a wish to preserve Effie's beauty and to keep her from exhaustion so they could go Alpine walking' or 'a revulsion with body odour and menstruation' (cited in Prodger 2013) that led to this? John explains that 'it may be thought strange that I could abstain from a woman who to most people was so attractive. But though her face was beautiful, her person was not formed to excite passion. On the contrary, there were certain circumstances in her person which completely checked it' (cited in Prodger 2013). In a letter to her father, Effie describes that John 'had imagined women were quite different to what he saw I was, and that the reason he did not make me his Wife was because he was disgusted with my person the first evening' (cited in Prodger 2013)—leading to the most popular theory[1]: John, familiar only with the smooth (marble) vulvas of classical art, was shocked and repulsed by the sight of *pubic hair* on his bride and could not desire his new wife.

(Re)Imagining the Past: Shifting Frameworks of Then

What ontological truth is relied on in this popular narrative? What implicit ideas about gender, gendered bodies, and sexual desirability and practice are (re)produced? I am struck first by how blame is located in the

[1] This theory has recently been questioned (Brownell 2013).

person/psyche of John rather than Effie. In contrast to a long tradition in which women's sexuality *has* been located as blameworthy (e.g. in sexual assault and rape), here it is John's failure to respond that is in need of explanation—he is a failed husband. In contrast, Effie's body occupies an ontologically unquestioned status—its desirability is not in doubt. Effie is not faulted for her hirsute state: neither her account to her father nor the popular theory suggests that *she* ought to change her body to conform to John's aesthetic preferences. Effie is *not* positioned as a failing/bad wife or woman. But this is not some feminist utopia: the narrative does rely on very traditionally gendered constructions of male and female bodies and sexuality, where women are positioned as the *recipients* of male sexual action, rather than active contributors *to* a sexual encounter—just 'lie back and think of England'. John's *fault* relies on us understanding him as the agent of sexuality and that particular sexual encounter. With Effie's embodied presence assumed naturally to excite male passion, she is situated as a passive object, the waiting recipient of John's active sexuality. These paired constructions render Effie both passive and faultless, and John blameworthy for his lack of action. We find familiar echoes of this story in contemporary western renderings of heterosex, including a trenchant sexual double standard meaning heterosex remains profoundly gendered (Farvid, Braun and Rowney in press). But it has major unfamiliarities, too, and we can use these to *undo* certain representations and positionings that have come to occupy places of truth. So what might the John and Effie story look like, in 2016?

(Re)Imagining the Past as the Present: John and Effie's Break-up, 2016

> **"When the clothes are off, she's just not that sexy"**
> ***John's* shocking late-night tweets suggest rumours are true. *Is Joffie* really over?**
>
> (*GossipRag*, 10 May 2016)

> **"Yes, it's over!"**
> ***Joffie* confirm rumours of split!**
>
> (*GossipRag*, 13 May 2016)

"John's addiction to porn ruined the romance"
Friends suggest it's John's fault!

(*GossipRag*, 14 May 2016)

"I tried everything!"
Effie reveals the truth behind *Joffie's* shock split!
"I was even booked in to get a designer vagina". In a revealing interview, Effie Gray, It-girl and now-former wife of TV art-celebrity John Ruskin, reveals the extent to which she tried everything, including considering labiaplasty, in an attempt to excite John's passions—which, she now reveals, remained dormant.

(*GossipRag*, 16 May 2016)

"nuff muff?"
Leaked pics reveal Effie's 70s-style free-wheelin' muff. Is that the *real* reason for *Joffie's* split?

(*GossipRag*, 19 May 2016)

"They're private! Please don't view or share them"
***Effie* begs fans not to spread leaked naked pics.**

(*GossipRag*, 20 May 2016)

"Muff no more?"
Effie spied leaving vaginal spa.

(*GossipRag*, 21 May 2016)

(Re)Imagining the Past: Through the Framework of Now

These headlines illustrate how the John/Effie scenario might play out in a 2016 (Britain) context (let us imagine the evening as if each had never engaged in a sexual encounter before[2]). Effie and John are a hot couple, regulars on the covers of celebrity magazines, TV, and gossip websites.

[2] Now, it is *highly unlikely* that their marriage night is either's first sexual encounter—with each other, or anyone—making lack of desire/annulment unlikely.

Their romance and marriage are for public consumption, likewise any rift and breakup. Rumours swirl. Tweets and leaked photos purportedly reveal truths about what really happened. Experiential accounts (from Effie) tell *a* story of their romance, their sex life—or lack of it!—and their marriage and split. Their 2016 story is highly *narrativised*.[3] So how might this story flow? What interpretative frameworks would *they* bring to it, would *we* bring to it?

There are some interpretative continuities between the then (mid-nineteenth century) and the now (twenty-first century). The idea of cultural influence on aesthetics remains. John v1848's desires were understood as shaped by the visual culture (fine arts) he was professionally immersed in. Pornography now takes centre stage. Alongside widespread and normative consumption among men, pornographically informed representational modes (including advertising, Gill 2008) mean pornography penetrates the *everyday* worlds of many western people (Häggström-Nordin et al. 2006). In some complex way, it seeps into our aesthetics and, perhaps more significantly, our affects (e.g. Paasonen 2011). It is therefore highly *unlikely* that John v2016 has never encountered what a real-life vulva actually looks like. Or is it? Airbrushing and censorship rules mean the vulval images he has consumed as objects of desire and arousal often resemble each other (Drysdale 2010)—but they may not closely resemble Effie Gray's vulva. Without real, fleshy, sexual experience with women, John v2016 operates in a mode of sexual knowing *and* unknowing. His aesthetic preferences and understanding of vulval normality have been shaped by fairly narrow representations of sexy female bodies and sexually-appealing vulvas. In 2016, the ideal *and* the 'normal' vulva is 'small, neat and tidy', with 'invisible' labia minora and limited or no pubic hair, and despite access to some creative responses that challenge this homogenised imaginary vulva (e.g. the 'Great Wall of Vagina'[4]), John's aesthetics and affects remain normative.

By 2016, we understand Effie's aesthetics, desires, and anxieties as also formed through the same sociocultural melange: post-sexual revolution, Effie and John share access to cultural expectations for being sexy. Lying

[3] Their original story also was, albeit in a different way.

[4] See: http://www.greatwallofvagina.co.uk/

back and thinking of England is not a viable option for Effie v2016; her body and sexuality require her attention and unlike Effie v1848, she is highly unlikely to present John with an unmodified vulva.[5] Teen Effie v2016 has only known a world where vulval modification is required as part of a desirable body. Cosmetic surgery is normalised (Blum 2003), and female *genital* cosmetic procedures are popular and regularly promoted (Braun 2005a, 2009a). The 'Brazilian' wax is frequently discussed[6]—Effie first saw it in the super popular, glamorous *Sex and the City* she sneakily watched as a child—and most of her friends are completely pubic hair-free (Braun et al. 2013; Fahs 2014; Herbenick et al. 2010; Terry and Braun 2013). Friends like Cameron Diaz[7] have advised her on what is, and is not, 'sexy' for her pubic hair ahead of her wedding night, and if Effie has decided to keep any, it will be trimmed and shaped. She booked herself into a spa for a vajacial—a 'facial' treatment for the vulva (Chung 2015)—to present John the smoothest vulva possible (and to manage the consequences of pubic hair removal such as ingrown hairs), but even though fellow celebrities have promoted the wonders of 'vajazzling' (Huffington Post 2010), she has decided to leave that for another time. Likewise, she is not sure she needs to dye her labia (Stewart 2010) just yet.

Effie v2016's world offers a smorgasbord of opportunities for vulva modification, but we can theorise these as obligation as well as opportunity: through an expanded mode of potentials, we are invited into diverse moments and modes of vulval attention and vulval vigilance, to ensure the perfect vulva. Vulval modification is not only normative, it is—for many—*mandatory*. Not a question of *whether*, but of *what* and *how*. The practices of vulval modification are not only aesthetic labour formed around management of the risk of having

---

[5] John v2016 is quite likely to have also removed or trimmed some of his pubic hair (Terry and Braun 2013); he *may* have considered some temporary pharmaceutical modification, to alleviate 'performance' anxiety.

[6] The poor Brazilian has suffered some 'challenges' in very recent times (Adams 2014).

[7] In what offers a compelling and distressing example of the way female friends' 'police' each other's bodies—something Winch (2013) has referred to as the 'girlfriend gaze'—Cameron Diaz notoriously forcibly 'insisted' that Gwyneth Paltrow modify her pubic hair, for the sake of her marriage, an event she has recounted publicly as humorous (see spookylorre 2013).

a 'wrong' vulva, but a normative compliance with expected—even unquestioned—embodiment. It is unimaginable that Effie, a popular 19-year-old 'It girl'[8] with a high public profile, who embodies (privileged white) hetero-feminine desirability, would not 'invest in' her body and her 'self', to present what she imagines to be, what she herself *believes* to be, the ultimately desirable body to John on their wedding night. All this is a lot of *work*—a point nicely captured by British feminist writer Caitlin Moran's (2011) description of her routine of preparation of her body before 'going out' into situations where a sexual encounter is on the menu. The female body—and the female psyche (Farvid and Braun 2013a, 2013b)—unworked on is situated as unfit for sexual presentation, not able to be desired, or not desirable *enough*. This makes the unmodified vulva a (legitimate) site of anxiety. Pregnant women, for instance, seek advice about what they should do with their pubic hair for the birth (e.g. Eckler and Parker-Court 2014). That women even consider the acceptability of an 'untamed bush' in childbirth demonstrates how much a modified vulva has become part of the imaginary apparatus of embodying not just a desirable, but an *acceptable*, female body.

Unlike 1848, Effie and John's aesthetic preferences will likely closely converge in 2016. Effie's modified vulva will probably satisfy John's anticipated/desired vulva. But what if—gasp—Effie has labia minora that *do* 'extrude' beyond the 'clam shell', the 'Barbie' vulva—as many women's do? What if these labia are asymmetrical? Or have some darker pigmentation? What if—bear with me—John simply cannot desire Effie's vulva? Although vulval appearance is claimed not to be important by many men (Horrocks et al. 2015), others indicate *strong* preference for certain aesthetics (e.g. YouTube features videos of men who admonish women with pubic hair), and this may be the case for John. Alternatively, what if John has difficulty responding sexually to a real woman after intense pornography consumption (Weiss 2013)? Despite Effie's 'nice, tidied up' vulva, success is not guaranteed. So *what if* John does not respond?

---

[8] I use 'It girl' as a heuristic tool, as the term evokes an almost incalculable sexuality and hipness that elides any of the work which goes into embodying such a position.

(Re)Making the Female Body, Now

Our twenty-first century interpretative framework for non-consummation would be very different to that of 1848: while John *may* be situated as a failed husband, Effie would *definitely* be positioned as a failed wife. I end this thought experiment by arguing that Effie, in having a body not 'desirable enough' for John, has failed in her duty as a twenty-first century woman: to *labour enough* on her body that it becomes unquestionably desirable, unquestionably conformist, yet still 'unique'. Given the nexus of discursive and ideological representations and resources she is immersed in, Effie v2016 will not think of herself and her tasks in terms of conformity (Gill 2008). What women do to their bodies is now typically made sense of—including by women themselves—through two dominant and interlinked explanatory frameworks: personal choice and personal aesthetic preferences (Braun 2005b, 2009b). Our choices and preferences are indelibly shaped by context, but we are active in enacting them. A 'labour' framework can move us beyond the 'dupe versus agent' arguments that have stymied some feminist debate, as it seems to position women as *inherently* agentic, no matter on what and how they labour, and whether that labour is towards or away from conformity. But we have to theorise labour *within* context, because the ways we labour, the point and purpose of that, is always responsive to context.

Imaging Herself a Good Woman: Effie v2016

In an exclusive post-breakup post-photo-leak interview, Effie offers her public some insight into her practices, preferences, and anxieties around appearance and John's failure to respond:

> John was hot—anyone would think so. And I thought our sex life would be great. But it wasn't. John just didn't seem to be that into me, he didn't find me hot. I don't know why! My body's not that different to what he looks at in mags and things.
>
> I've always waxed—it just feels cleaner, and I really like the smooth clean look. Who wants hair? It's dirty, and gets in the way. It looks and feels bet-

> ter without it, more natural. But John wasn't into me. So as crazy as it sounds, I thought I'd try something different—to give me an edge. I grew my muff out a bit—ick. But even that didn't make a difference.
>
> I tried everything. I even booked in with a surgeon to have a labiaplasty. One of my lips is a bit longer than the other—and you can see them. I've never liked them, and they worry me—even though many men say they don't mind. This is all about me, and being able to relax, and know my body is the way I want it to be. Being able to feel sexy. I haven't had it yet—John sent that nasty tweet, and after that it was clearly over. But I still plan to go ahead. I need to do it, for me.
>
> John always said it was him, not me. He's not gay, so I'll never really understand why he wasn't into me.
> (*GossipRag,* 31 May 2016)

What can we make of this (imagined) reveal? Effie v2106, a child of post-feminism, is a good subject of neoliberal times (Braun 2009b; Gill 2008; Gill and Scharff 2011). She thinks about herself in individualistic terms, as an independent woman who acts and chooses of her own free will. Context and culture (e.g. advertising, pornography, media) provide a net of information and resources from which she decides on how to be, on what it is she likes, but she does not see these as *telling her* how to look, as telling her what is 'hot'. She understands her aesthetics in interior terms, as reflecting her own inherently natural aesthetics.

This cultural narrative also situates the modified vulva within evolutionary logic—a progression beyond the inherent ugly, non-modified body, to a better-than-before state. Long-standing cultural associations of woman with (savage) nature, and the 'natural' female body as always-on-the brink-of-abjection (Braun and Wilkinson 2001) echo here. This orientation to evolution invokes the idea of a sexual marketplace, where value is accrued through the display of desirable sexual features, yet Effie v2016 is not a cold and calculating woman, callously motivated by what she sees as others' desires. Although 'what John may want' hovers nearby, Effie's story reveals that it is her own aesthetic preferences, her beliefs about what is sexy, that drive her actions. That there *is* a close resonance between her own preferences and what is culturally valued, between her own and John v2016's aesthetics, between her body and 'what he looks at' elsewhere, is happenstance. Effie understands bodily labour as part of what being a woman is—it is not modification; it is just a required part of living—and she is endlessly engaged in this project of herself, a project towards fulfilment, well-being, and happiness, towards *being her true self*. Her body, where it fails to meet her (or John's) aesthetic ideals, becomes a barrier to being the *real* Effie. So when John v2016 fails to respond in their sexual encounter, Effie has, effectively, failed at the key task of hetero-femininity: being attractive to, and therefore securing, a sexual partner/(future) husband. The excuse 'it's me, not you' is never quite reassuring; the female body always teeters on the edge of failure.

Reimagining Effie v2016 as Aesthetic Labourer

We do not tend to explain what women do with their bodies through a framework of 'labour', but we ought to view Effie v2016 as an aesthetic labourer, engaged in an ongoing job of *working* on her self—body *and* mind—to manage, present, and produce a body that is, effortlessly, 'It'. A labour framework orients to (feminist) work around 'emotional labour' (Hochschild 1983) and 'aesthetic labour' (Sheane 2012) which has recently blossomed in work studies (e.g. Entwistle and Wissinger 2006; Hall and van den Broek 2012; Warhurst and Nickson 2009). The concept of *aesthetic* labour, most regularly applied around the intersection of employees, their bodies, and their appearance/comportment/presentation, highlights aesthetics as an (often invisible) part of employee expectations, and the often invisible labour deployed in the doing of aestheticised identities/presentation in the workplace. If we transpose this onto the everyday living of the individual body/self—the key work object of the neoliberal subject—the framework fits perfectly.

By orienting to *work*, an aesthetic labour framework allows us to destabilise contemporary framings of vulval modification. It takes us away from personal preference, indulgence and pleasure, and even 'just what you do'-type understandings. By destabilising these, it provides a fruitful tool for *de-naturalising* the practices, affects (including desire and disgust), perceived obligations and 'preferences' that become normalised when, ontologically, the vulva shifts from being something that is 'just the way it is', to something that is always *potentially* different, always sitting on the edge of change. This re-ontologised vulva requires us to take responsibility for its state of being—and taking responsibility means *work*. With the vulva shifted into this tenuous ontological state, of never quite being, it becomes a mandated site of work—whether we depilate, whether we undergo a vajacial (sometimes to minimise the effects of depilation!), whether we contemplate labiaplasty, as Effie v2016 has done, or whether or not we actually do anything to it. Even 'doing nothing' requires us to do *some*thing (Blum 2003). Doing nothing with this re-ontologised vulva is now an action—it requires resistance to cultural imperatives and involves psychological and possibly emotion work.

Effie v2016 is employed in the individual (but collective) job of creating and presenting a (desirable) normative female vulva—and body—as if it is naturally and effortlessly like that. But although it *is* work on her body and her mind, Effie does not see it as onerous. Framing it as about prioritising *herself* and her desires, about 'pampering' herself, about taking the time and money to put into herself, to invest in herself, about how much she values herself and her body, elides the effort involved. But the invisibilised work towards this normative vulva is extensive. It requires planning and psychological vigilance, with daily attention given to its aesthetic state—inspections of hair, of labial appearance, and odour. It requires consideration of when and how hair removal is needed. 'Big days' like a wedding need to be planned for in advance. It requires money—the tools of this work are not freely available, and Effie often pays *others* to labour on her body: the woman who waxes; the woman who does the 'vajacials'. Effie is not only an aesthetic labourer, she is also an aesthetic consumer—and as with much consumption, relationships of exploitation are part of this.[9] To keep her edge, she needs to keep abreast of new products and practices. She has just read about Gwyneth Paltrow's latest thing—vaginal steaming[10]—which she is keen to try. She is also

[9] Exploitation in the beauty industries has been highlighted in relation to manicures and pedicures (see Nir 2015), revealing the erased 'dark side' of the (western) consumption of services from invisible bodies in global-cheap-labour movements.

[10] 'Vaginal steaming' refers to a practice whereby herb-infused steam enters the vagina through a combination of a steam-delivery device and an appropriate seating position; the claimed purpose ranges from pampering to fertility enhancement (Vandenburg and Braun 2016).

seeking the best 'odour-masking' product, having not yet found one she is happy with.

Around the edge of her existence, worry about the not-quite-rightness of her vulva teeters, pulsing in and out of consciousness, depending on what is coming up in her life. This reveals the psychological, emotional, and attentional energy, the emotional/aesthetic *labour*, she gives to this small body part, as well as the financial and time investment she puts into it. It might be on the way to (nearly) perfect, but a lot of time, energy, and money are required to get and keep it that way. And it is always on the brink of betrayal.

Inconclusion

I have used this thought experiment of imagining what John and Effie's 'failed' sexual encounter/marriage might look like if it happened *now*, to destabilise some of our contemporary taken-for-granteds. What this reveals is that the contemporary western vulva and the vulva of the nineteenth century are ontologically different objects. Although they share the same fleshy starting point, the actual product of experience and engagement currently offered up to women is a different one to that of Effie's time. A confluence of old ideas and new makes the contemporary vulva ontologically an object of incompleteness, an object of potentiality, an object of required engagement and work. This vulva, ontologically, is always never quite there, never quite finished, never quite 'fixed', never *just*, always potentially *improvable*. But more than this, it is now a *should-be-modified* body part.

Through this ontological state of uncertainty, a (cisgendered, western) woman in 2016 has a (likely) very different relationship with her vulva compared to 1848. She is 'invited' into an embodied regime of (endless) work to seek an (imagined) end-state of 'rightness'. But that state is either illusory—an apparition or a mirage—or transitory if achieved, and it soon seeps away (see also Dosekun, this volume). Even if her ideal material 'perfection' is achieved, shifts in representational context, in the discourse of what constitutes the perfect vulva, mean she is always vulnerable. Her own aesthetic preferences are not inherent, not fixed. They evolve and shape themselves in response to context and experience. The search for vulval normality/desirability is an ongoing task, for someone who cares. But even the woman who does not care—who does *not* work on the aesthetics of her vulva—has work to do, has to work to disengage from performed desirable hetero-femininity.[11] While 'opting out' is always possible (and potentially easier for women somewhat older than Effie), doing nothing is no longer the *default* position where the vulva is concerned. Dominant cultural narratives now position vulval modification as normative, and even as key to embodied heteronormative feminine success. Indeed, as the final (current) chapter of John and Effie's tumultuous relationship is revealed to the public, a culturally compliant Effie links her and John's reunion and happiness to a now-logical (but still extreme, and risky) vulval modification:

> **"Our sex life is amazing, and we're happier than I thought possible" Effie reveals labiaplasty was key in *Joffie* reunion.**
>
> (*GossipRag*, 18 September 2016)

References

Adams, E. (2014). Brazilian Wax in Crisis: A Report. *Racked*. [Online] http://www.racked.com/2014/12/15/7564641/brazilian-bikini-wax-pubic-hair-style

Blum, V. L. (2003). *Flesh Wounds: The Culture of Cosmetic Surgery*. Berkeley, CA: University of California Press.

Braun, V. (2004). A Sheath for a Sword? Culture, Shaping Bodies, Shaping Sex. In N. Gavey, A. Potts, & A. Weatherall (Eds.), *Sex and the Body* (pp. 17–34). Palmerston North: Dunmore Press.

Braun, V. (2005a). In Search of (Better) Sexual Pleasure: Female Genital 'Cosmetic' Surgery. *Sexualities, 8*(4), 407–424.

[11] It is problematic to essentialise queer women as a group, suggesting that they necessarily (all) sit outside such cultural imperatives, but their identities *may* give access to different investments and engagements with different potentialities than those typically accessed by heteronormatively invested straight women.

Braun, V. (2005b). Just a Nip and a Tuck? The Culture of Cosmetic Surgery. *Feminism & Psychology, 15*(3), 345–350.

Braun, V. (2009a). Selling the 'Perfect' Vulva. In C. Heyes & M. Jones (Eds.), *Cosmetic Surgery: A Feminist Primer* (pp. 133–149). Farnham, UK: Ashgate.

Braun, V. (2009b). 'The Women Are Doing it for Themselves': The Rhetoric of Choice and Agency Around Female Genital 'Cosmetic Surgery'. *Australian Feminist Studies, 24*(60), 233–249.

Braun, V. (2010). Female Genital Cosmetic Surgery: A Critical Review of Current Knowledge and Contemporary Debates. *Journal of Women's Health, 19*(7), 1393–1407.

Braun, V., & Kitzinger, C. (2001). The Perfectible Vagina: Size Matters. *Culture, Health & Sexuality, 3*, 263–277.

Braun, V., Tricklebank, G., & Clarke, V. (2013). It Shouldn't Stick Out from Your Bikini at the Beach: Meaning, Gender, and the Hairy/Hairless Body. *Psychology of Women Quarterly, 37*(4), 478–493.

Braun, V., & Wilkinson, S. (2001). Socio-Cultural Representations of the Vagina. *Journal of Reproductive and Infant Psychology, 19*, 17–32.

Braun, V., & Wilkinson, S. (2003). Liability or Asset? Women Talk About the Vagina. *Psychology of Women Section Review, 5*(2), 28–42.

Braun, V., & Wilkinson, S. (2005). Vagina Equals Woman? On Genitals and Gendered Identity. *Women's Studies International Forum, 28*(6), 509–522.

Brownell, R. (2013). *Marriage of Inconvenience: Euphemia Chalmers Gray and John Ruskin: The Secret History of the Most Notorious Marital Failure of the Victorian Era*. London: Pallas Athene.

Chung, M. (2015). What Happened When I Got a Vajacial–A Facial for My Vagina, *Huffington Post*. [Online] http://www.huffingtonpost.ca/madelyn-chung/vajacial_b_6647724.html

Drysdale, K. (2010). *Healing it to a Single Crease*. ABC Australia: Hungry Beast.

Eckler, R., & Parker-Court, J. (2014). Should You Get a Bikini Wax Pre-Childbirth? *Today's Parent*. [Online] http://www.todaysparent.com/pregnancy/giving-birth/debate-bikini-wax-pre-childbirth/

Entwistle, J., & Wissinger, E. (2006). Keeping Up Appearances: Aesthetic Labour in the Fashion Modelling Industries of London and New York. *The Sociological Review, 54*(4), 774–794.

Fahs, B. (2014). Genital Panics: Constructing the Vagina in Women's Qualitative Narratives About Pubic Hair, Menstrual Sex, and Vaginal Self-Image. *Body Image, 11*(3), 210–218.

Farvid, P., & Braun, V. (2013a). Casual Sex as 'Not a Natural Act' and Other Regimes of Truth About Heterosexuality. *Feminism & Psychology, 23*(3), 359–378.

Farvid, P., & Braun, V. (2013b). The 'Sassy Woman' and the 'Performing Man': Heterosexual Casual Sex Advice and the (Re)constitution of Gendered Subjectivities. *Feminist Media Studies, 14*(1), 118–134.

Farvid, P., Braun, V., & Rowney, C. (2016). No Girl Wants to Be Called a Slut!': Women, Heterosexual Casual Sex and the Sexual Double Standard. *Journal of Gender Studies*, online first.

Gill, R. (2008). Empowerment/Sexism: Figuring Female Sexual Agency in Contemporary Advertising. *Feminism & Psychology, 18*(1), 35–60.

Gill, R., & Scharff, C. (2011). *New Femininities: Postfeminism, Neoliberalism and Subjectivity*. Basingstoke, UK: Palgrave MacMillan.

Häggström-Nordin, E., Sandberg, J., Hanson, U., & Tydén, T. (2006). 'It's Everywhere!' Young Swedish People's Thoughts and Reflections About Pornography. *Scandinavian Journal of Caring Sciences, 20*, 386–393.

Hall, R., & van den Broek, D. (2012). Aestheticising Retail Workers: Orientations of Aesthetic Labour in Australian Fashion Retail. *Economic and Industrial Democracy, 33*(1), 85–102.

Herbenick, D., Schick, V. R., Reece, M., Sanders, S., & Fortenberry, J. D. (2010). Pubic Hair Removal Among Women in the United States: Prevalence, Methods, and Characteristics. *The Journal of Sexual Medicine, 7*(10), 3322–3330.

Hochschild, A. (1983). *The Managed Heart: Commercialization of Human Feeling*. Berkeley, CA: University of California Press.

Horrocks, E., Iyer, J., Askern, A., Becuzzi, N., Vangaveti, V., & Rane, A. (2015). Individual Male Perception of Female Genitalia. *International Urogynecology Journal, 27*(2), 307–313.

Moran, C. (2011). *How to Be a Woman*. London: Random House.

Nir, S. M. (2015). The Price of Nice Nails, *New York Times*. [Online] http://www.nytimes.com/2015/05/10/nyregion/at-nail-salons-in-nyc-manicurists-are-underpaid-and-unprotected.html

Paasonen, S. (2011). *Carnal Resonance: Affect and Online Pornography*. Cambridge, MA: The MIT Press.

Post, H.. (2010). Jennifer Love Hewitt Bedazzled Her Privates. *Huffington Post*. [Online] http://www.huffingtonpost.com/2010/01/13/jennifer-love-hewitt-beda_n_421751.html

Prodger, M. (2013). John Ruskin's Marriage: What Really Happened, *The Guardian*. [Online] http://www.theguardian.com/books/2013/mar/29/ruskin-effie-marriage-inconvenience-brownell

Sheane, S. D. (2012). Putting on a Good Face: An Examination of the Emotional and Aesthetic Roots of Presentational Labour. *Economic and Industrial Democracy, 33*(1), 145–158.

Spookylorre. (2013). Cameron Diaz–The too Much Pubic Hair Story. YouTube. [Online] https://www.youtube.com/watch?v=QWcaM_Y9Xt8

Stewart, D. (2010). My New Pink Button: 'Restore the Youthful Pink Color Back to Your Labia'. *Jezebel.* [Online] http://jezebel.com/5445537/my-new-pink-button-restore-the-youthful-pink-color-back-to-your-labia

Terry, G., & Braun, V. (2013). To Let Hair Be, or to Not Let Hair Be? Gender and Body Hair Removal Practices in Aotearoa/New Zealand. *Body Image, 10*(4), 599–606.

Vandenburg T., & Braun, V. (2016). 'Basically, it's Sorcery for Your Vagina': Unpacking Western Representations of Vaginal Steaming. *Culture, Health & Sexuality*, online first.

Warhurst, C., & Nickson, D. (2009). 'Who's Got the Look?' Emotional, Aesthetic and Sexualized Labour in Interactive Services. *Gender, Work & Organization, 16*(3), 385–404.

Weiss, R. (2013). Sexual and Relationship Dysfunction is the True Cost of Porn, *Huffington Post.* [Online] http://www.huffingtonpost.com/robert-weiss/sexual-dysfunction-pornography_b_2536216.html

Winch, A. (2013). *Girlfriends and Postfeminist Sisterhood.* Basignstoke, UK: Palgrave Macmillan.

4

Mapping 'Gross' Bodies: The Regulatory Politics of Disgust

Breanne Fahs

Introduction

Sara Ahmed said, 'Emotions should not be regarded as psychological states, but as social and cultural practices' (2004, 9). Critical feminist scholarship on embodiment and women's lived experiences of their bodies has resituated and reframed the way that social scientists understand the discipline, control, and regulation of bodies (Foucault 1995). As a malleable site of cultural anxieties (Bordo 2003), personal distress and self-objectification (Johnston-Robledo et al. 2007), pleasure and satisfaction (Fahs 2011b), cultural rebellion (Bobel and Kwan 2011), frank oppression (Owen 2012), or affiliation to various social identities (Hill Collins 2000), the body and its role as a social entity cannot be overstated. More specifically, psychologists, body image researchers, and critical feminist scholars have argued that women mould and shape their

B. Fahs (✉)
Arizona State University, Glendale, AZ, USA

A.S. Elias et al. (eds.), *Aesthetic Labour*,
DOI 10.1057/978-1-137-47765-1_4

bodies to emulate 'ideals' of youth, heterosexuality, ability, whiteness, and thinness (Bordo 2003; Ringrose and Walkerdine 2008; Tiggemann and Lewis 2004).

While most work focuses on cognitions or social interactions, less work has examined the affective and emotional components of bodily labour, that is, the way that emotions like disgust and dread may serve as regulatory devices for women to think about, and 'contain', their unruly bodies. Note that bodily labour also involves aspects of 'deep acting', where individuals modify their inner feelings, while aesthetic labour can sometimes involve either 'shallow acting', modifying expressions or performances of the self, or 'deep acting' (see Grandey 2003). While disgust as an emotion has appeared in some psychological literatures, most often framed as a device of moral regulation (Björklund and Hursti 2004; Inbar et al. 2012) and attitudes toward sexual minorities (Herek 1988), feminist theorists have not typically used disgust to examine the visceral qualities of body shame, dissatisfaction, and self-regulation among women. As such, this chapter draws from interviews from a diverse community sample of 20 women to examine how women use the emotion of disgust to police and regulate their own, and other women's, bodies. Specifically, I examine fatness, body hair and pubic hair, and menstrual sex as key sites to map 'gross' bodies in order to explore the outcomes and implications of women's self-regulation around body norms and practices.

Situating Disgust

Disgust has powerful implications for the regulation and control of women and their bodies. For example, disgust can increase the severity of moral judgements directed toward others, as it detaches people from the 'morally inferior' other (Schnall et al. 2008b). When people feel disgust, they create moral judgements rather than rational cognitions (Haidt et al. 1993), tying disgust to notions of cleanliness, goodness, and social ideals (Schnall et al. 2008a) as well as various social prejudices and cultural stereotypes (Taylor 2007).

Disgust also connects to social processes that stigmatise less powerful groups and regulate social behaviour and hierarchies. For example, people found women's public urination more disgusting (Eldridge 2010) and those more disgusted by fat bodies judged fat people as morally deficient and fully responsible for their own fatness (Vartanian 2010). People also rated crimes against the wealthy as more serious and more disgusting than crimes against the poor (Smith et al. 2013), constructed welfare recipients as more disgusting than others (Soldatic and Meekosha 2012), saw gays and lesbians as disgusting (Herek 1988), and rated the homeless as the most disgusting of all (Snow and Anderson 1993).

For women, disgust shaped ideas about the self (e.g. body image, sexual desirability, self-worth) and others (e.g. racism, homophobia, classism) (Hodson et al. 2013; Inbar et al. 2012). Bodily disgust has typically appeared in the literature as a cognitive facet of eating disorder behaviour (Abrams et al. 1993) and as connected to social identities like class (Lawler 2005) and race (Hill Collins 2000). While feminist scholars have framed notions of healthy embodiment and body-affirming practices for women and girls as central to wellness, women still struggle with a host of competing discourses about body affirmation and body shame (Johnston-Robledo et al. 2007). As women become neoliberal subjects, haunted by notions of consumerism and the body-as-product model, they utilise the rhetoric of 'choice' to construct morally good bodies (Gill 2007) and to frame bodies they must *not* become (Ringrose and Walkerdine 2008). The self *produced* within neoliberalism is laced with moral undertones about certain bodies as good and other bodies as morally repulsive (e.g. thin bodies as morally good versus fat bodies as morally corrupt, lazy, or bad).

Literature Review

Fatness

Fatness, at times symbolising self-indulgence and moral failure, permeates Western culture as the ultimate example of 'gross' bodies, particularly for women (Rothblum 1992; Wray and Deery 2008). Women engage regularly in weight loss and dieting in part to avoid an unfavourable fat identity (Dalley and Buunk 2009; Vartanian 2010), while fat women reported widespread fat prejudices that impacted well-being (Wray and Deery 2008). Fat women learned to divest themselves of sexuality and to feel 'uncultivated' and 'uncared for' (Murray 2004), leading at times to social withdrawal and invisibility related to spatial discrimination and microaggressions (Owen 2012).

Women and girls framed thinness as a requirement for feeling acceptable to themselves and others (Williamson 1998). For example, eating disorder diagnoses continue to rise, and mothers reported fears that children would gain weight (Jaffe and Worobey 2006). Even for groups who have historically embraced larger bodies (e.g. African-Americans and Latinas), increasing body distress and fear of fatness have emerged (Williamson 1998), though white women reported more body dissatisfaction and more idealisation around thinness compared to women of colour (Abrams et al. 1993).

Body Hair and Pubic Hair

Women's removal of their body hair has shifted from an optional form of body modification to a required and universally expected behaviour. Recent studies suggest that between 91 percent (Tiggemann and Kenyon 1998) and 97 percent (Tiggemann and Lewis 2004) of Australian women shaved their legs, 93 percent shaved their underarms (Tiggemann and Kenyon 1998), and over 99 percent of women in the UK have removed body hair at some point in their lives (Toerien et al. 2005). Pubic hair removal, too, has increased in frequency since the 1980s (Ramsey et al. 2009), as pornography and popular culture idealise prepubescent female genitals and promote hairlessness as the absolute default and as women want to achieve 'sexiness' and 'cleanliness' to feel normative (Smolak and Murnen 2011).

Women removed body hair to feel attractive, clean, and to enhance sexuality (Braun et al. 2013), though older age, feminist identity, and lesbian identity predicted decreased likelihood of body hair removal (Basow 1991; Toerien et al. 2005). Women who refused to remove their body hair felt negatively evaluated by others as 'dirty' or 'gross' (Toerien and Wilkinson 2003, 2004), while American women rated other women who retained their body hair as less sexually attractive, intelligent, sociable, happy, and positive compared to hairless women (Basow and Braman 1998), just as they described hairy women as less friendly, moral, and relaxed, but more aggressive, unsociable, and dominant compared to women who removed their body hair (Basow and Willis 2001). Further, women with negative attitudes toward body hair reported more body disgust (Toerien and Wilkinson 2004), stronger feelings that their bodies were unacceptable and unattractive in their natural state (Chapkis 1986), and more compliance with other restrictive body norms like dieting and plastic surgery (Tiggemann and Hodgson 2008). Conversely, *not* removing body hair also produced a variety of negative outcomes for women, ranging from fear of hate crimes (Fahs 2011a), accusations of failing as women (Fahs and Delgado 2011), and family and partner anger about their bodies (Fahs 2014).

Menstrual Sex

Women also face a barrage of messages that denigrate menstruation as negative, dirty, disgusting, and 'gross' (Fahs 2011b). Educational settings overwhelmingly promote negative views of menstruation, as girls learn to associate menstruation with fear, embarrassment, disgust, and revulsion (Havens and Swenson 1989). Nearly 43 percent of girls disliked their menstruating bodies (Rembeck et al. 2006), while adult women associated menstruation with uneasiness, pain, and maturity (Amann-Gainotti 1994). When selling menstrual products, advertisers portray women's menstruating bodies as unclean and unfeminine to market panty liners, pads, and tampons (Kissling 2006). Film portrayals also construct women's bodies as dirty, disgusting, and in need of sanitising, medicating, and managing (Kissling 2006).

Saddled with menstrual negativity in the broader culture, women also harbour shame, negativity, and disgust toward engaging in sex during menstruation. Less than 50 percent of college women engaged in menstrual sex and over one-third said they would never have menstrual sex; younger women, those in committed relationships, and those less disgusted by menstrual sex expressed more openness toward menstrual sex (Allen and Goldberg 2009). Engaging in menstrual sex correlated to comfort with sexuality, arousal to romantic activities, less disgust toward one's body (Rempel and Baumgartner 2003), and more partner support (Hensel et al. 2007). Further, lesbian and bisexual women (regardless of gender of partner) reported more positive feelings toward menstrual sex than heterosexual women (Fahs 2011b).

Research Questions and Method

Given the variety of ways that women internalise negative messages about their own and others' bodies, this study drew from several research questions to guide its analysis. First, how do women construct their own bodies as 'gross' and where does the language of 'gross' appear? Second, how do women discipline their own bodies by using narratives of the 'gross' female body? Third, how do narratives of 'gross bodies' connect to discourses of gender, power, and containment? Finally, how do women negotiate the tensions between their own ideas about their bodies and others' ideas about their bodies, particularly through a neoliberal and patriarchal lens?

This study utilised qualitative data from a community sample of 20 adult women (mean age = 35, SD = 12.01) recruited in 2014 in a large metropolitan Southwestern US city. A purposive sample was selected to provide greater demographic diversity in the sample: sexual minority women and racial/ethnic minority women were intentionally oversampled and a diverse range of ages was represented (35 percent ages 18–31, 40 percent ages 32–45, and 25 percent ages 46–59). The sample included 60 percent white women and 40 percent women of colour. For self-reported sexual identity, the sample included 60 percent heterosexual women, 25 percent bisexual women, and 15 percent lesbian women. Participants reported a range of socioeconomic and educational backgrounds, employment histories, and parental and relationship statuses. Participants were interviewed using a semi-structured interview protocol that lasted for approximately one-and-a-half to two hours, where they responded to 36 open-ended questions about their sexual histories, sexual and body practices, and feelings and attitudes about their sexuality and their body. All participants were interviewed by the author in a room that ensured privacy and confidentiality of responses. Questions included aspects of their best and worst sexual experiences, feelings about sexual satisfaction, and questions about body image and menstruation. For the purposes of this study, women were asked several questions about their bodies, including: 'How do you feel about your weight?'; 'What would it be like to gain one hundred pounds?'; 'How have you negotiated your body hair and how do you feel about shaving or not shaving?'; and 'What are your experiences with having sex while menstruating?' These questions were scripted but served to open up other conversations and dialogue about related topics, as follow-up questions were free-flowing and conversational. Because of the brief length of this chapter, responses were analysed for patterns related to women assessing their (quite frequent characterisations of their) bodies as 'gross', particularly the language used around their bodies as disgusting, repulsive, or distressing.

Results

Fatness

Feelings about weight elicited the language of disgust and 'gross-ness' in vivid ways, as women critiqued their own shape and size and imagined wanting to lose weight or alter their bodies. Lila[1] (36/White/Heterosexual) described her body as saggy and unattractive, saying: 'My boobs sag. I'm embarrassed in front of somebody else. I'm fat. I don't like my vagina itself. I think my labia minora are too long. They just hang down and I'm always embarrassed'. Martha (52/White/Heterosexual) felt upset when thinking about how she had recently gained weight, saying: 'I worked at a department store and I had to get clothes out of the dressing room. When I saw myself in the mirror, I was disgusted to be so heavy'. The notion of the body as unpleasant, foreign, disgusting, and unacceptable when fat appeared frequently in women's narratives.

[1] All participants have been given pseudonyms to ensure anonymity.

While women certainly identified their disgust related to their current weight, these feelings became exacerbated when they imagined gaining 100 pounds. When I asked women to imagine gaining 100 pounds, responses elicited powerful language around disgust and horror. As if they would become the most disgusting and despised sorts of people, Corinne (21/White/Bisexual) succinctly said: 'I would shoot myself in the head'. Felicity (20/White/Heterosexual) described distress at the idea of becoming fatter, saying: 'I would be insanely unhappy. It would be gross'. With an even more emphatic response, Zari (43/African-American/Heterosexual) described gaining 100 pounds as: 'Devastating. I would have a heart attack. I would be anorexic or bulimic. I have a fear of being fat, like a huge fear. I would be killing myself'. Here, the imagined 100 pound gain seemed too overwhelming to manage, with suicide and eating disorders as more acceptable responses than coping with the weight gain itself.

Body Hair and Pubic Hair

Women also frequently described their own body hair, and other women's body hair, using the language of disgust and 'dirtiness'. Emma (42/White/Heterosexual) said: 'I think not shaving feels dirty, dirty and lazy'. Yvonne (41/Mexican-American/Heterosexual) echoed these comments by discussing the labour she invested into her body hair removal: 'I shave my legs every single morning. I just don't like body hair. I feel manly and I like the smooth feeling after that you just shaved. When I don't I feel dirty, really dirty'. Hair as dirty, and women's hairy bodies as 'gross', led women to construct depilation as a required form of bodily labour.

Some women expressed emphatic disgust about body hair both for themselves and for other women; for example, Daphne (33/White/Heterosexual) noted that body hair made her feel physically sick: 'No, I can't grow out my body hair. God no. I will vomit. It really visually makes me want to vomit. When other women do it, just don't put your legs near me. I'm so weirded out by hair'. Bea (37/Filipina/Heterosexual) described vivid language around the smell of body hair: 'I tried growing my armpit hair once and that's when I was depressed and lazy and stinky but even when I'd take a shower for some reason it would still be stinky'. Occasionally, too, women received this sort of feedback from others; Gretchen (52/White/Heterosexual) described a gay male friend shaming her about body hair: 'I was laying on my stomach and he looked at my ass and he said: 'Your ass is as hairy as a guy's ass'. No one had ever said that to me before'. The visceral qualities of disgust, whether self-inflicted, imagined toward other women, or inflicted by others onto the body, reveal disgust as a powerful social regulator.

Menstrual Sex

Discussions of menstrual sex, for some women, also included the language of menstrual sex as 'gross' or 'disgusting', particularly for women who had sex with men. Sofia (42/Mexican-American/Heterosexual) described menstrual sex as dirty and physically sickening: 'I heard that you can get sick while you are on your period and you have sex. I worry about the mess we're making and I know it's just dirty'. Joyce (21/Filipina/Bisexual) also felt self-conscious about her 'gross' body during menstrual sex:

> I'm usually reluctant because it's made some sort of mess. The guy is thinking I'm gross and they don't want to be around me or they wouldn't want to have sex with me. I always think guys are disappointed when they find out I'm on my period.

Trish (19/White/Lesbian) described differences between menstrual sex with men and women, claiming that with women it felt necessary and less gross:

> With men you can still do it with a tampon in you and even if there's penetration. It's interesting and frustrating. It's mostly a negative experience because your hormones are off balance … With my dad I joked about getting my 'red wings'. It's something I've done often with women in part because it has to happen. Otherwise there are two weeks of the month you're not having sex!

Other women described more emphatic objections to menstrual sex, claiming that it repulsed them. Kathleen (49/White/Heterosexual) described feeling bad about her body during menstrual sex: 'My body doesn't feel like it stays as fresh, and my periods are really heavy now and kind of clotty, eew, gross. It just kind of seems gross now'. Corinne (21/White/Bisexual) described it the most negatively by linking menstrual sex with hating her period in general:

> I hate my period. I just want to get the blood out and be done with it. I wear gloves to take my tampons out and stuff. I hate menstrual sex too. I feel like it's dirty or yucky. My boyfriend likes it but I'm like, 'that's gross' or 'I just got some on the bed. That's disgusting. I need to wash the sheets'.

The perceived need to immediately rectify messes, or to feel dirty or gross during menstrual sex, reflected women's beliefs that they must manage their unruly bodies but also clean the house, fusing bodily and domestic expectations together.

Discussion

While this chapter only gives brief snippets of longer conversations about weight, body hair, and sex during menstruation, it highlights a variety of aspects of how women produce, discipline, express emotions about, regulate, and control their bodies. Specifically, disgust becomes a regulatory, politicised emotion that dictates specific rules and scripts about bodies and body practices. Notably, disgust also seemed to erase or obscure women's shared experiences with other women; rather than fighting back as a feminist collective or imagining the body as a site of rebellion, most women in this study constructed their bodies as singular, individualistic, and as something they alone needed to regulate and control in order to conform to societal expectations. Disgust, in essence, had an individualising effect on women, removing the social context of their bodies and enforcing a sharply neoliberal view of the body as labouring individually toward goodness/perfection/moral superiority. This mirrors Renata Saleci's (2011) claim that anger under neoliberalism becomes increasingly directed at the self; for the women in this study, disgust was directed not only at those perceived as lower on the social hierarchy but also at the self, particularly as women imagined their bodies as always/already failing. Perhaps because women experience strong emotions as 'within' themselves, these emotions do not always link up to political alliances with other women (e.g. seeing the disgust directed toward fatness as a social justice problem rather than a shaming, individualistic problem for individual women to 'fix'). Collective anger, on the other hand, has had strong political implications for collective social action (Holmes 2004).

Further, women in this study overwhelmingly overlooked or denied the ways that patriarchal culture imposed certain notions of 'good' or 'appropriate' bodies onto them. For example, when talking about weight and fatness, women talked about their weight as something they must control or else they would feel repulsive to themselves. The over-valuation of thinness in the economy of 'good bodies' seemed absent from these discussions. In general, women in this study did not direct a critical eye toward menstrual shaming or menstrual negativity in our culture, instead describing their hatred of their periods as something they, too, felt (and, in some ways, they implied that all women *should* feel this way). Scripts of rebellion against patriarchal control, or breaking free of menstrual negativity, or shamelessly embracing body hair, or testing the limits of their own fat-shaming tendencies, were largely absent in these narratives and stories. Instead, women described feeling burdened with the task of managing unruly bodies, maintaining 'appropriate' standards of cleanliness, hairlessness, and thinness, and hoping that they would not offend or otherwise step outside of the boundaries of appropriate bodies.

The language of 'gross bodies'—something this chapter highlights—thus permeates women's understanding of their own and others' bodies. The need to discipline their own, always-failing, always-in-need-of-maintenance, always-problematic bodies appeared both in overt and subtextual ways throughout women's narratives about their bodies. Being 'too much' represented a consistent fear in women's descriptions of fatness, body hair, and menstrual sex. Making a mess, too, seemed like a pervasive fear that women expressed, just as keeping body hair within certain limits (avoiding the 'too hairy' status) had central importance. Language of dirtiness, gross-ness, and repulsion showed up across identity groups, ages, and sexual orientations, both for women's *current* bodies and even for their *imagined future* bodies. With regard to the latter, the *hypothetical* musings of women elicited emphatic responses of disgust at a more visceral level; when women imagined gaining 100 pounds, responses that entailed eating disorders, intense distress, and even suicide reflected again the powerful regulatory politics of disgust and dread.

This chapter is limited by its rather short consideration of a very complicated topic, not to mention the particular aspects of the study's design. Word choice and interview characteristics may have impacted the results. Future research could explore studying each of these topics in more detail, interviewing men (which could yield important insights about men's disgust about their own, or women's, bodies; see O'Neill, this volume), having a larger sample size (and engaging with quantitative questions), and working to identify patterns along gender, race, class, and sexual identity themes. Studies might also look into how neoliberal sentiments in the media impact women's disgust about their own bodies.

Ultimately, the body serves as a mirror for the kinds of anxieties, hang-ups, entitlements, and pleasures people feel, and as such elicits intense emotional reactions worthy of further consideration and exploration. Disgust, in particular, can establish moral boundaries but also reveal much about deeply engrained prejudices and beliefs, particularly within a context that values neoliberal ideas of 'choice' and individual 'agency' about the body. Links between neoliberalism and disgust also move beyond 'choice' and 'agency' by showing us that good neoliberal subjects must demonstrate their ability to practice (seemingly effortless and pleasurable) self-care; those who resist such self-care practices, or who do not display significant disgust at the 'unkempt' body (e.g. hairy, fat, wild, and so on) lose their moral autonomy as neoliberal subjects (see Brown 2003). Further, the effort involved in beauty modification or 'self-care' remains unseen and unrecognised as labour at all but is instead understood (I think problematically) as an *inherently* pleasurable aspect of women's lives. These qualities make the intersection between disgust and women's bodies an ideal site for examining attitudes about gender, power, emotions, and the social contexts of neoliberal body aesthetics.

This chapter also points to the significance of critical feminist interventions related to the body, as feminist activism, feminist pedagogies, a strong feminist media presence, and feminist psychologies can meaningfully intervene into the lives of women as they develop ideas about bodies, sexualities, and social justice. Perhaps we can even one day imagine a radical potential in embracing 'gross-ness' as a form of bodily revolt, or using the visceral disgust people feel about bodies to transform their understandings of themselves, others, and their social world. In the meantime, a continued critical examination of the rhetoric of 'choice' about bodies, and its attendant philosophical and cultural anxieties, will yield important new directions for feminists interested in exploring 'gross' bodies.

References

Abrams, K. K., Allen, L. R., & Gray, J. J. (1993). Disordered Eating Attitudes and Behaviors, Psychological Adjustment, and Ethnic Identity: A Comparison of Black and White Female College Students. *International Journal of Eating Disorders, 14*(1), 49–57.

Ahmed, S. (2004). *The Cultural Politics of Emotions*. Edinburgh: Edinburgh University Press.

Allen, K. R., & Goldberg, A. E. (2009). Sexual Activity During Menstruation: A Qualitative Study. *Journal of Sex Research, 46*(6), 535–545.

Amann-Gainotti, M. (1994). Adolescent Girls' Internal Body Image. *International Journal of Adolescent Medicine and Health, 7*(1), 73–86.

Basow, S. A. (1991). The Hairless Ideal: Women and their Body Hair. *Psychology of Women Quarterly, 15*(1), 83–96.

Basow, S. A., & Braman, A. C. (1998). Women and Body Hair: Social Perceptions and Attitudes. *Psychology of Women Quarterly, 22*(4), 637–645.

Basow, S. A., & Willis, J. (2001). Perceptions of Body Hair on White Women: Effects of Labeling. *Psychological Reports, 89*(3), 571–576.

Björklund, F., & Hursti, T. J. (2004). A Swedish Translation and Validation of the Disgust Scale: A Measure of Disgust Sensitivity. *Scandinavian Journal of Psychology, 45*(4), 279–284.

Bobel, C., & Kwan, S. (2011). *Embodied Resistance: Challenging the Norms, Breaking the Rules*. Nashville: Vanderbilt University Press.

Bordo, S. (2003). *Unbearable Weight: Feminism, Western Culture, and the Body*. Berkeley: University of California Press.

Braun, V., Tricklebank, G., & Clarke, V. (2013). 'It Shouldn't Stick Out from Your Bikini at the Beach': Meaning, Gender, and the Hairy/Hairless Body. *Psychology of Women Quarterly, 37*(4), 478–493.

Brown, W. (2003) Neoliberalism and the End of Liberal Democracy. *Theory & Event,* 7(1). [Online] Retrieved from https://uranthplsc379.files.wordpress.com/2013/10/wendy-brown-neo-liberalism-and-the-end-of-liberal-democracy-theory-event-71.pdf

Chapkis, W. (1986). *Beauty Secrets: Women and the Politics of Appearance*. Boston: South End Press.

Dalley, S. E., & Buunk, A. P. (2009). 'Thinspiration' Vs. 'Fear of Fat': Using Prototypes to Predict Frequent Weight-Loss Dieting in Females. *Appetite, 52*(1), 217–221.

Eldridge, A. (2010). Public Panics: Problematic Bodies in Social Spaces. *Emotion, Space and Society, 3*(1), 40–44.

Fahs, B. (2011a). Dreaded 'Otherness': Heteronormative Patrolling in Women's Body Hair Rebellions. *Gender & Society, 25*(4), 451–472.

Fahs, B. (2011b). Sex During Menstruation: Race, Sexual Identity, and Women's Qualitative Accounts of Pleasure and Disgust. *Feminism & Psychology, 21*(2), 155–178.

Fahs, B. (2014). Perilous Patches and Pitstaches: Imagined Versus Lived Experiences of Women's Body Hair Growth. *Psychology of Women Quarterly, 38*(2), 167–180.

Fahs, B., & Delgado, D. A. (2011). The Specter of Excess: Race, Class, and Gender in Women's Body Hair Narratives. In C. Bobel & S. Kwan (Eds.), *Embodied Resistance: Breaking the Rules, Challenging the Norms* (pp. 13–25). Nashville: Vanderbilt University Press.

Foucault, M. (1995). *Discipline and Punish: The Birth of the Prison*. New York: Vintage.

Gill, R. (2007). Critical Respect: The Difficulties and Dilemmas of Agency and 'Choice' for Feminism. *European Journal of Women's Studies, 14*(1), 69–80.

Grandey, A. A. (2003). When the 'Show Must Go on': Surface Acting and Deep Acting as Determinants of Emotional Exhaustion and Peer-Related Service Delivery. *Academy of Management Journal, 46*(1), 86–96.

Haidt, J., Koller, S. H., & Dias, M. G. (1993). Affect, Culture, and Morality, or is it Wrong to Eat Your Dog? *Journal of Personality and Social Psychology, 65*(4), 613–628.

Havens, B. B., & Swenson, I. (1989). A Content Analysis of Educational Media About Menstruation. *Adolescence, 24*(96), 901–907.

Hensel, D. J., Fortenberry, J. D., & Orr, D. P. (2007). Situational and Relational Factors Associated with Coitus during Vaginal Bleeding Among Adolescent women. *Journal of Sex Research, 44*(3), 269–277.

Herek, G. M. (1988). Heterosexuals' Attitudes Toward Lesbians and Gay Men: Correlates and Gender Differences. *Journal of Sex Research, 25*(4), 451–477.

Hill Collins, P. (2000). *Black Feminist Thought: Knowledge, Consciousness, and the Politics of Empowerment.* London: Routledge.

Hodson, G., Choma, B. L., Boisvert, J., Hafer, C. L., MacInnis, C. C., & Costello, K. (2013). The Role of Intergroup Disgust in Predicting Negative Outgroup Evaluations. *Journal of Experimental Social Psychology, 49*(2), 195–202.

Holmes, M. (2004). Feeling Beyond Rules: Politicizing the Sociology of Emotion and Anger in Feminist Politics. *European Journal of Social Theory, 7*(2), 209–227.

Inbar, Y., Pizarro, D., Iyer, R., & Haidt, J. (2012). Disgust Sensitivity, Political Conservatism, and Voting. *Social Psychological and Personality Science, 3*(5), 537–544.

Jaffe, K., & Worobey, J. (2006). Mothers' Attitudes Toward Fat, Weight, and Dieting in Themselves and Their Children. *Body Image, 3*(2), 113–120.

Johnston-Robledo, I., Sheffield, K., Voigt, J., & Wilcox-Constantine, J. (2007). Reproductive Shame: Self-objectification and Young Women's Attitudes Toward their Reproductive Functioning. *Women & Health, 46*(1), 25–39.

Kissling, E. A. (2006). *Capitalizing on the Curse: The Business of Menstruation.* Boulder, CO: Lynne Rienner.

Lawler, S. (2005). Disgusted Subjects: The Making of Middle-Class Identities. *The Sociological Review, 53*(3), 429–446.

Murray, S. (2004). Locating Aesthetics: Sexing the Fat Woman. *Social Semiotics, 14*(3), 237–247.

Owen, L. (2012). Living Fat in a Thin-Centric World: Effects of Spatial Discrimination on Fat Bodies and Selves. *Feminism & Psychology, 22*(3), 290–306.

Ramsey, S., Sweeney, C., Fraser, M., & Oades, G. (2009). Pubic Hair and Sexuality: A Review. *The Journal of Sexual Medicine, 6*(8), 2102–2110.

Rembeck, G. I., Möller, M. M., & Gunnarsson, R. K. (2006). Attitudes and Feelings Towards Menstruation and Womanhood in Girls at Menarche. *Acta Paediatrica, 95*(6), 707–714.

Rempel, J. K., & Baumgartner, B. (2003). The Relationship Between Attitudes Towards Menstruation and Sexual Attitudes, Desires, and Behavior in Women. *Archives of Sexual Behavior, 32*(2), 155–163.

Ringrose, J., & Walkerdine, V. (2008). Regulating the Abject: The TV Make-Over as Site of Neoliberal Reinvention Toward Bourgeois Femininity. *Feminist Media Studies, 8*(3), 227–246.

Rothblum, E. D. (1992). The Stigma of Women's Weight: Social and Economic Realities. *Feminism & Psychology, 2*(1), 61–73.

Saleci, R. (2011). *The Tyranny of Choice*. London: Profile Books.

Schnall, S., Benton, J., & Harvey, S. (2008a). With a Clean Conscience: Cleanliness Reduces the Severity of Moral Judgments. *Psychological Science, 19*(12), 1219–1222.

Schnall, S., Haidt, J., Clore, G. L., & Jordan, A. H. (2008b). Disgust as Embodied Moral Judgment. *Personality and Social Psychology Bulletin, 34*(8), 1096–1109.

Smith, L., Baranowski, K., Allen, A., & Bowen, R. (2013). Poverty, Crime Seriousness, and the 'Politics of Disgust'. *Journal of Poverty, 17*(4), 375–393.

Smolak, L., & Murnen, S. K. (2011). Gender, Self-Objectification, and Pubic Hair Removal. *Sex Roles, 65*(7), 506–517.

Snow, D. A., & Anderson, L. (1993). *Down on Their Luck: A Study of Homeless Street People*. Berkeley: University of California Press.

Soldatic, K., & Meekosha, H. (2012). The Place of Disgust: Disability, Class, and Gender in the Spaces of Workfare. *Societies, 2*(3), 139–156.

Taylor, K. (2007). Disgust is a Factor in Extreme Prejudice. *The British Journal of Social Psychology, 46*(3), 597–617.

Tiggemann, M., & Hodgson, S. (2008). The Hairlessness Norm Extended: Reasons for and Predictors of Women's Body Hair Removal at Different Body Sites. *Sex Roles, 59*(11–12), 889–897.

Tiggemann, M., & Kenyon, S. J. (1998). The Hairlessness Norm: The Removal of Body Hair in Women. *Sex Roles, 39*(11–12), 873–885.

Tiggemann, M., & Lewis, C. (2004). Attitudes Toward Women's Body Hair: Relationship with Disgust Sensitivity. *Psychology of Women Quarterly, 28*(4), 381–387.

Toerien, M., & Wilkinson, S. (2003). Gender and Body Hair: Constructing the Feminine Woman. *Women's Studies International Forum, 26*(4), 333–344.

Toerien, M., & Wilkinson, S. (2004). Exploring the Depilation Norm: A Qualitative Questionnaire Study of Women's Body Hair Removal. *Qualitative Research in Psychology, 1*(1), 69–92.

Toerien, M., Wilkinson, S., & Choi, P. Y. L. (2005). Body Hair Removal: The 'Mundane' Production of Normative Femininity. *Sex Roles, 52*(5–6), 399–406.

Vartanian, L. R. (2010). Disgust and Perceived Control in Attitudes Toward Obese People. *International Journal of Obesity, 34*(8), 1302–1307.

Williamson, L. (1998). Eating Disorders and the Cultural Forces Behind the Drive for Thinness: Are African American Women Really Protected? *Social Work in Health Care, 28*(1), 61–73.

Wray, S., & Deery, R. (2008). The Medicalization of Body Size and Women's Healthcare. *Health Care for Women International, 29*(3), 227–243.

5

The Escalating Price of Motherhood: Aesthetic Labour in Popular Representations of 'Stay-at-Home' Mothers

Sara De Benedictis and Shani Orgad

Introduction

The devaluation of domestic, reproductive, emotional and maternal labour has been extensively critiqued by feminist scholars and activists. Women's domestic labour is normalised as 'housework', considered to have no material or economic recognition (Federici 2012), and childrearing and looking after the home are still often equated with 'doing nothing' (Crittenden 2010). Many have argued that cultural and media representations play a constitutive role in normalising the devaluation and thus exploitation of women's productive and repro-

S. De Benedictis (✉)
Division of Midwifery, University of Nottingham, Nottingham, UK

S. Orgad
Department of Media and Communications, London School of Economics and Political Science, London, UK

A.S. Elias et al. (eds.), *Aesthetic Labour*,
DOI 10.1057/978-1-137-47765-1_5

ductive labour. The media legitimise the continuing lack of social, political and economic recognition and reward of motherhood by symbolically naturalising and masking maternal labour, for example, by representing mothers' work as 'natural' and a product of intrinsic maternal love (Douglas and Michaels 2004). Building on this scholarship about the cultural construction of maternity, in this chapter we highlight aesthetic labour as a new(ly) added, previously unrecognised dimension of contemporary maternal labour that has emerged under neoliberalism.

In contemporary popular representations the 'good mother' is frequently articulated through, and celebrated and praised for, her sexually attractive look (Tyler 2011; Lachover 2013; Littler 2013). As noted by Jo Littler (2013, p. 229): 'now mothers themselves are encouraged to look "hot"'. However, we would argue that the immense *labour* required for this idealised maternal image is largely masked; the beauty *practices* involving self-surveillance, self-disciplining and self-blame underpinning a 'hot' look are denied.

Our analysis focuses on the middle-class 'stay-at-home mother' (hereafter SAHM), a maternal figure who, supposedly, is outside the neoliberal sexual contract (McRobbie 2009) which requires women to perform successful femininities simultaneously, as mothers and economic labourers and/or consumers. The SAHM's counterpart, the 'career mother' who participates in the workforce, is implied to invest in her appearance and aspire to normative beauty and active femininity (manifested in the glamorous images of attractive career women who successfully combine a job with motherhood). This contrasts with many popular representations depicting the SAHM's position outside the labour market, and her prime (perhaps exclusive) association with the domestic sphere which seemingly 'exempts' her from the demand to perform sexuality. The SAHM is supposedly not upheld by neoliberal demands of aesthetic labour and performance of attractive sexual appearance.

However, the following analysis shows that in some current popular representations the 'good' SAHM is required simultaneously to be a carer *and* to engage in intense aesthetic labour, which involves the exercise of bodily and beauty disciplining practices. Yet both the maternal labour of caring—which historically has been concealed and unrecognised—*and* the intense aesthetic labour she is now demanded to perform are marginalised, obscured and denied.

We start by briefly contextualising the remarkable visibility of the maternal in contemporary neoliberal media and culture in existing research, focusing on the construction of the SAHM. We then present our study of popular representations of SAHMs, based on two examples of SAHM figures: Jools Oliver and Bridget Jones. Our analysis highlights how aesthetic labour has become a central, even constitutive, feature of the good SAHM, and, while strongly demanded of SAHMs, is simultaneously masked. Thus, we conclude, echoing Ann Crittenden (2010), that aesthetic labour is now part of the endlessly rising and heavy 'price of motherhood'.

Maternity, Neoliberalism and Aesthetic Labour

Images of glamorous working mothers have come to typify the normative ideal of the woman who smoothly and successfully combines paid labour and maternal labour. Endlessly replicated in images of working mothers, most notably in women's magazines and advertisements, 'the woman with the flying hair' (Hochschild 1989, p. 1), is a (often white, middle-class, heterosexual) woman whose appearance connotes confidence, empowerment and a sense of liberation (Gill and Orgad 2015; Lachover 2013). Working on one's appearance has become a requirement for women to successfully combine motherhood and a career (see Introduction to this collection). Yet, as Hochschild (1989, pp. 59–60) observed some time ago, this image hides the 'intricate webs of tensions, and the huge, hidden emotional cost to women, men, and children of having to manage inequality'. This image obscures another fundamental aspect which has received prominence (and attracted scholarly scrutiny) more recently, namely, the pervasiveness of aesthetic labour in women's lives.

A growing body of scholarship on maternity under neoliberalism interrogates the incorporation, intensification and legitimation of aesthetic labour into maternal subjectivities (e.g. Allen and Taylor 2012; Ekinsmyth 2013; Boyer 2014). Mediated figures such as the 'yummy mummy' (Littler 2013) or 'pregnant beauty' (Tyler 2011) have emerged recently, emphasising how maternal identities are increasingly reliant upon and articulated through beauty practices and body projects such as dieting, exercise and cosmetic surgery (e.g. Goodwin and Huppatz 2010). Such practices are deeply entrenched in self-surveillance, self-regulation and 'disciplinary neoliberalism' (Gill 1995), underscored by the commodification of maternity under neoliberalism (Tyler 2011).

However, less scholarship explores how maternal subjects considered 'outside' of the labour market by 'choice' are shaped and affected by the demands of aesthetic labour. On the one hand, unlike her counterpart, the SAHM seemingly is outside the new sexual contract. She has 'opted out' (or never entered) the labour market, and her femininity relies exclusively on and is articulated through her role as carer. Indeed, the figure of the SAHM embodies the two fundamental prohibitions that 'good mothering' is often predicated upon in western popular representations: sexuality and work outside the home (Danuta and Harrison 2014). On the other hand, the SAHM differs from the traditional housewife due to her distinct positioning as a postfeminist neoliberal figure: 'she is not a productive labourer contributing directly to the neoliberal economy, yet she embodies the [...] values of choice, agency, individualisation and female liberation' (Orgad and De Benedictis 2015). Specifically, SAHMs' decisions to leave paid employment are depicted mostly as personal empowering choices, with the related barriers, constraints or regrets barely mentioned (Kuperberg and Stone 2008; Orgad and De Benedictis 2015). It is within this positioning, and the SAHM's embodiment as a postfeminist neoliberal figure, that aesthetic labour comes to play a constitutive (but simultaneously masked) role in her construction.

Popular Representations of SAHMs

We examine the construction of the SAHM figure in popular culture—a key site where ideas, fantasies and judgements about femininity and maternity are articulated, often becoming 'new forms of common sense' (McRobbie 2009, p. 33; Littler 2013). Specifically, we analyse two SAHM examples in popular media: celebrity Jools Oliver and the literary character Bridget Jones in *Mad About The Boy* (Fielding 2013). Our choice of examples was informed by a content analysis of news media representations of SAHMs (Orgad and De Benedictis 2015), which examined press coverage of SAHMs in UK newspapers during recession and post-recession (2008–2013). Situated in debates on mediated constructions of maternal femininities, postfeminism and neoliberalism, we explored whether the depiction of SAHMs reflects and reinforces neoliberalism's and postfeminism's entangled embrace of market values and emphasis on economic productivity through participation in the labour force, and consequently critiques SAHMs' 'opting out' and return to the domestic setting as attacking market productivity and capitalism. Contra to the expectation that the SAHM figure would be derided and denigrated for her absence from the workforce, we found that the SAHM is represented as 'a largely positive figure, whose "choice" is valued, recognised and endorsed, including by government (as long as she is middle-class and not dependent on benefits)' (Orgad and De Benedictis 2015, p. 15). This emphasis on SAHMs' decision as a private choice obscures the larger societal, political and economic explanations of SAHMs' experiences and enables their husbands' economic ultra-productivity, naturalising and re-securing gender inequality.

Our focus in this chapter on Jools Oliver and Bridget Jones illustrates the features of the white middle-class SAHM we identified in the content analysis: highly individualised, agentic and embodying personal and positive choice through stay-at-home motherhood. Developing this analysis, in what follows we critically unpack how the SAHM's maternal femininity—and its coupling with notions of agency, choice, individualisation and liberation—is predicated on naturalising and masking her maternal labour.

Performing and Masking Aesthetic/ Maternal Labour

Jools Oliver: The Successful SAHM

Celebrity Jools Oliver is an exemplary figure of a SAHM whose successful maternal femininity is predicated on her (constructed) ability to simultaneously perform the role of a caring mother outside the labour market, with being very attractive physically according to the heteronormative definitions of beauty. Jools is constructed across various popular representations as one half of the celebrity couple, Jamie and Jools Oliver. The couple began to occupy the media spotlight when Jamie became a celebrity chef through the UK television cookery programme, *The Naked Chef* (1999–2001). Since then the Olivers have retained a consistent presence in the media spotlight. Jamie's media narrative is emphasised as one of humble, working-class Essex roots, which he has transcended through his talents as a chef, sheer determination and hard graft to become a celebrity. Like celebrities more generally (see Littler 2004), the Olivers occupy a neoliberal vision of individualisation, meritocracy and social mobility and represent the benefits of the traditional nuclear family and familial harmony.

While Jamie's media persona is largely constructed through his success as a celebrity chef, television personality and health and food advisor, Jools' celebrity persona rests on, and is constituted in relation to, her role as a wife to Jamie, and mother to their four children. The repetitive narrative that is told across media sites is of Jools having been a model prior to meeting Jamie, and subsequently deciding to be a wife and SAHM. Jools was also employed as a television researcher, but this role receives little attention in her mediated representations. Her subjectivity is continually constructed in relation to the aesthetic, maternal or domestic, but the actual labour associated with these aspects is rarely made visible.

Jools is preened to perfection in public appearances and media interviews, the wife and mother who juggles responsibilities, but has not a hair out of place, and never displays a drop of sweat or remnants of baby vomit. The ex-model glides seamlessly and consistently between a slim pre-, during and post-natal body showing no markers of the huge labour required to achieve this appearance. Her beauty practices and fitness regimes are marginalised and barely commented on, as illustrated by her claim of just using organic face wash and moisturiser (Oliver in Everrett, 2012). She is positioned as simultaneously 'naturally' glamorous and sexual, and wholesomely motherly and domestic. The masking of the aesthetic labour needed to achieve this celebrity image is further enabled by the visual construction of her figure through a retro and austerity type aesthetic. The marketing for Jools' Mothercare clothing range, Little

Bird, plays upon the notion that her 'paired down' look and 'ordinary' angle of her celebrity persona, are effortless, usual, waking states. Photos taken through a Vaseline-smeared, Instagram-like frame, muted colours, and homemaking set-ups reinforce a 'smooth' and soft image of Jools as a 'natural' feminine wife and mother, blurring the labour this image underpins. This echoes postfeminist recessionary media culture, whereby 'conspicuous consumption accommodates a modesty that respects the economic times', creating social distinctions and moral consumer citizenship (Nathanson 2014, p. 140). On the very few occasions when her 'bodywork' is addressed, Jools is constructed as not only blessed with 'good genes' and 'metabolism' but also as refusing to partake in 'all this dieting rubbish' (D'Souza 2015). Her daily exercise is constructed as being *not* about aesthetics, but rather about health and strength.

The masking of Jools' aesthetic labour is coupled with the naturalisation of her maternal labour, exemplified by her repeated self-account of a woman who 'always knew' she 'wanted the babies, the baking and the roses round the door' (Oliver 2006, np). Crucially, Jools' role as wife and mother is constructed as an active choice. She comes into being in the media spotlight through a stated 'natural' calling to be a SAHM and to pursue motherhood as a career and, consequently, has not 'had a lie-in for about ten years' (Oliver in *The Daily Mail* 2012). The decision to be a SAHM is represented as necessary and ultimately Jools' choice, naturalising her maternity as an individual, instinctive life-calling, driven by 'natural' and 'innate' maternal feelings. She is constructed as always knowing that she 'didn't want a career' and was 'uncomfortable' in previous jobs, whereas now she is 'comfortable being a mum' (Oliver in Ford-Rojas 2012). Jools is represented as hovering in the wings to willingly support and complement her husband as they combine to form the image of the harmonious celebrity couple and nuclear family. She is depicted as dependent on her husband, Jamie, while his persona can stand alone as celebrity, chef or father. By contrast, Jools' celebrity is constructed exclusively through the prism of being an ex-model turned wife and mother. This construction, compounded by the rhetoric of choice, diffuses any tensions and the price that this 'choice' may entail.

Jools' lack of career gumption is sometimes represented as problematic between the couple:

> [Jools] hasn't got a mission, she just wants to be married to someone she loves and have a family and that's it, end of story. [...] It baffled me for ages, I almost felt she had a part of her life missing, then I thought, it's sweet and quite refreshing (Sawyer 2002)

In this extract, Jools' choice initially is presented as difficult but then as agentic, courageous and refreshing. She is constructed as shunning the postfeminist dictates of contemporary society for middle-class mothers to 'have it all'. In turn, staying at home comes to signify Jools' difference, novelty and uniqueness, despite this role having a substantial history in relation to the gendering of labour. Thus, Jools' representation as a SAHM would seem to defy the 'new sexual contract' (McRobbie 2009). She is constructed in opposition to postfeminist maternal figures that come into being through the emphasis on their roles as both economic labourers/consumers *and* carers (Allen and Taylor 2012; Ekinsmyth 2013; Littler 2013).

In a postfeminist twist, therefore, Jools simultaneously is represented through active femininity and an attractive appearance and constructed as a dependable wife and mother. Jools has capitalised upon her celebrity status as a SAHM to write children's books and design children's clothing lines that have become bestsellers for Mothercare. Yet, her maternal entrepreneurialism is constructed as only undertaken in her spare time and as 'small' sideline projects. Thus, Jools' role as an economic labourer is totally diminished, while the maternal and domestic are upheld as her main roles.

In sum, Jools' maternal and feminine body are the focus and site of her celebrity persona, her body and physical femininity are foregrounded in her mediated representations. Her figure as a SAHM and wife to Jamie underscores stereotypically feminine maternal and aesthetic roles to define her subjectivity. However, neither the labour these roles involve, nor the labour she performs which is considered socially to be economic (researcher, writer, designer) are acknowledged or recognised. Jools' sexual appearance and entrepreneurial subjectivity work to substitute her 'lack' of overt economic labouring, as well as her presented lack of drive to forge a career separate from her stated calling as wife or mother. Moreover, the aesthetic labour that is necessary to be the 'yummy mummy' she is, and the economic labour, emerges as 'naturally' constitutive of her persona, rather than the result of intense aesthetic and entrepreneurial labour.

Bridget Jones: The Failing SAHM

Helen Fielding's *Bridget Jones: Mad About the Boy* casts the postfeminist zeitgeist 20 years on from her 'girly' singleton days to her current status as a SAHM. Bridget Jones is now a 51-year-old widow and mother to two small children, residing in a middle-class North London neighbourhood. Bridget recounts her experiences in the familiar diary form and writing style of her early diaries (e.g. daily statistics) enhanced by her bemused experimentation with new media technologies like Twitter. She writes about her emergence from grief over her husband Darcy's death four years previously, her everyday struggles as a mother, and her consequent return to dating.

Darcy left Bridget financially secure, with no financial need to return to the workforce and she is represented as neither willing nor fit to do so. Her capacity to be an economic labourer is ridiculed through various grotesque meetings with the potential film production company that considers buying her contemporary adaptation of *Hedda Gabler*. These meetings specifically highlight the 'clashes' between Bridget's maternal identity and her (vaguely aspired to) professional identity. Bridget is never properly prepared for or focused during her meetings with the production team, almost always because she is preoccupied with issues related to her kids and their school.

Mothering is a new important object of Bridget's self-governing. The 'disciplinary neoliberalism' (Gill 1995) that in her 20s focused on self-monitoring her calorific intake, fluctuating weight and romantic relationships now extends to her maternal practices through Twitter and numerous parenting self-help books whose expert advice she tries to follow. Bridget constantly demands of herself and feels that she is being demanded by others (her mother, her children, other parents, her children's teachers, experts) to be a 'good mother'. This demand is accentuated and legitimised by her 'stay-at-home' status. Bridget is not in paid employment and, thus, has no 'real' career to excuse anything but 'perfect' mothering. When her son's teacher criticises her for neglecting his homework and assigning greater importance to 'sitting in the hairdresser's' (Fielding 2013, p. 233), echoing the stereotypical image of the lazy self-indulgent SAHM who deals with her 'excess' time by working on her appearance, Bridget defensively explains: 'I am a professional woman and am writing an updating of Hedda Gabbler by Anton Chekhov' (Fielding 2013, p. 233). Thus, Bridget marginalises her investment in and concern with her appearance, to highlight her focus with the 'important' matter: her professional identity.

But Bridget fails continuously. She and the readers know that rather than focusing seriously on her professional career, she has been procrastinating, working on her improbable screenplay and thinking about her toyboy, Roxter. When she is about to give a presentation after proudly describing her play as a 'feminist piece' (Fielding 2013, p. 221) she opens her laptop to reveal a girly homepage of Princess Bride Dress Up—a mark of her two incompatible worlds: career and mothering—in both of which she repeatedly fails. Thus, while Bridget's ability to be an economic labourer is deeply questioned, so is her ability to adequately perform her mothering role. She aspires to be a 'perfect mother' (Fielding 2013, p. 134), but consistent with her younger incompetent self, Bridget makes a clumsy mother, finding herself in endless comical situations related to parenting and schooling.

On the one hand, Bridget recognises the substantial labour involved in being a single SAHM. She reports in her diary on thoughts and moments that do not normally enter the dominant highly idealised 'Mommy Myth' (Douglas and Michaels 2004), such as exhaustion, annoyance and frustration with childcare. Bombarded by her children's relentless morning demands, she writes: 'Suddenly overwhelmed with exhaustion and desire to read paper in echoing silence. [...] Why can't everyone just FUCKING SHUT UP AND LET ME READ THE PAPERS?' (Fielding 2013, pp. 87–88). Simultaneously, she repeatedly rehearses to herself that her children must come first (Fielding 2013, p. 158) and she should not focus on men (Fielding 2013, p. 133), puncturing the 'masquerade of the doting, self-sacrificing mother' (Douglas and Michaels 2004, p. 6) that mothers are expected to adopt. Writing from a maternal perspective, in such a way that does not idealise, silence or denigrate the maternal, but rather attends to the mundane, messy realities and frustrations of motherhood, may contribute to complicating dominant maternal narratives (see Baraitser 2009). Thus, the character of 51-year-old Bridget might be argued to contribute to challenging the stronghold of the 'perfect mother' myth by voicing the difficulties and frustrations of maternal experience and by making visible the huge labour that mothering involves.

On the other hand, this recognition is constantly diffused and undermined. The comic, satirical features of Bridget's chaotic and clumsy parenting mask the immense labour demanded by and involved in single stay-at-home motherhood. Amusing situations, such as having to wash and change her children's diarrhoea and vomit-soaked sheets, largely obscure the physical and emotional work Bridget's mothering entails. They also diffuse the very painful feelings of self-blame and self-hate that she sometimes experiences as a mother, exemplified as she writes: 'Everything is completely intolerable, I hate myself, I'm a rubbish mother' (Fielding 2013, p. 135).

Recognition of Bridget's maternal labour is further obfuscated by her depiction as desperately dependent on her *au pair* to manage herself and her kids, from doing the daily school run to looking after sick children—'simple' and 'basic' tasks that Bridget is constructed as too inept (and lazy) to do alone. Bridget's self-mocking and self-disparaging of her poor performance in these maternal tasks reinforce the marginalisation and misrecognition of the significant labour they involve.

Importantly, Bridget's self-beratement, and others' judgements of her 'poor mothering', rely on oppositional figures of the 'perfect mother', against which such judgements are implicitly (and sometimes explicitly) made. Specifically, it is the SAHM mediated figure, such as Jools Oliver's, that is evoked: not only is she the perfect SAHM who has an absent partner and who (seemingly) has no childcare help, Jools (and similar SAHM figures) is also the sexual 'perfect body' model whose images Bridget frustratedly consumes in magazines. The perfect sexual SAHM is not only mediated; there is 'perfect Nicolette', a mother in Bridget's son's class, who constitutes an important reference point in the book (the stereotypical 'yummy mummy') against which Bridget measures herself: 'the Class Mother (perfect house, perfect husband, perfect children) [...] perfectly dressed and perfectly blow-dried with a perfect gigantic handbag' (Fielding 2013, pp. 4–5).

Just like 20 years ago, now in the shadow of these successful maternal feminine figures, Bridget aspires to '*work on herself*' (Gill 2007, p. 227, original emphasis). Her body is still presented as equally (if not more of) a fundamental source of her feminine identity. Twenty years wiser, struggling to control her unruly maternal body, Bridget recognises the acute oppressiveness of the unattainable and untenable beauty standards which women are demanded to meet. She questions: 'Why are bodies so difficult to manage?', stressing that bodies 'splurge fat unless you, like, STARVE yourself', subsequently listing 13 high-calorie foods she has consumed before noon and concluding: 'Put that in your pipe and smoke it, society!' (Fielding 2013, pp. 58–59).

Yet Bridget is depicted as unable *not* to surrender to a sisyphic body project to re-attain 'her sense of sexual self' (Fielding 2013, p. 33). She constantly self-monitors and struggles to discipline her body's shape and size, through endless dieting, physical exercise and reduction of alcohol intake. Echoing the (Christian) 'prohibition' on sexuality as underpinning 'good mothering' (Littler 2013; Danuta and Harrison 2014), Bridget is temporarily resolute about a 'focus on being a mother instead of thinking about men' (Fielding 2013, p. 33). However, she swiftly concludes that this prohibition is outdated; the age of 50s, she observes, was 'the age of Germaine Greer's "Invisible Woman", branded as non-viable, post-menopausal sitcom fodder', however 'now with Talitha school of branding combined with Kim Cattrall, Julianne and Demi Moore, etc. is all starting to change!' (Fielding 2013, p. 152).

Talitha's voice reverberates contemporary culture's hailing of women to makeover their ageing bodies and make themselves visible through 'cosmeceutical interventions' (Dolan and Tincknell 2013) and beauty practices. Thus, however satirical Bridget's obsessive self-monitoring is presented, as Rosalind Gill (2007, p. 228) observed of the first Bridget Jones novel and film, 'the satire is not straightforward', 'the body is represented as a chaotic and in need of constant discipline'. Just as the huge labour of her chaotic mothering is marginalised and ridiculed, so the intense aesthetic labour demanded of Bridget is masked, alongside its often painful consequences. The following example, of Bridget's dualistic self-surveillance—observing herself (in the diary) observing herself (in the mirror)—illustrates how humour and self-irony work to blur and divert difficult feelings like self-blame and self-hate, which are induced by 'body projects' and practices of 'disciplinary neoliberalism' (Gill 1995):

> Got home and surveyed self aghast mirror. Am starting to look like a heron. My legs and arms have stayed the same, but my whole upper body is like a large bird with a big roll of fat round the middle that [...] is about to be served up for an extended family's post-Hogmanay breakfast. (Fielding 2013, p. 48)

Thus, 51-year-old Bridget continues to be the woman who is endearing by virtue of her failing (McRobbie 2009). However, unlike her younger self, Bridget's mature self is characterised by an inner drive to compete against herself and other mothers, most notably 'perfect Nicolette'. Indeed, the 2013 diary is a space of 'inner-directed self-competition' (McRobbie 2015, p. 15) over becoming the 'Perfect Mother' (Fielding 2013, p. 134) and the perfect 'sensual woman' (Fielding 2013, p. 86). The outcome of this competitive self is constant self-beratement (McRobbie 2015), which feeds into and perpetuates extensive and ever-expanding types of labour she must perform.

Conclusion

As SAHMs, both Jools and Bridget perform similar aesthetic practices and 'body projects' (Tyler 2011) to those demanded from and exercised by their maternal and non-maternal counterparts within the labour market. Jools performs a successful and desirable maternal femininity, predicated on intensified aesthetic labour. Bridget performs a failed maternal subjectivity, continuously upholding Jools' norm of perfection and striving to achieve it, thus, conforming to and defining the norm by failing (McRobbie 2009, 2015).

Yet their aesthetic maternal labour is simultaneously masked, obscured and marginalised. The intense labour Jools invests in creating and maintaining her attractive appearance is smoothed and hidden by her celebrity persona. Bridget's aesthetic labour and continuous exercise of self-monitoring and self-policing is used primarily to create comic effect;

thus, even when it potentially exposes some of the painful and disturbing consequences of beauty and aesthetic practices, they are diffused and overridden by humour. The hiding of Jools' and Bridget's aesthetic labour supports their construction as dependent and domestic carers, rather than active aesthetic and maternal labourers. Thus, they demonstrate a new twist: not only must mothers look 'hot' (Littler 2013), they should keep and/or help keep invisible the price of living up to this demand by repudiating and plastering over aesthetic labour and its consequent injuries for confident selfhood (Gill and Orgad 2015).

Ultimately, then, the contemporary SAHM figure, embodied by Jools and Bridget, is doubly subjugated: her subjectivity is increasingly constituted through intensive (and oppressive) aesthetic labour, self-surveillance and beauty practices demanded by neoliberalism, while simultaneously constructed as dependent and relegated to the domestic sphere, *outside* the neoliberal market and its exclusive valuing of economic productivity.

The SAHM, by 'self-choosing' to 'opt out' of the labour market, has seemingly breached the 'new sexual contract', which demands women to be simultaneous economic labourers and carers (McRobbie 2009). She could, therefore, be a maternal figure that voices a critique of and resistance to the increasing capitalisation and commodification of neoliberal maternity. SAHM figures, like Jools and Bridget, could potentially muddy the myth of the perfect good-looking mother and expose the enormous price women are demanded to pay in trying to achieve this myth. However, as we have shown, rather than critiquing the neoliberal sexual contract, contemporary representations inscribe the SAHM into the realm of 'the perfect' (McRobbie 2015) through her individualised, autonomous, 'free' choosing to exercise aesthetic labour and body self-disciplining, and collude in its masking. In so doing, such media representations continue to play a fundamental role in the masking and marginalisation of maternal labour: domestic, childcare, emotional and now also the aesthetic.

References

Allen, K., & Taylor, Y. (2012). Placing Parenting, Locating Unrest: Failed Femininities, Troubled Mothers and Riotous Subjects. *Studies in the Maternal, 4*(2), 1–25.

Baraitser, L. (2009). *Maternal Encounters: The Ethics of Interruption*. East Sussex/New York: Routledge.

Boyer, K. (2014). Neoliberal Motherhood: Workplace Lactation and Changing Conceptions of Working Motherhood in the Contemporary US. *Feminist Theory, 15*, 269–288.

Crittenden, A. (2010). *The Price of Motherhood: Why the Most Important Job in the World is Still the Least Valued*. New York: Picador.

D'Souza, C. (2015). She's a Knockout. *The Sunday Times*. [online] Retrieved from http://www.thesundaytimes.co.uk/sto/style/living/Wellbeing/article1506137.ece

Danuta, S. W., & Harrison, L. (2014). Not Ready to Make Nice: Aberrant Mothers in Contemporary Culture. *Feminist Media Studies, 14*, 38–55.

Dolan, J., & Tincknell, E. (2013). *Representing Older Women in the Media: Key Issues*. Labour Party, House of Commons. [online] Retrieved from http://eprints.uwe.ac.uk/21953/3/Labour%20Commision%20Media%20-%20final.pdf

Douglas, S. J., & Michaels, M. (2004). *The Mommy Myth: The Idealisation of Motherhood and How it Has Undermined Women*. New York: Free Press.

Ekinsmyth, C. (2013). Mothers' Business, Work/Life and the Politics of 'Mumpreneurship'. *Gender, Place & Culture, 20*, 1–19.

Federici, S. (2012). *Revolution at Point Zero: Housework, Reproduction and Feminist Struggle*. New York: Common Notions.

Fielding, H. (2013). *Bridget Jones: Mad about the Boy*. London: Jonathan Cape.

Ford-Rojas, J. P. (2012). Jools Oliver Says Naming Her Daughter After a My Little Pony Toy Is Nobody Else's Business. *The Telegraph*. [online] Retrieved from http://www.telegraph.co.uk/women/mother-tongue/9495117/Jools-Oliver-says-naming-her-daughter-after-a-My-Little-Pony-toy-is-nobody-elses-business.html

Gill, R. (2007). *Gender and the Media*. Cambridge/Malden: Polity.

Gill, R., & Orgad, S. (2015). The Confidence Culture. *Australian Feminist Studies, 30*(86), 324-344.

Gill, S. (1995). Globalisation, Market Civilisation, and Disciplinary Neoliberalism. *Millennium—Journal of International Studies, 24*, 399–423.

Goodwin, S., & Huppatz, K. (2010). *The Good Mother: Contemporary Motherhoods in Australia*. Sydney: Sydney University Press.

Hochschild, A. with Machung, A. (1989). *The Second Shift: Working Families and the Revolution at Home*. London: Penguin.

Kuperberg, A., & Stone, P. (2008). The Media Depiction of Women Who Opt Out. *Gender & Society, 22*, 497–517.

Lachover, E. (2013). Influential Women: Feminist Discourse in Women's Business Magazines—The Case of Israel. *Communication, Culture & Critique, 6*, 121–141.
Littler, J. (2004). Celebrity and 'Meritocracy'. *Soundings: A Journal of Politics and Culture, 80–81*, 118–130.
Littler, J. (2013). The Rise of the 'Yummy Mummy': Popular Conservatism and the Neoliberal Maternal in Contemporary British Culture. *Communication, Culture & Critique, 6*, 227–243.
McRobbie, A. (2009). *The Aftermath of Feminism: Gender, Culture and Social Change*. London: Sage.
McRobbie, A. (2015). Notes on the Perfect: Competitive Femininity in Neoliberal Times. *Australian Feminist Studies, 30*(83), 3–20.
Nathanson, E. (2014). Dressed for Economic Distress: Blogging and the 'New' Pleasures of Fashion. In D. Negra & Y. Tasker (Eds.), *Gendering the Recession: Media and Culture in an Age of Austerity*. Durham/London: Duke University Press.
Oliver, J. (2006). *The Diary of an Honest Mum*. London: Penguin Books.
Orgad, S., & De Benedictis, S. (2015). The 'Stay-At-Home' Mother, Postfeminism and Neoliberalism: Content Analysis of UK News Coverage. *European Journal of Communication, 30*, 418–436.
Sawyer, M. (2002). Dish of the Day. *The Guardian*. [Online] Retrieved from http://www.theguardian.com/theobserver/2002/apr/14/features.magazine4
The Daily Mail. (2012). Jools Oliver, Mother of Daisy Boo and Buddy Bear, Urges Parents to Be More Imaginative with Baby Names. *The Daily Mail*. [online] Retrieved from http://www.dailymail.co.uk/tvshowbiz/article-2192491/Jools-Oliver-mother-Daisy-Boo-Buddy-Bear-urges-parents-imaginative-baby-names.html
Tyler, I. (2011). Pregnant Beauties: Maternal Femininities Under Neoliberalism. In R. Gill & C. Scharff (Eds.), *New Femininities: Postfeminism, Neoliberalism and Subjectivity*. New York: Palgrave MacMillan.

6

Holistic Labour: Gender, Body and the Beauty and Wellness Industry in China

Jie Yang

Introduction

There are two beauty salons in the community of Zhangqiu, Shandong Province, where I lived during my summer trips. The one I frequented is on the first floor of an apartment building. Walking into the salon, one sees a front desk decorated with bamboo plants—symbols of growth and good luck. To the left are couches facing each other, and between them is a low table spread with glossy beauty magazines, self-help literature offering 'chicken soup for the soul' and booklets on Confucianism and Buddhism proffering advice on how to cultivate *yuan* (the force to affect and attract people). Near the couches are jasmine plants and mints. Soothing Buddhist music and scents mingle throughout. People living or working in this building can come down for a massage, foot bath or

J. Yang (✉)
Department of Sociology and Anthropology, Simon Fraser University, Burnaby, BC, Canada

A.S. Elias et al. (eds.), *Aesthetic Labour*,
DOI 10.1057/978-1-137-47765-1_6

facial. Those working at nearby office buildings also pop in over lunch for beautification or relaxation. The dynamics of this salon seem to take what Meredith Jones (2012) calls 'lunch-hour' procedures to a new level, as people willing to consume these services here do not even need to go to the nearest high street or shopping mall.

In China, urban residential communities are equipped with facilities like this, sometimes called *yangsheng guan*, 'life-nurturing centers'. They provide relief and rejuvenation for residents through various forms of beautification and 'counselling'. People come to exchange ideas about beauty, health and life in general. They also confide in the beauty care workers, usually migrant women who are perceived as 'outsiders' detached from the affairs of this relatively close-knit community. Besides beauty care, the workers offer clients emotional, psychological and moral support.

This chapter is based on ethnographic work at these kinds of beauty salons in Beijing and Shandong Province.[1] I investigate the lives of beauty care workers (predominantly women) in order to understand their role in China's booming beauty economy and holistic wellness industry. While many workers believe beauty equals happiness and health, in their work, they offer something more: *quan fangwei fuwu,* 'holistic services'. To attract clients, they undertake training to improve their massage and beautification skills and various techniques of Chinese medical cosmetology. Many even seek training in psychological counselling or familiarise themselves with Buddhist, Daoist or Confucian doctrines, which are then deployed as both a marketing strategy and a resource for psychological relief. Unlike counsellors who start from the heart (the basis for cognition/emotion, virtue and bodily sensation), care workers begin with the body. They treat the body as the infrastructure for gaining access to beauty and physical and psychological health; that is, one can restore a full and positive relationship with oneself through the body. However, because of the important place of the heart in Chinese culture, beauty care workers cannot separate the body from the heart. Thus, they work at

[1] This chapter is based on a broader study on the beauty economy and the wellness industry in Beijing and Shandong Province since 2002. I interviewed both salon owners and employees (particularly those reemployed laid-off workers) (see Yang 2011).

the body-heart nexus and attempt to provide holistic care. Through body work, they aim to reach the hearts of the clients, from which they extract value for themselves and the neoliberal economy.

I want to argue that when beauty care workers promote the art of living as part of their market-based labour, they actually participate in a holistic mode of governance of life that supports state interests. Although beauty salons or *yangsheng guan* appear as 'depoliticised' spaces external to the family and the state, they actually dovetail with and confirm them. Furthermore, while they seem to enmesh the Confucian tradition of *xiushen* (cultivating the body) as part of the tradition of *yangsheng* (nurturing life), beauty workers deploy neoliberal techniques to entice citizens to strive for health and avoid becoming economic or societal liabilities. I demonstrate that beauty workers' holistic care constitutes an individual, medical and aesthetic solution to the broader social and economic problems that negatively impact individual bodies and health in China today.

Gender and the Beauty Economy in China

The development of the beauty industry in China profits from the transformation of gender ideologies during the post-Mao reform era. Unlike the more 'egalitarian' gender relationships of Mao's era (1949–1976), which saw women masculinised and mobilised to 'do whatever men can do', reform-era gender ideology naturalises and even essentialises gender differences (Rofel 1999; Yang 1999), highlighting the importance of hyperfemininity (beauty, youth and sexual desirability in women) and connecting gender to consumerism (Yang 2011). The state, in the midst of privatisation and marketisation, is now removed from the role of Big Brother. Without its direct regulation, extreme forms of exploitation have emerged. The focus of this chapter is the emotional and psychological labour of women care workers, which has become a site of value extraction and economic development.

Meanwhile, as Chinese living standards rise, so does the desire for beauty. The cosmetics industry has become the fifth largest consumer market in China (after real estate, automotive, clothing, and food and restaurant industry), with annual revenues exceeding RMB thirty billion and employing more than thirteen million people (Liu 2012). Issued in 2002, a set of guidelines called 'Medical Beauty Care Services Regulations' classified the industry into two categories: 'life cosmetology' and 'medical cosmetology' (Liu 2012). Life cosmetology, also called decorative cosmetology, uses technologies and cosmetics to fulfil clients' desire for beauty. It includes services like beauty consultation, skin care, makeup, body care and so on. Medical cosmetology has two subspecialties: 'modern' and 'Chinese'. Modern medical cosmetology includes tattooing, chemical and medical cosmetics, and plastic surgery. By contrast, Chinese medical cosmetology has the goal of building and strengthening the body and is supported by Chinese medical theory, targeting people with health problems or beautification needs. People consider Chinese medical cosmetology natural and safe. This is hardly the case for its modern counterpart, which is based mainly on Western biomedicine.

In general, Chinese medical cosmetology combines beauty and health care by using traditional Chinese medical methods that protect health and nurture life, including acupuncture, massage, traditional Chinese medicine and *gua sha*—a popular treatment for sunstroke involving scraping the client with special devices. A well-known story of the development of *gua sha* illustrates several key aspects of the beauty boom. Hao Wei was a laid-off factory worker from Anshan, Liaoning Province, who went to Beijing for training in *gua sha*, then returned to Anshan to set up her own physiotherapy centre, through which she offered treatment and *gua sha* training. She later provided free training to thousands of laid-off workers like herself, all while developing 41 franchised outlets nationwide. Eventually, Hao helped create the new professional title of Gua Sha Healthcare Specialist in China.[2] Her story highlights not only the growth of Chinese medical cosmetology but how it combines with personal struggle, socioeconomic transformation and the altered (and reduced) role of the government in providing for the marginalised. Indeed, in my interviews, I encountered many beauty care workers who, like Hao, had been laid off from state-owned enterprises as a result of

[2] Chinese version available at: http://www.people.com.cn/GB/shizheng/252/8276/8282/2039366.html

privatisation in China since the mid-1990s. Quite a few laid-off workers-turned-beauticians invoked the clever pun, 'We *quxian jiu guo*'—we use our curved bodies (curve, *quxian*) to save the country'—which can also be translated as 'saving the nation through indirect ways'. Instead of relying on the government for reemployment, these women have used their own bodies and skills to generate value; their bodies are like an infrastructure for them to rebuild confidence, identities and new lives in the private sector.

The Body, Biopower and Somatisation

We can view this strategic use of the body as taking part in 'biopower', a term first invoked by Michel Foucault (1978) to refer to a particular mode of power that administers life. As a juncture of power and life, biopower relates to the concerns of a government with fostering the life of the population through discipline and regulatory controls. Biopower emphasises the protection of life, rather than the threat of death. Rabinow and Rose (2006, pp. 199–200) advanced Foucault's definition of biopower by considering how it could be wielded from multiple sites of authority (the substate level, institutions, non-state bodies), rather than by the government only. This devolved mode of power can partly explain the multiple cultural, economic and political forces that characterise the reemployment experiences of Hao and that have spawned the beauty economy in China.

The Body as an Infrastructure

In my interviews, a key strategy beauty care workers adopt is to identify threats to the health and beauty of clients' bodies that can be reduced through beautification. They frequently underscore how beautiful looks can improve clients' health, advance their careers and better their marriage and even life course. Such body work exemplifies what Jose Gil (1998) calls the body's 'transductive' powers, that is, its potential to communicate and transform. Both the body of the client and that of the beauty care worker have an agentive force and act as 'infralanguage', like an infrastructure, triggering change in the superstructure through bodily transformations. They can then transduce and transform broader social and economic forces, such as employment, class status, gender and family relations—like Hao, who used her body to practice *gua sha*. She then became an entrepreneur and state-designated 'reemployment star' (Yang 2007), further impacting other laid-off workers through free training, helping them survive the market economy. Her body worked as a force that converged with and transduced other forces.

Beauty care work demonstrates the multiple engagements of the body with the world in terms of potentiality and the limitations (harm) imposed on the body by social, economic or moral forces. Gil's (1998) discussion of the body as infrastructure offers a dynamic framework to capture processes through which the body metamorphoses and simultaneously interacts with and transforms other forces. Treating bodily forces not according to their representational contents but their functions in their own right—how they may differ from the signs and symbols that are attached to them—Gil's (1998) notion of the body goes beyond cultural constructionism to resonate with a call for greater attention to the concrete bodily dimensions of emotion and subjectivity in anthropology (Jackson 1983; Lyon 1995).

Gil uses the notion of 'exfoliation' to refer to the way the body metamorphoses and 'turns onto' things, onto external space. In the case of China's beauty economy, through beautification or body-shaping techniques, one's bodily transformations may also change one's identity and interactions with the external world. Such 'bodily exfoliation' (or changes to the outer world that the body and its transformation take part in) provokes psychological transformations or, sometimes, an altered sense of self among both clients and workers, and yokes the self and the world (through consumption, labour, power dynamics, institutional structure of salons and the industry, and so on).

Gil's perspective makes it possible to show how the body, although a site of exploitation, is also agentic and transformative. But the body Gil discusses seems to be a unitary, natural body, rather than one situated in a specific 'body culture' (Brownell 1995) demarcated by class, gender, race or sovereign power. To extend Gil's work, I point out that the Chinese term for the body, *shenti*, includes two root words: *shen* and *ti*. Elvin (1989, p. 275) translates *shen* as 'body-person', conflating self and body, and implying a lived body with a life history. *Ti* denotes a physical body. *Ti* can also be used as a verb, meaning 'to contain', 'to intimate' and 'to understand', suggesting a lived body that acts, experiences and understands (Zhang 2007, p. 36). In this sense, both *shen* and *ti* can act as a subject with an experiential dimension (see also Brownell 1995).

Further, Brownell (1995) develops the notion of somatisation to refer to how social tensions are routinely expressed in bodily metaphors in China. She suggests that the boundaries between the body, the family and the state are more fluid than in the West. Individual bodies are conceptualised as interlinked; the boundaries between bodies seem fairly permeable (Brownell 1995, pp. 238–262). An individual's body is not entirely his or her own but is subject to demands and pressures from the state, family or community that challenge individual autonomy (Brownell 1995, p. 23). This notion of somatisation and its relationship with family and the state are manifested in the caring body of the beauty care worker, as well as in the bodies they care for and market to. Indeed, the rapid development of the beauty and wellness industries in China dovetails with government interests in both continued market development and social stability.

Holistic Body and Holistic Services

A beauty care worker in China plays multiple roles. She must be a professional, a mentor, a confidante—even a counsellor. As mentioned, many go further yet, dedicating themselves in a full-bodied manner in order to offer holistic care. This care requires sharp eyes, not only to identify the problems of the client's appearance but also to observe the verbal signals, body language and behavioural clues that can reveal how clients think in order to market the right products and services to them. In the holistic approach, care workers take the initiative to orient clients toward an appreciation for the benefits of products and services. They become physical conduits for their industry. As a folk saying goes, *Yan wei xin sheng, yu wei ren jing*, or 'One's speech reflects one's heart and inner movement and mirrors one's personality'. The owner of the beauty salon in my community in Zhangqiu highlighted the significance of observation and communication in this regard:

> We target mainly women … The purpose of our conversation with them is to identify whether they have money to purchase our products or services. Some rich women can be easily identified from their clothes and the way they carry themselves. Others who don't look like rich actually lead a well-to-do life with stable incomes like teachers, wives of local officials, we must pay attention to how to communicate with them, confident but humble in a way to attract them to stick with us.

In monthly training sessions with her employees, this owner stresses the importance of clients' first impressions. The first few sessions with a client are the opportunity to showcase a beautician's overall quality. Thus, the owner provides advice on workers' makeup, clothes, manners and communication skills for these early sessions. She sometimes asks all her employees to wear 'school uniform'-type clothing in order to show their youth and vitality. During traditional Chinese festivals she asks her employees to wear, for example, Han Dynasty-style outfits in order to charm and please clients and promote certain services. Having been trained in counselling, she actively imbues her management with precepts of (positive) psychology. She believes that positive heart-attitudes and pleasant manners on the part of beauticians play a crucial role in determining the quality of services. She expects physical, psychological and emotional performances from her employees.

However, my fieldwork revealed that this level of demand for holistic labour can have negative effects. The youngest beauty care worker at the Zhangqiu salon, a 21-year-old woman, told me that she would not do this job for long, as she found herself developing health problems:

> Before working at the salon, I was perfectly healthy, but now I have serious pre-menstrual pain; my back aches. I am the one who applies essential oil to clients. When you massage the oil to the client's body to detoxify, the toxins extracted from their bodies would be absorbed by my own body and ruin my body.

In this account, the worker's body has been enlisted to act as infrastructure for transducing other forces and extracting value for others, but as a result, her body also extracts negative value (harm) for itself. Another young worker in a *yangsheng guan* in Zhangqiu provided a similar account of negative effects of her work:

> Our wages are based on the number of clients we have and the amount of cosmetic products we can sell. To get more clients, you have to stay at work longer during lunch break … you don't want to leave for lunch when those office workers come here for a facial during their normal lunch break. When they come, you want to serve them and make them satisfied. Sometimes when there is no power for air conditioners, I use paper fans to make them feel cool and comfortable so that they would come again. With irregular meal times and hard physical labour, I have stomach problems and feel exhausted easily.

The bodies of these workers define their access to resources and are a means of survival, but at a cost. In fact, due to negative health outcomes, the workforce of the beauty salons in Zhangqiu is unstable. Some workers eventually move into retail jobs at department stores, while others, who have money and a stable clientele, open their own salons.

In the beauty industry, the body as a subject with its own bodily feelings is manifest in the unintended psychological, emotional and physical consequences of the labour of beautification. Some of the care workers I interviewed acknowledged that they sometimes had a hard time controlling their bodies: the gap between the will and the body seemed to show that the body is autonomous, with a memory of its own. No matter how willingly they wanted to serve return clients, their bodies would not always align with their thoughts. One young beauty care worker told me that she had difficulty 'squeezing' out a smile for a very important client.

> I have a long-term regular client; she first came to me for both facial and body massage. But one day, she went to a coworker for massage, telling me that that coworker has bigger hands; her massage is stronger and more comfortable. Indeed, my hands are smaller, more delicate on the face … Clients are very strategic. It's hard to make a living in this industry and we basically feed on our own bodies.

This worker said that on subsequent visits for facial massage by this client, her hands did not cooperate; her body opposed her will. While she tried her best to appear 'normal', she felt that she 'became' heavy-handed because of her body's 'opposition'.

The Body-Heart Affective Nexus

To feed clients' desire for services and products, care workers start from the body. As mentioned, however, their ultimate purpose is to reach the heart. They call this technique *gong xin,* or 'attacking or bombing the heart'. As one owner of a *yangsheng guan* in Zhangqiu remarked:

> We have to use our own bodies, appearance, and confidence to create an atmosphere that can touch the hearts of clients. You have to create and embody that *qichang* [an atmosphere that can be felt, that affects and is affected] and affinity so that people will be attracted and consume.

Thus, care workers' own bodies, makeup or beautification habits communicate with clients in such a way that clients are oriented toward beautifying their bodies and treating their bodies as a resource for enhancing income and social status, expanding personal connections and fostering entrepreneurship—having their own beauty salons and becoming boss of their own. In other words, these care workers try to orient clients to see the importance and value of an investment in their bodies. Clients' bodies can then act as infrastructure to access other resources and transduce forces for their own benefit. Care workers and their clients engage in the same behaviours to the same ends. They rely on essentialised gender ideologies by seeing their bodies, femininity or feminine beauty as important resources they can control and expand.

Interestingly, workers (and their trainers) emphasise not only the beauty of their bodies but also the 'beauty' (calm and contentment) of their hearts. As mentioned, they occasionally undergo training in counselling. They learn empathetic communication skills, speaking in soft tones and listening patiently to clients to establish bonds. They care for both the beauty and psychological health of the clients. They call this interaction *goutong* (channelling or interacting). These workers use their own bodies to increase the number and stability of their clientele, establish financial security or prepare for entrepreneurship (by opening their own salons).

The techniques of body shaping provide a good example of what I call the body as a transducive force. Body shaping is done through spa treatments, aromatherapy, essential oil scrubs and tightening therapy. These techniques help 'shape' or correct their clients' bodies. One body works on another through a kind of bodily intimacy and felt experience that requires tremendous mutual trust. The fitter the figure of the body-shaping specialist, the more persuasively and confidently she can show the efficacy of her services. Indeed, many workers who specialise body shaping treat their own bodies as instrumental to their success, as their bodies serve as transducers and infrastructure to access resources through the bodies and hearts of their clients. Their services perpetuate this idea, since they use the same argument on themselves as on their clients. This highlights a unique mode of biopower—body working on body. Care workers work on their own bodies to extend the reach of their bodies toward other bodies—those of their clients.

Emotional and Psychological Labour

In my interviews, many salon owners paid attention to the care and training of their employees. They indicated that beauty care is intimate body work and bodily interaction, very personal and intimate. According to the 2012 National Beauty Salon Customers' Consumption Survey in China, 36 percent of customers were willing to change beauty salons along with the change of beauticians; evidently, customers' trust in the salon lies in their trust in the beauticians (Liu 2012). Salon owners acknowledge that while a range of their services, including professional knowledge, consummate skills and idealised physical images, have a dollar value, some of their other services are priceless, including those that improve people's psychological 'beauty' and positive outlook on life. These services require a depth and genuineness of emotional care that cannot be measured or paid for.

A beauty care trainer in Beijing stressed the importance of emotional and psychological care in the beautification process, and of attending to the client's psychology when assuring the survival of a beauty salon. She herself had twice received training in counseling:

> We try our best to let those women truly feel as if they are 'back to their parents' homes' … they confide to us whenever they suffer at home or at work. In this context, the beauty concept can be extended from external beauty to the care and adjustment of the inside [their hearts].

The importance of the intensity of care, which reaches the heart, was echoed by others I spoke to, including a salon owner who had actually developed a typology of consumer psychologies in the beauty industry and strategies for dealing with each of these. Some of her perceptions are based on her essentialised ideologies about her female clients and their consumption patterns. First, she discussed the conformist mentality of rushing headlong into mass action. In beauty, the conformist mentality is ubiquitous, she argued, and determined by the special requirements of femininity. Driven by this mentality, females who love beauty blindly imitate others. They have a psychology of keeping up with the Joneses.

The second type of psychology, according to this owner, is that of the small-peasant-consciousness, focused on taking advantage of cheaper services and products. Beauty salons can make use of festivals to launch promotional activities, such as reducing the price to attract more clients. The expectation of enjoying the best beauty services at the most preferential prices is a common psychology of general beauty consumers.

The third type of psychology she proposed involves a competitive mindset desiring to be upper class. People in this group generally have no powerful social or educational background, but they have quickly become rich thanks to China's economic reform. They patronise beauty salons or purchase cosmetics because they are driven by a yearning for upper-class status or marriage with rich men. To them, walking into beauty salons is not only to consume; they also want to make friends with those who can afford a gold membership card. These are the customers that owners wish to hold onto, because they are willing to purchase expensive goods.

Fourth, we have the psychology of pursuing spiritual satisfaction. Besides material enjoyment, many people also place a high value on spiritual 'satisfaction'. Instead of simply improving their 'look', a lot of customers walk into beauty salons expecting the beauticians to bring them ease of mind and psychological relief.

Finally, this owner identified the crisis mentality of the end of youth as driving many of her customers. For females, the years between 35 and 45 represent a significant period in the psychology of beauty. During this period, they are concerned about small changes in their looks; they often feel uneasy and sad about their ageing appearance. So they walk into a beauty salon for help, hoping to delay the onset of old age, shaping their 'second youth'. They seem to reduce ageing to merely a state of the body, a matter of appearance and something that can be remedied and cured through consumption. These clients evince a great need to reshape their beauty when visiting beauty salons.

For the salon owner, developing such a rich typology demonstrates not only her fine observation of customers through years of holistic work but also a high degree of strategic thinking and psychology-imbued analysis in service of reaching the hearts of clients to enhance profit—all performed through the bodies of female care workers. This highlights how both gender and psychology constitute and contribute to the aesthetic labour and processes of neoliberalisation in China.

Conclusion

This chapter has explored the dialogic relationship between beauty and body—how the body acts as infrastructure and transducer to access other resources and forces, and how bodily changes through beautification trigger new ideas, new perspectives or even the formation of new subjectivities (based on gender, femininity, youth). I show that the meaning of body praxis is not always reducible to cognitive and semantic operations; bodily movement (or feelings) can express more than words can say. The body emerges as a subject with agentive force.

My work also operates at the level of recent social change, demonstrating the intensified gendered exploitation that has resulted from China's economic restructuring. The individual female body has become the site of extracting value and entrepreneurial capital, and an infrastructure for sustaining the neoliberal economy and social stability. In this way, beauty care work takes part in a new and unique form of biopower based on care (aesthetic, psychological), which serves the state by turning people away from other collective forms of remedy to growing inequalities; by emphasising individual and aesthetic solutions to people's problems, and by locating the source and treatment of problems in the individual.

There is a significant cost to this bodily and individualised mode of value extraction, including negative effects on the emotional and physical health of care workers. The growing beauty industry in China has a domain for promoting reemployment, particularly among women who were laid off from state-owned enterprises. However, with the state gradually withdrawing from the direct intervention in the market economy, the gendered reemployment pattern in the beauty industry has enhanced gender exploitation. It binds women to a new set of inequalities—first, by requiring their holistic labour in an environment of essentialised gender norms, and second, by placing them in a position to absorb the negative effects of their transducive work. These inequities lead to the exploitation of the female body, feminine beauty and feminine youth in creating a large consumer base for China's consumer capitalism.

References

Brownell, S. (1995). *Training the Body for China: Sports in the Moral Order of the People's Republic*. Chicago: University of Chicago Press.

Elvin, M. (1989). Tales of Shen and Xin: Body-Person and Heart-Mind in China During the Last 150 Years. In M. Feher (Ed.), *Fragments for a History of the Human Body* (pp. 266–349). New York: Zone Books.

Foucault, M. (1978). *The History of Sexuality: Volume I: An Introduction*. New York: Pantheon Books.

Gil, J. (1998). *Metamorphoses of the Body*. Trans. S. Muecke. Mineapolis: University of Minnesota Press.

Jackson, M. (1983). Knowledge of the Body. *Man, 18*, 327–345.

Jones, M. (2012). Cosmetic Surgery and the Fashionable Face. *Fashion Theory, 16*(2), 193–209.

Liu, Y. (2012). The Analysis of the Current Needs and Education in Chinese Medical Cosmetology. [Online] Retrieved from http://www.xahtxy.cn/2012/xsyj_0416/1338.html

Lyon, M. L. (1995). Missing Emotion: The Limitations of Cultural Constructionism in the Study of Emotion. *Cultural Anthropology, 10*(2), 244–263.

Rabinow, P., & Rose, N. (2006). Biopower Today. *BioSocieties, 1*, 195–217.

Rofel, L. (1999). *Other Modernities: Gendered Yearnings in China After Socialism*. Berkeley: University of California Press.

Yang, J. (2007). 'Reemployment Stars': Language, Gender and Neoliberal Restructuring in China. In B. McElhinny (Ed.), *Words, Worlds, Material Girls: Language, Gender and Globalization* (pp. 73–102). Berlin: Mouton de Gruyter.

Yang, J. (2011). Nennu and Shunu: Gender, Body Politics and the Beauty Economy in China. *Signs, 36*(2), 333–357.

Yang, M. M. (1999). *Spaces of Their Own: Women's Public Sphere in Transnational China*. Minneapolis and London: University of Minnesota Press.

Zhang, Y. (2007). *Transforming Emotions with Chinese Medicine: An Ethnographic Account from Contemporary China*. Albany: State University of New York Press.

7

The Entrepreneurial Practices of Becoming a Doll

Adrienne Evans and Sarah Riley

Introduction

> This room is her own office, where she creates fairytale beauty.
> (YouTube video on Anastasiya Shpagina 2012)

'Living dolls' is a term that emerged online during 2010 to describe a group of women who participate in the practice of appearing 'doll-like'. Living dolls take part in a number of beauty techniques in order to achieve a doll appearance through, for example, using wide-rimmed contact lenses, hair extensions and corsetry. An online

A. Evans (✉)
School of Media and Performing Arts, Coventry University, Coventry, UK

S. Riley
Aberystwyth University, Aberystwyth, Wales, UK

A.S. Elias et al. (eds.), *Aesthetic Labour*,
DOI 10.1057/978-1-137-47765-1_7

community also holds that the living dolls achieve their appearance through the use of photo-editing technologies (e.g. Photoshop) and/or surgery—including rib removal, eye widening, breast implants and liposuction.

Living doll cultural outputs exist on a range of social media platforms, including Facebook, Twitter, Instagram and blogging sites. But, the most dominant output takes the form of YouTube make-up tutorial videos on how to achieve a doll-like appearance. Through these tutorials living dolls become self-made celebrities, with a fan base who admire the dolls' ability to transform themselves into a stylised version of hyper-femininity.

Living dolls converge with the democratisation of celebrity and 'micro' celebrity, where categories of fame take shape through practices of tagging, sharing, remixing and the meme (Senft 2009). Online communities form who celebrate the dolls' digital embodiments of exceptional femininity, creating an 'affective economy' that includes the production of fan art, fashion blogs and attempts at imitating their favourite dolls—which themselves can take the form of YouTube make-up tutorials. Living dolls may also receive modelling contracts and opportunities to develop own-branded make-up ranges marketed in Central Europe and East Asia. These cultural outputs allow successful living dolls to take up entrepreneurial subject positions in relation to their aesthetic labour, creating possibilities for economic independence and geographical and social mobility.

The majority of the dolls who have a large online following have emerged from the post-Soviet states, largely from Russia and the Ukraine. These dolls include Olga Oleynik, Anzhelika Kenova, Valeria Lukyanova (also known as 'Human Barbie'), Alina Kovalevskaya and Anastasiya Shpagina (also known as 'Anime Girl'). Although other examples exist (notably the American Dakota Rose and the British Venus Angelic), the practice of becoming a doll is so significant in the Ukraine as to spark the term 'Barbie flu' to describe the large-scale uptake of doll-like appearance by Ukrainian women. The predominance of post-Soviet women in both the online bridal market and living dolls phenomena suggest useful comparisons might be made to enhance our understanding of new entrepreneurial modes of femininity enabled through new internet technologies, which we discuss below.[1]

In the film essay *Writing Desire*, feminist producer and artist Ursula Biemann (2001) reflects on the politics and commodification of women in the context of transnational capitalism and the marketplace of cyberspace. In doing so she turns to electronic media that have facilitated the mass exchange and migration of women from post-Soviet and East Asian countries into 'the West' through the online bridal market. She notes a contradiction between the internet brides' apparent adherence to 'traditional' notions of femininity, including the desire to make a home, take care of appearance and dote on a future husband, and their agentic actions and aspirations to migrate to 'the West' through the opportunities afforded by communication and internet technologies. Similarly Taraban notes that this 'intimate transaction' is predicated on the bride's 'ability to sustain the male fantasy of herself as a pre-feminist and hyper-feminine subject' (2006, p. 108). The internet bride thus constructs herself through notions of femininity unscathed by feminism, while being positioned within multiple gender ideologies. As Biemann argues, our very Western notion of the oppressed mail-order bride, whose lack of freedom is merely exchanged for a new restriction in marriage, is replaced with the 'juxtaposition of the two contradictory models—stereotypical inscription on the female body and female agency—[which] open speculative spaces in representation and broaden restrictive figures of femininity' (2001, p. 256).

The contradictions inherent in internet brides, and as we argue below, in post-Soviet living dolls, can be understood as part of a postfeminist sensibility. Postfeminism refigures particular tropes of femininity, often in contradictory ways. What constitutes a postfeminist sensibility and its imbrication within neoliberalism is discussed in detail by Gill (2008)

[1] We are aware of other parallels that could be drawn here, such as the promotion through online agencies of sex workers. This developing market provoked the rise of the Ukrainian feminist activist group, FEMEN, whose protests have largely concerned the growing sex tourism in the country. However, while acknowledging similarities in their digital formation, we feel that internet brides and living dolls movements share more in terms of notions of love/adulation, discourses of agency and the promise of migration.

and elsewhere in this book (also see Evans and Riley 2013, 2014). What we highlight here is how 'entrepreneurialism' is central to the self-reliant, flexible and choiceful performances of femininity that are privileged within postfeminism. As a particular 'mentality of governance', the 'enterprising self is both an active self and a calculating self, a self that calculates *about* itself and that acts *upon* itself in order to better itself' (Rose 1998, p. 154). Within the Western uptake of neoliberalism, women are understood as exceptional subjects of such entrepreneurial neoliberal subjectivity, empowered in new ways by engaging in consumer practices that enable them to transform their bodies into the image of their desire, with a flash of sassiness or attitude to show that the practice is choiceful and agentic (see Banet-Weiser and Portwood-Stacer 2006; Jackson et al. 2012; McRobbie 2009). Because postfeminism is understood as subverting traditional femininity from passive to active it provides the backdrop to legitimising a 'retraditionalisation' of gendered practices that were conceptualised by second wave feminists as patriarchal. Examples include a hyper-feminine appearance (McRobbie 2009), participating in practices of sexual objectification (Evans and Riley 2014) and the re-emergence of wedding culture (Broekhuizen and Evans 2014).

Following the fall of the Soviet bloc, constructs of self-expression, self-improvement and self-monitoring embedded neoliberal entrepreneurial subjectivity within the post-Soviet collective psyche (Makovicky 2014; Salmenniemi and Adamson 2015; Zhuzhenko 2001). This included new gender constructs that contrasted with previous representations of Soviet femininity (e.g. the 'dowdy' farmer's wife living under austere communist regimes). But while postfeminism has become a significant address, it is one of multiple gendered, classed, national and racialised discourses that young women must negotiate: including in relation to post-Soviet constructs of the sly, cunning, migrant white woman who exploits Western men while still retaining a meagre existence on the borderlines of poverty (e.g. in films such as *Birthday Girl*), or who live the extravagant life of an Oligarch successfully achieving post-Soviet desire for the freedoms and pleasures of participation in a neoliberal market economy (Zhuzhenko 2001). The hyper-femininity of post-Soviet constructs of femininity, be they would-be brides or living dolls, might therefore be understood as part of a transnational postfeminist femininity, which like neoliberalism generally morphs as it colonises new space by incorporating local understandings that make it more attractive.

Neoliberal modes of governance and their impact on subjectivity, in particular in the production of a postfeminist sensibility, are arguably important for considering the aesthetic labour of living dolls. But several other national and transnational factors are also at play, including the take up of a globalised digital media. The Orange Revolution, for example, saw the Ukraine employing new mobile and internet technologies to protest governmental corruption and electoral fraud. Western influence is clear in the generation of technology savvy youth emerging from a context where the creative and cultural industries had previously been suppressed, insular and marginalised (see, e.g. Pilkington et al. 2002). But the West is not the only influence. Historical geopolitics includes post-Soviet allegiances to other communist states (e.g. North Korea, China) and the physical geographic location of the post-Soviet, located between East and West (both with their own attendant but never homogeneous gender ideologies), provide opportunities for a range of cultural cross-overs that create some of the discursive space from which the living doll subjectivity has emerged.

Drawing on our own account of neoliberal postfeminist subjectivity,[2] we take a Foucauldian perspective in addressing the aesthetic labour of the living dolls. In considering the technologies of subjectivity (broad sense-making) that provide the cultural backdrop to living dolls, we argue that the aesthetic labour of doll identity is enabled by cultural and contextual shifts in new technologies and the intersections of gender, national identity and the cosmopolitan promise of social mobility, which turns feminine appearance into a business and consumer practice under the guise of Western concepts of freedom through consumption. We now develop our analysis by exploring the subject positions enabled by these technologies of subjectivity and the technologies of self (practices that enable the take up of subject positions) that post-Soviet living dolls may employ using a case study analysis of one of the most notable examples of the living dolls, Anastasiya Shpagina.

[2] See Evans and Riley (2014) for detailed discussion of the technologies of sexiness framework that draws on the work of Foucault's technologies of self and subjectivity and Butler's notion of performativity.

Anime Girl: The Fluid Brand

Anastasiya Shpagina (also known to her followers as Anime Girl or Ana) originates from Odessa in the Ukraine. Her self-narrative of becoming a living doll is repeated across the internet: suffering with acne as a teenager, Shpagina learnt how to use make-up to change the appearance of her skin. Becoming a beautician and hairstylist following her education, she began providing online tutorials that demonstrated how she produced her appearance. In her own YouTube biography she states that, 'My interest turned in hobby and then from hobby transformed into work'. Shpagina's self-representation of her folded hobby-work transformation maps onto the recognisable 'Do What You Love' (DWYL) ethic of flexible cultural industries labour that has been noted for its fit with new modes of feminine citizenship (Gregg 2008; McRobbie 2009). In Duffy's (2015) analysis of the feminisation of digital labour, for example, she defines this DWYL ethic as illusionary but affective, because it promises the aspirational dream of immersing oneself in feminine practices (e.g. fashion, beauty) while eliding the long hours and emotional, unpaid work required of this kind of labour. In Shpagina's embodiment of this DWYL ethic, her YouTube videos feature her transforming into, among others, Chi from the Chobits manga series, the virtual 'vocaloid' Hatsune Miku and various Korean K-pop stars (2NE1 singers Minzy, Bom, Dara and CL), as well as American actors and celebrities (e.g. Johnny Depp, Miley Cyrus, Megan Fox and Britney Spears).

With nearly one million YouTube subscribers and two hundred thousand Facebook followers, Shpagina represents a new media 'micro' celebrity through her participation in online platforms, attracting significant media attention in Europe and East Asia (specifically Japan, where her popularity led her to adopt the Japanese name Fukkacumi). Shpagina therefore offers an exceptional example of transnational (post-Soviet, Western and East Asian) entrepreneurial femininity, where aesthetic and emotional labours converge through neoliberal notions of the self-as-commerce-and-commodity and where identity and economic potential are located on the body.

Part of Shpagina's popularity in Japan is that she borrows heavily from the aesthetics of Japanese kawaii culture and shojo anime for what she terms her 'everyday' appearance.[3] Shojo is a subgenre of manga/anime (Japanese cartoon/animation style) that is aimed at teenage girls: it draws on kawaii culture, which constructs beauty through notions of cuteness. Although kawaii and shojo femininities are constructed through notions of childish innocence, an alternative postfeminist discourse of agentic sexuality as a source of female empowerment is also woven into contemporary manga comics primarily aimed at a male audience (Gwynne 2013). Gwynne, for example, analyses the character Sailor Moon (one that Shpagina imitates on YouTube), as a cute, wide-eyed 'nymphomaniac' (2013, p. 339) who is located in a narrative that articulates a set of contemporary moral panics around gender in Japan, including the emasculation of men by women's increased social and economic participation and young women/girls' sex-worker like attitude to sexuality (see, e.g. Roberson and Suzuki 2003).

Shpagina's online transformations at the intersections of kawaii, shojo and postfeminist cultural codes produce a version of femininity that is both recognisable and an extension of its own recognisability. Normative expectations for beauty and bodywork assume that women should work on, discipline and regulate their bodies (Bartky 1990; Wolf 1991). But, in the context of postfeminist sensibility, this aesthetic labour must be produced as though it were done for oneself, as the outcome of a savvy and knowing femininity that is agentic and self-determining (Evans and Riley 2014; Gill and Elias 2014; McRobbie 2009). With Anime girl, Shpagina's savvy and knowing femininity is underscored by its aesthetic retraditionalisation. By imitating 'the doll', her YouTube tutorials mix traits of cuteness, passivity and innocence with feminine appearance work.

[3] As suggested earlier, there has been a complex and hybrid blurring of cultural identity in Ukrainian youth culture, and there are complex racial politics at play in Shpagina's appropriation of Japanese kawaii culture—not least because kawaii fashion is itself so hybrid. Kawaii has been understood previously as a Westernisation of Japanese youth culture (Chua 2000), a resistance to national feminine expectations and an historical aesthetic (Iseri 2015). It works in parallel with other 'cute' cultures in East Asia, such as feizhuliu and sajiao in China, which also emerge 'post-socialist' and through a particular digital moment (Zitong 2013). Meanwhile, the living dolls movement has a complex set of racialised, ethnic and nationalistic discourses within it, especially in the context of the historical and contemporary Russo-Ukrainian conflict (see for example Valeria Lukyanova's *GQ* interview, Idov 2014).

In a Western context, the imitation of doll femininity could be understood as infantilising. But, the association of dolls with pre-feminist femininity fit for a patriarchal order is troubled through complex gender ideologies. As we have noted above, at first sight, the overlaps between the living dolls' post-Soviet femininity and the online bridal market make sense in a Western feminist analysis of female objectification and bodily commodification. However, these associations are too simple: traditional feminine passivity, the desire for domesticity and the appeals to the institution of marriage can also be understood as articulating a desire to migrate and gain some form of freedom (Biemann 2001; Taraban 2006). Moreover, Shpagina's articulation of this relationship is complicated by two further doubling acts. First, by the intended audience of other young women, since Shpagina's postfeminist revisioning of the online bride means that where once the spectator would have been male, Shpagina's audience consists largely of other women (see Winch 2013 for a discussion of the 'girlfriend gaze'). Second, its passivity is actively deconstructed in its very production into the make-up tutorial format, demonstrating femininity's performative nature.

With each of Shpagina's celebrity imitations, the female body project is shown as endlessly transformational and malleable. Beginning with a 'teaser' of the finished look, each tutorial takes the viewer through the required steps to achieve each given transformation. In the case, for example, of Miley Cyrus (Shpagina 2013), which has received over three and a half million views, we are shown the final look, before a subtitle instructs us 'Let's Start!'. A significant amount of time is given to the eyes. A wig is then modified, seemingly imitating Cyrus' own 'dramatic' haircut. A range of highlighters, blushers and concealers are used to shape the contours of the face, before finally a bright red lipstick is applied. The transformation into Miley Cyrus is completed with recognisable stylised body moves. Through a transformation performed on and through her own body, Shpagina presents back to us what is widely recognised about current feminine celebrity culture: its carefully stylised beauty practices to produce a (hetero)sexually attractive appearance.

Shpagina's YouTube videos represent a new form of digital self-branding and self-management, in which the self is worked on and produced as a commodity in its own right and in line with an expectation towards entrepreneurialism and the economisation of subjectivity (Rose and Miller 2013). The professionalisation of Shpagina as a brand is evident in her videos. Early videos were shot in a bedroom and maintained an amateurish feel reminiscent of bedroom culture. More recent videos are sleek and stylised, often taking place against a green screen, with the transitions and cuts appearing cleaner and more 'professional' and with English subtitles. Through her internet celebrity, she has gained several modelling contracts, most notably in East Asia, which make use of her ability to appear as an Anime character; she has sponsorship with make-up brands (largely Japanese) and has recently been developing her own line of make-up and wide-rimmed contact lenses.

As suggested above, the production of femininity through new internet technologies that facilitate participation also create affective economies, whereby Shpagina's affective value accumulates as her tutorials circulate in digital space. Affective economies create meaningful connections based on an affective relation between brand and consumer, and in playing with cuteness while demonstrating her own unique 'sellable' product (i.e. herself, skill and malleable appearance), Shpagina creates a transient affective community and scene of online belonging (Ferreday 2009) that celebrates her ability to transform the body:

> My God your skills are flawless girl! I would so hire you as my personal everyday makeup artist! I LOVE IT! YOUR GENIUS I SAY!
>
> You're probably the most talented makeup artist in the whole world. <3
>
> Anastasiya, you are absolutely beautiful <3 I admire your talent and passion c: You're an inspiration to me to express myself, and I thank you for that. Please, never stop doing what you're doing <33

The celebration of Shpagina's transformations emphasises her skill and technique, similar to that of the artist or expert. In our previous analysis of women's understandings of celebrity sexiness (Evans and Riley 2013), we suggested that in contrast to notions of 'natural' beauty, celebrity capital comes from the capacity to work on the self, through entrepreneurial brand-savvy skills, and the ability to spend time and money on self-appearance. YouTube commenters' reaction to Shpagina's 'talent', 'skills' and 'passion' represents a response to a form of entrepreneurial femininity produced through a highly visual transformation, which works on market values and that sells the self as a commodity. Like our previous analysis of sexy celebrities, the suggestion of reproducibility through the tutorial format is undermined by the imposition of skill, technique and labour that go into producing this appearance. Although giving the impression that these transformations are done in the service of allowing other women the opportunity to reproduce these imitations, by attributing some special proficiency in these imitations ('I would so hire you as my personal everyday makeup artist', 'the most talented makeup artist in the world') such aesthetic labour is constructed by Shpagina's community as one that is unique to her.

Shpagina is thus a brand: the girl who can transform herself into anyone through the medium of the makeover tutorial. The outcome is always stunning in terms of its reproduction of the character while always recognisable within wider cultural codes of Japanese cuteness aesthetic in terms of both appearance (e.g. wide eyes) and demeanour (e.g. not looking directly at the camera, hands covering the face). Even when imitating less traditionally feminine characters (men, evil characters such as Maleficent), the imitations are still evidently in keeping with Shpagina's brand: they are still 'cute', 'girly' and 'feminine' and so constitute repetition with difference.

Through all her online communication, Shpagina maintains her girlie-feminine image, which relies on a style of 'intimate transaction' based on emotion. For instance, her Twitter feed includes regular use of emoticons (e.g. in her Twitter bio: '♡ ^_^ ~Nothing's Impossible~'), alongside new fashion shots, appearances at digital industry events (e.g. Google) and teasers of upcoming tutorials. This form of digital emotional labour makes use of traditionally feminine characteristics that are a dominant part of the service sector and typically mapped in accounts of the work of airhostesses, hairdressers and other feminine-coded careers, who work to keep the customer happy (Hochschild 2002). Her fans celebrate her emotional labour, the pleasures of watching makeover videos and her skills and techniques through public statements of love and adoration. In addition, Shpagina's Twitter also includes acknowledgement of fan admiration in the form of retweets, which works to reinforce this affective community: 'i love you so much Ana:* ^_^ you are nice person:> love youuuuu <3'.

Although Shpagina has an affective community of fans, her performance is also regulated and disciplined by others. For example, in her public social media dispute with fellow living doll Valeria Lukyanova, fans criticised her behaviour for not appearing appropriately feminine or doll-like. Similarly her doll transformations are questioned through suggestions of photo-editing software or cosmetic surgery. The questioning of authenticity in her embodiment of postfeminist perfection also opens Shpagina up to affective forms of horror and disgust. For example, one comment on her YouTube video reads:

> FAKE ANOREXIC PIECE OF PLASTIC!
> YOURE THE REASON WHY YOUNG GIRLS DIE TO BE SKINNY!
> YOURE NOT INSPIRING ANYBODY! YOURE MAKING YOUNG GIRLS KILL THEMSELVES! STUPID FAKE BITCH!

We read this regulation as connected to notions of authenticity, which, for Western viewers at least, is bound up in notions of neoliberal subjectivity that all performances of identity should be about being 'your true self' (Bauman 2000). Such notions of authenticity have been recognised as important in the transformations produced by more traditionally Western make-up tutorials (Tolson 2010). They also inform the sense-making of reality TV's use of cosmetic surgery, where extreme body disciplining and surgical transformation are required to 'become the real you' (Banet-Weiser and Portwood-Stacer 2006; see also Banet-Weiser in this collection). Shpagina, by contrast, does not become 'who she really is'.

Thus, in doing transformation so well, Shpagina's beauty practices become a form of 'uncanny' aesthetic labour. In the uncanny, the familiar and recognisable becomes strange—a sensation that Freud (1919 [2003]) likens to a homeliness that has become unfamiliar, and so frightening or ghostly. Applying this to Shpagina, we could suggest that her aesthetic labour is very intelligible within current expectations for transnational postfeminist femininity (e.g. in its application of make-up, its girliness and passivity and its constant forms of self-transformation produced through a disciplining of the body through a variety of beauty practices). However, through its perfect replication of recognisable figures of femininity and the plastic malleability of its own body, it becomes inconceivable, unfamiliar and unreal, causing some to react with abject disgust.

Likewise, Attwood reads celebrity culture itself as producing a transformative space that threatens the binary between real and unreal, where practices such as cosmetic surgery create a liminal body 'hybrid, permanently in transition and animated by technology: a zombie' (2014, p. 9). This zombie-femininity, as in the above comment, also has the ability to contaminate others, turning young girls themselves into the living dead (Burke 2006; Ferreday 2009).

For all her adulation, the production by Shpagina of a constant aesthetic postfeminist transformation is also undercut by the neoliberal discourses of authenticity. Her aesthetic labour is neither 'true doll' nor 'real human'. Sitting liminally on the boarders of intelligibility it thus becomes 'like living as a fake' and pathologised as having 'illusions of wanting to be something you are simply not' (comments from YouTube). As long as neoliberal entrepreneurialism continues to value authenticity, Shpagina runs the risk of being 'discovered either to be impossible, sheer fantasy, or too possible, and toxic' (Berlant 2011, p. 24).

Transnational Postfeminist Aesthetic Labour

In Shpagina we see an example of exceptional transformational beauty practices, producing a postfeminist post-Soviet femininity that combines new modes of celebrity, a hybrid form of cultural expression, feminine expectations for passivity, cuteness and beauty-body work and practices of freedom through social and global mobility. Shpagina appears on the surface to embody aesthetic labour's postfeminist promise of constant self-transformation, built on the premise of being self-made and in control of her own mediated, marketable visibility. None of these are new to postfeminist subjectivity; indeed they are recognisable from previous analyses of postfeminist entrepreneurialism and postfeminist contradiction (see Banet-Weiser and Portwood-Stacer 2006; Evans and Riley 2014; Gill and Elias 2014). However, what is different in the phenomenon of the living dolls is that the aesthetic labour produced by Shpagina and others has become a digital global assemblage-like restructuring of post-Soviet femininity that includes constructs of pre-feminist and exaggerated hyper-femininity, feminist critique and a postfeminist sensibility, which makes its articulation both fascinating and unsettling.

In Shpagina's transnational performance of complex post-Soviet, Western and East Asian aesthetic labour, her 'conventional feminine vulnerability' sits comfortably alongside a femininity that appears to be cute, unknowing and girly-feminine; but like arguments about celebrity sexiness, its business savvy market-orientation could deem it calculated and strategic (Evans and Riley 2013). Shpagina's labour is the product of her own self-commodification, constantly transforming and becoming, producing herself as her own marketable product, complete with identity branding and a malleable appearance. Shpagina therefore offers an interesting example of the postfeminist contradiction structured by the promise of agentic freedom in the image of the successful, self-determining and self-made feminine subject, where the body has become a marker of achievement, identity and mobility.

In a recent piece for *GQ* magazine, it was suggested that Valeria Lukyanova's Human Barbie 'is not about submissiveness, fame, or snagging a husband. It could be about finding a way out, however random, bizarre, and costly the route appears from the outside. It could be about gaining some measure of freedom' (Idov 2014). Shpagina's aesthetic labour similarly embodies a governance of the self through forms of freedom. However, it is also one that makes sense only in the context of 'political exceptions that permit sovereign practices and subjectifying techniques that deviate from established norms' (Ong 2006, p. 12). Emerging both from its own cultural, social and political location, but performed transnationally and globally through its digital mediation, these new forms of aesthetic labour become inauthentic and uncanny: and are thus still often denied full participation and rendered near-unintelligible when considered through Western neoliberal notions of authenticity.

References

Attwood, F. (2014). The Uncanny Valley: Transformations of the Body and Debates About Sexualization. *International Journal of Cultural Studies, 18*(3), 269–280.

Banet-Weiser, S., & Portwood-Stacer, L. (2006). 'I Just Want to Be Me Again!' Beauty Pageants, Reality Television and Post-Feminism. *Feminist Theory, 7*(2), 255–272.

Bartky, S. L. (1990). *Femininity and Domination: Studies in the Phenomenology of Oppression*. London: Routledge.
Bauman, Z. (2000). *Liquid Modernity*. Cambridge: Polity.
Berlant, L. (2011). *Cruel Optimism*. London: Duke University Press.
Biemann, U. (2001). Writing Desire. *Feminist Media Studies, 1*(2), 251–258.
Broekhuizen, F., & Evans, A. (2014). Pain, Pleasure and Bridal Beauty: Mapping Affective Bridal Perfection. Journal of Gender Studies, online first.
Burke, E. (2006). Feminine Visions: Anorexia and Contagion in Pop Discourse. *Feminist Media Studies, 6*(3), 315–330.
Chua, B. H. (2000). Consuming Asians: Ideas and Issues. In B. H. Chua (Ed.), *Consumption in Asia: Lifestyles and Identities* (pp. 1–34). London: Routledge.
Duffy, B. E. (2015). The Romance of Work: Gender and Aspirational Labour in the Digital Culture Industries. *International Journal of Cultural Studies*, online first, 1–17.
Evans, A., & Riley, S. (2013). Immaculate Consumption: Negotiating the Sex Symbol in Postfeminist Celebrity Culture. *Journal of Gender Studies, 22*(3), 268–281.
Evans, A., & Riley, S. (2014). *Technologies of Sexiness: Sex, Identity and Consumer Culture*. New York: Oxford University Press.
Ferreday, D. (2009). *Online Belongings: Fantasy, Affect and Web Communities*. Oxford: Peter Lang.
Freud, S. (1919 [2003]). *The Uncanny*. London: Penguin Classics.
Gill, R. (2008). Culture and Subjectivity in Neoliberal and Postfeminist Times. *Subjectivity, 25*, 432–445.
Gill, R., & Elias, A. S. (2014). 'Awaken Your Incredible': Love Your Body Discourses and Postfeminist Contradictions. *International Journal of Media and Cultural Politics, 10*(2), 179–188.
Gregg, M. (2008). The Normalisation of Flexible Female Labour in the Information Economy. *Feminist Media Studies, 8*(3), 285–299.
Gwynne, J. (2013). Japan, Postfeminism and the Consumption of Sexual(ised) Schoolgirls in Male-Authored Contemporary Manga. *Feminist Theory, 14*(3), 325–343.
Hochschild, A. (2002). *The Managed Heart: The Commercialization of Human Feeling*. Berkeley and Los Angeles: University of California Press.
Idov, M. (2014) This Is Not a Barbie Doll. This Is an Actual Human Being. *GQ Magazine*. [Online] Retrieved from http://www.gq.com/story/valeria-lukyanova-human-barbie-doll

Iseri, M. (2015). Flexible Femininities? Queering Kawaii in Japanese Girls' Cultures. In C. Nally & A. Smith (Eds.), *Twenty-First Century Feminism: Forming and Performing Femininity* (pp. 140–163). Basingstoke: Palgrave Macmillan.

Jackson, S., Vares, T., & Gill, R. (2012). 'The Whole Playboy Mansion Image': Girls' Fashioning and Fashioned Selves Within a Postfeminist Culture. *Feminism and Psychology, 23*(2), 143–162.

Makovicky, N. (2014). Me, Inc.? Untangling Neoliberalism, Personhood and Postsocialism. In N. Makovicky (Ed.), *Neoliberalism, Personhood and Postsocialism: Enterprising Selves in Changing Economies* (pp. 1–16). Farnham: Ashgate.

McRobbie, A. (2009). *The Aftermath of Feminism: Gender, Culture and Social Change*. London: Sage.

Ong, A. (2006). *Neoliberalism as Exception: Mutations in Citizenship and Sovereignty*. London: Duke University Press.

Pilkington, A. H., Omel'chenko, E., Flynn, M., & Bliudina, U. (Eds.). (2002). *Looking West? Cultural Globalization and Russian Youth*. Cultures: Pennsylvania State University.

Roberson, J. E., & Suzuki, N. (Eds.). (2003). *Men and Masculinities in Contemporary Japan: Dislocating the Salaryman Doxa*. London: Routledge.

Rose, N. (1998). *Inventing our Selves: Psychology*. Power and Personhood: Cambridge University Press.

Rose, N., & Miller, P. (2013). *Governing the Present: Administering Economic, Social and Personal Life*. Cambridge: Polity.

Salmenniemi, S., & Adamson, M. (2015). New Heroines of Labour: Domesticating Post-Feminism and Neoliberal Capitalism in Russia. *Sociology, 49*(1), 88–105.

Senft, T. (2009). *Camgirls. Celebrity and Community in the Age of Social Networks*. New York: Peter Lang.

Shpagina, A. (2012). Anastasiya Shpagina Anime Girl Subbed (English). YouTube [video, online]. Retrieved from https://www.youtube.com/watch?v=-1tC6gmF79I

Shpagina, A. (2013). Miley Cyrus Makeup Tutorial. *YouTube* [video, online] Retrieved from https://www.youtube.com/watch?v=Oz3F9qPGlh0

Taraban, S. (2006). Birthday Girls, Russian Dolls, and Others: Internet Brides as the Emerging Global Identity of Post-Soviet Women. In J. E. Johnson & J. C. Robinson (Eds.), *Living Gender After Communism*. Bloomington: Indiana University Press.

Tolson, A. (2010). A New Authenticity? Communicative Practices on YouTube. *Critical Discourse Studies, 7*(4), 277–289.

Winch, A. (2013). *Girlfriends and Postfeminist Sisterhood.* Basingstoke: Palgrave Macmillan.

Wolf, N. (1991). *The Beauty Myth.* Vintage.

Zhuzhenko, T. (2001). Free Market Ideology and New Women's Identities in Post-Socialist Ukraine. *European Journal of Women's Studies, 8*(1), 29–49.

Zitong, Q. (2013). Cuteness as a Subtle Strategy: Urban Female Youth and the Online Feizhuliu Culture in Contemporary China. *Cultural Studies, 27*(2), 225–241.

8

PhD Barbie Gets a Makeover! Aesthetic Labour in Academia

Scarlett Brown

Introduction

During my PhD, at the suggestion of my supervisor and my sponsor organisation, I worked with a presence coach or 'image consultant', who helped me prepare for interviewing elites. I had been recruited to conduct research that addressed the poor representation of women on corporate boards, but I was told that my appearance was 'not professional enough', and that to do the PhD I needed to 'look good and sound right' (Warhurst and Nickson 2001, p. 2).

Employees needing to perform aesthetic labour as part of their day-to-day work has been noted in industries where the employers' appearance—the aesthetic quality of the body—is part of the work (Mears 2014) and

S. Brown (✉)
School of Management and Business, King's College London,
London, UK

A.S. Elias et al. (eds.), *Aesthetic Labour*,
DOI 10.1057/978-1-137-47765-1_8

in corporations where 'professionalism' is an aesthetic requirement (Witz et al. 2003). Aesthetic labour is not often associated with academia (see also Donaghue, this volume), partly due to academia's foregrounding of the mind over the body; however, social researchers have acknowledged the need to be self-reflexive and aware of how they may influence participants throughout the research process (Carroll 2013). This can include aspects of aesthetic labour.

In this chapter, I explore the role of aesthetic labour in academic research through an auto-ethnographic account (Alvesson and Sköldberg 2009) of preparing for and conducting elite interviews. I show how expectations about 'acceptable' professional appearance are embodied; they went from being something ascribed *onto* my body to something my body had to *do* (Crossley 1995). As a young, female, feminist academic preparing for interviews in professional environments, my aesthetic labour also reflected social expectations about (acceptable) femininity, the female body, professionalism and what it means to be a good researcher. This highlights how the body can be a site where conflicting discourses play out, and how the boundary between aesthetics and the self can become blurred.

To do so, I use Erving Goffman's work on stigma (Goffman 1963; see also Ellis 1998). Before conducting my research, I was told I was not professional enough, marking my appearance as something that needed fixing, making it abject (Mavin and Grandy 2014) and stigmatised. I was then taught how to look and behave professionally, a purportedly gender-neutral (but, in reality, highly gendered) concept, that requires aesthetic labour as a form of 'stigma management' (Goffman 1963). Through wearing the appropriate clothes and make-up, and learning different ways of speaking and interacting, I sought to conceal traits that might mark me as unsuitable for professional environments, such as my 'messy appearance', 'flushed skin' and 'energetic presence'. Initially, I saw this concealment as a uniform or mask, but over the course of the research I felt increasingly that professionalism was achieved as part of a full bodily performance and it is better conceptualised as an embodied practice (Entwistle 2000b).

Before exploring these processes, I will briefly discuss the wider literature on aesthetic labour to demonstrate its role in research and academia, particularly in professional environments. I then discuss my experience of preparing for elite interviews: how my appearance and body were criticised, stigmatised and disciplined to meet professional standards, under a neoliberal and postfeminist rhetoric of self-improvement (Gill 2007). Finally, I discuss how aspects of these standards ceased to be simply performative and became second nature, as part of successful, embodied 'stigma management' (Goffman 1963) and an internalisation of socio-cultural norms and expectations. This offers an embodied, gendered understanding of professionalism (Entwistle 2000a), as well as an understanding of how these norms become internalised.

Aesthetic Labour and Professionalism

Aesthetic labour is a current trend in work practices and workplace expectations, where importance is placed upon individuals' appearance, dress and other 'embodied dispositions' and the employee is expected to 'look good and sound right' (Warhurst and Nickson 2001, p. 2). Aesthetic labour builds on Hochschild's (1983) seminal work on emotional labour, a requirement that employees display certain (usually positive) emotions while at work. Building on this, aesthetic labour theorists foreground the body, looking at what the employee does to the surface of the body through dress, make-up and bodily maintenance, as well as 'what the body does' (Crossley 1995, p. 43). Owing in part to the connection with emotional labour and to creative and aesthetic work, aesthetic labour has been primarily discussed in relation to service, hospitality and retail sectors (Nickson et al. 2001; Tyler and Abbott 1998; Warhurst and Nickson 2007; Warhurst et al. 2001), and related to those in creative industries, such as hairdressers, models, actors or artists (Dean 2005; Entwistle and Wissinger 2006; Mears and Finlay 2005; Sheane 2012). Work that involves a bodily 'display' element has an even clearer connection with aesthetic labour: for a model, for instance, the look and appearance of the body is intrinsic to the work and the body is therefore 'the main commodity or tool of the trade' (Entwistle and Wissinger 2006, p. 776).

Aesthetic labour is also required in professional environments: employees are expected to dress and behave in line with corporate expectations and ensure they have the correct appearance, to 'get in and get on' in organisations (Witz et al. 2003, p. 42). Although in some cases this manifests as an explicit uniform (Freeman 1993) it more commonly falls under the label of professionalism (Collier 1998), where standards or rules are maintained through cultural expectations about what is presumed to make the individual successful or not. Professionalism is best exemplified in the (male) suit, which allows the wearer to become neutral—rendered invisible in professional environments (Entwistle 2000a; Hollander 1994; Kelan 2013). This means that norms of professionalism for women are much less clear-cut than for men, and women require higher levels of aesthetic labour to be deemed professional. There is a great deal of advice offered to women about how to align their appearance with professionalism (Entwistle 1997; Kelan 2013), and a trend towards personal consultancy and training in this area—such as the existence of image consultants or presence coaches (Hewlett 2014; Masciave 2014). Although professionalism is often primarily related to clothing, it also includes embodied elements such as mannerisms, demeanour and voice (Sinclair 2011). This is particularly the case at senior levels, where men and women are expected to display leadership qualities that are more frequently aligned with masculine traits (Kelan 2013).

Aesthetic Labour in Research

Although aesthetic labour has been discussed in a number of industries, it has not been identified in methodological literature as required for academic research. Qualitative research typically relies on face-to-face engagement, and many of the characteristics of good qualitative interviewing (rapport building; mutual disclosure; emotional intelligence and awareness; building common understanding with participants) are very similar to those seen in industries that require emotional labour (Carroll 2013; Dickson-Swift et al. 2009; Holmes 2010). Even where this is highlighted, the body and aesthetic labour tend to be largely absent from discussions about academic research (Spry 2001). This is partly due to a conceptual mind/body dualism, allocating knowledge, understanding and scholarship to the mind, and treating the body simply as a tool for data collection. This is problematic, Spry notes, because '[when] the body is erased in the process of scholarship, knowledge situated in the body [becomes] unavailable [...] [it] fixes the body as an entity incapable of literacy' (2001, p. 724). By acknowledging cases where aesthetic labour is required for research and treating the body as part of the scholarship, we may also reveal cases where awareness of the body helps the researcher better understand the phenomena (read: people) they are researching.

The success of qualitative interviews—particularly if understood as 'conversations with a purpose' (Mason 2011)—relies on the interviewer and interviewee establishing an interactional 'working consensus' (Goffman 1959) by performing their appropriate identity. Methodologically, this is more commonly discussed in terms of building 'rapport' (Mason 2011) as a way of ensuring the interviewee feels at ease and of gaining valid data from the interviews (Birch and Miller 2000). This is particularly the case with feminist research, which foregrounds the need for interviewers to attempt to equalise power relations in the interview by encouraging collaboration and mutual disclosure (Sinding and Aronson 2003). It follows that aesthetic labour in this context might mean dressing to make the interviewee feel comfortable rather than dressing authoritatively; however, these power dynamics are upended when the respondents have a higher status than the interviewer, as is the case when researching elites (Conti and O'Neil 2007). In this case, interviewers often have to work to uphold their legitimacy and be taken seriously (Conti and O'Neil 2007), and this may require dressing professionally or authoritatively.

Not Professional Enough

The inspiration for this chapter came from my experience of aesthetic labour during my PhD research. The project was a qualitative study into how men and women are recruited onto corporate boards in the UK, based on interviews with executive men and women. The PhD was funded through a collaborative studentship, and this meant that the project was outlined before I applied, and as part of the application I was interviewed by a panel of two academic supervisors, and the head of the search firm, or 'headhunters' who were co-sponsoring the research.

After the interview I was told that, while I was well suited to the project academically, there were concerns that my appearance and demeanour were 'not professional enough'. Given the seniority of the interviewees and that I would be a representative of the University and the headhunters, I would need to 'look good and sound right'. In short I was given an ultimatum: provided I could learn how to be professional, I could do the PhD.

Although for all intents and purposes I had been successful, this feedback made me hyper-aware and ashamed of my appearance (Mavin and Grandy 2014) in a way I had not experienced before. Rosalind Gill's (2009) description of rejection in academia summed it up perfectly: 'I felt shabby, a little bit less than the human being I want to be' (Gill 2009, p. 11). In some ways, reaching this age (22 at the time of interview) without feeling ashamed of my appearance is an example of my privilege—I am white-British, blonde, able-bodied, tall, middle class and well spoken—all traits that are aligned with normative expectations of professionalism (Witz et al. 2003) and 'acceptable appearance' (Mears 2014). On the other hand, I grew up in an old Welsh farmhouse to feminist, artist (read: 'hippie') parents. As a result I have high levels of cultural capital, low economic capital and little experience of professional environments or professionalism. Although I had achieved academic success to get here, I had little of the 'well-groomed, slim, sophistication' (McRobbie 2004, p. 102) that might mark me as successful in the business field. The decision that I was not professional enough could, in this case, represent a form of legitimated class antagonism (McRobbie 2004)—if one occurring between different kinds of middle classes, rather than against the working class. It also denigrated my feminist politics: I actively, politically, avoid being overly concerned with my appearance or my body. That I should now have to be aware and critical of my appearance and work on making it 'better', to conduct a project about women in senior roles in the workplace (at the behest of women in senior roles!) seemed like a strange and ironic twist.

Despite my frustration, making my appearance professional seemed a relatively easy thing to work on. I saw my body as 'software' (Witz et al. 2003) that could be moulded, designed and adapted; far easier, I thought, than if the concern had been with my ability to be an academic.

My friends were already calling me 'Grad School Barbie' (for being tall and blonde and loving academia); maybe I just needed the 'Corporate Barbie' clothes kit. Treating professionalism as something achieved simply by wearing the right clothes established emotional distance between my identity as a feminist researcher and the demand that I focus on my appearance—this distancing is common in employees performing emotional labour, who avoid emotional fatigue by compartmentalising real emotions away (Hochschild 1983; Carroll 2010). By establishing a distance between my self and my work—a distance that can be difficult to maintain in academia (Gill 2009)—I avoided taking the criticism personally, despite it being entirely personal. It was framed as helpful feedback to develop my skills as a researcher, rather than a negative attack on the self (Nath 2011). I kept seeing an advert for a clothing company that said: 'To crack the glass ceiling you don't need a sharp stick, you need a sharp suit'. I took this to heart, only in hindsight reflecting that this is exemplar of the postfeminist sensibility (Gill 2007)—a belief that my (appropriately dressed) body would be the key to my success, provided I could put the work into dressing it correctly.

To start, I had to learn the 'rules' of professionalism. My supervisor called in a favour and suggested I have sessions with an image consultant, who agreed to see me *pro-bono* as support for the research. She works with senior-level executives in helping them to develop their 'executive presence' (Masciave 2014)—displaying traits such as gravitas, confidence, poise and decisiveness (Hewlett 2014)—through having the correct appearance and self-presentation. These sessions were like a makeover programme (cf. McRobbie 2004); they involve 'transformation of self' with the support of an expert and start by outlining exactly what the 'problem' is. The image consultant has written a kind of self-help book based on her work and I agreed to be one of her case studies. Here is a quote from the text, outlining her impressions on our first meeting:

> *I arrived at the meeting early […] and sat where I could see [Scarlett] enter the café and lock in my own first impressions. I noticed the hair ["waist length, Rapunzel-like and blonde"] and glasses ["quirky-cool, geek-glasses with black frames"] immediately, of course, but what was most apparent about Scarlett, as 'presence detractors', were her energy and general disarray. As her presence coach,*

> *I don't want to turn Scarlett into a Barbie doll. I want to help her succeed. So the first step is to get a read on how she's presenting herself to others. This was the Five Facets scorecard I gave her:*
>
> - *Visual: messy, sloppy, writing on her arm.*
> - *Verbal: aggressive and buoyant, nice tone, very smart.*
> - *Kinesthetic: boisterous, puppy, flushed skin.*
> - *Sociability: fine.*
> - *Presence: scattered, young, energetic.*
>
> *Not bad, but not great. Definitely not who you want to send into an office environment to meet with a C-level executive for a research-gathering interview.*
>
> (Masciave 2014, p. 502)

This section clearly outlines the traits that need to be addressed: being 'messy, sloppy, scattered, *etcetera*; all are defined as unprofessional and unsuitable. The presumption on her part—and that of my sponsors—was that these traits would detract from the overall performance of professionalism and therefore disrupt the research interviews or risk losing the respect of my interviewees. At the same time, she insists that this be done in an authentic way; it is not achieved by turning me into a Barbie doll—a 'one-size-fits-all' cover for these traits—she wants to 'help me succeed'.

Next, I had to learn how to 'dress-for-success' (Entwistle 2000a). We went shopping and I was taught the intricate, detailed and specific rules: because of my age and fair colouring I should avoid clothes in colours and patterns that could make me look younger (pastels, pink and feminine patterns; blues, greens and greys are good), but avoid black and white (like a waitress). Clothes should be well-fitting and angular; jewellery should be silver, expensive and elegant. I should always carry a notebook, pen and handbag (dark colours, right angles, nothing untidy) and wear a watch (executives do not use their phone for timekeeping). I should wear make-up to 'neutralise' my skin tone (bronzer is good; blusher is bad for flushed skin) and tie my hair back (but avoid looking like a ballet dancer or school girl). There were also interactional rules: I had to practice lowering the volume, speed and enthusiasm in my speech; I should avoid gesticulating with my hands by keeping my hands fixed and solid in front of me; as an 'effervescent extrovert' I should 'let silence be my friend'. Even my involuntary reactions had to be addressed—to avoid my skin flushing, I should hold my wrist on a glass of cold water. These tips and snippets of advice, although often given light-heartedly and with a touch of self-conscious irony and 'knowingness' (Gill 2007), are presented as rules to be followed and as an individual plan for success—individualised and personalised forms of shaming and instruction (McRobbie 2004). This defines what is (un)acceptable and presents arbitrary, gendered, socially constructed rules as expert, and common sense (Mavin and Grandy 2014).

I was also struck by how often professionalism meant concealing or suppressing my sense of self and identity and/or disciplining my body. In taking traits that I was proud of (energetic, buoyant) or that I recognised but did not find problematic (general disarray, messy, scattered) and marking them as a problem to be fixed (presence detractors), they became stigmatised and labelled as potentially *discrediting*, or relating to my 'spoiled identity' (Goffman 1963), which had to be hidden during the research interviews. Nath (2011) outlines a similar occurrence in Indian call centre workers, who are required to use British or American accents to 'align with professional discourses' (Nath 2011, p. 712). This stigmatises their individuality and (racial) identity. The comments made about me were gendered—being labelled as 'aggressive' or 'boisterous' is akin to being described as 'bossy', as it refers to an outspoken or direct, unfeminine way of interacting, and the criteria are different for men. Similarly, with age, being 'young' and 'puppy[-like]' is a detractor from professionalism, and attempting to look older was part of the process. Claims to professionalism become a more palatable or acceptable form of racism, sexism or classism, which is cast as relating to the individual, rather than social expectations (McRobbie 2004). Professionalism—for those who are not white men—is, perhaps, better conceptualised by what is concealed, rather than what is achieved.

Being professional and hiding a stigmatised identity requires a great deal of exertion. Remembering all the rules, employing heightened social skills (Nath 2011), as well as the physical work required for 'beauty' (Black 2004) all became a kind of extra, unpaid labour. As with emotional labour, this was exacerbated by the effort required to maintain an outward projection that I felt was different to my internal identity

(Reay 2004). It is also physically uncomfortable, disciplined and disciplining: professional dress tends to be restrictive, tight and uncomfortable (Entwistle 2000b)—while I cannot speak for the male suit, nowhere is this more exemplified than in the wearing of a pencil skirt, tights and high-heeled shoes. This created a paradox where I had to wear physically uncomfortable, constraining clothing in order to feel socially appropriate and comfortable (Entwistle 2000b). Instances where I felt I had failed—mis-judged the outfit—or felt over- or under-dressed left me at risk of losing 'face' (Goffman 1963) and created discomfort, anxiety and hyper-awareness of my body, to the extent that it could eclipse my ability to concentrate in the interview. This shame also sometimes led to feminist *meta-shame* (Ellis 1998) where I felt ashamed for feeling ashamed about my appearance and was frustrated with the preoccupation with my appearance it was causing. Rather than disengaging me from the work, however, these negative emotions were a motivator. I devised solutions—I bought new outfits, learnt what worked and what did not, practiced my speech patterns, concentrated on lowering my energy and tone—and was determined to try harder, practice more and get better (Gill 2009).

At the beginning of the project, I had approached aesthetic labour with a kind of resigned cynicism (Fleming and Spicer 2003) and deliberately dis-identified with the Corporate Barbie image I was embodying; however as time went on, professionalism became easier and less conscious, until it felt second nature. It felt like a theatrical performance where the success was judged, not by an applauding audience, but by occasions of psychologically positive feedback when I was able to successfully 'pass' (Nath 2011). Fleming and Spicer (2003), in their research into the role of cynicism in corporate employees, argue that 'when we dis-identify from our prescribed social norms we often *still perform them*—sometimes better, ironically, than if we did identify with them (Fleming and Spicer 2003, p. 160). In this veil, professionalism becoming easier could be the performance becoming more polished and rehearsed; however this neglects the subjective, embodied and affective self who is giving the performance. Because professionalism required a full, embodied performance, practicing and embodying professional characteristics meant they became internalised, in a way they possibly would not have, if professionalism were gained simply by (cynically) wearing the right clothes.

Conclusion

In this chapter, I have outlined some of the social forces and discursive and embodied practices that shaped my PhD research, using aesthetic labour to make sense of my experience. In doing so, I offer an example of how aesthetic labour may be required for academics conducting research, particularly when studying environments or people that have implicit dress codes or expectations around professionalism. In hindsight, I wonder how successful I might have been had I attempted to 'stake a political claim to being shabby' (McRobbie 2004, p. 107). From a feminist perspective it could have been a political or radical act (albeit one that might have cost me the opportunity to do this PhD). While it would have affected my relationship with the gatekeeper organisation, I can only speculate as to whether remaining shabby would have affected the interviews or made me unable to conduct the study, or how the interviewees would have related to me had they been faced with PhD Barbie before she had her makeover. Unexpectedly, it gave me common ground with some of my interviewees: they discussed how professional appearance and fitting with corporate culture were important when seeking board roles, and one had (voluntarily) worked with an image consultant. This hints a potential methodological benefit to the aesthetic labour and an auto-ethnographic approach, as the demand that I be professional gave me greater empathy and understanding of the interviewees' perspective.

This also elucidates the value of understanding professionalism and aesthetic labour as stigma management (Goffman 1963). Being marked as unprofessional discredited my real identity, through a direct claim that it was unsuitable and had to be hidden (Nath 2011). From Goffman's (1963) perspective, hiding a discredited identity is never truly achievable; however, in this case I found some aspects of my hidden identity did not return. My taste in clothing has changed (tending towards blues and greys and away from patterns and colours) but the embodied and unconscious changes are most notable. My accent was not mentioned during the coaching, but I have lost the hint of a Welsh accent I had before; my hands sit still when I am talking, and overall my energy and tendency to talk too quickly have both reduced. While at the beginning I had to consciously enact bodily comportment in professional situations, I now find moments—returning to my family home, for instance—where I have to actively work to spread out, to occupy space, or to be louder, more energetic and less controlled in my speech.

Finally, I want to draw attention to how the embodied nature of aesthetic labour means bodies can become sites for powerful discourses, expectations and social forces to play out, and that these can become internalised, sometimes despite our best intentions. Acknowledging the body as central to the 'modern person's sense of self-identity' (Shilling 1993, p. 3) alongside aesthetic labour's necessarily embodied nature (Warhurst and Nickson 2007) demonstrates how discourses around 'acceptable' appearance and ways of being can become internalised, and how the individual's sense of identity can be influenced through the inscribing of these discourses. Throughout this research I gradually adopted these discourses so well that professionalism no longer feels like an entirely false performance. It is lived and embodied, and sits alongside other aspects of my re-fashioned self: someone who is professional, dresses-for-success, while still on occasion being 'messy, scattered, young and energetic'.

References

Alvesson, M., & Sköldberg, K. (2009). *Reflexive Methodology: New Vistas for Qualitative Research*. London: Sage.

Birch, M., & Miller, T. (2000). Inviting Intimacy: The Interview as Therapeutic Opportunity. *International Journal of Social Research Methodology, 3*(3), 189–202.

Black, P. (2004). *The Beauty Industry: Gender, Culture, Pleasure*. London: Routledge.

Carroll, K. (2013). Infertile? The Emotional Labour of Sensitive and Feminist Research Methodologies. *Qualitative Research, 13*(5), 546–561.

Collier, R. (1998). 'Nutty Professors', 'Men in Suits' and 'New Entrepreneurs': Corporeality, Subjectivity and Change in the Law School and Legal Practice. *Social and Legal Studies, 7*(1), 27–53.

Conti, J. A., & O'Neil, M. (2007). Studying Power: Qualitative Methods and the Global Elite. *Qualitative Research, 7*(1), 63–82.

Crossley, N. (1995). Merleau-Ponty, the Elusive Body and Carnal Sociology. *Body and Society, 1*(1), 43–63.

Dean, D. (2005). Recruiting a Self: Women Performers and Aesthetic Labour. *Work, Employment and Society, 19*(4), 761–774.

Dickson-Swift, V., James, E., Kippen, S., & Liamputtong, P. (2009). Researching Sensitive Topics: Qualitative Research as Emotion Work. *Qualitative Research, 9*(1), 61–79.

Ellis, C. (1998). 'I Hate My Voice!': Coming to Terms with Minor Bodily Stigmas. *The Sociological Quarterly, 39*(4), 517–537.

Entwistle, J. (1997). 'Power Dressing' and the Construction of the Career Woman. In M. Nava, A. Blake, I. MacRury, & B. Richards (Eds.), *Buy This Book: Studies in Advertising and Consumption*. London: Routledge.

Entwistle, J. (2000a). *The Fashioned Body: Fashion Dress and Modern Society*. Cambridge: Polity.

Entwistle, J. (2000b). Fashion and the Fleshy Body: Dress as Embodied Practice. *Fashion Theory, 4*(3), 323–348.

Entwistle, J., & Wissinger, E. (2006). Keeping up Appearances: Aesthetic Labour in the Fashion Modelling Industries of London and New York. *The Sociological Review, 54*(4), 774–794.

Fleming, P., & Spicer, A. (2003). Working at a Cynical Distance: Implications for Power, Subjectivity and Resistance. *Organization, 10*(1), 157–179.

Freeman, C. (1993). Designing Women: Corporate Discipline and Barbados's Off-Shore Pink-Collar Sector. *Cultural Anthropology, 8*(2), 169–186.

Gill, R. (2007). Postfeminist Media Culture: Elements of a Sensibility. *European Journal of Cultural Studies, 10*(2), 147–166.

Gill, R. (2009). Breaking the Silence: The Hidden Injuries of Neo-Liberal Academia. *Secrecy and Silence in the Research Process: Feminist Reflections*, pp. 228–244.

Goffman, E. (1959). *The Presentation of Self in Everyday Life*. Reading: Penguin.

Goffman, E. (1963). *Stigma: Notes on the Management of Spoiled Identity*. Englewood Cliffs, NJ: Prentice Hall.

Hewlett, S. A. (2014). *Executive Presence: The Missing Link Between Merit and Success*. New York: Harper Collins.

Hollander, A. (1994). *Sex and Suits: The Evolution of Modern Dress*. Brinkworth: Claridge Press.

Holmes, M. (2010). The Emotionalization of Reflexivity. *Sociology, 44*(1), 139–154.

Hochschild, A. (1983). *The Managed Heart*. Berkeley and Los Angeles, California: University of California Press.

Kelan, E. (2013). The Becoming of Business Bodies: Gender, Appearance, and Leadership Development. *Management Learning, 44*(1), 45–61.

Masciave, C. (2014). Executive Presence for Women 1: The Five Facets Approach to Get the Job You Deserve. *Eden Image Coaching Series, 1*.
Mason, J. (2011). *Qualitative Researching*. London: Sage.
Mavin, S., & Grandy, G. (2014). Bodies, Appearance, Abjection: Women Elite Leaders' Intra-Gender Experiences. *74th Annual Meeting of the Academy of Management 2014*, 1–5 August 2014, Philadelphia, USA.
McRobbie, A. (2004). Notes on 'What Not to Wear' and Post-Feminist Symbolic Violence. *The Sociological Review, 52*(2), 97–109.
Mears, A. (2014). Aesthetic Labor for the Sociologies of Work, Gender, and Beauty. *Sociology Compass, 8*(12), 1330–1343.
Mears, A., & Finlay, W. (2005). Not Just a Paper Doll: How Models Manage Bodily Capital and Why They Perform Emotional Labor. *Journal of Contemporary Ethnography, 34*(3), 317–343.
Nath, V. (2011). Aesthetic and Emotional Labour Through Stigma: National Identity Management and Racial Abuse in Offshored Indian Call Centres. *Work, Employment and Society, 25*(4), 709–725.
Nickson, D., Warhurst, C., Witz, A., & Cullen, A. (2001). The Importance of Being Aesthetic: Work, Employment and Service Organization. In A. Sturdy, I. Grugulis, & H. Willmott (Eds.), *Customer Service: Empowerment and Entrapment*. London: Palgrave.
Reay, D. (2004). Cultural Capitalists and Academic Habitus: Classed and Gendered Labour in UK Higher Education. *Women's Studies International Forum, 27*, 31–39.
Sheane, S. (2012). Putting on a Good Face: An Examination of the Emotional and Aesthetic Roots of Presentational Labour. *Economic and Industrial Democracy, 33*(1), 145–158.
Shilling, C. (1993). *The Body and Social Theory*. London: Sage.
Sinclair, A. (2011). Leading with Body. In E. Jeanes, D. Knights, & P. Martin (Eds.), *Handbook of Gender, Work and Organization* (pp. 117–130). London: John Wiley and Sons.
Sinding, C., & Aronson, J. (2003). Exposing Failures, Unsettling Accommodations: Tensions in Interview Practice. *Qualitative Research, 3*(1), 95–117.
Spry, T. (2001). Performing Autoethnography: An Embodied Methodological Praxis. *Qualitative Inquiry, 7*(6), 706–732.
Tyler, M., & Abbott, P. (1998). Chocs Away: Weight Watching in the Contemporary Airline Industry. *Sociology, 32*(3), 433–450.
Warhurst, C., & Nickson, D. (2001). *Looking Good and Sounding Right: Style Counselling and the Aesthetics of the New Economy*. London: Industrial Society.

Warhurst, C., & Nickson, D. (2007). Employee Experience of Aesthetic Labour in Retail and Hospitality. *Work, Employment & Society, 21*(1), 103–120.
Warhurst, C., Nickson, D., Witz, A., & Cullen, A. (2001). Aesthetic Labour in Interactive Service Work: Some Case Study Evidence from the 'New' Glasgow. *Service Industries Journal, 20*(3), 1–18.
Witz, A., Warhurst, C., & Nickson, D. (2003). The Labour of Aesthetics and the Aesthetics of Organization. *Organization, 10*(1), 33–54.

Part II

Risk, Work and (Post)Feminist Beauty

9

The Risky Business of Postfeminist Beauty

Simidele Dosekun

Introduction

Women in Africa, in their diversity, have long 'dressed up', that is fashioned selves and subjectivities through changing styles of beautification, adornment, clothing and display. Africans are also longstanding consumers and participants in transnational media and commodity cultures. Indeed the multi-disciplinary literature on dress in Africa shows that for women there, just like women elsewhere, central to the imagination and presentation of 'stylish' and 'modern' femininities is participation in the transnational, keeping up with new trends abroad (for example, Allman 2004; Dogbe 2003; Mustafa 2002). Necessarily, *structurally*, African women fashion themselves in 'the linkages between local and transna-

S. Dosekun (✉)
Media, Film and Music, University of Sussex, Falmer, UK

A.S. Elias et al. (eds.), *Aesthetic Labour*,
DOI 10.1057/978-1-137-47765-1_9

tional circulations of images, objects, events, and discourses of dress and adornment' (Mustafa 2002, p. 178). They dress 'in the interstices of multiple cultural and socioeconomic grammars—colonial, local, global, and neocolonial' (Dogbe 2003, p. 382).

In the city of Lagos, Nigeria, both in the flesh and in local media representations, a new transnational style of femininity is increasingly visible. This style, which I call 'hyper-feminine' or 'spectacularly feminine,' is characterised by the extravagant use and combination of normatively feminine elements of dress including cascading hair extensions or 'weaves'; long and brightly painted acrylic nails; heavy and immaculate make-up; false eyelashes; towering heels; masses of jewellery and accessories, and so on. The style looks like that of the luminous new figure of the 'post-feminist masquerade' as Angela McRobbie describes it, 'triumphantly re-instating the spectacle of excessive femininity'; 'weighed down with bags, shoes, bracelets and other decorative candelabra items, all of which need to be constantly attended to'; 'endlessly and repetitively done up' (2009, pp. 66–67).

Postfeminism is a contemporary cultural sensibility that proclaims and celebrates that women are now 'empowered' and 'equal,' hence able to return 'freely' to 'all things feminine and 'girly'' (Lazar 2009, p. 375). This centrally implicates their styles of dressing up and appearing. Women are invited to style themselves as postfeminist subjects by spectacularly putting on their femininity. In practice this means the disciplinary consumption of a growing basket of fashion and beauty goods and services, and women subjecting their embodied appearances to an ever expanding and intensifying regime of self-scrutiny (for example, Banet-Weiser 2013; Blue 2013; Evans and Riley 2013; Gill 2007; McRobbie 2009). Yet in a postfeminist discursive logic, the spectacularisation and 'maintenance of the feminine body [are] steeped in the rhetoric of choice as an endless series of supposedly positive and empowering, autonomous consumer decisions for women' (Blue 2013, p. 665).

Whereas postfeminism has been overwhelmingly conceptualised and researched as a Western cultural phenomenon, I take a view of it as *transnational* (Dosekun 2015a). The transnational designates that which exceeds and crosses boundaries of nation-state and region without thereby erasing or negating them (Grewal 2005; Hegde 2011). It is constituted by heterogeneous and historicised 'connectivities' such as media networks, commodity circuits and migratory and diasporic flows, through which discourses, capital, commodities and people travel (Grewal 2005). As a thoroughly mediated and consumerist entanglement of meanings and practices, postfeminism travels via transnational media and consumer connectivities especially. From happy rhetorics of 'girl power' to the highly mediated figure of 'Kim Kardashian' and the new norms and technologies of spectacular femininity that she embodies, postfeminism is broadcast and sold across borders. It interpellates subject-consumers that have the material, discursive and imaginative capital to buy into it, their diverse locations and histories notwithstanding. Thus while postfeminism may be understood to have emerged in the West in response to a specific Western feminist time, it must also be understood to have since exceeded these origins, and to have 'gone global,' as it were, in ways that are not merely derivative or linear.

This chapter is concerned with educated and class-privileged Lagosian women between the ages of 18 and 35 who dress up in hyper-feminine style. It draws on a larger research project that enquired into the kinds of feminine subjectivities that such women are performatively constituting in and through their style, to which the short answer is that they see themselves as cosmopolitan postfeminist subjects (Dosekun 2015b). The present focus is on what the research participants revealed to be the relative risks of their dress style, their constructions of their 'choice' to take on or consent to such risk, and their strategies to try and mitigate it. The chapter is based on discursive analysis of qualitative semi-structured interviews with 18 women, and on a feminist poststructuralist understanding of power as productive, as constituting the subject, its desires and its self-government or self-conduct (Butler 1997, 1999; Davies et al. 2002; Rose 1998).

I argue that with the postfeminist intensification of feminine beauty norms and the attendant, commodified proliferation of beauty technologies or 'solutions,' the pursuit of beauty comes to pose heightened, embodied and psychic risks for women. These risks compel what I theorise as 'aesthetic vigilance'. Aesthetic vigilance is a calculative and self-governmental labour of *risk-managing* one's attachments to beauty and its technologies. It includes the taking of 'aesthetic rest'. This is the practice of taking a deliberate break from the laborious and risky pursuit of beauty so as to be fortified to later return to it. The chapter emphasises how the research participants construct their vigilant practice as a new feminine competence and indeed a further site and mark of feminine empowerment precisely because it allows them to continue their quest for beauty. Thus, I argue that as a new form of knowledge, aesthetic vigilance is a postfeminist and neoliberal rationality of power in that it makes the women's subjection to these forms of power seem reasonable and manageable (Davies et al. 2002), and thereby delimits their visions of resistance.

Attached to Beauty, Consenting to Risk

In terms of their hyper-feminine dress practice, the women in my research positioned themselves as agentic and individualised subjects who freely and actively chose their style. Furthermore, they emphasised that the choice was above all to see and please *themselves*. For instance, one participant, Adaeze,[1] explained her love of dressing up in spectacular style with the comment: 'even if I'm at home, I wanna look a certain way, it's not even about, it's not about how other people perceive me, it's for me. It's like looking good makes me feel good'. Looking good, being pretty, beauty in a word, was the central motivation for and desired effect of the women's dress practice. Women often experience or envision beauty as unattainable or elusive, a perfect state that is rarely if ever present (for example, Coleman and Figueroa 2010; Evans and Riley 2013). But not so for those in my research. From their weaves to their pedicures, the myriad constituent elements of the women's dress promised to compliment, accentuate, conceal, transform and so on. Beauty was now thoroughly technologised and commodified, hence with sufficient effort, skill and disposable income, beauty was *attainable*, albeit iteratively.[2]

Diane, for example, explained her love of wearing weaves and her accumulation of about ₦1 million (roughly $7000) worth of the femi-

[1] All names are pseudonyms.

[2] The British women in Evans and Riley's (2013) research, figured as 'ordinary women', also see beauty as attainable for such reasons but not for themselves, rather for celebrities with time and material means.

nine commodity in terms of her love of 'looking good'. Stating that she was 'into makeup a lot,' another woman, Ima, remarked that she felt 'prettier' with it, as did Alero who described a daily process of applying and perfecting her makeup, on which she spent up to an hour. Bisi, conversely, reported that she was not really into makeup. Detailing that she wore 'white powder, fake eyelashes, eyeliner and clear lipgloss or red lipstick,' Bisi explained that it was because she considered her makeup regimen light and her face otherwise relatively bare that she always wore false lashes, to get the additional effect that she evocatively called 'the oomph'. As Bisi and other participants variously elaborated it, the 'oomph' was a certain lift. It was an interiorised and embodied sense of self-confidence and empowerment that beauty promised. Bisi subscribed strongly to such postfeminist promises. She believed that 'looking good' enabled a woman to face and take on the world. She was insistent that a woman should always dress for herself therefore:

> not even for your boyfriend, not for your husband, for your *self.* Cause if you wear something and you don't feel you look good, other people will automatically, they'll feel that vibe about you … When I dress up, I feel like I glow and I'm happy and I'm comfortable and I'm confident. Wherever I go, nobody can put me down.

Although insisting on such self-pleasing, self-regarding and self-empowering postfeminist discursive positions, in the course of their interviews the women also revealed a range of disciplinary norms and external considerations and pressures that governed or guided their 'choice' of style. Here I will highlight examples that implicated some of the style's risks. Sade, who worked in the Nigerian media industry, cited and naturalised the 'standard' of appearing on local television in a weave. She recounted that having duly worn the hairstyle for work, she had suffered the loss of some of her own hair due to the friction and pulling of the weave on her scalp. Hair loss was a risk, a possible adverse outcome, of wearing weaves. Another participant, Misan, shared that she did not like to wear acrylic nails. She later described the accoutrement as 'really terrible' because 'after you take it [off] your [own] nails get really weak'. However, Misan, an entrepreneur in the local fashion and beauty sector, explained that due to pressure and advice from her female clients to dress like she was 'earning some money,' to look like a modern and upwardly mobile career girl in other words, one of her new year's resolutions had been to more regularly affix false nails. Tobi, a presenter on local television, spoke of having worn false nails for years before stopping because she was experiencing the kind of bodily damage to which Misan was referring. Yet she was now back to the beauty technology, she explained, because: 'One day I was on TV and my friend says, she sends me a message that "babe, fix your nails, they look horrible" (*laughs*)'.

I asked Tobi if she worried about the risks involved in her renewed consumption of acrylic nails. Her reply: 'Yes I do … but you know what these are necessary evils, ugh! (*putting on a falsetto voice*) A girl has to be a *girl!*' The very notion and language of 'necessity' is a governmental rationality of power. It works to pre-empt critical questioning or resistance and instead invite and naturalise the subject's compliance. In this case the necessity of which Tobi spoke was to be 'appropriately' subjected, embodied and thereby recognised and recognisable. The necessity was to '"cite" the norm in order to qualify and remain a viable [gendered] subject' (Butler 2011, p. 177). Alero also spoke in terms of gendered necessity, normativity and therein belonging, in her case with regard to the wearing of high heels. Referring to the potential physical pain of such shoes, which was yet another risk of the research participants' spectacularly feminine style, she said: 'Some heels are comfortable but even when they are not comfortable and you go out, you just have to manage, just, yeah, swallow the pain'. She further justified the logic and ostensible reasonability of swallowing the pain of high heels by claiming that it was a shared feminine experience: 'I am not the only one suffering with that. It's a group thing … everyone has to just (*pauses*), it's just, I mean like they say "beauty is pain."' In this formulation, stepping into a feminine community of pain was not only something that a woman did, it was constitutive of being or becoming a woman. Thus, painful shoes were constructed as a feminine inevitability.

Sharon also cited the notion that beauty is pain, a notion that I would insist is a patriarchal rationality. She named herself as a 'lover of heels,' happily adding 'the higher the better'. To my question about the comfort of such style, Sharon reflected that 'of course' one's feet would eventually begin to hurt 'but it's worth it, it's totally worth it so I don't think—"beauty is *pain*" they say'. Sharon's view that the reward or promise of beauty was 'totally worth' the price of pain, and her consequent practice of paying the price, vividly illustrates the poststructuralist theoretical insight that a key modality of power is to work *through* rather than against desire (Butler 1997; Davies et al. 2002; Petersen 2008). '[D]iscursive constructions take hold—take hold of the body, take hold of desire … rigidly colonizing the flesh' (Petersen 2008, pp. 55–56). Indeed, inciting the subject's desires and inviting its psychic attachments renders power all the more effective or stubborn. In what follows, I argue that my research participants' consenting to the risky technologies and practices of spectacular postfeminist beauty rendered their attachment to this style of beauty 'cruel' because it meant attaching and consenting to 'compromised conditions of possibility' (Berlant 2006, p. 21).

Cruel Attachments and Cruelly Optimistic Vigilance

An attachment to a state such as feminine beauty or to a putatively beautifying object like high heels is cruel if this state or object 'contributes to the attrition of the very thriving that is supposed to be made possible in the work of attachment in the first place' (Berlant 2006, p. 21). According to Lauren Berlant, such an attachment is therefore also 'cruelly optimistic' because it draws the subject repeatedly back to the desired state or object and its putative promises. Cruel optimism keeps the subject 'in proximity to the scene of desire/attrition' (Berlant 2006, p. 21). It keeps women like Sharon and Alero dressing up and stepping out in their painful heels over and over again, as heard above. It leads them to push through and rationalise the pain rather than try to avoid it, by wearing comfortable shoes, say. More cruelly optimistic in my hearing of the research participants was their attachment to the beauty technologies of hair weaves, false eyelashes and acrylic nails. Repeatedly, the women expressed a knowledge or recognition that these technologies were 'not good' for their own hair, eyelashes and nails, respectively, some instances of which I have cited above. At times speaking from personal experience, other times commenting more generally, they explained that wearing weaves could cause one's hair to thin or fall out; that in the process of removing false lashes, one's real lashes could be lost too; that acrylic could cause one's own nails to weaken and break.

Yet in most cases where the women noted such risks, they did not talk of therefore rejecting or resisting the beauty technology in question. Instead, knowing the risk, their predominant practice was to anticipate and manage it. *Their predominant practice was one of risk-management, in short.* Risk-management is a core entrepreneurial logic and value, and thus it is a core mentality and practice of the ideal responsibilised, calculating and enterprising neoliberal subject (Binkley 2006; Leve et al. 2012; Rose 1998). The inflection of such a neoliberal mentality with postfeminist beauty standards, or what we can understand as the growing imperative for women to be aesthetic entrepreneurs, meant, for those in my research, engaging in a strategic 'on-off' beauty practice. The women's practice was to give oneself occasional reprieve from the hyper-feminine beauty technologies viewed or experienced as risky, to enable one's relative recovery from them, so as *to better withstand the subsequent redeployment of the very same technologies.* In the interviews this on-off practice was often expressed in terms of allowing one or another part of one's body, and sometimes one's mind, to 'breathe' or 'rest'.

Consider Ima who said that she kept her false nails on for about a month and then after taking them off: 'I would let my [own] nails breathe for like maybe two weeks or another month and do it again'. Folake similarly explained why she had recently taken off her false eyelashes:

> cause I wanted my natural lashes to breathe and you know the longer you do them [that is, false eyelashes], the more you do them, it weakens your natural lashes … So I just, I was just like let me take a break, take a break you know and not do it too much.

I propose to understand this on-off beauty practice as 'aesthetic vigilance,' a new and specialised postfeminist and neoliberal form of aesthetic labour. As I have begun to outline above, aesthetic vigilance is an entrepreneurial practice of risk-managing one's spectacularly feminine appearance. It is a labour of vigilance specifically, a mental and interiorised rather than physical or surface labour, because it entails keeping a reflexive and watchful eye on one's attachment to and consumption of cruel hyper-feminine technologies, as well as scheduling and juggling periods of what I call 'aesthetic rest'. The aim of this labour is to forestall the renouncement of the cruel beauty technologies by pre-empting or minimising the embodied and/or psychic loss that they may engender. Aesthetic vigilance is a cruelly optimistic practice, then, because its aim and intended effect is to sustain cruel feminine attachments.

To put the point conversely, aesthetic vigilance and its constitutive rationalities work to forestall resistance. Detailing how she wore make-up every working day for her television show and then most weekends when 'you have somewhere to go', Tobi welcomed the odd day that her face could have 'off':

> Sometimes I don't go out on Saturday. I *loooove* the fact that on days like that my face can *rest*. I'm not wearing *any* makeup. Cause I mean I feel, I feel that once I give my face that rest, once I put it on again, I'll be looking too *fine!*

Berlant notes that 'the return to the scene where the [cruel] object hovers in its potentialities' may not always '*feel* optimistic' (2006, p. 20, original emphasis). The surrender to one's cruel attachments may be tinged with dread or ambivalence or disappointment in one's self, for instance. But a happily optimistic affect is clearly palpable in Tobi's remarks above. This followed from her reasoning, maybe experience too, that for having had brief respite from makeup she would look even better with it subsequently. I asked Tobi if one day was 'rest enough' for her face:

Tobi: It's not but what can I do?
Simidele: Eh how much rest would you need ideally, to now be back to–
Tobi: Cause I've been putting on—like maybe if I can do, if I can do two days without makeup I will be happy, I will be happy.

Tobi returned to an implicit logic of 'necessary feminine evil' to account for her resignation to the fact that although one makeup-free day did not really suffice as aesthetic rest, it was all she tended to have.

The necessary evil here was the normative requirement to wear makeup in both her professional and social lives, a norm that she left completely unquestioned, again as the logic of 'necessity' encourages. In Tobi's comments above, the said necessity of makeup had the further governmental and depoliticising effect of constructing aesthetic vigilance as also necessity, the reasonable and indeed fortunate 'solution' to her beauty dilemma. Tobi's logic distilled to the following: because it was necessary for her to wear makeup virtually every day, what was also necessary was to find some time and space to give her face a breather. She depicted the breather as empowered though brief. Aesthetic rest constituted a certain 'me-time,' that is to say a postfeminist, putatively indulgent break from the very demands of postfeminism itself (Lazar 2009). The rest was framed as further empowering, moreover, because further beautifying.

Other women similarly represented their practice of aesthetic vigilance as recursively empowered and empowering by representing it as the informed, responsible and rational thing to do to continue to achieve their desired look. In this the women further positioned themselves as knowing, agentic and empowered postfeminist consumer subjects. Diane interpellated me as also knowing when, describing her typical routine for getting dressed, she made an aside about her use of an exfoliating face scrub: '[I] use my scrub cause I use makeup every day to work—like we all know makeup is not good for the skin, your skin has to breathe, and with the kind of job I do I see people every day so I know I have to look nice every day'. According to Diane, a corporate customer service representative, her face scrub was a tool to risk-manage the potentially adverse effects on her skin of her daily professional need for makeup. Yet it seemed that she also had to risk-manage her use of the scrub! Having first stated that she used it 'probably like twice or once a week,' Diane later made an apparent error and said that she used it 'every morning'. She promptly corrected herself: 'not every morning cause it's not good'. From my own feminine consumer subject position, I took it that Diane meant that too-frequent use of an exfoliating face product could be harsh on the skin.

In this example, the commodified 'solution' (makeup) to the putative core and foundational feminine problem of 'inadequate beauty' could engender a new beauty problem ('bad skin') for which there was another commodified solution (exfoliating scrub) which could engender yet other beauty problems, and so on. For this kind of iterative and frankly exhausting feminine beauty dilemma, aesthetic vigilance—watching, gauging, weighing, timing, spacing—became the resolution. Again the possibility of resistance, such as not wearing makeup in the first place, was not so much as mooted. As is quite clear in this example from Diane, the ostensible solution of aesthetic vigilance also relied on considerable class privilege, on having not only an array of beauty commodities but also the time and energy to deploy them.

Adaeze provided another example of a potentially iterative beauty problem that called for both a watchful eye and an extensive wardrobe. To the unstated yet implicit (and of course racialised) problem of 'inadequate hair,' she indexed wigs as a second or backup solution to weaves should the latter have proven too cruel. She did so while proposing that there was a psychic aspect to why women might return to feminine technologies like weaves that they deemed risky:

> You know it's addictive though, like the weave for instance. I started wearing wigs because the weave does actually damage your hair so just, you have to change things up. But you get so used to how you look that when you don't have a weave, you don't think you don't look good [*sic*]. If you don't have [false] eyelashes, if it's something you're used to, you don't feel you look good.

What Adaeze was suggesting as addictive was beauty and its promises. This suggestion, or what I have theorised in this chapter as the cruelty of being attached to beauty, is utterly crucial. It allows us to not see the women in my research as somehow 'silly', or self-destructive, for continuing to use beauty technologies that they actively worried about and recognised or in some cases experienced as potentially harmful. Rather, we see that a certain sense of self and self-recognition was not only founded but also persisted in and through their risky beauty practice. We see that the subject might, as Adaeze put it, 'get so used to' looking and feeling a certain way. The concepts of cruel attachments and cruel optimism:

> allow us to encounter what is incoherent or enigmatic in our attachments, not as confirmation of our irrationality, but as an explanation for our sense of *our endurance in the object*, insofar as proximity to the object means proximity to the cluster of things that the object promises' (Berlant 2006, p. 20, original emphasis).

And, indeed, if we understand the subject as dependent on power for its very existence, rendered a subject *by* power, we understand that to 'desire the conditions of one's own subordination is thus required to persist as oneself' (Butler 1997, p. 9).

Yet as Butler (1997) further argues, the subject founded by power is not determined by it but is rendered agentic by its very subjection, and so able to resist. One participant, Tinu, spoke of having become aware of what she deemed an unhealthy, creeping dependency on her false eyelashes. She vividly described how she sometimes saw herself when she was not wearing the lashes: 'I feel something is wrong with my face. I look at the mirror, I'll say "Oh God what is wrong, why am I looking so pale, so ugly and I'm looking sick?"' Problematising this as a self-alienation and misrecognition, Tinu took up an opposing 'natural beauty repertoire' that promised a more authentic and healthy sense of self, saying of her false lashes: 'I wanna be myself without them. I still wanna be myself and still feel great'. For this reason, she explained, she now 'deliberately weaned' herself off the lashes. Unlike aesthetic vigilance, which I have argued bolsters postfeminist disciplinary norms and imperatives by promising the subject an imminent and improved return to them, Tinu was referring to an act of resistance, of trying to sever her cruel attachments.

However, Tinu revealed that her spectacularly feminine dress choices were guided by other imperatives, too. Tinu was an actress in Nollywood, the booming Nigerian film industry. She explained that when she had to appear for public events in her professional capacity, she put her false lashes back on. She described the lashes for this purpose as like her 'trademark,' and as enhancing her celebrity 'packaging'. Here Tinu was speaking of aesthetic labour as it has tended to be conceptualised, namely 'the embodied *work* some workers have to do to maintain their bodies for particular forms of employment' (Entwistle and Wissinger 2006, p. 776, original emphasis). But as heard from her and the other women in my research—and as in this edited collection as a whole—to understand women's contemporary beauty practices and pressures the conceptual demarcation of paid work as a distinct aesthetic sphere no longer holds. Neoliberalism hails subjects 'as entrepreneurs of themselves or, more precisely, as *investors* in themselves, as human capital that wishes to appreciate' (Feher 2009, pp. 30–31, emphasis added), while postfeminism promises women that their 'capital' lies especially in beauty. Thus it is that under conditions of neoliberal postfeminism, women are hailed and guided to be entrepreneurial in their pursuit of beauty.

Conclusion

Individualised and responsibilised, called by ever-increasing consumer options, obliged to exercise 'choice,' *per force* the entrepreneurial neoliberal subject becomes a risk-taker. Based on interviews with young and class-privileged women in Lagos, Nigeria, who dress up and appear in spectacularly feminine style, this chapter explored the risks involved in their intensified and hyper-technologised postfeminist beauty practice. It showed how the consumption of new or increasingly normative beauty technologies posed both physical and psychic risks for the women, to which they tended to consent as a means to access the highly desired promises of beauty. I argued that the women's beauty practice was characterised by entrepreneurial calculations of risk-reward, then, including a knowing and concerted effort to manage what became construed as beauty's 'necessary' risks.

The chapter introduced the concepts of 'aesthetic vigilance' and 'aesthetic rest' to theorise the research participants' particular risk-management strategies and practices. These entailed keeping a keen eye on one's beauty practice so as not to fall into beauty's traps, and taking mini-breaks from beauty to later become all the more beautiful. I cast aesthetic vigilance and aesthetic rest as cruelly optimistic for further binding or attaching the women to disciplinary power. Indeed they are especially effective and insidious vehicles of power, I would argue, because they appear not only reasonable but also empowered and empowering, even somewhat subversive. In subscribing to such logics, being passionately attached to the terms and tools of their spectacularly feminine style, the women took up subject positions as aesthetic entrepreneurs: subjects guided by the fundamental postfeminist and neoliberal rationality that, for women, beauty is a most serious business.

References

Allman, J. (Ed.). (2004). *Fashioning Africa: Power and the Politics of Dress.* Bloomington: Indiana University Press.

Banet-Weiser, S. (2013). Am I Pretty or Ugly? Girls and the Market for self-Esteem. *Girlhood Studies, 7*(1), 83–101.

Berlant, L. (2006). Cruel Optimism. *Differences: A Journal of Feminist Cultural Studies, 17*(3), 20–36.

Binkley, S. (2006). The Perilous Freedoms of Consumption: Toward a Theory of the Conduct of Consumer Conduct. *Journal for Cultural Research, 10*(4), 343–362.

Blue, M. G. (2013). The Best of Both Worlds? Youth, Gender and a Post-Feminist Sensibility in Disney's *Hannah Montana. Feminist Media Studies, 13*(4), 660–675.

Butler, J. (1997). *The Psychic Life of Power: Theories in Subjection.* Stanford: Stanford University Press.

Butler, J. (1999). *Gender Trouble: Feminism and the Subversion of Identity* (2nd ed.). New York and London: Routledge.

Butler, J. (2011). *Bodies that Matter* (2nd ed.). London and New York: Routledge.

Coleman, R., & Figueroa, M. (2010). Past and Future Perfect? Beauty, Affect and Hope. *Journal for Cultural Research, 14*(4), 357–373.

Davies, B., Flemmen, A. B., Gannon, S., Laws, C., & Watson, B. (2002). Working on the Ground. A Collective Biography of Feminine Subjectivities: Mapping the Traces of Power and Knowledge. *Social Semiotics, 12*(3), 291–313.

Dogbe, E. (2003). Unraveled Yarns: Dress, Consumption, and Women's Bodies in Ghanaian Culture. *Fashion Theory: The Journal of Dress Body & Culture, 7*(3/4), 377–396.

Dosekun, S. (2015a). For Western Girls Only? Postfeminism as Transnational Culture. *Feminist Media Studies, 15*(6), 960–975.

Dosekun, S. (2015b). *Fashioning Spectacular Femininities in Nigeria: Postfeminism, Consumption and the Transnational.* Unpublished PhD Dissertation, King's College London.

Entwistle, J., & Wissinger, E. (2006). Keeping up Appearances: Aesthetic Labour in the Fashion Modelling Industries of London and New York. *The Sociological Review, 54*(4), 774–794.

Evans, A., & Riley, S. (2013). Immaculate Consumption: Negotiating the Sex Symbol in Postfeminist Celebrity Culture. *Journal of Gender Studies, 22*(3), 268–281.

Feher, M. (2009). Self-Appreciation; or the Aspirations of Human Capital. *Public Culture, 21*(1), 21–41.

Gill, R. (2007). Postfeminist Media Culture: Elements of a Sensibility. *European Journal of Cultural Studies, 10*(2), 147–166.

Grewal, I. (2005). *Transnational America: Feminisms, Diasporas, Neoliberalisms.* Durham and London: Duke University Press.

Hegde, R. (2011). Introduction. In R. Hegde (Ed.), *Circuits of Visibility: Gender and Transnational Media Cultures.* New York: New York University Press.

Lazar, M. (2009). Entitled to Consume: Post-Feminist Femininity and a Culture of Post-Critique. *Discourse and Communication, 3*(4), 371–400.

Leve, M., Rubin, L., & Pusic, A. (2012). Cosmetic Surgery and Neoliberalisms: Managing Risk and Responsibility. *Feminism and Psychology, 22*(1), 122–141.

McRobbie, A. (2009). *The Aftermath of Feminism: Gender, Culture and Social Change.* London: Sage.

Mustafa, H. (2002). Portraits of Modernity: Fashioning Selves in Dakarois Popular Photography. In P. Landau & D. Kaspin (Eds.), *Images and Empires: Visuality in Colonial and Postcolonial Africa.* Berkeley: University of California Press.

Petersen, E. B. (2008). Passionately Attached: Academic Subjects of Desire. In B. Davies (Ed.), *Judith Butler in Conversation: Analysing the Texts and Talk of Everyday Life.* New York; London: Routledge.

Rose, N. (1998). *Inventing Our Selves: Psychology, Power, and Personhood.* Cambridge: Cambridge University Press.

10

Dream Jobs? The Glamourisation of Beauty Service Work in Media Culture

Laurie Ouellette

Introduction

In May 2015, the *New York Times* exposed harsh working conditions in the city's thriving, and deeply feminised, nail industry. Based on interviews with dozens of female workers, journalist Sarah Maslin Nir, author of 'The Price of Nice Nails' and the follow-up investigation 'Perfect Nails, Poisoned Workers,' reported that many salons charge new manicurists up to $100 for the 'opportunity' to get their foot in the door, exploit undocumented workers and adhere to a racial hierarchy that values light-skinned Koreans over Latinos and African Americans (see Nir 2015a, 2015b). Many women reported working long hours without job security or health benefits, and the average wage hovered around only $35 a day,

L. Ouellette (✉)
Communication and Cultural Studies and Comparative Literature,
Minneapolis, MN, USA

A.S. Elias et al. (eds.), *Aesthetic Labour*,
DOI 10.1057/978-1-137-47765-1_10

or $3 an hour. Manicurists were also exposed to serious health risks associated with the toxic chemicals used in nail products, including chronic migraines, respiratory problems and miscarriages.

As the expose went viral, commentators expressed shock and outrage, consumers promised to tip better and patronise nontoxic salons and Governor Andrew Cuomo announced that every nail salon in New York would 'hence be required to post a workers bill of rights' stating minimum wage requirements and safety measures that owners are required to provide, including face masks and gloves (Grynbaum 2015). While these reforms are laudable, the nail scandal was perceived as an isolated local problem unrelated to the politics of work in the burgeoning beauty and style industries more broadly. Feminist media and cultural studies scholars have also tended to overlook the labour of cosmetologists, hairdressers and other aesthetic service providers, despite an upswing of attention to work in recent years. While there are excellent ethnographic and historical accounts (Gill 2010; Kang 2010; Willett 2000; Yang 2011), this literature has not been put into conversation with important new scholarship on gender and cultural labour, creative industries, immaterial and affective labour and related topics (Conor et al. 2015; Duffy 2015; Gregg 2011; Mayer 2011; Weeks 2011; Wissinger 2007). This gap is especially notable given the feminisation of beauty service work and the centrality of appearance to postfeminist and neoliberal models of subjectivity (Gill 2007).

As Angela McRobbie observes, recent decades have seen a burgeoning culture of 'pampering yourself' with beauty treatments marketed not only as a requirement of normative femininity, but also as a 'resource to be mined for added values which can enhance performance in the workplace' (2002b, p. 100). Women, she notes, are especially called upon to maintain a 'stylish and attractive' image through meticulous grooming and aestheticised care of the self as a requirement of employability and career advancement. The term aesthetic labour is used to describe this process of monitoring and 'maximising' one's appearance and self-presentation (Mears 2014), particularly in the expanding service sectors, so that employers can profit from the results. Increasingly, aesthetic labour also seeps beyond the official workforce into practices of self-branding which have intensified in tandem with the freelance economy

(Banet-Weiser 2012; Hearn 2008; Ouellette and Hay 2008). The imperative to look good, in other words, is increasingly tied to the demands of postindustrial work and the enterprising forms of personhood valued by free market societies.

Given the rising demands of aesthetic labour, it is no surprise that the beauty and style industries (hair, skin, nails, tanning, waxing, permanent makeup, wardrobe consultation) have boomed in recent decades. According to the Professional Beauty Association (2014), these industries are an 'engine of job growth for the U.S. economy,' with the US Bureau of Labour Statistics reporting that the number of personal appearance jobs will increase 14 percent between 2012 and 2022. Not coincidentally, beauty service labour is also integral to the makeover regime, the quintessential technology for regulating self-enterprising female subjects under postfeminism and neoliberalism. No longer confined to women's culture, the makeover has been mainstreamed as a 'go to' solution to a wide range of problems, including uncertainties and difficulties at work. While many scholars have critiqued the gender, age, class and racial politics of mediated makeover culture and its dubious claims of empowerment (Banet-Weiser and Portwood-Stacer 2006; McGee 2005; Ouellette and Hay 2008; Ringrose and Walkerdine 2008; Skeggs 2009; Tincknell 2011; Weber 2009), little has been said about the *occupational labour that underpins the makeover regime.*

This chapter approaches aesthetic labour from the vantage point of people who earn a living providing aesthetic services. I construct an alternate genealogy of the makeover regime by tracing the rising visibility of salon work in media culture and showing how previously feminised and devalued beauty service labour is now celebrated as creative, glamorous and enterprising. Contra to the *Times* expose, the low-paid and often insecure workers who make developments like aesthetic labour and makeover culture possible are increasingly cast as having 'dream jobs' in alluring industries, as epitomised by a surge of reality shows (*Nail Files*, 2011–2013; *Nail'd It*, 2014–present) that associate the nail industry with opportunities for artistry, celebrity and self-branding. While this cultural trend acknowledges the desire for creative and meaningful work that has always drawn women to salons, it ultimately dresses up the exploitative and risky dimensions of a gendered field in glittering new terms.

The Allure of Salon Work

Historically marginalised and hidden from view, the labour required to maintain attractive and well-groomed individuals is increasingly visible and celebrated across popular media culture. Whereas once salon workers 'stood somewhere above domestic servants but below school teachers in social status' (Blackwelder 2003, p. 3), today they are posited as glamorous, creative and aspirational. Magazines, television and social media have helped to construct a new category of celebrity that is the pinnacle of this trend. 'Celebrity' stylists, hairdressers, skin specialists and other aesthetic professionals permeate red carpet culture and appear to enjoy nearly as much fame and fortune as their clients. These celebrity figures often double as makeover experts, launch lucrative brands and accumulate millions of followers on platforms like Instagram. At the same time, high-end salons increasingly describe staffers as 'art directors', 'creative directors' and other euphemisms borrowed from Hollywood. Digital games set in salons invite children and adults to cast themselves in this role. In 2009, The Sims introduced a stylist occupation for players who want their characters to 'influence the look of the townsfolk and make money doing it'. Sims stylists, says the manufacturer, are highly 'creative individuals' who enjoy a glamorous lifestyle and a flexible schedule cutting hair, applying makeup, performing makeovers on clients and dashing around town promoting their brands and services.

The TV industry has also embraced the salon as the raw material for a slew of reality entertainment. While makeover shows were proliferating, a parallel strand of programming revolving around workers who provide beauty and spa treatments, tanning sessions, haircuts, hair blowouts, manicures, body sculpting and other aesthetic services was also taking shape. The British series *The Salon* (2003–2004) set this trend in motion by building a fully operational salon on a studio stage with 20 cameras and 30 microphones. Hair stylists and other service providers doubled as talent, and the public was invited to come in for haircuts and beauty treatments including spray-on tans, manicures, massages, waxing, Botox and makeup applications while TV viewers looked on five days a week. The debut episode served as public relations for the salon industry, informing viewers that British consumers made 'more than three hundred million visits to salons and spas each year, spending £4.1 billion annually'. While hairdressers were acknowledged to earn only three hundred pounds per week on average (roughly four hundred and seventy US dollars), the salon was pitched as an exciting and (potentially) lucrative workplace: 'Hairdressing is not just about perms and blue rinses,' it is 'glamorous,' 'exciting,' 'passionate,' 'sexy,' 'challenging' and 'cool,' claimed the narrator. With the power to 'change the way we look and feel,' hairdressers are becoming 'demi-gods' who enjoy a new 'level of celebrity,' with the most talented and ambitious among them earning 'ten times' the average amount and enjoying an upscale lifestyle signified by 'fancy cars' and trendy clothes.

In the United States, dozens of reality shows have subsequently taken TV viewers behind the scenes of the beauty and style industries, and the trend shows no sign of abating. Shows like *Blow Out* (2004–2006), *Split Ends* (2006–2009) and *Shear Genius* (2007–present) also operate as career manuals by educating potential workers and consumers about the routines, requirements and rewards of aesthetic service work. These productions downplay the more mundane and exploitative dimensions of salon work, and accentuate its fun, hip, creative and self-enterprising possibilities. This is accomplished by setting the programmes in posh, celebrity-studded salons in media capitals like New York and Los Angeles, and by staging serialised talent competitions in which stylists compete for artistic recognition, glamorous apprenticeships, endorsement deals and cash prizes. The celebration of the hair stylist as an *aesthetic entrepreneur* who embodies creativity and self-enterprising skills is echoed across industry discourse and occupational advice. While *US News and World Report's 2014 Guide to Best Jobs* acknowledges that most hairdressers are not salaried employees, that many work part time, and that the median hourly wage is only $11.12 (or $23,140 per year), it casts the 'booming' occupation as a beloved 'calling' for creative types. The brochure for The Beauty School Network (2015, np) which represents cosmetology schools, recruits 'individuals from all backgrounds' who have a 'passion for hair, makeup and style,' want to avoid the 'drudgery of an office,' desire the 'freedom of an entrepreneur' and hope to 'work with celebrities' or break into the 'world of entertainment and fashion'. In her advice book *It's Not Really About the Hair* (2011, p. 12), celebrity stylist/TV personality Tabatha Coffey compares herself to Bill Gates and Steve Jobs, who were not 'artists in the traditional sense,' but whose 'wild creativity has changed the way we understand the world'.

The Salon as Creative Industry

This discourse stitches the salon into the wider celebration of creative work. In *The Rise of the Creative Class* (2002, p. 68), Richard Florida situates hair styling within a 'creative class' of designers, editors, actors, financiers, scientists and others who 'engage in work whose function is to create meaningful new forms'. In the chapter 'The Machine Shop and The Hair Salon,' he claims that if offered a choice between a well-paying job with benefits and security at a machine shop and a lower-paying job with fewer benefits and more risks at a hair salon, most people will choose to work at the salon. This, he contends, is because styling hair is a 'creative' occupation that involves more flexibility, artistry and autonomy than machine labour. Business writer Virginia Postrel (2004, pp. 180–181) echoes this analysis, claiming that as capitalism and everyday life have become more aestheticised and demand for 'aesthetic workers has exploded,' new career options have 'opened up' for women and men who might once have pursued 'less expressive' crafts like waitressing or truck driving. Work such as hair styling, which was once considered an 'effeminate and low-prestige' profession, will become more desirable and prestigious as more and more people seek out creative occupations, she contends (Postrel 2004, pp. 180–181).

This discourse conflates beauty service work with more lucrative 'creative' careers that require access to college and graduate degrees. However, while Florida describes his own hairstylist as a creative genius who drives a BMW, most people who work in salons are minimally paid. This conflation is partly legitimated by drawing the hair stylist into an expanding culture and knowledge sector in which the pleasure of work is presented as a substitute for material compensation. As Andrew Ross points out, the artist has been appropriated as the ideal model for many cultural and knowledge workers. Historically unattached and 'adaptable to circumstance' (Ross 2003, p. 144), the artist presents a romanticised template for navigating the shift from 'social welfare systems, union contracts and long term job security' (Ross 2009, p. 4) to a flexible, insecure and contingent workforce (Ross 2009, p. 2). Artists also come with training in 'sacrificial labour,' which means they are 'predisposed to accept nonmonetary rewards—the gratification of producing art—as partial compensation of their work, thereby discounting the cash price of their labour (Ross 2003, p. 142). Drawing from Ross, Micki McGee proposes that 'artistic mentality' has been extended across the postindustrial workforce: Artists now provide an 'ideal work model' for everyone because 'passion for what they do motivates them to tolerate long hours for low (or no) pay and a mindset of contingency' (2005, p. 136).

According to McGee, the artist and the equally celebrated entrepreneur have merged in the celebration of creative labour, to the extent that both figures are driven by the 'desire for unalienated labour, for engagement in one's work' (2005, p. 136). Whereas artists labour for minimal compensation, entrepreneurs are expected to invest countless hours of overtime in order to establish and brand themselves (McGee 2005, p. 136). These expectations merge in the DWYL (Do What You Love) ethic associated with 'new employment spaces where pleasure, autonomy and income seemingly co-exist' (Duffy 2015, p. 2). Digital cultural production is one such space. In her study of female fashion and beauty bloggers and vloggers, Brooke Duffy observes a 'forward looking and entrepreneurial enactment of creativity' that she calls 'aspirational labour' (2015, p. 3). Aspirational labourers accept low pay, contingency and risk not just because they 'love' beauty and style, but also because they would like to reap social and economic rewards down the road. Relatedly, Kathleen Kuehn and Thomas Corrigan (Kuehn and Corrigan 2013) develop the concept of 'hope labour' to explain why people participate in unpaid online social production. While digital free labourers value the sense of control over their creative energies that posting content affords, they also hope for unlikely outcomes that are typically 'beyond their control', such as landing a glamorous job in the media and culture industries (Kuehn and Corrigan 2013, p. 17).

Similar processes are at work in the celebration of beauty service work as simultaneously creative and enterprising. The glamourisation of the hair stylist as creative entrepreneur extends the expectation of sacrificial labour to a gendered industry that has always been poorly paid and precarious, and has become even more so as salons move away from paid employees and categorise workers as independent contractors (Covert 2015). The fame and fortune of the celebrity stylist, moreover, provides a new justification for additional forms of hope and aspirational labour. For instance, career manuals with names like *Million Dollar Stylist* (Breslin 2014) encourage hair stylists to launch their own YouTube sites and use social media to brand themselves and cultivate 'celebrity' clienteles, while reality shows narrate unlikely situations in which unknown and aspiring stylists strategise to parlay uncompensated labour (including working as unpaid talent for the TV show) into media visibility, cash prizes, future work, celebrity status and brands of their own.

Angela McRobbie (2002a) argues that the designation of more and more service sector occupations (such as hairstylist) as creative constitutes a 'break' with expectations of work. As the 'flamboyantly auteur relation to creative work that has long been the mark of being a writer, artist, film director or fashion designer' (McRobbie 2002a, p. 517) is extended across the workforce, service labour is constituted less as an economic exchange (wages for work) than a venue for self-realisation. The suggestion that everyone now has the 'chance to fulfill their creative dreams' obscures unequal access to economic and cultural capital, and rationalises the offloading of job security and risk onto individuals. When this logic is applied to the beauty service industries, it justifies low wages, minimally compensated training periods, precarious contracts, rising expectations of unpaid promotional labour and self-branding, and anti-union policies.

Making over Beauty Service Labour

The making over of the hair stylist as an aesthetic entrepreneur also conceals the social and educational inequalities that have historically drawn mainly working class women and women of colour to the field. Just as scholarship on cultural and creative labour can help demystify the glamourisation of salon work, historical accounts of women's beauty service labour are helpful for unpacking the intertwined gender, race and class politics of this development. As many historians have shown, cosmetology offered one of the earliest opportunities for white working class women and women of colour to earn an independent living. From the beginning, Julie Willett documents, salon workers were entrenched in a 'pink collar ghetto where hazardous working conditions, low wages, and long hours were common' (2000, p. 4). Yet, hairdressing also offered women a 'meaningful work culture' (Willett 2000, p. 35). Like dressmaking and millinery trades, it presented an opportunity for creativity and an 'artisanal sense of self rarely associated with the realm of women's wage work' (Willett 2000, p. 36). Beauty shops owned by women were also among the earliest avenues for female entrepreneurialism. The recent glamourisation of salon work through an appropriation of the 'artistic mentality' (McGee 2005) is not a complete break from the past, but a radical rewriting under neoliberal logics. Cast as aesthetic entrepreneurs who love what they do and may become rich and famous, stylists are shown to embrace the aestheticisation, flexibility, creativity and self-enterprising required of postindustrial workers in an industry that is assumed to have overcome gender segregation.

The symbolic de-gendering of the salon has been crucial to its positioning as a creative industry. While salon work is still feminised—84 percent of individuals in personal appearance occupations are women, compared to 47 percent of employed individuals in the overall US workforce (Professional Beauty Association 2014)—heterosexual men are highly visible as aesthetic entrepreneurs. While gay men have long been considered 'style mavens' due to their perceived association with hip urban style and femininity (Lewis 2008), glamorous male stylists who flaunt their heterosexuality are now commonplace in media culture. Unlike barbers, they exude stylishness, work in aestheticised settings and have female as well as male clients. At a time when male-coded industrial jobs are declining in the West and men are moving into service fields, the male stylist mediates and buffers the 'feminisation of work'. *The Salon* made a point to feature heterosexual men as trendsetting stylists, conveying the idea that the modern aesthetic entrepreneur has transcended the ghetto of women's work. Likewise, the US show *Blow Out* followed a 'defiantly straight' male celebrity stylist who ran a posh salon in Beverly Hills, and eventually became a judge on *Shear Genius*, a competition to crown the 'best hair stylist in America'.

The masculinisation of salon work has a history with implications for labour organising. As Willett points out, efforts to professionalise hair-styling were led by middle class white men, who sought to disassociate the occupation from 'women's work' by casting male stylists as artists and women as 'mere gossip mongers' (2000, p. 5). Subsequent attempts by male barber unions to organise female hair stylists were also fraught with gender hierarchies and tensions. Many white and African American women were ambivalent about or resisted collective bargaining because they worried they would be disempowered (Willett 2000). This is not surprising, considering the gender hierarchies inherent to pro-union advocacy efforts exemplified by a 1960 American Federation of Labour and Congress of Industrial Organizations (AFL-CIO) educational film about hair salons and barbershops. The film began by announcing that a growing number of men were choosing the 'beautification of women as a career'. Inside a beauty salon we meet a white man in a tailored suit, whose job is to provide a 'creative vision' to female haircutters in lab coats. By the time the camera zooms in on a Union Shop sign, which as we were told by the narrator is a 'symbol of good barbering,' male take-over of salon work has been established. While collective bargaining has waned in the barber trade and the vast majority of hair salons are non-unionised, creativity is now evoked as a way to make beauty service work compatible with masculinity.

Many historians argue that early beauty shops were more than work-places: they were social institutions that nourished female sociality and 'community and political goals' (Willett 2000, p. 4). For African American women especially, beauty culture was 'tied to a wider ethical and political culture' (Black 2004, p. 29) in which salons played a central role. Neighbourhood beauty shops served the needs of Black communities during Jim Crow and simultaneously advocated to end segregation, in some cases operating as outposts of the civil rights movement (Gill 2010; Willett 2000). While these businesses have declined as corporate chains have proliferated, the Black-owned beauty shop—like the barbershop—remains symbolically tied to a history of racial solidarity and struggle (Mukherjee 2006). This legacy is downplayed in contemporary media culture, where salon work is presented as multi-cultural, but a postracial mentality that assumes the aims of the civil rights have been accomplished and racial discrimination no longer exists prevails.

As Gavin Mueller (2012, np) points out, postindustrial creative work is often mediated as multicultural, as exemplified by televised talent competitions filled with 'young diverse creative types' set in 'hip urban locales'. Likewise, salon work is also represented as a multicultural environment where difference is embraced and inequalities are assumed to be well in the past. Talent competitions routinely cast people of colour as registers of multicultural hipness, conveying the notion that racial discrimination (such as the treatment of New York manicurists) has no place in contemporary salon work. Likewise, the role of the Black salon in nurturing African American communities is erased by a cluster of docusoaps revolving around African American stylists including *LA Hair* (2012–present) and *Cutting It: In the ATL* (2015–present). While these productions promote diverse understandings of beauty and showcase the artistry and skill involved in styling Black women's hair, they distance modern aesthetic entrepreneurship from any wider ethical and political agenda. While the salons featured cater to mainly African American clienteles, stylists are cast as self-enterprising individuals who are largely preoccupied with building their personal brands and achieving celebrity status. The marketing for *Cutting It,* which follows 'talented,' 'glamorous' and 'headstrong' salon owners in Atlanta, promises shifting alliances, 'competition at its most cutthroat' and schemes to 'soak up every last dollar Atlanta has to offer'. *LA Hair* follows 'celebrity hair' stylist Kim Kimble, who runs an upscale Hollywood salon and claims to have A-listers like Beyoncé 'on speed dial'. Kimble's salon is a glamorous venue for brushing up against Black actors, performers and musicians. Working there is presented as a lucky break for stargazing stylists. The chance to 'do what you love' while servicing celebrities and learning the ropes of self-promotion is presented as a reward onto itself (wages, tips and benefits are never mentioned).

The TV show *Houston Beauty* (2013–present), set at the nation's oldest Black-owned beauty school, points to the stakes of this discourse. Franklin Beauty School was formed in 1915 by a self-made African American cosmetologist who got her start selling homemade beauty products. Besides training hairdressers who could serve the city's African

American community, the school promoted desegregation and served as an advocacy organisation working to raise wages and improve benefits in the cosmetology field. This history is shorn from the reality programme, which casts the school as an outdated institution in which elderly African American instructors demonstrate technical skills on worn mannequins in fluorescent-lit classrooms with peeling paint. Franklin Beauty has seen better days, and despite the attempt to modernise the curriculum for the benefit of ratings by staging competitions and having the students perform pro bono 'challenges' like making commercials for the school, the footage presents a stark counterpoint to the posh, 'artistic' salons celebrated on other reality shows. Yet, even here, the glamourisation of salon work is evident. Students who drop in and out of the programme based on financial aid, and who sometimes sleep in their cars, speak about their 'passion' for cosmetology and their ambition to become celebrity stylists, sometimes referencing TV programmes they have seen. They have been taught by contemporary media culture that salon work is a path to a more creative, enterprising and glamorous future. While institutions like Franklin Beauty School were part of an ethical and political culture that valued collectivity, community and shared responsibility, the new mantra of aesthetic entrepreneurship dovetails neatly with the neoliberal assumption that individuals who fail to achieve a dream job have no one but themselves to blame.

This message is made especially clear on *Tabatha's Salon Takeover* (2008–2011), a show that enacts the makeover as a solution to 'failure' in the salon industry. The premise is that most independently owned salons fail within three years of opening. Attributing this problem to the behaviour of owners and staffers, 'expert' Tabatha Coffey promises to turn around flagging and 'at risk' businesses in just a few weeks. On each episode, she targets a salon, diagnoses problems and implements changes and reforms. Salon owners are coached to 'manage through creativity' and stylists learn to find their passion and take 'ownership' of their performance and sales. Surveillance cameras are installed to document unambitious work ethics, inappropriate attitudes and other problems and 'tough love' is deployed to correct them. By making over those whose occupational labour underpins the makeover regime, the show brings the concept full circle. While makeovers rely on aesthetic services (such as a new haircut) to create 'better'—that is, appropriately aestheticised and self-enterprising—citizens and workers, the impetus here is to retool the capacities of hair stylists and others who make a living in the beauty and style industries, providing the aesthetic services upon which the makeover regime depends. As we have seen, these capacities are connected to the celebration of creativity and are also integral to the postfeminist aestheticisation of subjectivity, and the shifting demands and conditions of postindustrial labour more broadly. Billed as a creative enterprise for all, the salon—perhaps even more than the artist's workshop—provides an ideal setting for making over the workforce through the vicarious instruction that television provides.

Conclusion

Putting scholarship on creative and cultural labour into conversation with beauty service labour, this chapter has shown how the glamourisation of the hair stylist in contemporary media culture obscures risky and exploitative working conditions. While these conditions are not entirely new, they have intensified and are increasingly normalised as the price to be paid for autonomous and expressive work. The subjugated history of the salon as a site of female solidarity and racial activism denaturalises the figure of the self-interested aesthetic entrepreneur who overlaps with and has arguably outpaced the artist as a model postindustrial worker. This history also confirms that creativity is not a ruse: women's attraction to cosmetology has always been rooted in the gratification of artisanal production. Today, however, the rising status of the salon as a creative industry and the allure of celebrity have infused beauty service work with new hopes and additional justifications for sacrificial labour. The positing of the salon as a 'cool job in a hot industry' (Neff et al. 2005) by countless magazine articles, Instagram posts and TV programmes makes it more difficult to form solidarities or struggle for creativity at work as a 'basic human right', not an excuse for precarity and exploitation (Ross 2009, p. 47). While the *New York Times* exposé led to local reforms, the decks are stacked against a true democratisation of creativity by the glamourisation of the salon as a site for 'dream jobs'.

Notes

1. Thanks to Jo Littler for pointing this out to me.
2. The American Federation of Labour and Congress of Industrial Organizations (AFL-CIO) is a national trade union centre and the largest federation of unions in the United States.

References

Banet-Weiser, S. (2012). *Authentic TM: The Politics of Ambivalence in a Brand Culture*. New York: NYU Press.

Banet-Weiser, S., & Portwood-Stacer, L. (2006). 'I Just Want to Be Me Again!' Beauty Pageants, Reality Television and Postfeminism. *Feminist Theory, 7*(2), 255–272.

Beauty School Network. (2015). 8 Reasons Why You Should Attend Cosmetology School. Beauty School Network. [Online] Retrieved from http://www.beautyschoolnetwork.com/8-reasons-why-you-should-attend-cosmetology-school

Black, P. (2004). *The Beauty Industry*. London: Routledge.

Blackwelder, J. K. (2003). *Styling Jim Crow: African American Beauty Training During Segregation*. College Station: Texas A&M University Press.

Breslin, M. (2014). *Million Dollar Stylist*. New York: RMNC Publishing.

Coffey, T. (2012). *It's Not Really About the Hair: The Honest Truth About Life, Love and the Business of Beauty*. New York: IT Books.

Conor, B., Gill, R., & Taylor, S. (Eds.). (2015). *Gender and Creative Labour*. Malden, MA: Wiley-Blackwell.

Covert, B. (2015). Why Your Salon Doesn't Have Any Employees. *Think Progress*. [Online] Retrieved from http://thinkprogress.org/economy/2015/06/03/3665054/hair-salon-wage-theft/

Duffy, B. E. (2016). The Romance of Work: Gender and Aspirational Labour in the Digital Culture Industries. *International Journal of Cultural Studies*, 19(2), 441-457.

Florida, R. (2002). *The Rise of the Creative Class*. New York: Basic Books.

Gill, R. (2007). Postfeminist Media Culture: Elements of a Sensibility. *European Journal of Cultural Studies, 10*(2), 147–166.

Gill, T. (2010). *Beauty Shop Politics: African American Women's Activism in the Beauty Industry*. Urbana: University of Illinois Press.

Gregg, M. (2011). *Work's Intimacy*. New York: Polity.

Grynbaum, M. (2015). New York Nail Salons Now Required to Post Workers' Bill of Rights. *New York Times*. [Online] Retrieved from https://www.google.com/?gws_rd=ssl#q=Grynbaum+nails

Hearn, A. (2008). Meat, Mask Burden: Probing the Contours of the Branded Self. *Journal of Consumer Culture, 8*(2), 197–217.

Kang, M. (2010). *The Managed Hand: Race, Gender and the Body in Beauty Service Work*. Berkeley: University of California Press.

Kuehn, K., & Corrigan, T. (2013). Hope Labour: The Role of Employment Prospects in Online Social Production. *Political Economy of Communication, 1*(1), 9–25.

Lewis, T. (2008). *Smart Living: Lifestyle Media and Popular Expertise*. New York: Peter Lang.

Mayer, V. (2011). *Below-the-Line: Producers and Production Studies in the New Television Economy*. Durham, NC: Duke University Press.

McGee, M. (2005). *Self-Help, Inc: Makeover Culture in American Life*. New York: Oxford University Press.

McRobbie, A. (2002a). Clubs to Companies: Notes on the Decline of Political Culture in Speeded up Creative Worlds. *Cultural Studies, 16*(4), 516–531.

McRobbie, A. (2002b). From Holloway to Hollywood: Happiness at Work in the New Cultural Economy. In P. du Gay & M. Pryke (Eds.), *Cultural Economy: Cultural Analysis and Commercial Life* (pp. 97–114). London: Sage.

Mears, A. (2014). Aesthetic Labour for the Sociologies of Work, Gender, and Beauty. *Sociology Compass, 8*(12), 1330–1343.

Mueller, G. (2012). Reality TV and the Flexible Future. *Jacobin*. [Online] Retrieved from https://www.jacobinmag.com/2012/10/reality-t-v-and-flexible-future/

Mukherjee, R. (2006). The Ghetto Fabulous Aesthetic in Contemporary Black Culture. *Cultural Studies, 20*(6), 599–629.

Neff, G., Wissinger, E., & Zukin, S. (2005). Entrepreneurial Labour Among Cultural Producers: 'Cool' Jobs in 'Hot' Industries. *Social Semiotics, 15*(3), 307–334.

Nir, S. M. (2015a). The Price of Nice Nails. *New York Times*. [Online] Retrieved from http://www.nytimes.com/2015/05/10/nyregion/at-nail-salons-in-nyc--manicurists-are-underpaid-and-unprotected.html?_r=0

Nir, S. M. (2015b). Perfect Nails, Poisoned Workers. *New York Times*. [Online] Retrieved from http://www.nytimes.com/2015/05/11/nyregion/nail-salon-workers-in-nyc-face-hazardous-chemicals.html

Ouellette, L., & Hay, J. (2008). *Better Living Through Reality TV: Television and Post-Welfare Citizenship*. Malden, MA: Blackwell.

Postrel, V. (2004). *The Substance of Style: How the Rise of Aesthetic Consciousness is Remaking Commerce, Culture and Consciousness*. New York: Harper Perennial.

Professional Beauty Association. (2014). *Economic Snapshot of the Salon and Spa Industry*. Scottsdale, AZ: Professional Beauty Association.

Ringrose, J., & Walkerdine, V. (2008). Regulating the Abject. *Feminist Media Studies, 8*(3), 227–246.

Ross, A. (2003). *No Collar: The Humane Workplace and its Hidden Costs*. Philadelphia: Temple University Press.

Ross, A. (2009). *Nice Work if You Can Get It: Life and Labour in Precarious Times*. New York: NYU Press.

Skeggs, B. (2009). The Moral Economy of Person Production: The Class Relations of Self-Performance in Reality Television. *Sociological Review, 57*(4), 625–644.

Tincknell, E. (2011). Scouring the Abject Body: Ten Years Younger and Fragmented Femininity Under Neoliberalism. In R. Gill & C. Scharff (Eds.), *New Femininities: Postfeminism, Neoliberalism and Subjectivity* (pp. 83–95). New York: Palgrave Macmillan.

U.S. News and World Report. (n.d.). Best Social Service Jobs: Hairdresser. [Online] Retrieved from http://money.usnews.com/careers/best-jobs/hairdresser

Weber, B. (2009). *Makeover TV: Selfhood, Citizenship and Celebrity*. Durham, NC: Duke University Press.

Weeks, K. (2011). *The Problem with Work: Feminism, Marxism, Antiwork Politics, and Postwork Imaginaries*. Durham, NC: Duke University Press.

Willett, J. A. (2000). *Permanent Waves: The Making of the American Beauty Shop*. New York: NYU Press.

Wissinger, E. (2007). Modeling a Way of Life: Immaterial and Affective Labour in the Fashion Modeling Industry. *Ephemera: Theory and Politics in Organization, 7*(1), 250–269.

Yang, J. (2011). Nennu and Shunu: Gender, Beauty Politics and the Beauty Economy in China. *Signs, 36*(2), 333–357.

11

Skin: Post-feminist Bleaching Culture and the Political Vulnerability of Blackness

Shirley Anne Tate

Introduction

Skin bleaching/lightening/toning, a transracial multi-billion-dollar global enterprise, involves transnational pharmaceutical/cosmetics companies and local entrepreneurs. About 15 % of the world's population consumed skin lighteners in 2014, with sales projected at US 19.8 billion dollars by 2018 (Neilson 2014). Japan is the largest market and pills, potions, creams, soaps, lotions, suppositories, injections, lasers and intravenous drips are global lightening technologies. Irrespective of its globality and transraciality, skin bleaching/lightening/toning as pathological sticks to African and African descent women's skins whether poor 'bleacher' or 'celebrity lightener/toner' because of colourism and post-enslavement's

S.A. Tate (✉)
Associate Professor in Race and Culture, Centre for Ethnicity and Racism Studies, School of Sociology and Social Policy, University of Leeds, Leeds, UK

Research Associate, Nelson Mandela University, Port Elizabeth, South Africa

A.S. Elias et al. (eds.), *Aesthetic Labour*,
DOI 10.1057/978-1-137-47765-1_11

skin colour preferences for lightness/whiteness. As consumers, women enter the global market in lightness in a beauty culture which negates the racialised gender power relations and social structuration of colourism, positioning bleached skin as 'post-Black feminist'. Specifically bleached skin counters second-wave Black feminism's embrace of Black anti-racist aesthetics' ideology of 'naturalness'. This epistemological break challenges hegemonic Black feminist aesthetics as well as denoting a new racialised aesthetic sensibility in the contested 'post-race' afterlife of 1970s Black feminism as it comes up against neoliberal discourses on individualism, choice and empowerment (Gill and Scharff 2011). For some, going beyond the politics of 'natural skin' reproduces post-feminist Blackness as a site of political vulnerability when skin is devalued by bleaching/lightening/toning. However, I will argue that bleachers' readings of the global skin trade do not mean that they have fallen prey to white supremacy as they 'shade shift'. Instead, this change is a critique of existing pigmentocracy enabled by their post-Black feminist self-positionings.

The Politics of Black Women's Skins

We cleanse, moisturise, perfume, exfoliate and care for skin because of our normalised hygiene and beauty standards. As sexualised, skin is caressed to know the beloved through touch, to touch them while being touched (Derrida 1993). We inhabit skin but it is not an organ which is noticeworthy until it is problematised. That is, until we begin to think about 'race' and skin. Then skin takes on a different tenor as it marks those who are racialised 'others' versus the non-racialised norm. As racialised, skin becomes a boundary marker for otherness as well as signifier of societal positionings of subalternity or dominance. This makes us remember that skin is our very interface between ourselves and the social world. This link between the psyche and the social forges what Didier Anzieu (1989) calls 'the skin ego', which as we would expect is not at all 'race'/gender neutral but deeply textured by racialisation, racism, anti-racism, sexism and discourses of Black and feminist anti-racist aesthetics.

Black African descent women's skins occupy a political space of simultaneous value and disvalue within the Black Atlantic diaspora through which 'the racialised gender skin ego' is formed. Its disvalue is textured by a whiteness which sets itself up as the only skin and beauty ideal with lightness on Black skin in second position. Darker skin has historically not been the location of skin value in the Black Atlantic because of the pigmentocracy established by white supremacy, afro-pessimism and African descent phobia over the long period of 'discovery', enslavement, colonisation and (post)colonialism. Black aesthetic colourism has also set up skin shade hierarchies of its own in which 'ethnic ambiguity' (Sharpley-Whiting 2007) and 'mulatticity' (Bonilla-Silva 2012) are at their pinnacle in the twenty-first century.

In the twenty-first century, we still have ongoing Black Nationalist and second-wave Black feminist skin battles over darker skin aesthetics. These battles seek to re-value and continue the re-valuing of darker skin on Black women's bodies, a skin which is placed as politically and physically vulnerable to attack from colourism and whiteness. As such, we are warned against the insidious enslavement of Black psyches through global white supremacy and colourism which lead to darker skinned women continuing to inhabit negative aesthetic space. We see this call to arms to re-value vulnerable darker skin, for example, in the film *Dark Girls* (Duke and Channsin Berry 2012) which speaks against the deep-seated bias against darker skinned women within African American culture.

It is important that we remember to keep the necessity for a racialised gender analysis at the forefront because of the continuing focus on femininity and beauty as being the preserve of the lighter-skinned Black woman while no such socially instituted masculine aesthetic preference exists within either colourism or pigmentocratic regimes. Fanon's (1986) historico-racial schema and racial epidermal schema need to be re-inscribed at an aesthetic level to take note of both gender and skin tone difference. This is so as both Black women and men are beaten down by 'tom toms, slave ships and cannibalism' but darker skinned women are racially branded as irredeemably ugly and the occupiers of the zone of aesthetic negativity even in the twenty-first century. This aesthetic negativity was asserted in 2014 by *US Weekly* 'Best Dressed List' winner and star of *12 Years a Slave,* Lupita Nyong'o. The only location in which darker skin has value on a woman's body is on the catwalk or in advertising where their bodies and body parts then become the location of 'the strange', 'the exotic' and the 'racially different' which show off the product to be consumed to good effect or which also appeals to the growing global Black middle/elite classes. An example of the latter is Nyong'o as face of the *Lancôme Advanced Génifique Serum* campaign in 2015 along with Lily Collins, Penélope Cruz and Kate Winslet.

As Black Nationalism interpellated 'bearers of the race' and Black second-wave feminism's location for/of theorising, Black women's bodies and the skins which cover them continue to be objects of super-surveillance from within Blackness itself so as to ensure they are free from artifice of any kind. This surveillance is seen as politically necessary because artifice like hair straightening, weaves, extensions, coloured contact lenses as well as skin lightening through bleaching agents or make-up would point to the profound negative impact of white supremacy on Black psyches. That is, it would show a Black 'desire to be white' because these aesthetic practices are defined as 'mimicking whiteness'. This is an ideological position which has been prevalent since the 1930s across the Black Atlantic (Weinbaum et al. 2008; Tate 2009) and has impacted Black second-wave feminism. For example, in *Talking Back: Thinking Feminist, Thinking Black*, bell hooks (2014) critiques the hair straightening phenomenon as one which was dynamised by white capital and the political economy of racism in the USA in which Black people participated as willing dupes of capitalism while forgetting the rationale for radical Black politics. Straightened hair on Black women's bodies was essential for the production of an image that could cross-over and speak to the common concerns of whiteness while attracting the dollars of Black communities (hooks 2014). We see a similar argument in terms of mimicking whiteness on skin and hair in the words of Margaret Hunter (2005, p. 3):

> Skin color bias creates many painful experiences for women of color especially darker-skinned women. This has led many women to try to alter their appearances through skin bleaching, make-up application, use of colored contact lenses, dieting, hair straightening and hair extensions and even cosmetic surgery.

Both hooks and Hunter have a carefully drawn boundary around what skin racialised as Black should look like as they critique the skin and hair politics of white supremacy which mean that approximation to whiteness is the ideal. Of course, this means that second-wave feminism in line with the Black anti-racist aesthetics (Taylor 2000) which emerged from Black Nationalist politics operates within authenticity regimes, as in a Black woman's skin is this or that shade. Notwithstanding this authenticity trope, the necessity for approximation to the ideal racialised as white has been shown to impact partner choices and intimate relationships, employment opportunities, promotion prospects, judgements of beauty and ideas about one's educability, for example (Herring et al. 2004). Thus it is that the twentieth- and twenty-first-century continuation of the political necessity for Black 'pride' and Black 'naturalness' in hair and skin exemplified by hooks and Hunter emerges from a specifically Black anti-racist aesthetics fight back against white supremacy which appeared from at least the 1930s. This was carried, for example, by Garveyism (USA/Jamaica), Rastafarianism (Jamaica), Black Power (the USA, UK, Anglophone Caribbean), Afro-Black aesthetics (Brazil), Black Consciousness (South Africa) and *Negrissmo* (Dominican Republic). We see this fight back as well in the charge that skin bleaching/lightening/toning is pathological practice which locates Black psyche and skin, 'the racialised skin ego', as a site of white supremacy.

Skin Bleaching/Lightening/Toning as Pathological Practice: Black Skin as Site of White Supremacy?

As the introduction makes clear, skin colour transformation through bleaching/lightening and toning is a global, multi-billion-dollar, cross racial/gender/sexuality/age/class pharmaceutical and cosmetics enterprise from which no country is exempt. Why then is it specifically Black women's skins that are problematised with the pathology of 'wanting to be white'? Why is it so very important to mark Black women who bleach as 'enslaved' to white supremacy? Why is it that white women who also bleach their skins are just seen as enhancing their looks, for example, through removing age spots? These questions point us to the need to look at how it is that aesthetic racialisation works silently within the Black Atlantic in which the unmarked white ideal continues to be peddled by cosmetics companies, advertisers and entrepreneurs alike. These questions also make us note that the dictates of Black Nationalism and second-wave Black feminism on mimicking whiteness can as easily be co-opted by those white supremacists who think that the ideal beauty is white and by the medical profession who both then label skin bleachers as pathological.

As a constructed pathological zone of white supremacy, obviously bleached Black skin is further negated by the state drawing on Black Nationalist, second-wave Black feminist and white supremacist ideas of the necessity for 'natural Black skin'. I say 'obviously bleached' here because medicalised 'lightening' and 'toning' conducted in clinics in Harley Street using glutathione intravenous drips, microdermabrasion and laser treatments do not seem to cause dis-ease in the way that skin-bleaching agents do because of what is seen as the minimal physical harm to skin and body caused. This masks the class disparities between 'bleaching' marked as poor, working class and lightening/toning marked as middle/elite class practices. Physical harm from under the counter bleaching agents such as hyper-pigmentation, skin blistering, stretch marks and kidney problems do make skin bleaching an important health concern for Black communities around the world. This problem has been dealt with by different nation states in a number of ways. For example, by public health campaigns such as Jamaica's 'Don't Kill the Skin' (Brown-Glaude 2007), Ghana's 'I Love my Natural Skin Tone—Say No to Bleaching' and Senegal's 'Nuul Kukk—Black is So Beautiful!' These campaigns are all focused on 'loving' the natural Black skin you are in which should not be tampered with. However, they do not look at the underlying reasons for skin lightening practices in societies in which those who are lighter skinned continue to control the economy and political life even in states which are seen as Black and homogeneous (Brown-Glaude 2007; Fritsch 2014; Pierre 2013). The case of Jamaica shows that as such these campaigns are doomed to fail. The UK has been waging a silent war on skin bleaching by being active in the seizure of products that contain the banned substances hydroquinone and mercury by Local Authority Trading Standards Services, while other states have banned bleaching products. For example, this occurred in South Africa in the 1980s when the apartheid regime banned the extremely dangerous level of 12 % hydroquinone in cosmetics and in the early 1990s when the medical profession and the Anti-Apartheid Movement called for a ban on skin-bleaching products (Thomas 2009). The state then sees Black skin and Black bodies as vulnerable and in need of protection as a public health issue and also one that needs law to reinforce the need to end Black women harming their skins. Black skin is thus a matter of the public interest in the UK and elsewhere as Black people must be protected from their own pathological practices because they have imbibed white supremacy. What this does not at all take account of, as intimated above, is the political and libidinal economies of racism and colourism within which darker Black skin is uneasily located within a global market in lightness.

The Global Market in Lightness: Post-feminist Skin and Countering Second-Wave Black Feminism

The political economy of racism within 'post-race' states such as the UK and USA ensures that racial hierarchies are kept in place, 'race' circulates freely as biology and defines our lives even though we all know it is a social construct, and being white ensures privilege and power for those bodies racialised as white (Mills 1997; Yancy 2008). In such a context 'post-race' neoliberal racialisation also means that white and lighter Black skins have more societal value than others as said above. There are also psychic attachments and affective relationalities of Black skin based on Black Nationalist and second-wave feminist politics which as phobic or philic libidinal economy attaches to racialised skin. Indeed, for Frank Wilderson (2010, p. 7):

> libidinal economy functions variously across scales and is as 'objective' as political economy. It is linked not only to forms of attraction, affection, and alliance, but also to aggression, destruction and the violence of lethal consumption… it

> is the whole structure of psychic and emotional life…]something more than but inclusive of or traversed by… a 'structure of feeling'; it is a dispensation of energies, concerns, points of attention, anxieties, pleasures, appetites, revulsions, phobias capable of great mobility and tenacious fixation.

Even though it is material, an organ of the body, we can see from the discussion above on skin and white supremacist, Black Nationalist and second-wave Black feminist ideology that Black skin is part of this libidinal economy as racialised skin structures psychic and emotional life through its political and affective relationalities. Indeed, for Kobena Mercer (1994) skin signifies politically and affectively as does hair in terms of Blackness, specifically in relation to the need for naturalness.

Post-feminism offers us all an opportunity to actively other both this second-wave Black feminist and Black Nationalist skin established as vulnerable even as Black women's skins are centralised in representation through intense ongoing discussion about skin bleaching/lightening/toning and state intervention to save Black skins. There is also continuing media exposure of celebrity African American women's bodies which have also been 'outed' as bleached/lightened/toned at different points in their careers. Beyoncé's stage persona is an example of this as she can be seen to be part of the luxury lifestyle, consumption, bling and hyper-aestheticisation focus on the Black woman's body which are an integral part of hip-hop culture but which time and again returns the body of the lighter-skinned woman to a position of aesthetic prominence. This is in opposition to a post-feminism which does not return to a single standard of beauty (Tasker and Negra 2007) so it could be the case that Black post-feminism encompasses the consumption aspects but illustrates the pervasive normative whiteness of post-feminism's ideology. Black women's bodies then could racialise a post-feminism which is still largely focused on white middle/elite class culture within which Black women's skins are still not valued in accordance with their identifications or Black generated aesthetic standards. That is, a post-feminism in which Black women's skins, their plurality, are annihilated in representations of celebrities chosen by white owned media because we still continue to see the replaying of Beyoncé, Nicki Minaj and Rhianna as what Black women must be like globally in their bleached and hypersexualised modalities.

There is still second-wave Black feminist fight back against this. In a discussion at The New School in New York City entitled 'Are You Still a Slave: Liberating the Black Female Body' the panel, including bell hooks, discussed the politics of representation, 'race', gender, sexuality, 'choice', 'freedom' and feminist politics. As part of this discussion, hooks spoke about people 'bleaching their skin and committing suicide' because they feel there is no place for them. In making this statement as part of a panel on continuing mental slavery in terms of white supremacy, hooks replays the second-wave Black feminist message on Black pathology to a twenty-first-century audience most possibly inured to post-feminism and 'post-race' ideology. This can be claimed because the juxtaposition of skin bleaching and suicide already gives the impression of 'racial suicide' being committed in the act of bleaching. hooks also held forth on Beyoncé's *Time* magazine (2014) cover for *Time*'s '100 Most Influential People' in which she stated that the cover was an example of 'imperialist, white supremacist, racist patriarchal' imaging of the female body and that Beyoncé had colluded in her 'construction as a slave' because it was not a 'liberatory image'. She also called Beyoncé a 'terrorist' especially with regard to the impact on young girls and her playing into the major attack on feminism in US society which has come from visual media, television and videos (Crosley Coker 2014). hooks then clearly wraps the singer's image up with post-feminism in US society in which Beyoncé is part of the dominant standard of beauty and a part of the problem as women are asked to uphold impossible beauty standards.

Beyoncé, whatever we might think of her, is known to have lightened her skin since the days of Destiny's Child and has appeared in public and on some of her album covers visibly much lighter. If we recall, there was also a media storm over her skin being visibly lightened in L'Oreal advertisements and her album covers. Beyoncé has identified herself as a feminist only not of the second-wave Black feminist hooksian position but perhaps more of a third-wave Black (Lee 2010) or hip-hop feminist (Pough 2004). She has final cut approval of every image of herself that appears in the public domain, and she has power over what she wears and of how she is seen because she manages herself. She invests power in her skin as much as in what she chooses to wear so she has taken control of that image that hooks calls 'child-like' and thrown it back as a challenge to the magazine's audience as she stares them down. No sexual appeal then, no demure, enticing smile, no sign of vulnerability, not slave but mistress of all who look her in the eyes as affect flows from image to viewer.

Post-feminist Blackness Does Not Mean Skin's Political Vulnerability: Critiquing Pigmentocracy

Staying with Beyoncé as hooks' dupe of post-feminism's ideology and white supremacy's slave might be quite apposite here as we move to looking at critiquing pigmentocracy and skin's political vulnerability. In the song *Pretty Hurts* (2014), Beyoncé critiques beauty standards with her lyrics: 'Perfection is the disease of our nation. Try to fix something but you can't fix what you can't see. It's the soul that needs the surgery'. The music video shows contestants in a beauty pageant eating cotton wool balls and throwing up to remain slim, rubbing petroleum jelly on their teeth, buffing and using cream on their skins, as well as exercising interminably to attain the perfection that is needed because they are slaves to a beauty standard inculcated into them by their parents; indeed, 'mama says it's not what's in your head that counts', just only the surface, the skin. Interestingly, Miss Third Ward (Beyoncé) did not win the pageant, but a much lighter-skinned, light blonde-haired woman did as Beyoncé looks on with an unvoiced question 'why her and not me—is she better?' One wonders if 'Miss Third Ward' was a play on 'Miss Third World' and thereby itself a critique of the existing standards of light/white beauty within international beauty pageants such as *Miss Universe* and *Miss World*. To coincide with her music video, the singer started a website '#What is Pretty?' and asked fans to submit their beauty definitions. In both of these actions, Beyoncé seems to push against existing beauty standards in which the lightest skinned and those women who possess physical features racialised as white still remain at the top of the beauty hierarchy within the USA (Hunter 2005). Her lyrics and her website are provocations on the continuing pigmentocracy in the USA if not the world within which she is a global celebrity.

Beyoncé reiterates a Black Nationalist and second-wave Black feminist position without occupying either of those political spaces overtly. She is not a second-wave Black feminist still encased in the necessity for Black women's respectability in order to ensure uplift, but one of Shayne Lee's (2010) 'sexual revolutionaries'. As a third-wave Black feminist within the world of hip-hop, she disassociates herself from the straight-jacket of second-wave and Nationalist Black body politics which insists on 'naturalness'. So for her as we see from her own lightening practices, 'natural' Black skin does not mean untouched by lightening chemicals, processes, make-up or re-touching as there is a positive embrace of beauty culture. Within that embrace of lightening culture as exemplified in the face and body of Trinidadian US star Nicki Minaj, we see a re-versioning of 'natural' to be that which is also purchased and read as enhancement through involvement in the market in aesthetics and body transformation in which the body and the money spent on it are a necessary part of celebrity status.

The standard Black and white media, including YouTube, position on Black celebrities who bleach is to 'out' them through before and after photographs allied with descriptions of them as people with psychological problems who suffer from self-hate and want to be white or, in the case of multi-millionaire rapper Lil' Kim, to be Asian/white. To hate one's own skin is indeed a very serious affliction and one which I do not want to minimise as problematic in any way. What interests me about this hate though is that we never hear about hating to be 'white' skinned. We do not even hear about this in the curious 2015 case of that Black passer, Rachel Dolezal, who stated that she does not put on 'blackface' as a performance but she identifies as Black and called on trans metaphors to talk about feeling like a Black person trapped in a white body.

What would happen if we turned the perspective on self-hate on its head and instead saw skin bleaching/lightening/toning as also giving us the possibility to critique the political and libidinal economies of the twenty-first century's continuing pigmentocracy (Tate 2016)? Going back to Beyoncé's *Pretty Hurts* illustrates this critique as the lighter-skinned, blonder-haired and thinner woman wins the pageant and we are told 'it's the soul that needs the surgery'. I would like here to read 'soul' both as related to the nation and its aesthetic preferences and hierarchies as well as the self. It is the communal and individual soul that needs the surgery to begin to see that it is not perfected embodiment including lighter skin that is essential to a woman. This is a state of affairs in which mothers and significant other women participate in order to reproduce societal beauty regimes and body norms as they relate Black women's selves solely to their bodies and not their minds or intellect. This is the norm that needs to be surgically removed alongside the pervasive beauty ideology of the 'nearer to white the better' both of which asks that as Black women we try to fix something which we cannot see but which has been labelled as problematic.

It is this wilful not seeing that is perhaps the moment which enables critique of twenty-first-century pigmentocracy through skin bleaching. If it is indeed global white supremacy which drives the practice as some would say (Blay 2011; Hunter 2011; Glenn 2008), then skin bleaching points to the persistence of this ideology as well as Black skin resistance to it. Black women who bleach/lighten/or tone do that for a variety of reasons, none of which relate to 'wanting to be white' (Charles 2009; Hope 2011; Brown-Glaude 2007; Tate 2009, 2016). As women lighten, they declare their awareness of the political and libidinal economies of racialised skin shade within which they find themselves in societies not of their own making. As they bleach, they refuse the vulnerability of Black skin by showing instead its ability to change and also as a by-product that there is no such thing as natural Black skin or one natural Black shade for that matter. They use what could be called a 'bad' object of colonialism/(post-)colonialism as a 'good' object to racialise post-feminism's engagement in choice, hyper-aestheticisation and consumption and to highlight that skin colour emerges through aesthetic labour. The lightening technologies and products such as intravenous glutathione as well as *Nadinola* bleaching cream used by Black women today have transracial reach as they are used by white women as well. In fact, the history of the development of make-up and beauty culture in the West has largely been about 'white face' women produced through bleaching and make-up (Dyer 1997; Poietivin 2011; Roberts 2014). So it is white women who want to be white after all—notwithstanding Dolezal—and in fact for whom there is a necessity to be white so as to preserve white supremacy (Tate 2016).

Conclusion

Perhaps it is time to consign the founding aesthetic myth of racism that Black women want to be white to the dustbin of history as all indications show that *some* Black women want to be lighter Black shades and not mimic white ones (Tate 2009, 2016). What this means is that Black skin's political vulnerability relates to the conversation which needs to be had within Black communities about the continuation of colourism, the necessity to continue to be anti-racists within a world of 'post-race' sensibilities which deny neoliberal racialisation, as well the removal of the ethical obligation not to bleach as a pre-requisite for Black respectable womanhood.

References

Anzieu, D. (1989). *The Skin Ego: A Psychoanalytic Approach to the Self.* New Haven: Yale University Press.

Blay, Y. A. (2011). Skin Bleaching and Global White Supremacy: By Way of Introduction. *Journal of Pan African Studies, 4*(4), 4–46.

Bonilla-Silva, E. (2012). The Invisible Weight of Whiteness: The Racial Grammar for Everyday Life in America. *Ethnic and Racial Studies, 35*(2), 173–194.

Brown-Glaude, W. (2007). The Fact of Blackness? The Bleached Body in Contemporary Jamaica. *Small Axe, 11*(3), 34–51.

Charles, C. A. D. (2009). Liberating Skin Bleachers: From Mental Pathology to Complex Personhood. *JENdA: A Journal of Culture and African Women Studies*, 14: online.

Crosley Coker, H. (2014). What Bell Hooks Really Meant When She Calles Beyoncé A 'Terrorist'. *Jezebel.* [Online] Retrieved from http://jezebel.com/what-bell-hooks-really-means-when-she-calls-beyonce-a-t-1573991834

Derrida, J. (1993). Le Toucher. Touch/To Touch Him. *Paragraph: The Journal of the Modern Critical Thought Group, 16*(2), 122–157.

Duke, B., & Channsin Berry, D. (2012). *Dark Girls.* [film] Image Entertainment: United States.

Dyer, R. (1997). *White: Essays on Race and Culture.* London: Routledge.

Fanon, F. (1986). *Black Skin White Masks.* London: Pluto.

Fritsch, K. (2014). 'Trans-Skin': Analyzing the Practice of Skin Bleaching Among Middle-Class Women in Dar es Salaam, *Ethnicities*, online: 1–22.

Gill, R., & Scharff, C. (2011). Introduction. In R. Gill & C. Scharff (Eds.), *New Femininities: Postfeminism, Neoliberalism and Subjectivity* (pp. 1–19). Palgrave Macmillan: Basingstoke.

Glenn, E. N. (2008). Yearning for Whiteness: Transnational Circuits in the Marketing and Consumption of Skin Lighteners. *Gender and Society, 22*(3), 281–302.

Herring, C., Keith, V., & Horton, D. H. (2004). *Skin Deep: How Race and Complexion Matter in the 'Color-Blind' Era*. Chicago: University of Illinois Press.

hooks, b. (2014). *Talking Back: Thinking Feminist, Thinking Black*. London: Routledge.

Hope, D. (2011). From Browning to Cake Soap: Popular Debates on Skin Bleaching in the Jamaican Dancehall. *Journal of Pan African Studies, 4*(4), 165–194.

Hunter, M. (2005). *Race, Gender and the Politics of Skin Tone*. London: Routledge.

Hunter, M. L. (2011). Buying Racial Capital: Skin Bleaching and Cosmetic Surgery in a Globalized World. *Journal of Pan African Studies, 4*(4), 142–164.

Lee, S. (2010). *Erotic Revolutionaries: Black Women, Sexuality and Popular Culture*. New York: Hamilton Books.

Mercer, K. (1994). *Welcome to the Jungle: New Directions in Black Cultural Studies*. Abingdon: Routledge.

Mills, C. (1997). *The Racial Contract*. Ithaca, NY: Cornell University Press.

Neilson, S. (2014). Why Are Women Still Dying to Be White? *IOL News*. [Online] Retrieved from http://www.iol.co.za/lifestyle/style/fashion/why-are-women-still-dying-to-be-white-1705800

Pierre, J. (2013). *The Predicament of Blackness: Postcolonial Ghana and the Politics of Race*. Chicago: Chicago University Press.

Poietivin, K. (2011). Inventing Whiteness: Cosmetics, Race and Women in Early Modern England. *Journal of Early Modern Cultural Studies, 11*(1), 59–89.

Pough, G. (2004). *Check It While I Wreck It: Black Womanhood, Hip-Hop Culture and the Public Sphere*. Lebanon, New Hampshire: Northeastern University Press.

Roberts, B. (2014). *Pageants, Parlors and Pretty Women: Race and Beauty in the Twentieth Century South*. Chapel Hill: The University of North Carolina Press.

Sharpley-Whiting, T. D. (2007). *Pimps Up, Hos Down: Hip Hop's Hold on Young Black Women*. New York: New York University Press.

Tasker, Y., & Negra, D. (2007). *Interrogating Feminism: Gender and the Politics of Popular Culture*. Durham: Duke University Press.

Tate, S. A. (2009). *Black Beauty: Aesthetics, Stylization Politics*. Aldershot: Ashgate.

Tate, S. A. (2016). *Skin Bleaching in Black Atlantic Zones: Shade Shifters*. Basingstoke: Palgrave Macmillan.

Taylor, P. C. (2000). Malcolm's Conk and Danto's Colors, or: Four Logical Petitions Concerning Race, Beauty and Aesthetics. In P. Zeglin Brand (Ed.), *Beauty Matters* (pp. 57–64). Bloomington, Indiana: Indiana University Press.

Thomas, L. (2009). Skin Lighteners in South Africa: Transnational Entanglements and Technologies of the Self. In E. N. Glenn (Ed.), *Shades of Difference: Why Skin Color Matters* (pp. 188–210). Palo Alto, CA: Stanford University Press.

Weinbaum, A. E., Thomas, L. M., Ramamurthy, P., Poiger, U. G., Dong, M. Y., & Barlow, T. E. (2008). The Modern Girl Around the World: Cosmetics Advertising and the Politics of Race and Style. In *The Modern Girl Around the World: Consumption, Modernity, Globalization* (pp. 25–54). Durham: Duke University Press.

Wilderson III, F. (2010). *Red, White and Black: Cinema and the Structure of US Antagonisms*. Durham: Duke University Press.

Yancy, G. (2008). *Black Bodies, White Gazes: The Continuing Significance of Race*. Lanham: Rowman and Littlefield.

12

'Being a Better #Freelancer': Gendered and Racialised Aesthetic Labour on Online Freelance Marketplaces

Monika Sengul-Jones

Introduction

In 2011, after some success working on the online freelance marketplace oDesk, a twenty-something woman living in a southwestern city in the USA uploaded a fan video to her YouTube channel about her experiences. Recorded in her bright suburban kitchen, the young woman looks straight into the camera to casually describe to a presumed audience of other novice freelancers the steps necessary to 'being a better #freelancer'. But only four years later, in early 2015, by her own evaluation my informant had decidedly less confidence in online marketplaces as a conduit to her financial or personal freedom. In fact, she was tired and had stopped freelancing altogether.

M. Sengul-Jones (✉)
Department of Communication and Science Studies Program, University of California, San Diego, CA, USA

Department of Communication, University of Washington, Seattle, WA, USA

A.S. Elias et al. (eds.), *Aesthetic Labour*,
DOI 10.1057/978-1-137-47765-1_12

I begin by describing her experience to highlight this chapter's focus: a discussion of the relationship of online freelance marketplaces—which are themselves nested within a commercial internet economy—to the experiences of novice freelance writers using them, and together how this plays a role in producing the *aesthetics* of online freelancing. My chapter is part of a wider auto-ethnographic study concerned with gender and forms of digitally mediated writing work. This piece draws on interviews with six freelance writers who self-identify as women who have had success using US online freelance marketplaces. Four reside in the USA, one in Central Europe, and one in India. All reported native fluency in English.[1] I focus on women's experiences in part because in North America, freelance writing work is largely women's work. The 'Freelance Industry Report 2012' estimates that 71 per cent of freelancers in the USA identify as women between the ages of 30 and 50 (Gandia 2012). While research on journalism in the USA shows that though employment in media organisations remains male-dominated, the reverse is true for freelance journalists and editors, whose ranks are mainly women (McKercher 2009).

In this way, my chapter contributes to empirical research about how economic restructuring engenders precarious working conditions and affects the autonomy of cultural and information technology (IT) workers on a global stage (Cohen 2012; Gill 2009; Gregg 2011; Hesmondhalgh 2007; Hesmondhalgh and Baker 2010; Huws 2010; McRobbie 1998; Neff 2007; Neff 2012). Existing research foregrounds the role of 'work-*style*' (Deuze 2007; Gregg 2011)—cultural work is 'cool'—to the reproduction of insecure, precarious, and 'risky' working conditions (Gill 2002; Neff et al. 2005). As I will explain, I am concerned with naming the ways that freelancing online contributes to *subject formation*—or, the way that freelancers identify with, and find meaningful, the structures of power they are embedded within. I will examine two underexplored features of online freelancing, notably the way in which profiles and client feedback become mechanisms of disciplinary power.

[1] I do not ask my informants about their citizenship. I chose not to use pseudonyms for my informants or to relay many demographic details in order to avoid inadvertently classifying them to my readers according to my own categories. Instead, I seek to show how classifications about them emerged as a part of their experience using marketplaces online.

My informants describe choosing to freelance online because the workstyle offers them the opportunity to proactively manage uniquely difficult life circumstances—where divorce, taxing work environments, layoffs, lack of family/community support, or geographic marginalisation often are mixed together, and freelancing is described as an attractive alternative to unemployment, under-employment, or a toxic corporate workplace. In this chapter I discuss how this is facilitated, but also at what cost.

'Work Differently': The Rise of Online Freelance Marketplaces in the US Internet Industry

Following the 2008 financial crisis in the USA, online freelance marketplaces such as oDesk have been celebrated as new conduits to income, particularly for women and the underemployed (Abate 2009; Fost 2009; *Palm Springs Examiner* 2012; Oakland Examiner 2012; Hsu 2014; Komando 2010; Kowarski 2011; Shellenbarger 2008). Online staffing marketplace platforms such as Elance and oDesk (which merged in 2013 and rebranded as Upwork in 2015) are examples of US 'on-demand' or 'service economy' companies that sell convenience and a flexible workstyle as the outcome of their software.[2] While software companies have made headlines in the USA, online marketplaces account for less than 1 per cent of total spending in the global marketplace for contingent, temporary, outsourced, and contract labour (Karpie 2013). In this way, 'on-demand' software companies can be understood as drawing increased attention to debates about worker flexibility, in addition to finding new ways to facilitate existing trends in the global economy.[3]

---

[2] Networked 'on-demand' marketplace technology companies in the USA include Amazon's Mechanical Turk (for cognitive piecework), Uber (freelance taxi drivers), freelancer.com ('knowledge' work), and TaskRabbit (service-related domestic tasks). Many require a US social security number to work, including Amazon's Mechanical Turk; Elance-oDesk-Upwork do not. On Elance more than twenty thousand freelancers are registered from over twenty-five countries.

[3] These companies define themselves as neutral software companies facilitating peer-to-peer connections, not as companies with a responsibility to the workers as employees (Isaac and Singer

Online marketplaces are also important sites for feminist research on gendered and racialised forms of self-presentation for work. Marketplaces technically and visually resemble other social media platforms, including those that are not explicitly designed for getting paid work. But freelancers using marketplaces are aware that their profiles are, or may be, cross-referenced in the broader media ecosystem. The networked 'super public' (Boyd 2006) where self-presentation takes place suggests that the gendered discursive frames shaping self-presentation online will be relevant to my informants' experiences. In this arena, research on women and girls representing themselves in a 'post-feminist' mediated context have shown that the online media ecosystem pressures women, particularly young women, to present themselves in 'sexy' ways or through identification with formations of femininity (Ringrose 2013, p. 101) Meanwhile, research on selfies (and their pathologisation) indicates that self-representations (be they visual or textual, but especially the visual) in a networked social circuit are subject to social policing and surveillance, particularly for women and people of colour (Senft and Baym 2015, p. 1592). As doxxing directed at users who identify as women and feminists online attests, deviation from social norms around appropriate displays of femininity as 'empowering' sexualisation (see Gill 2008) can be punishing—including threats of mass violence, rape, and death (Citron 2014). In other words, existing research on gender and self-presentation online suggests that novice freelancers looking for work online are situated within a minefield of existing, and complicated, discursive frames about appropriate displays of self.

Yet online marketplaces are explicitly designed to facilitate paid writing work—they are not sites of unpaid labour veiled in discourses of sociality or pleasure. This fact is what often drew my informants to the sites in the first place; all my informants had heartfelt, if not even romantic, justifications for pursuing freelance writing work as a professional project, including the dignity that a writerly life confers upon writers and the

2015). 'Defendants hold themselves out as nothing more than a neutral technological platform, designed simply to enable drivers and passengers to transact the business of transportation', the California Labour Commissioner's Office wrote about Uber as quoted in an article for the *New York Times*. 'The reality, however, is that defendants are involved in every aspect of the operation' (Isaac and Singer 2015).

aim of doing meaningful intellectual work to earn a living. But on sites specifically designed to facilitate paid work, freelancers face additional constraints. Feminist research on gender and office workplaces suggests that women face contradictory messages about being 'professional', where signs of femininity are often devalued. Sociological research on the role of race, gender, motherhood, and disability in hiring decisions demonstrates that these discursively constructed subject positions are very real liabilities. Identifying as non-white, non-male, non-able bodied, or a mother introduces discriminatory consequences including lower call backs to job applicants, lower wages, and lack of promotion (Ameri et al. 2015; Bertrand and Mullainathan 2004; Correll et al. 2007). Researchers have theorised that women manage these pressures at the level of the body, by wearing make-up (Dellinger and Williams 1997) and shopping for and wearing feminine, but conservative, clothing (Trethewey 1999).

In this chapter I contribute to this literature with a new focus on freelancers working online. I analyse online and interview data to discuss how novice women freelance writers working on US online marketplaces manage the contradictory imperatives about appropriate displays of femininity, racial identity, and professionalism in an online mediated 'super public' (Boyd 2006) where the impulse is to self-broadcast. There are many ways to enter into such analysis. My chapter focuses on freelancers' reported interactions using two technical features typical to online marketplaces: the profile page and the mechanisms to receive client feedback. My analysis is material-discursive (Alaimo and Hekman 2008): I foreground how these mechanisms work and how women use them—how they are made real. I posit that reports of successes among my informants are achieved due to the aesthetic 'body-work' they do in order to *make* the mechanisms *work*. My chapter provides empirical evidence for the Foucauldian concept of self-disciplining as 'body-work' that the editors of this collection explain is extending into, and shaping, formations of labour in the early twenty-first century. Freelance online marketplaces are a space where aesthetic 'body-work' is localised in a very specific way. When the profile and client feedback mechanisms are understood as disciplinary technologies, it becomes clear how the aesthetic of freelancing as a conduit to self-improvement relies on reinscribing gendered and racialised subject positions among novice women writers. In the next two sections, I will describe how freelancers use the profile page and client feedback mechanisms and how these constitute disciplinary technologies elicit 'body-work'.

'I Guess It Looks Like Me': Discipline, Apology, and Making the Online Profile

On marketplaces, the profile is the technical portal to the freelancer. An assembled visual display of freelancers' skills, keywords, pay rate, photo, portfolio, client feedback, hours worked, skill test results, name authenticity, contact options, and more, the profile is the site for career description and identity verification. The profile is also a technology that disciplines the freelancer into a gendered, neoliberal subject position. Indeed, a profile is not an unusual feature on the social web. But given the public nature and searchability of freelancers' profiles, I argue this is a space where freelancers are policed according to discursive norms about gender and race. Some forms of self-presentation are more appropriate for freelancing than others, a benchmark that is measured by payments and call backs. When freelancers decide they are failing to meet these norms, they proceed with caution and retreat to apology, holding themselves responsible. Meanwhile, they make the profiles *work* by doing their best to meet the implicit norms.

In describing their experiences using marketplace platforms, my informants reported that the labour of profile maintenance, along with writing proposals and setting prices, is a central part of being a freelancer.[4] One informant described an underdeveloped profile as the mark of an amateur—'it takes work to do this', she said. Another described browsing others' profiles and reading inspirational articles about successful freelancers, to find models of effective self-presentation, their reports echo research by digital media scholars on reputation building as being a large

[4] While it is not in the scope of this paper to analyse the processes that go into writing proposals or setting prices and pay rates, I do not intend to minimise their importance to my informants. Rather, meaningfully unpacking these processes would require a second chapter.

part of the ongoing aesthetic labour required to manage a digital profile (see Abidin 2014).

However, while they took pleasure in the fact that freelancing as a career move was a conduit to a new life, my informants were often apologetic when describing their profiles. 'I don't do enough' was a common refrain, alongside comments such as: 'I should also be blogging'; 'Yeah, I should also tweet'; 'I need to really update my website'; 'They say you need to feed your audience, I am not feeding them enough'. But more than apologising for their lack of time, my informants were apologetic about their choices in self-presentation, which gave them anxiety. 'I should have a professional photo taken', said one. 'Mine isn't very good', said another, 'but I guess it looks like me'. 'I worried about showing my face in my profile', said a third, who was concerned about an ex-partner finding her online. She posted a photo of her face half hidden behind a book. She also wanted to use a pseudonym and was frustrated when she could not because of site rules about name verifiability through governmental identification checks. A fourth joked that in the amount of time she spent dressing for and editing her profile photo: 'I could have learned a new skill'. A fifth informant used a carefully stylised selfie, which she had modified using photo-editing software, to give a message of youthfulness and demonstrate her social media savvy. This aesthetic of freelancing evokes a positive, career-building, style that requires freelancers to labour in order to look the part, and to downplay any liabilities they might have—including fears of stalking or a sense that their physical appearance is less than ideal.

The imperative to post photographs is not surprising given the self-centred visual culture of social media (Marwick 2013). But for job seekers in the USA, the advice is unusual. In general, human resource departments instruct prospective employees *not* to share personal data, including photographs. Title VII of the 1964 Civil Rights Act prohibits discrimination by employers against employees, including potential employees, on the basis of race, gender, religion, nationality, and other identity categories. But freelancers, as independent contractors, do not qualify for legal protection under Title VII. As a result, the pressure to post photos of themselves on their profile pages may be the consequence of an internet culture that values images as vehicles for cultural messages about aptitude, race, class, age, and intelligence, among other cultural narratives.

The fact that my interviewees said they were 'not doing enough' and apologised for not meeting implicit standards could be interpreted as resistance to the imperative to broadcast or brand themselves online. My informants were self-aware, and describe using social media with caution. But a closer reading showcases how their response is a subtle reinforcement of a gendered subject position. Apologising for 'not doing enough' may challenge the aesthetic of freelancing that prioritises constantly sharing images of oneself, but their apologies also mark the double-bind women experience looking for work while a woman online—and their resistance to posting is also a way of avoiding the pitfalls of oversharing or losing work for not being seen as an ideal worker. Apologising is a linguistic act that reproduces socially marginal subject positions (see Lakoff 1973).

For instance, one of my informants suggested that women 'who share too much' online are responsible for losing jobs or being stereotyped: 'Did you hear about the woman who was fired from her job for a tweet that people misunderstood? You have to be careful that *everything* you do is professional'. I was surprised by this comment, as this freelancer keeps her Facebook and Twitter profiles public, actively posts, in addition to maintaining two marketplace profiles. She also shares articles she writes in the first-person, crafting her stories out of her personal experiences. But I believe that her concerns, and choice to write in the first person, are not in contradiction. Rather they index the opaque set of discourses framing what a 'professional freelancer', and 'woman writer', should look like online. There's a certain banality to having photos of oneself online. It is not only expected, but can be a source of affirmation and conduit to recognition and more work. At the same time, women who find themselves harassed or out of work are often the first to be blamed for causing their own misfortune, for not conforming to the most appropriate, authentic, or ingenious performances of femininity. These mixed messages are one of a host of paradoxes typifying freelancing as a space for self-invention, and the aesthetic labours required to sustain this work.

Self-Subordination and Shadowy Work: Client Feedback and Racialised Erasures

One crucial mechanism to getting paid, and rehired, is client feedback. Stars, grades, endorsements, and surveillance track records are all mechanisms marketplaces implement to facilitate a trust among users. In this section, I will describe how client feedback as a technical tool guaranteeing freelancer legitimacy functions when freelancers subordinate themselves to the requests of clients, illustrating the ways that discursive frames about femininity and race work through the commercial marketplace interfaces.

I asked my interviewees about their first successful work experiences online. Most described taking on low paid, odd jobs for individuals or small businesses. In the course of completing these jobs, there were occasions where they confronted sexist or discriminatory demands. Most expressed awareness that the demands of a project may change as it progresses, but sometimes the adjustments mandated they adjust their expectations of integrity. For instance, a freelance writer who lives in India was commissioned by a client in the USA to write a series of blog posts about golf. She reviewed the blog's existing page and presumed she would write the posts under her own name and use her own photo. Enthusiastic about adding this series of posts to her portfolio, she wrote them up but was then surprised when it came time to publish:

> They wanted a white woman's photo and name, believing that an American audience wouldn't want to know what an Indian had to say about golf. And they admitted that without knowing where I was from, it wasn't apparent from my writing that I wasn't American.

A stock photo and fake name would hide her Indianness, but the request was emotionally taxing. She believed the quality of her writing should transcend national origins. 'It wasn't apparent from my writing that I wasn't American', she repeated. Yet in order to receive compensation and maintain a positive relationship with the client, she was tasked with masking complex, asymmetrical global labour configurations and subordinating her identity to the client's vision of appropriate figures of authority in golf. Technologies in place for feedback and compensation required she make these concessions invisibly. Meanwhile, the freelancer who represented herself with a 'selfie' was also asked to mask her identity:

> Oh my goodness, it was so odd. The only thing he wanted me to do was go on dating websites and write messages to women that I found were interesting. This was all based on his tastes that he had told me … It was my first gig, and I needed the feedback. It wasn't paid well, but he gave me excellent feedback … I would message a lot of women. You know, guys have to do a lot of work in order to get a bite.

This freelancer had accepted her first job. Her commitment was for a month. She did the work because she wanted a good review and payment.

Another freelancer describes managing a sexist client using deference. He would write inappropriate comments directed both at her and women in general. She wanted to keep him placated until she was paid and got her review, so she would walk around her living room then write 'snarky comments' in a document and then 'rewrite them so they address the same issue but without the snark'. She described her technique:

> I was raised in a house where we had lots of ways of saying things directly but from behind the bush. I used to be amazing at this indirection. I lost the neck, so to speak, as I got older. Now, I'm learning I can still be very polite if I have time to write it out.

Once paid, she raised her rates in order 'to price myself out of working with him'. Their experiences illustrate how client feedback functions as a disciplinary device, shaping how freelancers make sense of their subject positions through racialised and gendered erasures.

Surveillance as a form of client feedback also serves as a disciplinary device—one of a range of new modes of worker control. Not all my research participants disliked surveillance. In fact, one of my informants, whom I introduced in the beginning of the chapter, described her appreciation for a neutral surveillance in her YouTube video about freelancing:

> So, when you're logged in, oDesk takes pictures of you 'on the clock'. It's really cool ... and it's convenient. Just a way to guarantee [to the hiring user] that you're working. That's one of my most favorite things about oDesk.

She said she prefers remote, private surveillance to other forms of client engagement, which can be disruptive, too public, or too intimate. For her, the technology of surveillance is also a conduit of autonomy.

In each of these examples, mechanisms facilitating client feedback also serve as disciplinary technologies. These are touchstones marking the material-discursive ways novice women writers make themselves into online freelancers. When they make the technologies 'work'—through the 'body-work' of self-monitoring, self-policing, deference, and appreciation of surveillance—freelancing becomes their conduit to a different, and new, life. 'My freelance career would not have happened prior to the internet', said one informant who used Elance for two years. But there are costs. Achieving the aesthetic of freelancing is exhausting—it requires subjects to manage paradoxes that refuse easy answers. The costs are also social: the 'body-work' of individual women that makes discourses about professional performance responsibility real reinforces cultural narratives about online marketplaces as neutral technologies, naturalising deviance from implicit norms as a problem that individuals are responsible for solving.

Concluding Remarks

My informants reported success in transforming their working lives. I wish to applaud these changes as real and worthwhile. Yet their successes do not occur in isolation, nor are they absent of influence from discourses about race and gender in the ways they pertain to both self-presentation and doing freelance paid work online. As I have described, when freelancers craft professional identities as writers online they are beholden to multiple, paradoxical constraints in ways that are distinct from other online economies of sociality, celebrity, or fame. My chapter offers suggestive analysis about how freelancers consider, and manage, paradoxical messages about appropriate demonstrations of professional self-presentation online. I describe how their 'body-work' makes the profile and client feedback work for them.

As a researcher concerned with naming the ways that freelancing online contributes to *subject formation*—or, the way that freelancers identify with, and find meaningful, the structures of power they are embedded within—this chapter brings to light the ways that online freelancers who do not identify as white males manage contradictory imperatives about appropriate displays of gender or racial identity and professionalism at the level of the body. Importantly, this chapter discusses how the tools that help freelancers lead a different life and be a better #freelancer—such as bootstrapping an online profile, accepting self-erasure, or preferring a surveillance video camera to other forms of monitoring—may relieve some of life's pressures at the expense of introducing new stresses, most of which are, ironically, invisible in a hyper-visible networked media system.

Acknowledgements I thank my informants for their time and honesty. I am also grateful for guidance and feedback, throughout my research and in developing this book chapter, from Lisa Cartwright, Allaine Cerwonka, Bridget Conor, Laurel Friedman, Eva Fodor, Kirsten Foot, Rosalind Gill, Dan Hallin, Lilly Irani, Amanda Menking, Lisa Nakamura, Lucy Suchman, Cristina Visperas, and Emily York. Special thanks to the editors, Ana Sofia Lemos De Carvalho Elias, Rosalind Gill, and Christina Scharff for the invitation and thoughtful and supportive editorial work.

References

Abate, T. (2009). Web-Based Hiring Halls Filling Workforce Gaps. *San Francisco Chronicle*. [Online] Retrieved from http://infoweb.newsbank.com/resources/doc/nb/news/126399790BA260D8?p=AWNB

Abidin, C. (2014). Instagram: A Repository of Taste, a Brimming Marketplace, a War of Eyeballs. In *Mobile Media Making in an Age of Smartphones* (pp. 119–128). Palgrave Macmillan: Basingstoke.

Alaimo, S., & Hekman, S. J. (Eds.). (2008). *Material Feminisms*. Bloomington, IN: Indiana University Press.

Ameri M., Schur, L., Adya, M., Bentley, S., McKay, P., & Kruse, D. (2015). The Disability Employment Puzzle: A Field Experiment on Employer Hiring Behavior. Cambridge, MA: National Bureau of Economic Research. [Online] Retrieved from http://www.nber.org/papers/w21560.pdf

Bertrand, M., & Mullainathan, S. (2004). Are Emily and Greg More Employable than Lakisha and Jamal? A field Experiment on Labour Market Discrimination. *American Economic Review, 94*(4), 991–1013.

Boyd, D. (2006). Super Publics. *Aporia*. [Online] Retrieved from http://www.zephoria.org/thoughts/archives/2006/03/22/super_publics.html

Citron, D. (2014). *Hate Crimes in Cyberspace*. Cambridge, MA: Harvard University Press.

Cohen, N. S. (2012). Cultural Work as a Site of Struggle: Freelancers and Exploitation. *tripleC*, 10(2): 141–155.

Correll, S. J., Benard, B., & Paik, I. (2007). Getting a Job: Is There a Motherhood Penalty? *American Journal of Sociology, 112*(5), 1297–1339.

Dellinger, K., & Williams, C. L. (1997). Make up at Work: Negotiating Appearance Rules in the Workplace. *Gender & Society, 11*(2), 151–177.

Deuze, M. (2007). *Media Work*. Cambridge: Polity.

Fost, D. (2009). In Hard Times, Freelancers Turn to the Web. *New York Times*. [Online] Retrieved from http://www.nytimes.com/2009/03/13/business/smallbusiness/13freelance.html?pagewanted=all&_r=0

Gandia, E. (2012). Freelancer Industry Report. *International Freelancers Academy*. [Online] Retrieved from http://www.internationalfreelancersday.com/2012report/

Gill, R. (2002). Cool, Creative and Egalitarian? Exploring Gender in Project-Based New Media Work in Europe. *Information, Communication & Society, 5*(1), 70–89.

Gill, R. (2008). Empowerment/Sexism: Figuring Female Sexual Agency in Contemporary Advertising. *Feminism & Psychology, 18*(1), 35–60.

Gill, R. (2009). Creative Biographies in New Media: Social Innovation in Web Work. In A. C. Pratt & P. Jeffcutt (Eds.), *Creativity, Innovation and the Culture Economy* (pp. 161–175). New York: Routledge.

Gregg, M. (2011). *Work's Intimacy*. Cambridge: Polity.

Hesmondhalgh, D. (2007). *The Cultural Industries* (second ed.). London: Sage.

Hesmondhalgh, D., & Baker, S. (2010). 'A Very Complicated Version Of Freedom': Conditions and Experiences of Creative labour in Three Cultural Industries. *Poetics, 38*(4), 5–20.

Hsu, T. (2014). Freelance Workers a Growing Segment of California Economy. *L.A. Times*. [Online] Retrieved from http://www.latimes.com/business/la-fi-contract-economy-20140803-story.html#page=1

Huws, U. (2010). Expression and Expropriation: The Dialectics of Autonomy and Control in Creative Labour. *Ephemera: Theory & Politics in Organization, 10*(3/4), 504–521.

Isaac, M., & Singer, N. (2015). California Says Uber Driver is Employee, Not a Contractor. *New York Times*. [Online] Retrieved from http://www.nytimes.com/2015/06/18/business/uber-contests-california-labour-ruling-that-says-drivers-should-be-employees.html?_r=0

Karpie, A. (2013). oDesk and Elance Merger: The Next Era of Online Staffing Begins. *Staffing Industry*. [Online] Retrieved from http://www.staffingindustry.com/site/Research-Publications/Blogs/Andrew-Karpie-s-Blog/oDesk-and-Elance-Merger-The-Next-Era-of-Online-Staffing-Begins

Komando, K. (2010). Find Legitimate Work-from-Home Opportunities Online. *USA Today*. [Online] Retrieved from http://infoweb.newsbank.com/resources/doc/nb/news/12E6AD0E85FB5B58?p=AWNB

Kowarski, I. (2011). Freelance Jobs: Half of all New Jobs in Recovery. *Christian Science Monitor*. [Online] Retrieved from http://www.csmonitor.com/Business/2011/0613/Freelance-jobs-Half-of-all-new-jobs-in-recovery.

Lakoff, R. (1973). Language and Woman's Place. *Language in Society, 2*(1), 45–80.

Marwick, A. (2013). *Status Update: Celebrity, Publicity, and Branding in the Social Media Age*. New Haven: Yale University Press.

McKercher, C. (2009). Writing on the Margins: Precarity and the Freelance Journalist. *Feminist Media Studies, 3*(9), 370–374.

McRobbie, A. (1998). *British Fashion Design: Rag Trade or Image Industry?* London: Routledge.

Neff, G. (2007). The Lure of Risk: Surviving and Welcoming Uncertainty in the New Economy. In J. Amman, G. Neff, & T. Carpenter (Eds.), *Surviving the New Economy* (pp. 33–46). Boulder, CO: Paradigm Publishers.

Neff, G. (2012). *Venture Labour: Work and the Burden of Risk in Innovative Industries*. Cambridge, Mass: MIT Press.

Neff, G., Wissinger, E., & Zukin, S. (2005). Entrepreneurial Labour Among Cultural Producers: 'Cool' Jobs in 'Hot' Industries. *Social Semiotics, 15*(3), 307–334.

Oakland Examiner. (2012December, 31). Things to Do While Seeking Employment. [video] *Oakland Examiner*.

Palm Springs Examiner. (2012, December 27). How Moms Are Making Extra Income by Working from Home. *Palm Springs Examiner*.

Ringrose, J. (2013). Are You Sexy, Flirty, or a Slut? Exploring 'Sexualization' and How Teen Girls Perform/Negotiate Digital Sexual Identity on Social Networking Sites. In R. Gill & C. Scharff (Eds.), *New Femininities: Postfeminism, Neoliberalism, and Subjectivity* (pp. 99–116). Basingstoke: Palgrave.

Senft, T., & Baym, N. K. (2015). What Does the Selfie Say? Investigating a Global Phenomenon. *International Journal of Communication, 9*, 1588–1606.

Shellenbarger, S. (2008, July 20). Amid Scams, Some Do Find Work at Home—Most Opportunities Part Time, Low Paying Skilled It, Freelancing Can Be an Exception. *Seattle Times*. [Online] Retrieved from http://infoweb.newsbank.com/resources/doc/nb/news/12212258F64F5DB8?p=AWNB

Trethewey, A. (1999). Disciplined Bodies: Women's Embodied Identities at Work. *Organization Studies, 20*(3), 423–450.

13

Seriously Stylish: Academic Femininities and the Politics of Feminism and Fashion in Academia

Ngaire Donaghue

Introduction

What does one wear to work in the life of the mind? The establishment of 'seriousness' as a cardinal academic virtue is reinforced via a series of distinctions between the high-minded concerns worthy of scholarly pursuit, and the materialistic, venal and/or frivolous concerns of secular life. The historical marginalisation of women in academia is also reinforced by these distinctions—despite the mass entry of women into academia over the past 40 years, a masculine hegemony continues to set the terms on which women can be accepted into and succeed within academia, and 'feminine' interests and concerns are treated with suspicion and/or contempt (Bagilhole 2002). Yet although the force of male hegemony in the academy is considerable, it is by no means uncontested; for many decades, women have fought against the assumption that academic

N. Donaghue (✉)
School of Humanities, University of Tasmania, Sandy Bay, TAS, Australia

A.S. Elias et al. (eds.), *Aesthetic Labour*,
DOI 10.1057/978-1-137-47765-1_13

recognition is contingent on eschewing femininity and have sought to find modes of embodiment that acknowledge the presence of women in academia *as* women (Showalter 1997). Women in academia thus face a dilemma in crafting and communicating what we might think of as (borrowing from Gill and Scharff 2011) 'academic femininities'—modes of self-presentation that allow them to simultaneously address the requirement to demonstrate intellectual seriousness, while also refusing to accept the traditional exclusion of markers of femininity from the academy.

I adopt the term 'academic femininities' to highlight the connections between the enactment and experience of feminine identities within academia and the broader currents of neoliberalism and postfeminism that Gill and Scharff (2011) have identified as crucial shapers of 'new femininities'. In particular, work around new femininities draws attention to the neoliberal requirement for people to understand themselves as autonomous, independent, enterprising individuals who are both free to choose their actions and accountable for the consequences of their choices (Rose 1996). The connection with new femininities also foregrounds the 'postfeminist sensibility' (Gill 2007) that, among other things, locates the body as a key site of feminine identity/subjectivity as well as emphasising a distinctive break between the experiences and agendas of so-called second and third wave feminists (Tasker and Negra 2007). Many of the issues confronted by women in academia are not new, yet, as I will argue below, young feminist women in the academy experience significant tensions in relation to second wave feminism. The struggle of women to be respected and included across the many facets of academic life is, of course, far more complex than how to dress; nevertheless in exploring how issues of aesthetic self-presentation are discussed among young academic women, I hope to show how elements of both neoliberal and postfeminist sensibilities are entangled with personal agendas and feminist politics in everyday decisions about 'what (not) to wear'.

The use of clothing to communicate academic femininities is complicated by the troubled relationships between feminism and fashion. The fashion-beauty complex has been a major site of feminist critique (Bartky 1990; Wolf 1990), and feminists of the so-called second wave, in particular, often actively denounced participation in its practices. The grounds on which the fashion-beauty complex has been critiqued are wide-ranging and include: its uses as a means of creating and amplifying sexual difference (Dworkin 1974); its role in disciplining the female body, extracting labour, reproducing feminine helplessness/weakness and its sometimes painful and physically restricting/deforming elements (e.g. Bartky 1990; Wolf 1990); and its material economic effects and exploitative labour practices (Jeffreys 2005). More recently, fashion-beauty practices have become a site of contention between second and third wave feminists, as the later generation of feminists set aside many of the critiques listed above and focused on reclaiming a normative feminine aesthetic as a means of repudiating the cultural devaluation of femininity and celebrating some of the pleasures of a 'girlie' aesthetic (Baumgardner and Richards 2000; Henry 2012). Beauty-fashion practices have come to be understood within postfeminist culture as a key means for achieving empowerment; dressing the body becomes a project of self-enhancement and self-expression, a means of working on and improving the self (Gill 2008; Gill and Donaghue 2013; Gill and Scharff 2011). Success in achieving a desired look is understood as promoting 'confidence', which in turn further empowers the confident woman in prosecuting her agenda as she goes about her daily life (Thompson and Donaghue 2014).

In exploring the role of aesthetic self-presentation in constructing academic femininities, I draw on material sourced from 'academic style' blogs that form a subgenre within the much broader 'personal style' blogs (Rocamora 2011). A suite of such blogs appeared around 2010 and were active through 2014. These blogs provide some insight into how issues of aesthetic self-presentation are negotiated in the everyday practices of academic women, although of course it is important to recognise that the material on the blogs is constructed in awareness of, and is in some ways oriented to, its public audience. In this analysis, I focus on two blogs in particular: *In Professorial Fashion* and *Academic Chic*. These are two of the more active blogs in this space, with frequent contributions in the comments section from writers of other academic fashion blogs. Both of these are group blogs with three core bloggers each, plus occasional guest posts. The main bloggers are all young women, the majority are white (one blogger on Academic Chic identifies as Asian American) and identify as heterosexual (one blogger on Academic Chic identifies as lesbian). The bloggers at *In Professorial Fashion* are all tenure-track assistant professors in humanities fields at North American universities; the *Academic Chic* bloggers are senior graduate students, involved in teaching undergraduate students, in humanities at a large Midwestern American university. As well as sharing pictures of outfits, fashion tips and anecdotes of academic life, on these sites the bloggers and their communities of commenters discuss how their clothing choices are implicated in a range of issues they face as academic women. These issues include: managing the tension between approachability and authority in the classroom; ensuring that they are taken seriously by colleagues; managing the perceived tension between displaying a normative feminine aesthetic and having claims to feminist politics recognised and respected; and the disruptive potential of feminine aesthetics for stereotypes of what it means to be feminist.

Being Taken Seriously as a Professional

One of the frequent topics of discussion and advice for young women in academia concerns how to dress in order to be taken seriously. This concern is often focused on the classroom, and how to strike a balance between looking formal enough to signal leadership and authority while remaining approachable to students. These discussions orient—sometimes explicitly, but often not—to the idea that there is something culturally incongruent about young women in positions of authority and/or as serious scholars, and that their rightful claims to these positions will need to be established in each new situation that they enter:

> I have always been of the mind that dressing professionally instils a sense of decorum and formality in the classroom and, given that I look somewhat young, I have used a more formal dress code to set myself apart from my students and to garner authority (*Academic Chic*).

Concerns about authority are also tempered with the desire to appear approachable and relatable to students:

> As a graduate student you inhabit a somewhat hybrid space between faculty and undergraduates. While some may want to dress more somber and

> professional to visually push themselves into that former category, I've always found an advantage to letting students see that I am not so far removed from where they are (*Academic Chic*).

Separately from concerns about constructing an identity as a teacher, the academic women on these blogs also ponder the role of their outfits in influencing their interactions with other colleagues, particularly those they don't know well. For example:

> I can't go into detail in this public forum, but I will say that I was recently and rather obviously underestimated in this way in a casual meeting with new colleagues. I wasn't meeting with students that day, so I came to campus in a trouser-jean-based 'business casual' ensemble. And now I wonder if I could have prevented this error through sartorial means. I am thus inspired to up the profesh-factor in my attire for each and every day on campus this term. And we'll just see if I can change certain people's responses to me through clothing alone (*In Professorial Fashion*).

Clothing is understood as providing a context for other actions, as creating expectations in others that will colour other aspects of these encounters. As in the extract, the 'wrong' outfit—one that is too casual—can misrepresent the 'true' academic inside the clothes. Although the fault is located in the misreader, the responsibility for correcting it (and preventing similar future mistakes) is given to future outfits. This taken-for-granted acceptance of the onus to avoid such misreadings illustrates the ease with which the responsibilising dynamics of neoliberalism infiltrate the everyday practices of life while barely even drawing notice, let alone resistance (although it is worth noting that in a separate post, another blogger on this site does mount a critique of the gendered ways in which casual attire is read in academic settings).

In addition to 'sending the right signals' with clothing, the role of appearance in enhancing subjective feelings of competence and confidence was also widely discussed. Particularly in discussion of some of the more nerve-wracking occasions of an early academic career—job interviews, conference presentations, first lectures to new groups of students—the power of a well-chosen outfit to instil a sense of confidence was drawn on repeatedly: 'Clothing can, as I think we'll all attest, lend us confidence, empower us, even' (*In Professorial Fashion*). The pairing of confidence and empowerment is a key plank of postfeminist culture (Gill 2008; McRobbie 2009; Thompson and Donaghue 2014). Contemporary career guides for young women reinforce the neoliberal ethos of self-determination—young women are exhorted to be more confident and to 'lean in' to their careers, boldly asserting their rights and taking their 'place at the table' rather than waiting to be invited (e.g. Sandberg 2013). Invoking the power of clothes to enhance confidence thus pre-emptively defends an interest in personal aesthetics against potential critique—who would have the right to deny a young woman a means of confidence as she makes her way in the world, merely to make an abstract political protest? Confidence serves as a bottom line argument in many of these discussions—'at the end of the day, wear whatever makes you feel most confident', is a typical refrain. Whatever other considerations may go into composing an 'academic outfit'—and as I will discuss below, there are many—enhancing confidence trumps them all.

Being Taken Seriously as a Feminist: The Problematics of the Pantsuit

Although frustrations about being underestimated by colleagues and mistaken for students were widely expressed, it was issues around how to communicate feminist identity that provoked the most political discussion among the bloggers. Questions and anecdotes around this issue recurred frequently, and were treated as the most difficult of all the questions around dressing as a woman in academia:

> The question about what signals feminism, sartorially, is something that's at the heart of IPF's 'mission' and something that's been discussed a good deal here. While the academic world might sometimes treat the question of fashion as frivolous and unimportant, clothing is still often intimately associated with who 'counts' as appropriately feminist, inside and outside the academy. (*In Professorial Fashion*)

There are many issues negotiated by academic women here that are reflected in the discussions on the blog, but a central one concerns how an academic woman's clothing and grooming practices position her in relation to markers of normative femininity. There are complex tensions to be negotiated here. On the one hand, an unreflexive adoption of normative modes of femininity can suggest a lack of awareness (or worse, complicity) regarding the privileges accorded to women who show willingness to comply with patriarchal views about the qualities that are valuable in women. On the other hand, eschewal of all forms of femininity can be seen as buying in to the cultural devaluation of femininity and the masculine hegemony of academia (Bagilhole 2002).

The 'pantsuit' (sometimes 'polyester pants') is used across the blogs as a kind of shorthand for a bland, apparently sexless style of dressing that is associated with some older women in academia. The extract below comes from a 'panel discussion' on *Academic Chic*, in which the sartorial challenges for young feminist academics are constructed as a reflection of broader generational issues within feminism. Here, the bloggers are concerned with how their own clothing choices—which reflect an interest in fashion and a preference for pencil skirts and high heels over pant suits and 'sensible shoes'—are read by those around them, particularly more senior women:

A: Yes, I wonder about that professor all the time. She is very much a pantsuit kind of lady and I think it is a very specific and conscious style choice.

E: I agree, and I think it has a lot to do with when she came of age in academia.

A: Yes, she came of age in academia during the feminist political movement.

S: From all my fashion history readings, when I see the pantsuit I think of how, in the 80s, it was a symbol of women breaking further into male dominated work spheres and were borrowing from male aesthetics to fit in.

A: Yes, S., but are we still doing that? I think it is becoming more muddled … I do still think the suit has masculine connotations and is still associated with power. I think boxy cuts are also still associated

> with power because they resemble the ideal male body. I'm not sure if the idea behind the woman in the suit has changed all that much from the 1980s.

Although this exchange apparently relates to an actual person in their department, it also draws on a more generalised figure ('a pantsuit kind of lady') that embodies an implicit censoriousness and strictness that is often used by younger (third wave) feminists to characterise an 'older generation' of feminists (Henry 2012; Scharff 2010, 2012). The discussion here has overtones of the postfeminist splitting of 'the past' from 'the present' in ways that imply that the (putatively no longer relevant) agendas of second wave feminists can serve to blind them to the new gender-related issues being navigated by younger feminists. The exchange ends with A expressing a guarded criticism of the persistence of the pantsuit; what was an understandable and perhaps necessary adoption of a masculine aesthetic in order to break into male-dominated spaces is seen as having perhaps outstayed its welcome and usefulness, and now works to reinforce an association between masculinity and power. But it is not so much concern with this professor's outfits, so much as what her persistence in sticking with that aesthetic means for whether she (and others) correctly reads the intention of *their* aesthetics that most concerns the bloggers.

The possibility that a feminine aesthetic can undermine one's claims to a feminist identity in the eyes of other (often older) feminists is also central to the following extract from *In Professorial Fashion*:

> I've been thinking a LOT about how I perform gender at work of late … as a 'femme' straight woman in Women's and Gender Studies, I sense, occasionally, that I don't look like a feminist 'should'. And this results in my being spoken to dismissively … Sometimes I get this kind of treatment at academic conferences. And sometimes it happens in meetings outside of my home department. More recently, a visiting scholar who is a well-known queer theorist spoke to me—or rather, over me—in that familiar dismissive tone. She didn't like my response to one of her questions—and, frankly, I might word it differently if I had a do-over. But it wasn't a stupid or naively liberalist point. And it wasn't a response that should have resulted

> in her dismissing me as a 'particular kind of North American liberal feminist'. As she spoke this phrase, she looked me up and down in a way that suggested that I LOOKED like THAT kind of (politically irrelevant) person to her. (*In Professorial Fashion*)

The central issue here concerns whether and how dressing in a normatively feminine style can interfere with having one's claims to feminist identity and politics recognised and respected. The disparaging reference to the 'North American liberal feminist' suggests that a normative feminine presentation is a sign that one is uncritical of the ways in which femininity draws various (illegitimate) forms of privilege from patriarchal structures and participates in the ongoing subjugation of women to restrictive and oppressive standards of beauty (e.g. Jeffreys 2005). This (inferred) critique is rebuffed in a comment made in response to the post above by another woman assistant professor:

> It's ironic because to me, dismissing the feminine is very reminiscent of old school second wave liberal North American feminist. So this is a long way of saying that performing a femme gender identity is transgressive in its own way. If we're supposed to be wearing boxy blazers, shapeless polyester pants and masculine power pieces to be accepted into the old boy's club (by imitating their styles), then we are simply reproducing the existing sartorial norms. If historically the 'femme' in the academy were wives and secretaries, then bringing the femme into the professoriate is important. (comment on *In Professorial Fashion*)

This comment reflects a counter point of view—widely endorsed across the blogs—that dressing in a feminine manner is not only acceptable, but is in fact a form of transgressive political action. She argues that academic femininities are an important means of demanding that women in the professoriate be recognised *as* women, in the full variety of aesthetic presentations that they may choose. But in its focus on the importance of diversity of modes of self-presentation among academic women, this comment glosses over the substantive critiques made by feminists of the specific practices and functions of normative femininity. It engages only at the symbolic level, and in doing so marginalises any critical engagement with the politics of the reproduction of particular, patriarchy-sanctioned modes of femininity, the many forms of labour and bodily disciplining required to achieve them, and the privileges that are attached to conforming to those prescriptions. Not only are these key elements of second wave critiques of the fashion-beauty complex (Bartky 1990; Dworkin 1974; Wolf 1990) dismissed by a sole focus on symbolic representation, more concerning is the lost opportunity for productive dialogue across these positions. What possibilities might there be for the creation of 'looks' that *both* incorporate (elements of) traditional feminine aesthetics *and* also address (some of) the critiques made by members of the second wave? Such questions are pushed aside by a simplistic inter-'wave' battle over the complex tensions structuring the relationship between feminism and femininity.

Despite this critique, academic style blogging and the aesthetic self-presentations that it promotes can be framed as a form of intervention against both historical and continuing sexism within the academy. In the extract below, the writer makes a case for celebrating normative feminine aesthetics as a means of disrupting stereotypical assumptions about feminism that may alienate students, and for opening up spaces in which some of the assumptions about 'appropriate' forms of self-presentation for academics can be exposed and interrogated:

> Thus, despite the seeming frivolity of things like style blogs, I think there's something quietly radical about what we've all embarked on here in our various ways: demonstrating the different ways of dressing like a feminist. While many of the privileges that underwrote my mom's versions of feminism are replicated in the blog world (and the rest of the world, generally) and could stand to be more clearly interrogated, there's a fantastic level of discussion about what style means and allows. Further, interactions with students (female and otherwise) act as a continual reminder of the work that needs to be done and, while I'm not always as up front about my feminism with them as others, I like to think that my clothes are performing an important pedagogical interruption to their assumptions about 'what a feminist looks like'. (*In Professorial Fashion*)

'Authentic' Self-Expression Versus 'Passing' and Privilege?

A recurring issue across the blogs involved the idea of 'earning' the right to show an interest in matters of fashion and personal style. In the extract below, one of the writers at *In Professorial Fashion* mulls the question of whether the quality of her work and position in the academy should be enough to vouch for her scholarly and feminist credibility without her personal styling calling either into question:

> I'm left with the sense that if I continue to dress and look the way I do, I'll have to fight harder to be taken seriously. So, do I change, or do I fight? To date, I've chosen to fight harder. Because this feminist LOVES colouring her hair, playing with fashion, and accessorizing. Because when I've tried other costumes and self-representations, they've felt less authentic somehow. And I know we're all performing gender in one way or another. However, this performance, the one I do now, is the one that—despite all the styling—is less work for me. But maybe I *should* work harder. I'm not so naive as to believe that my relatively normative gender performance is natural. So maybe it's appropriate to work against type, to consent less—and in less visible ways—to my own subordination (through high heels, for example) and/or objectification (through make-up and hair dye, for example) in culture. And maybe I should be modelling alternative gender performance/s for my students.
>
> Or maybe, just maybe, my current performance does this already. I'm already here in the university, after all. And the authority of the institution as well as the quality of my work should reinforce my politics, shouldn't it?… Furthermore, do my long hair, make-up, and high heels really undercut the positive endorsement by my peers of the research I've done and continue to pursue? I'd love to hear what you think, internet. Because I'm not sure where I stand anymore.

But this extract is not a straightforward claim that her scholarly work entitles her to a certain reading of her aesthetic choices. Rather, it encapsulates the many different considerations that she grapples with in trying to come to a position on the politics of her aesthetics. She eloquently describes a tension between experiencing an affinity with certain modes of self-presentation and knowing that this sense of 'authentic' self-expression is constructed and mediated by a whole slew of forces that maintain an interest in the continued subjugation of women. It is also one of the few instances across the blogs in which the labour associated with executing these looks is acknowledged ('all the styling'), although that is mitigated by the claim that the forms of labour involved are 'less work' (for her) than a different performance of gender. And although she alludes to the pedagogical value of interrupting students' expectations about how feminists do/should look (as discussed above), there is here a rare sense of genuine dilemma about how all these competing considerations should, in the end, be resolved.

Despite the many (re)affirmations of the political value and merit in rejecting the exclusion of the feminine from academic spaces, in many posts on the blogs writers acknowledged the need to make their self-presentations political. When dressing in a way that attracts privilege (in wider Western culture, if not so clearly within academia), it is not necessarily clear to the casual observer that there are reflexive politics at play: 'I think we've also discussed before how, at some point, our words are important because you're not subverting if you're just passing' (*Academic Chic*). In some ways, these blogs can be understood as 'footnotes' to the texts of self-styling. They provide the words that decide in favour of one reading of an outfit over another; the existence of these blogs may partly reflect a frustration expressed by one of the *Academic Chic* bloggers wishing, in reference to her discussion of one of her outfits, that she could 'put that on a billboard above my head'.

Conclusions

Much of the scholarship around clothing choices and self-presentation has operated through the conceptual apparatus of habitus (Bourdieu 1996; Entwistle and Rocamora 2006). But habitus suggests a kind of thoughtlessness, or taken-for-grantedness, about these daily enactments of taste that is at odds with the highly self-conscious and accountable presentations that characterise academic style blogs. Post after post on these blogs describes the active and effortful processes around building an outfit that will (ideally) send the desired signals to its various audiences while also heading off potential misreadings from those who don't understand (or endorse) the meanings that it is indented to convey. As Martin Roberts (2007) has argued, displays of taste, such as those made through aesthetic self-presentations, can perhaps be better thought of as elements in the entrepreneurial construction of a self. For the ideal neoliberal worker, work is an expression of the self, something reflecting who one is rather than simply what one does (Rose 1996). And given that the body is such a central site of the self—particularly for young women—the self-styling practices that are illustrated and discussed on the blogs can be understood as part of the wider task of constructing one's 'academic femininity', of embodying an identity that simultaneously evokes an irrepressibly unique, autonomous, self-knowledgeable individual while also demonstrating an apparently seamless alignment of this 'authentic' self with the capacities and commitments necessary to perform the many and varied elements of the role of a contemporary academic.

A striking feature of the material on the blogs is the way it illustrates a tension between understanding how to be recognised in certain ways within existing academic dress codes, while at the same time also wanting to challenge those codes and the ideologies underlying them. Bloggers were well-aware that dressing in their preferred, normative feminine styles could (and sometimes did) lead others to question both their seriousness as scholars and their feminist politics. Yet at the same time, they challenged the legitimacy of this reading and frequently argued that it is politically necessary for feminists to embody a wide range of modes of femininity in order to lay to rest the notion that femininity is incompatible with intellectual seriousness. This form of subversive femininity was seen as having especially important pedagogical value, both in challenging students' preconceptions about feminism and also in being more accessible and approachable—meeting students where they are.

Some of the complexities around adopting a normative feminine aesthetic can be understood in terms of the 'femininity versus feminism' dilemma identified by Riley and Scharff (2013) in their analysis of beauty practices among feminist-identified women. However, one striking difference is that the women writing on these blogs, unlike Riley and Scharff's participants, externalised the dilemma—it was a question of whether their displays of femininity would lead *others* to read them as 'not feminist', rather than an internally felt contradiction or struggle. Although the *existence* of earlier feminist critiques of the fashion-beauty complex was acknowledged, there was very little sense of substantive engagement with the *content* of those critiques. It is as though the actual issues identified and railed against by earlier feminists have been relegated to the past, without the need to actually address them. The invoking of 'pastness' as a kind of evidence of irrelevance is a discursive strategy that is characteristic of postfeminism (McRobbie 2009). Furthermore, the issue of whether normative femininity can be compatible with feminist identity was treated in a strikingly all-or-nothing way; there was little sense that it might be worthwhile to attempt to make space for some of the repudiated aspects of femininity within the academy while also taking seriously at least some of the issues identified in feminist critique of the fashion-beauty industry. An all-or-nothing analysis puts all of the emphasis on the symbolic aspects of normative femininity: it marginalises any extended consideration of the aesthetic labour required to achieve certain kinds of 'looks', the constraints on activity imposed by some elements of some of these outfits, or the bodily disciplines required to produce/maintain the figures that inhabit the pencil skirts that exemplify the 'femme' aesthetic.

One way of understanding the near absence of discussion of internal struggles with these issues is that aesthetic entrepreneurship, and the neoliberal subjectivity of which it forms part, requires us to own fully each of our choices. In this sense, and particularly on a public blog, there is perhaps little room for the kind of feminist compromise articulated by some of Riley and Scharff's participants, in which the apparent contradiction of simultaneously critiquing and participating in feminine fashion-beauty practices is understood as the result of the inability of anyone, feminist women included, to simply 'step out' of culture and decide to be unaffected by its pressures and pleasures. But while this is understandable, it may be that the certitude with which normative femininity is celebrated prevents a more sophisticated—and also pedagogically valuable—engagement with the complexities of feminist engagement with normative feminine aesthetics in the construction of academic femininities.

References

Bagilhole, B. (2002). Challenging Equal Opportunities: Changing and Adapting Male Hegemony in Academia. *British Journal of Sociology of Education, 23*(1), 19–33.

Bartky, S. L. (1990). *Femininity and Domination: Studies in the Phenomenology of Oppression*. New York: Routledge.

Baumgardner, J., & Richards, A. (2000). *Manifesta: Young Women, Feminism, and the Future*. New York: Farrar, Straus and Giroux.

Bourdieu, P. (1996). *Distinction: A Social Critique of the Judgement of Taste*. London: Routledge.

Dworkin, A. (1974). *Women Hating*. New York: E. P. Dutton.

Entwistle, J., & Rocamora, A. (2006). The Field of Fashion Materialized: A Study of London Fashion Week. *Sociology, 40*(4), 735–751.

Gill, R. (2007). Postfeminist Media Culture: Elements of a Sensibility. *European Journal of Cultural Studies, 10*(2), 147–166.

Gill, R. (2008). Empowerment/Sexism: Figuring Female Sexual Agency in Contemporary Advertising. *Feminism & Psychology, 18*(1), 35–60.

Gill, R., & Donaghue, N. (2013). As if Postfeminism Had Come True: The Turn to Agency in Cultural Studies of 'Sexualisation'. In S. Madhok, A. Phillips & K. Wilson (Eds.), *Gender, Agency, and Coercion* (pp. 240–257). Basingstoke: Palgrave Macmillan.

Gill, R., & Scharff, C. (Eds.). (2011). *New Femininities: Postfeminism, Neoliberalism and Subjectivity*. Basingstoke: Palgrave.

Henry, A. (2012). Fashioning a Feminist Style, or, How I Learned to Dress from Reading Feminist Theory. In M. Jolles & S. Tarrant (Eds.), *Fashion Talks: Undressing the Power of Style*. Albany, NY: SUNY Press.

Jeffreys, S. (2005). *Beauty and Misogyny: Harmful Cultural Practices in the West*. New York: Routledge.

McRobbie, A. (2009). *The Aftermath of Feminism: Gender, Culture and Social Change*. London: Sage.

Riley, S. C., & Scharff, C. (2013). Feminism Versus Femininity? Exploring Feminist Dilemmas Through Cooperative Inquiry Research. *Feminism & Psychology, 23*(2), 207–223.

Roberts, M. (2007). The Fashion Police: Governing the Self in *What Not to Wear*. In Y. Tasker & D. Negra (Eds.), *Interrogating Postfeminism. Gender and the Politics of Popular Culture*. London: Duke University Press.

Rocamora, A. (2011). Personal Fashion Blogs: Screens and Mirrors in Digital Self-Portraits. *Fashion Theory, 15*(4), 407–424.
Rose, N. (1996). *Inventing Our Selves: Psychology, Power, and Personhood*. Cambridge, England: Cambridge University Press.
Sandberg, S. (2013). *Lean in: Women, Work, and the Will to Lead*. New York: Random House.
Scharff, C. (2010). Young Women's Negotiations of Heterosexual Conventions: Theorizing Sexuality in Constructions of 'the Feminist'. *Sociology, 44*(5), 827–842.
Scharff, C. (2012). *Repudiating Feminism: Young Women in a Neoliberal World*. Ashgate.
Showalter, E. (1997). The Professor Wore Prada. *Vogue, 187*, 80.
Tasker, Y., & Negra, D. (Eds.). (2007). *Interrogating Postfeminism: Gender and the Politics of Popular Culture*. Durham, NC: Duke University Press.
Thompson, L., & Donaghue, N. (2014). The Confidence Trick: Competing Constructions of Confidence and Self-Esteem in Young Women's Discussions of the Sexualisation of Culture. *Women's Studies International Forum, 47*, 23–35.
Wolf, N. (1990). *The Beauty Myth*. New York: Random House.

14

How to Do Feminist Mothering in Urban India? Some Reflections on the Politics of Beauty and Body Shapes

Shilpa Phadke

Introduction

One morning I was tweezing the tiny hair on my upper lip when my 3-year-old burst into the bathroom.

A: *What are you doing?*
Me: *I'm taking out my moustache.*
A: *But girls don't have moustaches.*
Me: *Yes we do. But fewer women than men grow them. Though some do.*
A: *That means girls also have moustaches?*
Me: *Yes.*

My daughter was only three but the questions had already begun.

S. Phadke (✉)
School of Media and Cultural Studies, Tata Institute of Social Sciences, Mumbai, India

A.S. Elias et al. (eds.), *Aesthetic Labour*,
DOI 10.1057/978-1-137-47765-1_14

In continuing my exploration of feminist mothering in urban India this chapter examines some negotiations that self-identified feminist women with daughters engage in the process of mothering. An earlier paper reflects on feminist mothers' reflections of sexuality and risk in the ways in which they were raising their daughters (Phadke 2013). Other ongoing work looks at reflections on child sexual abuse and the moral panic raised by recent incidents of assaults on children in schools. This chapter examines feminism's relationship with the politics of beauty asking how (mostly middle-class) feminist mothers in urban India negotiate their own relationship with their bodies/beauty (configured by neoliberal contexts), even as they try to provide good examples for their daughters. While this chapter focuses on the mothering of girls, this is not intended to suggest that boys are not impacted by sexist cultures or indeed that feminist mothering is any less relevant in raising boys.

I interviewed twelve women for the study this chapter is based on, among which are four academics, three journalists, three women who work with non-governmental organisations and two writers, one of whom writes for children.[1] As evinced by their occupations, these are privileged women, most of whom have a post-graduate education. Of these, eleven have one daughter each and one has two daughters. Two have daughters in their twenties; five have daughters in the age group of ten to thirteen; and six have daughters in the age group of five to nine.[2] Two are single mothers and four have adopted their daughters. All of them currently live in one of the large metros of the country.

The women interviewed are not intended to be representative of feminist mothers in urban India. Nor are these narratives representative of middle-class women, though all interviewees are located within a broadly defined middle class in India. Rather my intention is to use these narratives to gesture towards the contradictions and ambiguities that we are compelled to negotiate as feminists who are parenting girls in a cultural context that is deeply contradictory (Phadke 2005, 2012). Being able to

[1] All names have been changed.

[2] This number adds up to thirteen as I have counted the woman with two children separately for her two daughters.

critique cultural norms around the reification of particular ideologies of idealised femininity places feminist women in a peculiar location, since our intellectual understanding of these discourses does not always enable us to be completely free of them. This tension has been articulated by feminist scholars who have introspected on the tension between their politics and practices around feminism and femininity (Riley and Scharff 2012; Throsby and Gimlin 2010).

From the perspective of being feminist mothers the tension is heightened by internal pressure to not just be a good feminist but also to be a good mother. The challenge then is twofold—to be good feminists and to be good mothers. The question that this raises is whether being good feminists automatically makes us good mothers. Is feminist mothering, by virtue of this political location, good mothering? Despite these dilemmas, I am aware that this is a very privileged location.

As in my earlier piece on the theme, I use the collective pronoun 'we' rather than 'they' to locate myself as both subject and object of the research gaze (Phadke 2013). Indeed, I have often reflected on my own negotiations with varied forms of patriarchy and have watched my own subversions and rebellions with pleasure and my conformity with some anxiety. In placing myself squarely within my research, I encounter some of the pitfalls Throsby and Gimlin (2010) suggest in their own engagement with the politics of writing the researcher's body into the research, notably the danger of one's own narrative upstaging those of the respondents. My own location within the frame of my research has meant that my interviews are dialogues—I share my stories as much as my interviewees share theirs, which is often facilitated by a shared class location. My interviewees are often as invested with the concerns of this work—for us it is at once political and deeply personal.

In the first section I reflect on the transformations India has seen since the early 1990s and what it means to be a feminist mother in post-globalisation India. The next section draws on mothering narratives focussing on concerns related to body hair, colour and weight. In the third section I attempt to think through the inevitable contradictions that arise when a feminist politics encounters the fashion-beauty complex in the context of mothering.

Temporality: Parenting in Neoliberal India

Bringing up our daughters in the early twenty-first century comes with its own set of peculiarities and it is worthwhile briefly dwelling on these temporal peculiarities. Processes of globalisation have transformed visions of both beauty and the body in India. The 1990s marked a more global vision of both what it meant to be beautiful and what was considered a desirable body shape. In 1994, two Indian women won the Miss Universe and Miss World beauty contest titles. In 1996, *Cosmopolitan* magazine launched its Indian edition. These might seem to be insignificant markers but they signalled the beginning of a transformation in how both beauty and bodies were envisioned in India. (John 1998; Oza 2001; Phadke 2005; Sangari 2004). Post-globalisation India has created an increase in the aesthetic labour that women are expected to perform on their bodies. It is no longer enough to be virtuous, one must also be sexually desirable—defined in increasingly narrow ways in body shapes and clothing—and even as one is expected to be articulate and 'modern', one must nevertheless not be feminist for that is undesirably strident (Phadke 2005).[3]

Many of my interviewees have to varying degrees reflected on patriarchal body-focussed cultures in relation to our own adult bodies but find that contemplating the impact of these on our daughters is very different. Being a girl or a young woman in the early twenty-first century is very different than when I or indeed my interviewees were growing up in the 1970s, 80s and 90s, respectively. For us, the opening of the economy is something that happened when we were children or adolescents or young adults. We grew up in an economy where there was considerably less available in terms of consumer choices. Many of us also grew up in a political context that was articulated as socialist and so any kind of overt consumption, usually referred to as 'conspicuous consumption', was suspect. There was one state-run television channel.

[3] As Talukdar and Linders (2013) argue concerns about body shape and size are overwhelmingly located among those women for whom liberalisation had opened up career and other opportunities and for which the symbolic value of a fit, often read as healthy and active body, were a distinct advantage.

In contrast, we are bringing up our daughters in a world saturated with images—images we cannot possibly hide from our daughters. Simultaneously, we live in a time that is demanding more images from our girls, images they are in many ways delighted to provide. Kyla laughs as she describes taking her daughter out to a meal with her friends: 'The phone camera was the extra person at the table—always present, with the girls all taking pictures of themselves and each other'. There's something performative about this moment—a performance that must be recorded for posterity. In the twenty-first century, these circulating images bring ever more scrutiny into the lives of young women, who must then submit to the circumscribing gaze, engaging in continuous aesthetic labour to produce 'perfect' selves. As Meera puts it:

> For me and my friends—those who had daughters who grew up in the 1990s—the first generation of post-liberalisation children. And our questions really were: 'What is it that we want to pass on? What do we not want to pass on?' This is not to suggest that we've reached the gold standard—but just to ask what is important to us, as feminists?

Tara agrees:

> I don't want to say 'in our time', but … it was different. I find it easy to be a feminist mother, I have so many friends who are, but I wonder, will my daughter find it easy to be a feminist as she grows up?

What we are engaging with then is both parenting in a particular time but also, simultaneously, in a particular moment for feminism in this country and elsewhere. It is a time when feminism as a politics is increasingly derided in the mainstream and claiming feminism requires more gumption than it did two decades ago (Phadke 2015). Meera and Tara both unconsciously use the collective pronoun, 'we', and this is a sub-text that continued through my conversations with the women I interviewed. Even as women spoke about themselves, they spoke about what it meant to be part of a movement, to belong and to find oneself navigating the waters of feminists mothering both alone and with others.

What We Say, What We Do: Narratives on Body Hair, Size and Skin Colour

My hair stylist who runs her own salon talks worriedly about some women who bring daughters as young as 11 years of age to have the hair on their arms and legs waxed. There is a misconception, she says, that if you start early, they will have less body hair as they get older, thus making their lives easier. However, my stylist was questioning the age rather than the practice itself; that body hair is something all women must manage is a taken-for-granted assumption.[4]

For feminist mothers, however, the dilemma of hair is not just about the regimes about beauty and the creation and valourisation of pre-pubescent looking bodies. The anxiety now is magnified both by the inability to extricate oneself from these demands as well as the concern that one is giving mixed messages to one's daughter. Am I sending the message: 'Do as I say, not as I do', to my daughter? I worry that my daughter will watch me shave my legs and think that hair is undesirable, and so I lock the bathroom door, hiding the act of shaving almost as a guilty secret. As someone who has been conditioned into the 'hair is unsightly' school of thought, I'd like very much for my daughter to be free of it.

Using a double negative, Priya emphatically argued: 'It's not as if I don't want my daughter to ever wax or shave, but I do want her to understand the sexist ideologies that such practices are part of. I want her to not hate her body'. When I point out the several negatives she uses, Priya laughs: 'I should have said—I want her to love her body—is it telling that I didn't? How hard is this world we live in for young women'. Tara shrugs self-deprecatingly: 'I worry about my own politics sometimes, because I worry that my daughter has some hair on her shoulders. I hope she does not find this something she has to deal with as she grows older'. Tara's comment suggests that we cannot but be aware of the onslaught of cultural demands of beauty that our daughters are likely to face and are

---

[4] In the USA, Breanne Fahs' (2011) pedagogic experiment with her students—where the women stopped removing body hair and men shaved theirs—also pointed to the complex cultural nuances in which body hair is located, including the colour of the skin, the colour of the hair, the thickness of the hair and the visibility of the hair.

anxious both about this pressure as well as our own apparent inability to adequately live our politics in our personal lives.

Kyla suggests that peer pressure matters too, even as she injects a note of practicality:

> My twelve year old wanted to use hair removal cream on her underarms since her friends do. I let her. One of her friends also waxes her arms and legs and has a boyfriend—my daughter is very impressed by her 'bad girl image'—the idea of rebellion. I don't say anything though. I talk to her about techniques of hair removal and what they mean in terms of effort and time. Even if I tell her hair is ok, her peer group is not telling her it is ok and that matters to her.

Feminist mothers then are articulating an interesting problematic here—in an ideal world they would want their daughters to not care about body hair at all, to be in that sense different and freer than their mothers are. In a more pragmatic sense, they concede that it would be all right if their daughters chose to remove body hair so long as they did it with an awareness of the patriarchal discourses within which it is embedded, that is, to be as their mothers are. What does it mean then to 'settle' for an awareness of the patriarchal discourses within which we live our lives? Why is it that so many could not envisage a world in which hair and its discontents will cease to matter? How much power do we assign to the codes of body and beauty regimes, even as we hope that things might be different?

Skin colour is a further significant issue in a country that is deeply racist and casteist. One woman wrote in an article about the pain of being the mother of a dark daughter and her hope that she will somehow be able to raise her daughter to look beyond the stereotypes that associate fairness with virtue and darkness with its lack (Ruth 2015). Everywhere one turns one finds an advertisement for fairness cream, including more recently one to make your 'vagina' fair.[5] So pervasive is the obsession with fairness that in 2009 a campaign titled 'Dark is Beautiful' was launched to attempt to address skin colour based prejudice.[6] The dismay with the

[5] See: http://www.mid-day.com/articles/now-vaginal-whitening-cream-that-promises-fairness-within-4-weeks/183036

[6] More information on this campaign is available at: http://darkisbeautiful.blogspot.in/p/about-us.html

regime of fairness is visible among many mothers, not just self-identified feminists.

Both Maitri and Vani talk about how their daughters have been bullied in school for being dark. Vani, herself, is much fairer and this has been a source of additional angst for the daughter:

> I tell her that she's lucky that she has her father's colour as also his lean build. I tell her that if she had my colour, maybe she would also have had my large build with its concomitant issues. I feel strange saying that. In another context I would never mention fat or weight to her but here in order to contextualise I did. One thing I've learnt about parenting is that you always take back your words. I also wanted to point out to her that we're all dealing with some unhappiness on how we look. Lookism is so all pervasive.

What does it mean when a feminist mother says that we are all dealing with unhappiness about the way we look—the acceptance that there is no way out of this quagmire? Vani would not otherwise present size as a problem to her daughter but in the face of what seems to be her daughter's 'bigger' problem, colour, she feels compelled to place the two next to each other to suggest: 'all of us have problems'. She does this in full awareness that this is not ideal at all, but perhaps important to her daughter's self-esteem at that precise moment.

Despite our awareness of the ways in which our bodies are sought to be disciplined into specific shapes, most articulated the inability to be completely unaffected by it. Ratna recounts intervening to ensure her daughter was not harangued about weight. At the same time, she expresses dissatisfaction with her own weight:

> I wasn't happy at all about putting on weight. I've been fat and I've been thin and thin is better. But I intentionally don't make comments about my weight in front of my daughter. In third grade her Physical Education teacher told her she needed to lose weight to run faster. She was running for her school and was slightly chubby. I pulled her out of that class immediately. I told her not to worry about getting fat—but despite this she tells me now, 'I will never get fat'.

Scholarly work in the area of fat studies has produced narratives that suggest that the mother-daughter relationship is significant in the creation of negative meanings in relation to body weight (Donaghue and Clemitshaw 2012; Maor 2012). While all of these studies are located in non-Indian contexts, my interviewees' narratives suggest that they at least appear to believe that what they say will impact how their daughters feel about their bodies.

Maitri suggests that whatever one might say or do it is hard to counteract the outside effects:

> My daughter worries about her weight, tells me Ma you are feeding me too much and I am getting fat. Also, in the extended family people constantly comment on her weight and how she should try and lose it—she struggles with it. I tell her that at the end of the day it is your privileges of education, social security, and unconditional love surrounding you which gives (or should give) you the confidence to carry off your different body type without any worries.

Alka, Leela and Revathi discuss conversely the travails of having been too thin as adolescents, Leela and Revathi of having taken much longer than their peers to grow breasts and their hope that their daughters would be more comfortable with their bodies.

Who is this woman we all want our daughters to be? This woman who is confident about herself and her body, who is concerned about her health but not her size for its own sake. If we worry that none of us are quite yet that woman, then is this woman imaginary? What might we do to 'guide' our daughters in this direction, even as we struggle with our own awareness of our imperfections? Can we counteract the effects of the other narratives, most notably media narratives that our daughters are constantly subject to?

Our own stories of growing up are embedded in how we parent. Meera says:

> I was always tall and large—my mother was very small and petite. But I didn't have a bust earlier and people would tell me 'when you grow up…'. This would make me very conscious and I hated it. When my daughter was

> about eight years old, she was a little glutton, she loved food. She started being what people would call 'plump'—and others would tell me she is a girl and you should make her lose weight. This annoyed me intensely. Then I was away for a year on work and by the time I returned, she had put on four inches in height and had become rake thin. Then the outsiders' narrative was about how she had pined for her mother, or alternately how much her mother used to feed her. It was all just so annoying... She's now very conscious of her weight though in an athletic way—this may have something to do with my being so indisciplined and letting myself go. I wonder if my complete rejection of any kind of diet was a good thing.

Meera's narrative strikes at the heart of the contradictions that underlie the good mother, bad mother narratives woven in complicated ways with the idea of feminist mothering. The good mother must both feed her daughter well and yet ensure that she does not get too fat. If the mother travels and her daughter gets thin, it is because the child missed the 'heartless' mother. The feminist in the mother argues that she should not worry about her daughter's weight, but the mother who is also embedded in a cultural context that includes ideas about valued femininity thinks that perhaps both over- and underweight are not a good thing. The feminist mother who has chosen not to be concerned about her weight now worries that her own lack of concern has pushed her daughter to be too careful. The questions and counter-questions only multiply.

I too am conscious in an on-and-off way about my own weight, usually when I am in a room full of thin well-dressed women, but in relation to the things that worry me about myself, my shape is certainly not a priority. I have a reasonable self-image often centred around my mind rather than my body. If I think about my body, I think of its capabilities—can I climb a mountain, or perform a difficult *yogasana*—rather than its shape. And yet, I wonder if I am being too cerebral in my approach. Is the body a machine, subservient to the mind? Have I internalised the mind-body dichotomy entirely? A woman I met, to whom I described my research, responded by saying:

> If I had a daughter, I'd want her to share my comfort with my body, curves and all. I'd like her to respect her body and take good care of it. I hope she can enjoy her body more than I do.

When I relay this comment and my own concerns to Tara, she laughs: 'Yes. I wonder too if all this attention we lavish on our minds is worth it. Perhaps some hedonistic body-centred love would be good for us'.

The Cartesian mind-body dichotomy and the lessons of the Enlightenment that privilege the mind and the capacity for rational thought are perhaps ones that we, as feminist mothers, have learnt too well. However, in some of the articulations in my interviews I hear more than the whispers of a desire to undo those shackles to expand our imaginations and our concerns to include our bodies not only for what they can do, but for themselves: to enjoy the body for perhaps more than just its capacities.[7] What might this enjoyment of our bodies entail?[8] Further, how does our privileging our minds over our bodies impact our daughters? Conversely, if we participate in the fashion-beauty complex as feminists, will our daughters read this as contradictory, even hypocritical?

Navigating Feminist Politics and the Fashion-Beauty Complex

The expression of concern about how body and beauty regimes appear to our daughters mediated both by the outside world and, perhaps more significantly, by ourselves suggests the assumption that our interventions are relevant and will change the way our daughters see the world.

Leela is very certain about why she does not take her daughter to the beauty salon. 'I don't like her to sit there, watching me get primped—I do not want her to watch the number of things that go into a woman looking the way she does'. Megha, however, does not seem to believe the parlour will scar her daughter: 'I've taken her to the beauty parlour with me—I don't think it has adversely affected her'. Prerna agrees:

[7] An explication of what this stretching of the imagination might mean for the ways we envisage our bodies is beyond the scope of this chapter, as well as my own current imagination.

[8] One way to enter into this debate but one well beyond the mandate of this chapter is to begin an enquiry into the incendiary politics of self-care articulated in a variety of different ways by feminists.

> I have taken her to a beauty parlour. Earlier we used to take her to a local place, where mostly men go. One day she did not want to go there so I took her to a more expensive place. She liked this place very much and asked if we could go there again. I am a lazy person and do I do not do much by way of beautification but I don't mind if others do. It's fine with me if she does—for me this is the idea of agency. I realise that an image that comes to her of beauty is something I cannot control much—her life, where we live there are many different ideologies—I hope this will give her the space to make choices. She asks me why I don't use make up to which I simply say that I don't like it.

Alka disclaims: 'I hate dressing up, seldom use make up, never go to a beauty parlour except for a haircut'. Revathi avers: 'I am not big on beauty rituals. I do facials at home once in three months—seeing the face packs is an occasion for great hilarity for my daughter'. Vani talks about how hard it is for her daughter to have a non-conventional mother and how she sometimes tries to redress the balance:

> All my daughter's friends have more conventional moms, who dress in a particular way that I don't, and she ends up being the backward one in the group. Once when I painted my nails, she was very excited. I've had to compromise to let her feel more comfortable and more mainstream.

Meera says:

> When she was in school, there was a school play and the teacher told the students to do their make-up at home. I went to the teacher and asked her how she could assume that everyone had make-up at home. Some of us don't use any. I told my daughter that I was not going to buy make-up for this play.

Meera's anecdote, reflecting the assumption about the presence of make-up in the home, is telling. If you have a mother at home, she must have some make-up, the sub-text being that women are inevitably engaged in the process of beautifying themselves in ways that need artifice. Meera overtly resists this, presumably even at the cost of marking her daughter as different. Vani on the other hand chooses to 'compromise'.

How do our daughters respond to these multiple, sometimes mixed messages we send? Meera avers:

> I went through a hippy kind of phase but then went back to not being interested. My daughter also went through an identical phase—being outrageous and then lost interest. She is very good-looking and there was a point when she was obviously aware of it and would dress with this awareness. But, today she dresses very simply. So simply, that I tell her myself sometimes, to wear some *kajal* (eye liner). She hasn't bought clothes for herself for the last ten years, everything she wears, I've bought her.

Maitri adds: 'My daughter is now so socially conscious that she won't even buy a good pair of shoes. I'm the one who's nagging her to wear better footwear'.

What does it mean when our daughters learn the lessons we try to teach too well? Meera says: 'I always wanted her to be straight and narrow and now she is…', she trails off. In an earlier paper I examined the fear that feminist mothers expressed that our daughters will somehow reject feminism (Phadke 2013). This anxiety that one has somehow taught one's daughter not to care about appearance at all is perhaps a mirror image of that fear. And yet it is not at all clear to any of us what it is exactly that we want. We want for our daughters to be comfortable in a world that is largely hostile to women who do not conform. Yet we want our daughters to be feminists, a politics that brings with it the promise of non-conformity.

What We Want: Some Inconclusive Thoughts

What does it mean to be a feminist mother in twenty-first-century urban India, a moment when it is increasingly undesirable to be a feminist? It is already clear that being feminists is not going to be as obvious a choice for our daughters as it was for many of us. As women embedded in a post-globalisation socio-cultural context we navigate the demands to engage in aesthetic labour to produce smooth, hairless, odourless, slim, fair bodies. In our body-beauty regimes and our mothering practices we sometimes find ourselves veering precariously towards post-feminist understandings of choice and agency (Gill 2011; McRobbie 2004). Our awareness of the contradictions we literally embody unsettles us, even as we strive to think through ways to do justice both to our politics and to our commitment to facilitate 'happiness', that most elusive of conditions, for our daughters.

Even as this chapter elucidates some narratives from our individual and collective struggles to be good feminists' and 'good mothers', what it does not capture is that despite the dilemmas and the fear that one's best is not going to be good enough, there is the sheer joy of trying. As feminists and mothers, we think (and plot) a great deal about how we might achieve a better world for all our daughters. Motherhood is not something that happens to us, *we take on* the challenge of feminist mothering. My interviews were full of laughter, wry, sarcastic, and sometimes full throated and really amused. These interviews were not the first time the feminist mothers I spoke to had discussed their practices of mothering. I would like to reiterate the use of the collective pronoun 'we'—for many, being mothers is feminist work to raise strong, resilient, questioning women (and concomitantly thoughtful feminist men), not as an individual exercise, but as part of a larger women's movement. Despite our awareness of the ambiguities as we attempt to live the political in the often fraught and very intimate space of mothering, not a single one of us would choose to not be a feminist. This endeavour poses unquestionable challenges but also brings deep satisfaction and comradeship.

Acknowledgements I would like to thank the thoughtful and analytical women I interviewed for our continuing conversations and solidarity. I would also like to thank Rosalind Gill, Christina Scharff, Ana Sofia Lemos De Carvalho Elias and the two anonymous reviewers for their insightful and generous comments on an earlier draft of this chapter.

References

Donaghue, N., & Clemitshaw, A. (2012). 'I'm Totally Smart and a Feminist … and yet I Want to Be a Waif': Exploring Ambivalence Towards the Thin Ideal Within the Fat Acceptance Movement. *Women's Studies International Forum, 35*, 415–425.

Fahs, B. (2011). Breaking Body Hair Boundaries: Classroom Exercises for Challenging Social Constructions of the Body and Sexuality. *Feminism and Psychology, 22*(4), 482–506.

Gill, R. (2011). Sexism Reloaded, or, It's Time to Get Angry Again! *Feminist Media Studies, 11*(1), 61–71.

John, M. E. (1998). Globalization, Sexuality and the Visual Field. In M. E. John & J. Nair (Eds.), *A Question of Silence? The Sexual Economies of Modem India*. Kali for Women: New Delhi.

Maor, M. (2012). Fat Women: The Role of the Mother–Daughter Relationship Revisited. *Women's Studies International Forum, 35*, 97–108.

McRobbie, A. (2004). Post-feminism and Popular Culture. *Feminist Media Studies, 4*(3), 255–264.

Oza, R. (2001). Showcasing India: Gender, Geography and Globalization. *Signs, 26*(4), 1067–1095.

Phadke, S. (2005). Some Notes on the Construction of Urban Women's Sexuality in India. In R. Chandiramani & G. Misra (Eds.), *Gender, Sexuality and Rights in South and South East Asia: Exploring Theory and Practice*. New Delhi: Sage.

Phadke, S. (2012). But I Can't Carry a Condom! Young Women, Risk and Sexuality in the Time of Globalisation. In S. Srivastava (Ed.), *The Sexualities Reader: Oxford India Studies on Contemporary Society*. Delhi: Oxford University Press.

Phadke, S. (2013). Feminist Mothering? Some Reflections on Sexuality and Risk from Urban India. *Journal of South Asian Studies, 36*(1), 92–101.

Phadke, S. (2015). Risking Feminism: Voices from the Classroom. *Economic and Political Weekly, 50*(17), 63–70.

Riley, S., & Scharff, C. (2012). Feminism Versus Femininity? Exploring Feminist Dilemmas Through Cooperative Inquiry Research. *Feminism & Psychology, 23*(2), 207–223.

Ruth, S. (2015). What It's Like to Be the Parent of a Dark Skinned Girl. *Youth Ki Awaaz*. [Online] Retrieved from http://www.youthkiawaaz.com/2015/09/parent-of-a-dark-skinned-child/

Sangari, K. (2004). New Patriotisms: The Beauty Queen and the Bomb. In R. Ivekovic & J. Mostov (Eds.), *From Gender to Nation*. Zubaan: New Delhi.

Talukdar, J., & Linders, A. (2013). Gender, Class Aspirations, and Emerging Fields of Bodywork in Urban India. *Qualitative Sociology, 36*(1), 101–123.

Throsby, K., & Gimlin, D. (2010). Critiquing Thinness and Wanting to Be Thin. In R. Ryan-Flood & R. Gill (Eds.), *Secrecy and Silence in the Research Process: Feminist Reflections*. London: Routledge.

Part III

Empowerment, Confidence and Subjectivity

15

'I'm Beautiful the Way I Am': Empowerment, Beauty, and Aesthetic Labour

Sarah Banet-Weiser

Introduction

The early twenty first century has given rise to an ongoing girls' 'confidence movement' (Gill and Orgad 2015). This movement is decentralised, taking place in non-profit organisations, state-funded initiatives, advertising campaigns, marketing, and social media. Hundreds of organisations have emerged globally that focus on the empowerment of girls and women (Banet-Weiser 2015). Corporate culture has also joined the empowerment conversation, creating a slew of campaigns and advertisements shown on television and social media. One after another, companies like Verizon, CoverGirl, Always, and Dove have churned out emotional advertising campaigns, urging us to pay closer attention to

S. Banet-Weiser (✉)
School of Communication, Annenberg School for Communication and Journalism, University of Southern California, Los Angeles, CA, USA

A.S. Elias et al. (eds.), *Aesthetic Labour*,
DOI 10.1057/978-1-137-47765-1_15

girls and the opportunities available to them both personally and professionally. Ostensibly, the varied strands of the girls' empowerment and confidence movement seek to mobilise publics to collective action and to create a collective subjectivity around the need to be more gender inclusive.

Alongside a cultural landscape of protest and challenge against wide-reaching gender discrimination we have also seen a rise in creative industries that correspond with neoliberal capitalist imperatives about the self-governed entrepreneur. This mobilisation takes many forms and targets many demographics, from classic Silicon Valley tech start-ups to ecommerce to YouTube and other social media partnerships. The cultural and economic conditions of neoliberal capitalism have transformed the nature of creative work, and digital media in particular are shaped by a utopic vision that technological spaces afford possibility for anyone who wants to take advantage of these spaces (Gill and Pratt 2008; McRobbie 2015). While women are notoriously underrepresented in leadership positions in the tech industry, in the realm of social media entrepreneurship, girls have had more of a presence, especially in those areas that are seen as traditionally feminine, such as fashion blogging, shopping sites, and beauty vlogging (Duffy 2015; Banet-Weiser and Arzumanova 2013).

In this essay, I focus on the intersection between the recent increase in girls' empowerment and confidence campaigns and the growing presence of a particular genre of entrepreneurship on YouTube: the make-up tutorial, or beauty vlogging. On the face of it, there is a seeming contradiction between initiatives that claim to empower girls and women to *resist* unrealistic and exclusionary standards of beauty, and media productions that instruct or discipline them along these same lines, offering tutorials on how to precisely *achieve* these very same standards. Yet, I argue in this essay that corporate confidence campaigns and beauty vlogging together produce a gendered logic that is not contradictory but rather complementary. This gendered logic centres the 'empowered' feminine body as the source of aesthetic labour. The audiences for the corporate campaigns, as well as the fan bases for beauty vlogs, are encouraged to perform aesthetic labour on their own bodies. To demonstrate how this is achieved, I first analyse two recent commercially visible advertising initiatives, Always' #Like a Girl and CoverGirl's #GirlsCan. Both of these campaigns address discriminatory practices that exclude or diminish girls. I then focus on the recent rise in YouTube beauty vlogging as a potentially lucrative practice for girls and young women.

Despite the fact that these tutorials instruct girls how to apply makeup and thus discipline themselves in conventional hetero-feminine ways, they also, like the confidence campaigns, position girls as self-empowered and entrepreneurial. This contemporary iteration of empowerment prominently positions the individual girl as what Angela McRobbie calls a 'better economic subject' in a context of aesthetic labour and neoliberal entrepreneurialism (McRobbie 2009). This is where the corporate confidence campaigns and beauty vlogging intersect, because in both, girls and young women are encouraged to be good economic subjects, in both the production and consumption realms.

The Confidence 'Movement' and Empowerment Initiatives

In 2013, Facebook's COO, Sheryl Sandberg, published her feminist ode and self-help guide for women, *Lean In*, and it has remained a bestseller ever since, spawning a range of 'Lean In' franchises, such as the Lean In Foundation, the #BanBossy campaign, and others. The argument in the book suggests that women feel that their accomplishments are not as great as those around them (especially men), and this then becomes a barrier to a successful career trajectory (Sandberg 2013). Sandberg's advice is for women to overcome this 'confidence gap' (Kay and Shipman 2014) by being more assertive in their careers and to develop the self-confidence in order to do so. And, according to her, self-confidence is the key to success.

As I have written elsewhere, the 'confidence gap' is a signifier of what is understood as a general emergence (since the 1990s) of a particular 'crisis in girls' (Banet-Weiser 2015; Hains 2012; Gill and Orgad 2015). This crisis is ostensibly evidenced by widespread exclusion of girls from math and science programmes in schools, rising numbers of white, middle-class girls with eating disorders and other body-image issues, and reports of general low self-confidence that is seen to emerge from media representations of hyper-sexuality (Hains 2012; Projansky 2014). This is the conversation that Sandberg is attempting to join; the efforts to encourage younger girls to be more confident will presumably address the confidence gap that Sandberg identifies in the corporate environment.

So, alongside the efforts to empower girls through external mechanisms such as policy and education, there has also been a mandate to 'empower oneself'. Empowering oneself as an individual is a key logic within neoliberal capitalism, which privileges the individual entrepreneur as a primary subjectivity (Cruikshank 1999; McRobbie 2009). This neoliberal focus on the individual is the crux of efforts to build confidence in girls and women. While the focus on building confidence for adult women typically addresses lack of ambition and expressiveness in the workplace, for girls and young women, the confidence issue is located squarely on the body and in one's self-image. In response to the confidence gap, a range of cultural organisations and corporate and non-profit campaigns have emerged with the goal of encouraging girls to be more confident in their bodies and self-image.

Always' #Like a Girl (A#LAG)

Always, the feminine hygiene company owned by Proctor and Gamble, debuted their #LikeAGirl campaign in the summer of 2014. The company hired Lauren Greenfield as the director of the campaign ad. Greenfield is known for her monographs Girl Culture and THIN, and for her critically acclaimed documentary *Queen of Versailles;* she is publicly and politically invested in girl culture. The A#LAG campaign has as its website tagline, 'Fighting to Empower Girls Everywhere', and the company has partnerships with UNESCO as part of their Global Puberty Education program as well as the Lean In Foundation and the Girl Scouts.

Clearly, this campaign is part of a constellation of corporate players invested in resolving the 'girl crisis' through ads and campaigns that encourage empowerment and confidence among girls and young women. These corporate campaigns are examples of a shifted form of corporate social responsibility, where the socio-political goals of the company are not attached to a particular politics such as fair trade or environmentalism, but rather to the formation of gendered subjectivity. While the campaign gained considerable visibility throughout 2014, it wasn't until a shortened version of Greenfield's ad aired on the US Super Bowl broadcast in February 2015, that the campaign became hypervisible.

A#LAG begins with Greenfield posing as director of a shoot asking young women, in their late teens and early 20s, to 'show me what it looks like to run like a girl'. From the beginning of the ad, the focus on gendered subjectivity is the female body—bodies that move, throw, run—and it is through the body that empowerment can be realised. The young women answer Greenfield by running in exaggerated movements, flailing their arms, fussing with their hair. They run slowly, inefficiently, and in an unfocused, untrained manner. Follow-up questions, such as 'show me what it looks like to fight like a girl' and 'to throw like a girl' have similar results: flailing arms, laughing, clearly ineffectual body movements. The ad then cuts to text, saying: 'We then asked young girls the same questions'. The ad then depicts younger girls (one identifying as 10 years old, with others looking even younger), with Greenfield asking the same question. In contrast, the young girls respond earnestly, in force, running, fighting and throwing with strength and confidence. One young girl, when asked what it means to run like a girl, says 'it means run as fast as you can'. The ad then cuts to text, 'when did doing something like a girl become an insult?' Clearly, the ad implies the answer to its question: it makes a point of representing two different female age groups and suggests that 'like a girl' becomes an insult in adolescence. The narrative of the ad then changes, offering more empowered responses: one young woman who is asked 'what advice do you have to girls who are told you run like a girl, hit like a girl, throw like a girl, swim like a girl?', answers:

> Keep doing it 'cause it's working [...] It doesn't matter what they say. I mean, yes, I kick like a girl, and I swim like a girl, and I walk like a girl, and I wake up in the morning like a girl because I am a girl. And that is not something that I should be ashamed of, so I'm going to do it, anyway. That's what they should do.

The ad ends with text: 'Let's make #LikeAGirl mean amazing things. Join us to champion girls' confidence at always.com'. The ad clearly intends to intervene in the early onset of the confidence gap before it crystallises into a full-blown crisis for individual women. By asking viewers to 'join' them in championing girls' confidence, Always positions itself as part of a broader confidence movement. Yet it is also part of a media and popular culture context. Always is a company that needs to sell products—and feminine hygiene products no less—in order to survive. Feminine hygiene products necessarily direct our attention to the body, and indeed, the route to self-confidence, as demonstrated in the ad, is through the body and how the body moves.

CoverGirl's #GirlsCan (CG#GC)

CG#GC also maintains a focus on the body as the route to empowerment, yet it also implies that confidence is something unrelated to the body. Like A#LAG, CG#GC also placed its ad in a media moment of hyper-visibility, the closing ceremonies of the 2014 Winter Olympic Games in Sochi. The ad features celebrities such as Queen Latifah, Katy Perry, Janelle Monae, Sofia Vergara, and others. The narrative of the ad is simple: beginning with Ellen DeGeneres (spokesperson for CoverGirl) boldly stating: 'Girls can't. Sometimes you hear it, more often you feel it'. The narrative of the ad that girls *can't* quickly gives way to girls *can*, with celebrities forcefully contradicting cultural stereotypes about girls and women using their own success as evidence; Queen Latifah says: 'I heard that girls couldn't rap. I rap. Girls couldn't own their own businesses? I own my own business'. Pink insists that girls can rock, Janelle Monae points out that girls can dance 'crazy'. DeGeneres offers this overly vague and broadly ambitious advice: 'I've learned you just have to be yourself'. The ad is highly produced and, like A#LAG, is custom-made for social media with the already established hashtag. The ad ends with the traditional CoverGirl tagline: 'Easy, Breezy, Beautiful'.

Indeed, all of the women who are depicted in the ad *are* conventionally beautiful, and all have high visibility in part because of the way they look. Even the unnamed hockey player in the ad dramatically removes her helmet to reveal long curly hair and striking blue eyes. In other words, it is *through* a celebration of beauty that Procter and Gamble creates a rallying cry for female empowerment. After all, the ad ends with the mandate for girls to be easy, breezy, and beautiful. The continued focus on traditional, normative beauty as a pipeline to empowerment belies the generality of 'girls can', as it is *specific* girls who 'can'.

Both Always and CoverGirl are attempting to not only recognise the importance of building confidence in girls, but are also obviously tapping into a consumer audience of girls and women as users of feminine hygiene products and make-up. This may signal economic empowerment, but it is also about anchoring the *individual* girl to discourses of empowerment. The message of these ads places the responsibility on the young women who are the consumers for their products. There is an absence of collectivity in these ads, and there is no gesture toward empowerment through solidarity. Rather, girls and women individually need to lean in, be confident, to stop thinking 'I can't'. This relieves institutions of the burden of having to grapple with restructuring their own gendered asymmetries.

Girl Entrepreneurship and Make-up Tutorials

One way that gendered asymmetries have been restructured by girls themselves is through the production of content on digital media. Current data indicates that girls and women use online media more than boys and men; the 2013 Pew Research Center report, 'It's a Woman's (Social Media) World', finds that three out of four women online use social networking sites, and women are significantly more likely to use Facebook, Pinterest, and Instagram (Duggan 2013). The presence of girls producing media online gives us something important to celebrate, given the historical exclusion of girls from fields in technology, media production, and science. Yet, the spaces where girls are being encouraged to produce and make media are also conventionally feminine; as Brooke Duffy has argued, the genre of make-up tutorials, fashion blogs, haul videos, fitness tutorials, and so on are clearly feminised spaces, with many producers garnering contracts with corporations and media companies and creating economically successful careers from these entrepreneurial endeavours (Duffy 2015).

The kind of labour involved in creating and curating digital spaces such as beauty vlogs is aesthetic labour, and the girls and women who produce these sites could be called aesthetic entrepreneurs. Yet, as with other forms of neoliberal entrepreneurship, only specific vloggers, usually those who conform to conventional norms of gender, race and class, are actually financially successful (Nathanson 2013; Mears 2014). The creators of these videos instruct viewers how to construct a hyper-feminine aesthetic, through the application of make-up, honing the body, buying the proper clothes, and so on. These cultural productions involve labour that produces one's body as conventionally feminine, and the producers in turn guide viewers on how to deploy the same kind of labour on their own bodies. Importantly, producing and uploading make-up tutorials is big business for media companies such as YouTube, where the search for 'beauty' is among the top search categories, and beauty vlogger Michelle Phan is one of the most viewed vloggers on YouTube.

Beauty vlogging is invested in perpetuating a conventional understanding of beauty and femininity through instruction, where disciplined citizens teach others how to become similarly empowered, visually appealing feminine subjects. We see here the intersection of corporate confidence campaigns and beauty vlogging, as both media productions encourage women to discipline themselves as economic subjects, in both production and consumption. The labour of beauty vloggers is complicated (as most labour is), and the outcome of the labour is particularly suited to both a neoliberal capitalist context and what Catherine Rottenberg calls 'neoliberal feminism' (Rottenberg 2014). The increasing popularity of beauty vlogging emerges within the context of the 'confidence movement' discussed earlier, a movement that ostensibly encourages girls to focus on personality traits and work ethics situated *outside* the body. Indeed, much of the confidence movement explicitly focuses on the low self-esteem and low self-image of girls and women that results from hyper-sexualisation of the body, especially in media and popular culture. Yet, as the success of beauty vlogging shows us, one of the most lucrative career options where women are apparently confident and self-assured is precisely that which brings focus back to the body—and a particular body at that, one that conforms to a conventional understanding of beauty and hyper-femininity. So while beauty vloggers are celebrated for their entrepreneurialism, they achieve this success by becoming 'the object of desiring gazes' (Nathanson 2013).

The Body

In many ways, it is quite obvious that beauty vloggers are focused on the body; after all, the tutorials are meant to instruct viewers how to not only ornament their faces with make-up using specific mechanisms and techniques, but how to change their faces, how to hide parts of their faces, and how to embellish and/or mask their faces. In fact, a good proportion of the tutorials is about contouring the face with make-up, a technique that is about hiding pieces of one's face, literally painting these pieces into shadows. I'd like to call attention, however, to the ways in which this kind of instruction functions as a disciplinary technique that not only produces but *reproduces* the feminine body. The aesthetic labour of the beauty vloggers is also reproductive labour, working to continually reproduce a conventional, idealised definition of beauty.

In 1997, Sandra Lee Bartky, writing about the ways in which female docile bodies are disciplined through work on the body, pointed out that applying make-up is portrayed in fashion magazines and cosmetics ads

> as an aesthetic activity in which a woman can express her individuality. In reality, while cosmetic styles change every decade or so, and making up the face is, in fact, a highly stylised activity that gives little rein to self-expression. Painting the face is not like painting a picture, at best, it might be described as painting the same picture over and over again with minor variations. (Bartky 1997, p. 33)

According to Bartky, applying make-up is an 'aesthetic activity', a routine everyday ritual of disciplined femininity.

Of course, in contemporary beauty vlogging, applying make-up is also an aesthetic activity. But Bartky is commenting on what is largely a private activity, where women apply make-up in private as a daily routine. With beauty vlogging, we need to reframe the individual routine activity as an act of aesthetic labour where women produce tutorials that reveal the steps, the sequence, and the technique of make-up application for an audience of viewers. This positions the beauty vlogger as a master at these techniques, and encourages mastery with her viewers. These are all ways in which the make-up tutorial publicly acknowledges the labour aspect of what Bartky called an 'activity'. In other words, the labour of the beauty vloggers is acknowledged by the viewer. But the acknowledgement of aesthetic labour is not the same as recognising it as *work*, because beauty vloggers often say (in their online bios and in the vlogs themselves) that they produce vlogs simply because they 'love to put on make-up!' The aesthetic labour involved in producing beauty vlogs is not typically recognised as labour. Rather, it can be considered what some members in social media communities call DWYL: 'Do What You Love'. As Duffy has detailed, the notion of loving what we do, or 'passionate work', functions in the marketplace to not only romanticise work but also to displace risks from institutions and corporations onto individuals (Duffy 2015; McRobbie 2015). This 'labour of love' can be underpaid (or even unpaid), but the lack of compensation is masked by what Duffy calls the 'romance of work'.

Thus, this kind of aesthetic labour, which also reproduces the feminine body, is not always identified or recognised as 'work', either by practitioners or consumers. And again, beauty vloggers are not simply disciplining what Bartky called 'docile bodies'; rather, the women who create vlogs and those who consume them are not only subject to external controls that regulate their bodies, but are encouraged to self-regulate and to modulate their own bodies. Through the use of these tutorials, girls transform *social* risks—the 'crisis in girls'—into problems of *individual* self-care. Consider Michelle Phan, who has been called the pioneer of beauty vloggers. She began posting make-up tutorials on YouTube in 2007 and is now the most popular beauty vlogger on YouTube, with 374 videos and 7,413,236 subscribers. Her online popularity has paid off: the cosmetics company Lancôme (whose parent company is L'Oréal) sponsored Phan as an 'official video make-up artist' in 2010, and she has introduced her own make-up line called Em Cosmetics, backed by L'Oréal. It is estimated that she is now worth $84 million (Moore 2014). Phan says about her labour as a beauty vlogger: 'It doesn't even feel like a job', and adds: 'I'm learning so much and meeting so many wonderful people'. The article continues, 'Makeup is now her full-time job' (Ricapito 2010).

What are we to make of the fact that beauty vlogging is one of the most prevalent forms of 'how-to' videos on sites such as YouTube as simultaneously there is a 'confidence movement' that encourages girls to be 'beautiful the way they are'? Beauty vloggers demonstrate in painstaking detail how to achieve an ideal of beauty, yet corporate confidence campaigns tell girls and women to resist unattainable ideals of beauty. Despite this seeming disconnect, the message of beauty vloggers, like that of corporate confidence campaigns, is self-empowerment. Obviously, beauty vloggers explicitly suggest that viewers can become empowered by disciplining their bodies according to the tutorial. However, the success of beauty vloggers ostensibly works as a double form of empowerment: not only cultural but also economic—which is achieved through a focus on their own bodies, as they transform their face and body for their fan base in exchange of material compensations. Simultaneously, the general philosophy of the make-up tutorial rests on the promise of empowering their fan base: you can be anyone you like, and beauty is a mere make-up brush stroke away—you just have to work at it. Beauty is achievable through labour, and not just any kind of labour, but labour as dedicated practice, repetition, and mastery.

Authenticity

One of the features of beauty vlogging is the performance of authenticity by the vloggers. The success of vloggers depends on their fan base believing that they are 'ordinary' women whose labour is based in passion and love for putting on make-up, not in a sheer desire to be discovered by the industry or for financial success. Of course, beauty vloggers are creating media in order to become successful. Beauty vlogging is part of celebrity culture and neoliberal entrepreneurialism, even as the aesthetic labour of the beauty vloggers is carefully constructed to be authentic and passionate and not profit-driven.

Indeed, the cultural economic context of neoliberal entrepreneurialism provides the backdrop for the cultural circulation of a mythology about the openness of capitalism and the freedom of online production, which is key to the continued creation of make-up tutorials. The ideas that *anyone* can have a successful start-up, that self-branding is a primary mechanism to become visible, and that 'everyone is creative' help provide the ideological scaffolding for girls and young women to become beauty vloggers (McRobbie 2015). A crucial component of this ideology is celebrity culture, though a particular kind of celebrity, what Alice Marwick and danah boyd call micro-celebrity (Marwick and Boyd 2011). Micro-celebrity is a kind of celebrity that is ideally suited to online media, because it involves a performance of self that is designed to be consumed by fans, and part of the labour of the micro-celebrity is careful management and cultivation of those fans (Marwick and Boyd 2011, p. 140). As Marwick and boyd (and others) have demonstrated, celebrity culture has changed in an era of networked media, where traditional control and management mechanisms have shifted so that creating and maintaining a celebrity persona is now something 'ordinary' people who aren't conventionally famous can now access. Indeed, the production of micro-celebrity within networked media presents opportunities for 'ordinary' people to create lucrative careers based on things like blogs, social media, and beauty vlogging. Graeme Turner calls this process the 'demotic turn', which refers to the 'increasing visibility of the "ordinary person" as they turn themselves into media content through celebrity culture, reality TV, DIY websites, talk radio, and the like' (Turner 2006, 153).

Indeed, the celebrity of beauty vloggers absolutely depends on not losing one's 'ordinariness'. It is *precisely* the ordinariness of beauty vloggers, or their authenticity, that makes them consumable as celebrities to their online fan base. As Elizabeth Nathanson has shown, their ordinariness is the substance of authenticity in this context (Nathanson 2013). Beauty vloggers trade in on their authenticity as earnest every-girls who simply liked to put on make-up and then found a lucrative career guiding viewers to acquire skills. Aesthetic labour here is expressed in earnest terms as just doing something one loves to do, and the focus on love and ordinariness obscures the mechanisms that are needed to produce these videos, including professionalisation, access to products and technology, and, in some cases, corporate sponsors (Duffy 2015).

Beauty vlogs utilise authenticity in a number of ways, from the 'naked' (no make-up) faces of the vloggers at the beginning of each video, to the constant appeals to the fans that 'this [smoky eye, concealer, face mask] is something everyone can do easily', to the positioning of themselves as close, intimate girlfriends of the fan base. As Nathanson comments on beauty vlogs like Phan's: 'Their videos [...] replicate the experience of applying makeup in one's bathroom mirror, conveying an immediacy that constructs a sense of authenticity' (Nathanson 2013, 147). The relative amateur quality of the actual videos, where the vloggers often adjust the camera during the video, or accidently move their faces out of the video frame, is another component of their authenticity. Consider again in this regard Michelle Phan. One of the keys to her success is her authenticity and earnest address: it is often noted how beauty vloggers produce their videos with a simple laptop, often in their bedroom, thus encouraging an 'anyone can do it!' message. As Phan puts it: 'I don't want people to think they need a perfect amazing lighting video. If it's authentic and has a great message, people will watch' (Mau 2014). The amateur quality of the video is clearly one of the most important elements of the beauty vlog, as the point of the media production is to transfer make-up application skills to the millions of followers who will be reproducing this labour on themselves.[1]

Phan herself is also recognised for her authentic appeal; she is charmingly self-deprecating in her videos and speaks intimately to her audiences, noting how difficult it was for her to learn some techniques, thus establishing make-up routines as something any girl or young women can do if they just practice. For example, her bio on YouTube states, 'Teaching and inspiring everyone to become their own best makeup artist:) So sit back, enjoy and let's play with makeup!' The use of 'play' here, rather than 'work', situates her aesthetic labour as fun rather than a job. She, like most beauty vloggers, also embodies 'niceness', a sort of adorable girl-next-door banality. This performance of authenticity removes the threat that might come from the fact that she makes money off her tutorials, reassuring the fans that she is 'just like them', a girl who loves to put on make-up and look beautiful. Her authenticity also provides a counter-narrative that creating these tutorials and managing a fan base *is* laborious. For example, in her vlog, '#NoFilter Beauty Tutorial', the importance of not only being authentic but instructing fans on the importance of authenticity is the central message. Phan films herself against a simple blue backdrop and conveys a girlish innocence with a pink sweater

[1] Though Phan produces what seem to be high production videos and has now created tutorials with romantic narrative scripts involved, such as 'First Kiss' or 'Prom Night'.

and a large hair bow. She begins with 'A selfie is like a self-portrait—you want to capture the best version of yourself, right? And after that, there are so many filters you can choose to enhance your portrait. Well, in this video, I'm going to show you how to enhance your skin without the need for a filter' (Phan 2014). Authenticity is also an important element within corporate confidence campaigns, which communicate their message with a sentimental earnestness about a girl's 'true' self.

Entrepreneurialism

There are necessary cultural and economic conditions that allow for the emergence of beauty vloggers as a particular kind of success story. YouTube make-up tutorials can be seen as a quintessential neoliberal industry in that the focus is on the individual entrepreneur who mobilises her own creativity and gumption into a lucrative career. Yet, beauty vloggers' entrepreneurialism is not the brutal entrepreneurial spirit of the male Silicon Valley entrepreneur but a welcoming embrace, an invitation to perform labour in the name of desire, personal fulfilment, and being 'nice'.

The tutorials are also an example of the ever-expanding reach of neoliberal markets, as they ostensibly disrupt the economic model of cosmetics industry while simultaneously creating new markets. Indeed, as Susan Murray (2012) has pointed out, YouTube has become the exemplar of social media industry, where videos go viral and generate income for users and producers. Yet despite the apparent openness of YouTube, where anyone can upload a video, the company, now owned by Google, has quickly capitalised on the success of its users. As Murray has argued, the YouTube partner program, as well as the numerous 'creator institutes' the company sponsors, allows the company to maintain control over its content and revenue streams even as it retains its feel as a non-hierarchical social media space. Writing about the YouTube creator institute, where intrepid entrepreneurs can receive training on how to be a successful online media producer, Murray (2012) points out that it is clear that YouTube is not attempting to identify artists to cultivate their craft but rather looking for individuals who can create new markets. Many of the most popular beauty vloggers are YouTube partners.[2]

To be an entrepreneur means that one is forward-thinking, with a vision of how self-starting in one media platform can lead to another. Online beauty tutorials have proven to be a success in this realm as well, as popular online aesthetic entrepreneurs such as Michelle Phan and Zoella have expanded their brands from their YouTube channels to magazine covers, make-up lines, and sponsorship from major cosmetic labels. Zoella, a British beauty vlogger, became the first YouTube beauty star to appear on the cover of a mainstream magazine, *Company*. The editor of *Company*, Victoria White, explained the choice to feature Zoella on the cover through the language of entrepreneurialism: 'Vloggers like Zoella have given young women hope that girls just like them can become successful from their bedrooms. Unlike the Big Brother pipe dreams of the 90s, it is a fame based in hard work' (Wiseman 2014). Beauty vloggers also routinely promote make-up brands in their tutorials, displaying the product for the camera and often mentioning the 'good deal' they got on the product. Duffy calls this standard routine of beauty vlogging 'entrepreneurial brand devotion', where digital content creators such as beauty vloggers demonstrate their loyalty to specific brands with the aspiration to become more formally aligned with these companies.

One central characteristic of neoliberal entrepreneurialism is a mandate to 'empower oneself'; and again, this is also the crux of the 'confidence movement', which revolves around self-confidence in girls and women. The dual contexts of neoliberal entrepreneurialism and the 'confidence movement' for girls and women incorporate the aesthetic labour involved in beauty vlogging. The campaigns examined earlier demonstrate that 'confidence' for women is often understood through/within the body, a point that is dramatically emphasised in beauty vlogs.

---

[2] The YouTube partner program is an even more direct link to the company's profit agenda. When videos begin to generate views in the thousands, YouTube may invite media producers to be 'partners' where they can earn money from advertising, and users share in the revenue generated when people watch. Partners must agree to allow what YouTube deems as 'relevant' advertising to be placed alongside and also within their videos.

Conclusion

For many girls and young women, a great deal of self-confidence generates in the body and in one's self-image. Girls are seen to have plummeting self-confidence in adolescence and young adulthood, so marketing initiatives and advertising such as Always and CoverGirl, among others, have shifted their tactics and target this demographic with messages that focus on self-love, self-image, and body positivity.

But the trajectory has an ultimate goal: to insure that women are better, more confident economic subjects, not feminist subjects. Indeed, the empowerment initiatives like Always and CoverGirl are about targeting consumers, which suggests an economic empowerment. The focus on economic empowerment of girls and women allows for beauty vlogging to be a career trajectory at precisely the same moment when the confidence movement is directing girls and young women to *not* focus on their body. Thus, while the two cultural phenomena—the confidence movement and beauty vlogging—seem to oppose each other, within the context of neoliberal entrepreneurship, they actually support and legitimate each other. In so doing, the goal of both corporate confidence campaigns and beauty vlogs is to discipline girls and women to become better economic subjects.

Acknowledgements I am grateful for the research help and feedback from Melina Sherman and Inna Arzumanova.

References

Banet-Weiser, S. (2015). 'Confidence You Can Carry!': Girls in Crisis and the Market for Girls' Empowerment Organizations. *Continuum: Journal of Media and Cultural Studies, 29*(2), 182–193.

Banet-Weiser, S., & Arzumanova, I. (2013). Creative Authorship: Self-Actualizing Individuals and the Self-Brand. In D. Gerstner & C. Chris (Eds.), *Media Authorship*. New York: Routledge.

Bartky, S. L. (1997). *Femininity and Domination*. New York: Pyschology Press.

Cruikshank, B. (1999). *The Will to Empower: Democratic Citizens and Other Subjects*. New York: Cornell University Press.
Duffy, B. E. (2015). The Romance of Work: Gender and Aspirational Labour in Digital Culture Industries. *International Journal of Cultural Studies, 25*, 1–17.
Duggan, M. (2013, September 13). It's a Woman's (Social Media) World. *Pew Research Center*.
Gill, R., & Orgad, S. (2015). The Confidence Cult(ure). *Australian Feminist Studies, 30*(86), 324–344.
Gill, R., & Pratt, A. (2008). In the Social Factory?: Immaterial Labour, Precariousness and Cultural Work. *Theory Culture Society, 25*(1), 1–30.
Hains, R. C. (2012). *Growing up with Girl Power: Girlhood on Screen and in Everyday Life*. New York: Peter Lang.
Kay, K., & Shipman, C. (2014, April 14). The Confidence Gap. *The Atlantic Monthly*.
Marwick, A., & Boyd, D. (2011). To See and Be Seen: Celebrity Practice on Twitter. *Convergence, 17*(2), 139–158.
Mau, D. (2014, January 30). How the Fastest-Rising Beauty Vloggers Found YouTube Success. *Fashionista*.
McRobbie, A. (2009). *The Aftermath of Feminism: Gender, Culture and Social Change*. London: SAGE.
McRobbie, A. (2015). *Be Creative: Making a Living in the New Cultural Industries*. London: Wiley.
Mears, A. (2014). Aesthetic Labour for the Sociologies of Work, Gender, and Beauty. *Sociology Compass, 8*(12), 1330–1343.
Moore, L. (2014, February 20). Her Blog, Her Brand. *New York Times*, p. 3.
Murray, S. (2012). Amateur Auteurs: The Cultivation of Online Videos Content Producers. In D. Gerstner & C. Chris (Eds.), *Media Authorship*. New York: Routledge.
Nathanson, E. (2013). Dressed for Economic Distress: Blogging and the 'New' Pleasures of Fashion. In D. Negra & Y. Tasker (Eds.), *Gendering the Recession*. Durham, NC: Duke University Press.
Phan, M. (2014). #NoFilter Beauty Tutorial, YouTube [video] Retrieved from https://www.youtube.com/watch?v=2UZMhv87OjU
Projansky, S. (2014). *Spectacular Girls: Media Fascination and Celebrity Culture*. New York: NYU Press.
Ricapito, M. (2010, May 28). Viral Videos: Michelle Phan's Rise to Youtube Stardom. *Vanity Fair*.

Rottenberg, C. (2014). The Rise of Neoliberal Feminism. *Cultural Studies, 28*(3), 418–437.

Sandberg, S. (2013). *Lean in: Women, Work, and the Will to Lead.* New York: Knopf.

Turner, G. (2006). The Mass Production of Celebrity: Celetoids, Reality TV and the 'Demotic Turn'. *International Journal of Cultural Studies, 9*(2), 153–165.

Wiseman, E. (2014, July 19). Lights Camera, Lipstick: Beauty Vloggers Are Changing the Face of the Beauty Industry. *The Guardian.*

16

'Just Be Confident Girls!': Confidence Chic as Neoliberal Governmentality

Laura Favaro

Introduction

> Confidence is the new sexy
> (Bobbi Brown Cosmetics, 2014)

In our injurious patriarchal cultures, unconfidence is almost inescapable when inhabiting womanhood. However, recently the promotion of self-confidence has surfaced as the site for expanded, heightened and more insidious modes of regulation, often spearheaded by those very institutions invested in women's insecurities. This notably includes consumer women's magazines. Contemporary publications are marked by an intensified preoccupation with taking readers 'from crisis to confidence', offering even dedicated sections (e.g. 'confidence revolution' and 'Bye-bye body hang-ups' in *Cosmopolitan UK*) and issues—see, for example, *Elle UK*'s

L. Favaro (✉)
Department of Sociology, City, University of London, London, UK

A.S. Elias et al. (eds.), *Aesthetic Labour*,
DOI 10.1057/978-1-137-47765-1_16

January 2015 'Confidence Issue: A Smart Woman's Guide to Self-Belief'. Clearly, this sector is a fundamental player in the confidence movement-market, bringing together a range of interested parties, not least 'love your body' (LYB) advertisers like Dove (see Gill and Elias 2014), and enjoying an extensive audience reach, both in terms of numbers and geography—a reach increased to unprecedented degrees by online versions.

This chapter asks: how is (the turn to) confidence articulated in magazines for—and mostly by—young women? What does the rise of self-confidence as primary imperative for the production of successful femininity suggest about the operation of power at the current conjuncture? I focus on five popular websites/online magazines produced in the UK but globally accessed: *cosmopolitan.co.uk*, *elleuk.com*, *femalefirst.co.uk*, *glamourmagazine.co.uk* and *sofemenine.co.uk*. The analysis is divided into two main sections, each exploring a different data type: first, 80 editorial features applying a 'love your self' (LYS) approach and, second, 30 interviews conducted between December 2014 and July 2015 with writers and editors of these publications.[1] Uniquely, then, the chapter throws light both on confidence texts and on those producing them in widely read media spaces. Participants were all female, white, mainly in their mid-twenties to early thirties (coinciding with the target readership), middle-class and London-based.[2]

The analysis interrogates what I have labelled 'confidence chic'—pointing to the gendered, classed and commercial nature of the phenomenon under study, as well as its entrenchment within economies of visibility (in new media, neoliberal times; see Banet-Weiser 2013). I apply a feminist discursive Foucauldian-influenced approach, a key concept being that of 'governmentality', namely the contact between the (objectifying) technologies of domination of others and the (subjectifying) technologies of the self (Foucault 1988). Ultimately, this chapter argues that confidence chic is an emergent gendered technology of neoliberal governmentality variously related to proliferating feminisms.

[1] This chapter is part of a larger research project that additionally examines online magazines produced in Spain, and which includes a third data type: user discussions about sex and relationships on the sites' forums/boards. 'Confidence chic' is pervasive here too, with typical peer-to-peer advice being: 'just be confident girls!'

[2] My utmost gratitude to all the research participants.

Confidence Chic: Notes from the Web

Psycommerce as Confidence Expertise

> Feel Like the Queen of Confidence with these Expert Tips.
> (*cosmopolitan.co.uk*, 2014)

In women's magazines, 'lack of self-confidence' is normalised as a universal peculiarly female malady. However, this malady has solutions—individualised ones. The confidence chic regime exhorts women to undergo intense, constant self-scrutiny and self-work according to knowledges and procedures specified by experts. This notably involves the 'psy' professions (Rose 1998) and the newer authorities associated with the 'self-esteem industry' (Banet-Weiser 2013). Indeed, the power/knowledge apparatus of confidence chic seams gendered psychotherapies with commodity logic, as illustrated by hybrid 'psycommercial' positions such as: 'dating guru and head and shoulders Date Night Confidence Coach'.

Since self-confidence is allegedly not innate in women, 'working on your confidence is a life-long task', magazines assure readers. This legitimises an editorial bombardment of advice features ranging from how to 'become confident', 'boost your confidence' to 'maximise your potential', with 'confidence commandments' for every minutia of women's lives—from the meeting at work to the 'bikini body' to fellatio. All this is informed by the general premise that becoming confident: 'it's all in the power of thought'. Influenced by the positive psychology movement, the confidence project is undertaken via the application of techniques imparted by experts—but in the arena of the intimate and quotidian. Readers are urged to engage in an enterprising subjectivity labour of confidence individually and at all times through the conscious direct manipulation of thought, taking 'mental shifts' toward a '#PMA' (positive mental attitude). The ultimate exhortation to women is, then, to 'Zap your negative thinking' and 'Think yourself confident!' 'Whether you're in the bedroom or boardroom'. Below I centre on the realms of the body and intimate relationships.

'Confidence Is Sexy': Enlisting Labour

In apparent opposition to the obsession with (highly sexualised) female bodies in contemporary hyper-visual culture, suffusing women's magazines is the claim 'confidence is sexy'. Moreover, some texts *equate* sexiness with confidence: 'Sex appeal *is all about* self-confidence', 'real sexiness *is* true confidence!' (my emphasis). Likewise, beauty magnates tell readers that 'beauty is all about confidence'. The relationships features accordingly assert that 'to attract love' 'what really works is looking at the *inner* you and doing the *inner* work necessary'. As an agony aunt further explains in response to 'My weight is making me nervous to register for online dating': 'The important thing is to feel confident, be confident as confidence is attractive regardless of your size'. Note in these two quotes the resort to 'overwording' (Fairclough 1992), even italicisation for additional emphasis. This suggests ideological struggle, intense preoccupation with winning consent for a particular representation or (new) meaning—in this case complicated/challenged by adjacent weight loss content, and more broadly the centrality of the beauty sections in these magazines/sites, which are then further divided into dedicated subsections on skin, hair, make-up, nails and even cosmetic surgery in *sofeminine.co.uk*. Discursively mystifying this is the 'inside' dictate: 'love yourself on the inside', 'confidence is an inner issue', 'seductiveness comes from within' and so on, which also normalises the new realms of femininity labour.

Magazines promote the seemingly radically woman-friendly new precept 'love your body and he'll love it too'. This deceptively simple idea not only invisibilises likely conflicts with everyday experience, but it also effectively renders women responsible for body love *and* body hate in intimate relationships. Such state of affairs is discernible in this agony aunt response to 'My husband ogles at other women!':

> Men are drawn to confidence and if you are feeling a little low about yourself atm [at the moment] then this may be why he is looking at the maid that is more forward and comfortable in her own skin. Remind him why he married you and bring out your best side again! (*femalefirst.co.uk*)

In these media female insecurity is the ultimate male repellent, a total 'turn off'. 'He's not there to reassure you about yourself', *sofeminine.co.uk* adds. Even more worryingly, a piece titled '30 Things MEN Wish Women Knew' builds on the premise 'Insecurity isn't sexy!' as follows: 'A bit of self-dignity and self-confidence in who you are and what you want is HOT. If you can't respect yourself, he won't respect you'.

As a new requisite of the (hetero)sexiness imperative, 'confidence' adds *yet more levels of labour* to the project of successful femininity. Although becoming a 'queen of confidence' is allegedly 'all in the mind ladies', it is inseparable from 'keep[ing] up the self-maintenance' (e.g. 'make sure you've waxed'), dressing for (hetero)'sex-cess' (e.g. in 'killer heels'), wearing a 'full face of make-up', buying a 'push-up Super Egoboost bra' and performing a boudoir striptease for 'your man' Dita Von Teese-style—'exuding confidence', of course. That is, confidence chic weaves the remodelling of the psyche with aesthetic and sexual labour, much of which is grounded in the heteronormative, pornified, body-fixated consumerist culture of postfeminism—the very culture seemingly being contested.

Battle the Negative Self: Toxic Women

A notion of female toxicity informs confidence magazine content. Autocritique and negativity are presented as natural tendencies in women, which are profoundly toxic both for themselves *and* others. Here the familiar language of 'flaws' and 'battles' departs the corporeal as its (main) target to enter the arena of the psyche. A 'madeover' positive subjectivity is promoted as panacea for all ills: 'Stop looking in the mirror and bashing your body… Battle the negative self talk… Remember love your self and everything else will follow suit'. Confidence surfaces, then, as a depoliticised, straightforward self-governing venture of rational choice and active appropriation.

The ideological discourse of 'toxic insecurity' not only blames women for feeling unconfident but also for putting their relationships at risk and unjustly affecting their (male) partners (see Favaro in press). Increasingly, magazines and advertisements also accuse mothers for 'passing' body insecurities onto their daughters and stress peer judgement. These dynamics of culpability operate to turn the critical gaze away from socio-political and economic structures and institutions—not least sexual politics—and to constitute women as *pathological*, and so legitimate subject-objects of intervention.

Confidence chic is a sinister regime. Despite the apparent promotion of positivity, self-acceptance and the insistence on insecurities as individual self-sabotage with no external basis (excepting possibly other toxic women), at the heart of LYS/B is a female body that is always already unruly, flawed and difficult to love. The following extract from *cosmopolitan.co.uk* exemplifies this contradictory discursive landscape: 'Body confidence = great sex. It just takes a mental makeover… The day of your big date is not the time you realise your legs resemble the Amazon jungle'. In addition to humour, the notion of producer-as-consumer that is key to women's magazines also facilitates a body shaming which would otherwise more readily risk criticism. By speaking from the position of 'us girls' and 'sisterly honesty', body hate—the prerequisite for the body love business—can be safely maintained. For example, among 'A woman's top 20 confidence boosters!' a *femalefirst.co.uk* feature consistently written in the first-person plural includes (emphasis added):

> Looking good in a photograph–There is always an apprehension that you will be able to see *that awful spot*, or *your double chin* will appear, or *your arm will look fat* from the side–when one turns out well we are generally surprised!

Magazines therefore continue to endorse—indeed benefit from—the hostile fragmentation, micro-scrutiny and shaming of female bodies, namely the very body hate discourses purportedly under challenge. But in an ideological sleight of hand it is women/readers who are figured as their toxic (re–)producers.

'Accept Responsibility': Managing Injury

In the spirit of neoliberalism, confidence chic interpellates women as autonomous, freely choosing, perpetually self-regulating, transformative and adaptive actors who are entirely self-reliant, responsible and accountable for their life, and whose value is largely measured by their capacity to self-care and self-improve. In particular, to be a 'confident chick' is to govern oneself taking an entrepreneurial approach informed by positive psychology. This involves incessant calculation—and 'appreciation'—of distinctive personal strengths ('assets'), along with advanced skills of self-management such as identifying and rationalising 'bad body triggers'. Women are equally expected to employ micro-techniques for the cultivation, enhancement and maintenance of positive outlooks and self-regard, through exercises like gratitude reflections and repeating affirmative mantras in front of a mirror.

Women's magazines are remarkably insistent on the idea that 'the greatest enemy of true self-confidence is *comparing yourself* (my italics), exhorting readers to instead 'just focus on being uniquely YOU!' This is informed by the values of authenticity and singularity of contemporary self-branding culture, inducing into being the entrepreneurial femininities of 'creative fashionistas' and 'trend setters'. The otherwise intensely promoted culture of comparison (certainly, it is a pillar of the industry) here hampers the competitive drive and work toward maximising unique personal qualities and developing differentiation (e.g. in your 'fashion mojo'), hence hampering too the cycle of consumption.

The 'no comparison!' confidence commandment also fits within the programme of sociocultural desensitisation that confidence chic entails. As exemplary neoliberal technology, it is structured by a violent ethos of self-determination that repudiates notions of social/external constraints, pressures or influences. Arguably due to the current difficulty (see next section) of completely ignoring the cultural injuries inflicted upon women, some are at times acknowledged—but only to be disavowed a few lines later to again blame and responsibilise women and to incite the labour of positive subjectivity, for example: 'Fatphobia is everywhere in the media… Negative thinking will damage you more than fashion mags'. Other editorial features interpellate the by now normative media literate consumer, with calls to 'be critical of these kinds of images', essentially exculpating the media industry.

Following neoliberal logics, then, the injunction is to deny *external* injury. Low self-esteem, feelings of vulnerability, victimhood and dependence upon external factors are rearticulated as 'self-pity, insufficient personal drive and a lack of personal responsibility for one's own life' (Baker 2010, p. 190). One illustration is the following extract from an article on 'How to be confident': 'Only you can help you. Want the truth? You have to stop blaming others for your low self-esteem and accept some responsibility'. This contrasts with the propagation of injury claims concerning society by heterosexual white men, as part of a rearticulated backlash against the upsurge of feminist ideas and activism in the 2010s (García-Favaro and Gill 2015). Women's magazines are also capitalising on the logics of victimisation or oppression, as discussed in the next section, which turns to the interviews I conducted with writers and editors of these media.

The Confidence R/evolution: Notes from the Office

'A Cultural Backlash': Claiming Injury

In the interviews, producers claimed that the sector is subjected to high levels of deeply unjust, 'aggressive', 'focussed' criticism: 'Women's magazine bashing is a thing … which is unfair'. Furthermore, conjuring an idea of irrational attack, my research participants argued that this occurs 'no matter what we do'. Critique was disavowed by describing publications a 'best friend', 'loyal', 'honest', 'a source you can trust'. Evoking both the individualism and gender essentialism driving these media, many likewise drew on the notion of 'a girl's YOUniverse' (*Cosmopolitan*), speaking about the magazine as a 'women's safe place' that is 'all about you' and the things (all) 'women really care about'. Moreover, for an editor-in-chief: 'Our publication encourages young women to feel good about themselves, that they're great as they are'. Swinging their dilemmatic (and problematic) relatability-aspiration pendulum, also repeatedly mobilised was an ideology of 'best': 'It's aimed at making you look and feel and do the best you can', insisted a features editor. This was again used to counter claims that these publications are detrimental as misguided and unfair. One freelance writer protested: 'Me and my friends that write for magazines spend a lot of time actually trying to help people with their weak spots'.

Others spoke of a distinctively contemporary backlash against these publications:

> There's been a cultural backlash against women's magazines because we are perceived—I would argue incorrectly—as being out of touch, telling women that they're not right, they need to be thinner, healthier, lalala. That we're not funny, that we're not intelligent, and that we're out of touch with this growing new wave of feminism, etcetera.

Against this, magazine producers repeatedly asserted: 'We have changed since the 90s and the noughties'. In particular, in the words of a staff writer: 'When we're talking about the shift in women's magazines, at the core of everything we do is [...] always trying to enforce positive messages'. In what follows I examine how magazine professionals explain the rise of LYS/B.

Creating Confidence Chic

The writers and editors of women's magazines were keen to highlight that LYS/B—often described as a shift in focus from 'looking' to 'feeling' good, from 'looks' to 'health' and 'well-being'—is 'such a subtle difference but it's huge'. This suggests how in these media: 'Working within tight restrictions of format and expectation, small changes become heavily symbolic' (Murphy 2013, p. 178). Such recent editorial modification was variously explained. Some of the interviewed journalists pointed to a conscious response to critiques: 'I know in the past is like "there's models that are too thin and features that aren't very encouraging", but we're trying to address that'. Others similarly mentioned a personal motivation rooted in a concern about the role of magazines regarding the well-being of readers:

> I remember reading a stat when I was first starting out about 'women read magazines and afterwards they feel worse about themselves' and I found that really sad and I've always had that at the back of my mind that I wanna go against that ... that's what my passion is.

However, paralleling the discursive moves in the editorial content, any critical allusion to the media was quickly followed by a statement that would redirect the gaze toward women(-as-problem), such as: 'Women have a natural tendency to feel insecure'.

Consumer demand was also emphasised: 'We are setting the agenda but we are also just *reporting* on the agenda, we are giving people what they want', a digital health editor stated. This discourse was used to support both 'body love' *and* 'look good' content. The former would be depicted as a response to an 'awakening' or 'backlash' by women against beauty standards that were unachievable and thus 'alienating them', with many stressing a producer-as-consumer identity: 'We're all just women … feeling the same things everybody else is feeling'. Mirroring contradictions in the magazine texts, this was often followed by claims like: 'Women still want to know how to be thin. They always will'. In this regard, I was repeatedly 'reminded' of the following: 'We have an editorial and journalistic responsibility to make sure that what we are giving people is going to be ethical and good and positive, but also we are business not charities, we have to sell'. In addition to blaming consumers' disinterest ('women like reading about diets'), magazine professionals argued that the potential expansion of LYS/B is restricted by the nature of the genre. Significantly, advertisers must not be 'alienated' by editorial and veto the critique of some issues (e.g. plastic surgery or photoshopping). 'All the content that is produced in the magazine is assessed through the filter of "what will our advertisers think about this"', explained a content director.

Generally leaving as quickly as possible the topic of editorial-advertising relationships, writers and editors would also highlight that 'at the end of the day women's magazines are creating an aspirational world'. Any potential critique of this was hastily pre-empted. Notably, these content producers would validate the pleasures of the aspirational, for example, as indulgent escapism or inspiring 'blueprint for how you ought to be living'; and evoke the figure of the media-savvy, freely choosing consumer, for example, women are not 'stupid', understand how marketing works, and can 'make their own choices' and 'informed decisions'.

More cynically, LYS/B was also sometimes described as the result of wanting to promote aspirational elements like being 'skinny', 'but in a way that is less dangerous and means we won't get into trouble'. Indeed, participants spoke of women's magazine producers 'checking themselves in fear of being scrutinized or told off'. Interestingly, this never involved, say, higher-level journalists or media watchdogs. It was instead attributed to social media call-outs for 'realism' and 'honesty' by 'literate' and 'discerning' readers—and to feminists: 'People do self-censor and check themselves because they're so over-analysed by feminists, popular mainstream feminists who have a massive following, the bloody *Vagenda*'.

Launched in 2012 as an online magazine and adapted into a book in 2014, *The Vagenda* self-describes as 'a big "we call bullshit" on the mainstream women's press' (*vagendamagazine.com*). Interestingly, this feminist media was frequently cited as a key catalyst of the shift to LYS/B. One staff writer put it as follows:

> [Women's magazines] were basically making women feel bad about themselves, and perpetuating this thing that women should be ashamed, women should try and be better. 'You're fat, that's not good enough. You need to be thin, and pretty and perfect in every single way, and be able to afford everything'. *The Vagenda* said: 'Hang on. This is not okay.' Then, suddenly, all the women's magazines, because they're in decline anyway, because print is in decline, it was the perfect opportunity to come out and be like: 'Hey, here's the new way'.

Whilst there were a handful of critiques (Favaro 2016), in general women's magazine producers enthusiastically endorsed this 'new way'. Such 'trend that is happening everywhere' was explained as 'an amalgamation of everything', 'a shift in mentality, a shift in historical context, a shift in so many things that is informing us … working together'. Next I further explore a crucial underpinning factor: Feminism.

F-ing up the Glossies

Dramatically reversing a well-documented feature of postfeminism—namely the disarticulation of a feminist identity (Scharff 2012)—most research participants eagerly defined themselves, the *glossierati* and women's magazines as 'utterly 100 % feminists'. As explained by a features writer:

> So one, we have a lot of feminist voices who write in women's magazines [gives examples]. We tackle a lot of feminist issues [gives examples]. And also a women's magazine office is one of the most feminist places you could possibly work: I'm surrounded by women, I have creative control or financial control, business control … which is why it's frustrating when people always hold us up as prime examples of people who are failing feminism. It's upsetting, because actually the work we do, how we work *is* feminist.

According to most editors and writers, there is a 'huge sense of feminism' as magazines 'champion other women' and work to 'empower', 'celebrate', 'inspire' and 'make women strong'. Speaking to previous critiques, these journalists also repeatedly asserted that 'we are very, very much *not* man pleasing' (anymore). An 'it's always about doing it for yourself' rationality was presented as key to the 'undercurrent of female empowerment' in these publications.

Women's magazines were claimed to additionally champion the ('new') principle that 'you can be feminist and love fashion with a passion and love beauty', 'waxing and high heels', want to know 'how to have good sex' and 'to put on make up right'. This was at times expounded in explicit alignment with 'modern feminists' such as *Grazia* columnist Polly Vernon. Certainly, the tenets of her 'hot feminism' pervade contemporary glossies. This includes battling 'feminist fatigue' through 'rebranding feminism', 'encouraging women—fat, thin, whatever—to self-identify as hot' and embracing the figure of a 'shavy-leggy, fashion-fixated, wrinkle-averse, weight-conscious kind of feminist' (Vernon 2015, p. 13).

The magazines' identification with feminism was also associated with a 'new wave of women's journalism', now that 'it's not a dirty word anymore'. A features editor described such new landscape like this:

> Lena Dunham and *Girls* and female empowerment is in. These were buzzwords that now are fashionable, and the advertisers find a turn on rather than a turn off. It legitimizes this stuff that probably we always wanted to write. That being said, I also think that Twitter … mainly Twitter, but all

> social media, is very female focused and it's mostly female users. If you piss off a huge chunk of Twitter users, they will let you know. That's a PR disaster. That influences a lot of what people are producing as well.

Therefore, the editorial inclusion of feminism partly emerges as necessity, since otherwise magazines 'get called out on it thanks to social media'. This account by a freelance writer further elucidates the editorial approach to the current cultural climate:

> Now there's a massive trend for it, to be really empowering for the reader because feminism is obviously finally coming to full force. That's a massive consideration for everyone … especially because you've got all these groups like No More Page 3 and Everyday Sexism. It's not just magazines and online things. It's all the social media. It's almost like a complete package that all this is going on at the same time. It's all bouncing off each other.

The constitution of feminism as trend and commodity evident in the interviews is reflected in the magazine content, as in this *sofeminine.co.uk* article 'Monday To Friday Feminism: How To F Up Your Week':

> In case you haven't noticed, the whole feminist movement is making a big comeback and that means it is time to clarify what being a feminist actually means, and how you can incorporate it into your daily routine … spice up your week with some feminism.

A number of critical voices spoke of 'tokenism' and 'just lip service' to feminism, arguing that the 'big players … cover it because it's news, because it's popular', and (hence) 'to keep up with their competitors and with online'. Whilst in agreement, others still saw potentialities in this. For instance, one freelance writer applauded the rise of LYS/B in the following manner:

> It's a commercial reaction to a new voice that's coming through women like Caitlin [Moran] and Lena Dunham that says 'there is an alternative life available here. It doesn't have to be a life of self-hatred and comparison to other women and silence in times of distress or marginalisation'.

Only certain feminisms have been upgraded from passé to cool, however. *The Vagenda* was repeatedly depicted as 'totally and utterly anti-women', unsupportive, despotic and mean. It was claimed to be 'doing the movement a disservice' with their 'negativity' and 'huge ranty raging', and especially through 'alienating the idea of feminism for people who would otherwise just accept it'; a growing investment by large commercial entities operating, then, 'from within' to (re)de-radicalise imaginaries, among other things (see Favaro 2016). Beyond feminism as 'a basic thing of equality' and 'do whatever the fuck you wanna do', in line with the postfeminist sensibility there was a general abhorrence of 'hardcore', 'intensely feminist women', their purported hairy armpits, man-hatred and disrespect for other women's choices. The glossy happy feminism of individualistic go-getters intensifies the abject state of the 'feminist killjoy', alongside other 'affect aliens' (Ahmed 2010, p. 158). Negative affect is rapidly silenced, and with that goes the transformative force of collective anger at structural realms of injury and injustice. Under confidence chic anger only flows inward.

Conclusion

Confidence chic is an assemblage of diverse—often contradictory—lines of thought and will, acts and counter-acts, interventions and developments ranging from marketing strategies in the fashion-beauty-complex to a call-out culture in the digital mediascape. This transnationally travelling technology of governmentality has roots in the 'state of esteem', a form of citizenship and self-government linking power and subjectivity in modern democracies (Cruikshank 1993). It is also part of the more recent neoliberal turn to happiness, connected to the impact of positive psychology, and, relatedly, the popularity of therapeutic cultures and feel-good self-help industries (Davies 2015). And it is deeply aligned with the postfeminist sensibility (Gill 2009), evident, for instance, in the emphasis upon individual empowerment and choice, (hetero)sexiness as power and a reasserted gender essentialism. But LYS/B in women's magazines is also partly a response to longstanding critiques, for example, for promoting unrealistic beauty standards, being stubbornly 'man-pleasy', judgemental, and, ultimately, harming women. It is often pushed by young female professionals who sympathise with these critiques, claim to feel 'passionate and strongly about women's confidence and their self-image', and identify as feminists. Indeed, confidence chic is related to proliferating feminisms. Some contest dominant forms of power. Others are embedded within them. In this regard a vital influence is 'neoliberal feminism', palpable in the compliancy to corporate values, the interlacing of positive affect and intensified individuation, alongside the concern with (some) gender inequalities and simultaneous avoidance of confrontation and emphasis upon 'internal obstacles' (Rottenberg 2014). Confidence chic constructs an active subject wholly responsible for her self-care, enhancing her own well-being, rationally calculating her 'assets', 'maximising her potential' and 'achieving success'—a hyper-autonomous, deeply individuated woman who can thereby more effectively meet the demands emanating from patriarchal neoliberal capitalism. Such mode of subjectification involves a versatile equilibrium between self-scrutiny and self-appreciation, self-capitalisation and self-realisation, 'self-discipline and enthusing the self run parallel' (Bröckling 2005, p. 21). These micro-practices of self-government interconnect with the biopolitical management of women via apparatuses of power/knowledge increasingly centred on inserting positive affect within infrastructures of measurement, discipline and exploitation.

When for many the injuries of postfeminist (and gendered 'austerity') culture were becoming insufferable and thus no longer silenceable, power relations are revitalised by translating feminist sentiments into an ethos of individual capacity, realisation, worth, and well-being—re-conducting the desire for change toward the self, replacing social emancipatory struggles for personal entrepreneurial ventures and 'interiorised affective spaces' (Rottenberg 2014, p. 424); and rendering normative new forms of violence. The inner-directed quasi-feminism of confidence chic works to countervail the more radical energies within the heterogeneous field of reinvigorated feminisms (McRobbie 2015)—some of which would underscore the necessity for collectivist projects. Others might offer intersectional insights into structural domination and privilege, whilst queer politics destabilise sex/gender boundaries. And others still kill joy with their anger at the socio-political forces responsible for women's discontents and insecurities. Sara Ahmed would usefully encourage us to consider whether this duty to confidence could be about leaving collective 'feelings of structure' (Ahmed 2010, p. 216) safely unexplored, and the 'narrowing of horizons, about giving up an interest in what lies beyond the familiar' (Ahmed 2010, p. 61). Maybe the way to 'give ourselves that well needed boost' (*femalefirst.co.uk*) begins with *refusing* the imperative to be confident.

References

Ahmed, S. (2010). *The Promise of Happiness*. Durham, NC: Duke University Press.

Baker, J. (2010). Claiming Volition and Evading Victimhood: Post-feminist Obligations for Young Women. *Feminism & Psychology, 20*(2), 186–204.

Banet-Weiser, S. (2013). 'Am I Pretty or Ugly?' Girls and the Market for Self-Esteem. *Girlhood Studies, 7*(1), 83–101.

Bröckling, U. (2005). Gendering the Enterprising Self: Subjectification Programs and Gender Differences in Guides to Success. *Distinktion, 11*, 7–23.

Cruikshank, B. (1993). Revolutions Within: Self-Government and Self-Esteem. *Economy and Society, 22*(3), 327–344.

Davies, W. (2015). *The Happiness Industry: How the Government and Big Business Sold Us Well-Being*. London: Verso.

Fairclough, N. (1992). *Discourse and Social Change*. London: Polity Press.

Favaro, L. (2016). *Technologies of Gender and Mediated Intimacy*. Unpublished Ph.D. thesis, University of London, London.

Favaro, L. (in press). Postfeminist Sexpertise on the "Porn and Men Issue": A Transnational Perspective. In K. Harrison & C. A. Ogden (Eds.), *Pornographies: Critical Positions*. Chester, UK: University of Chester Press.

Foucault, M. (1988). Technologies of the Self. In L. Martin, H. Gutman, & P. Hutton (Eds.), *Technologies of the Self: A Seminar with Michel Foucault* (pp. 16–49). London: Tavistock.

García-Favaro, L., & Gill, R. (2015). 'Emasculation Nation Has Arrived': Sexism Rearticulated in Online Responses to Lose the Lads' Mags Campaign. *Feminist Media Studies*, online first.

Gill, R. (2009). Mediated Intimacy and Postfeminism: A Discourse Analytic Examination of Sex and Relationships Advice in a Women's Magazine. *Discourse and Communication, 3*(4), 1–25.

Gill, R., & Elias, A. S. (2014). 'Awaken Your Incredible': Love Your Body Discourses and Postfeminist Contradictions. *International Journal of Media & Cultural Politics, 10*(2), 179–188.

McRobbie, A. (2015). Notes on the Perfect. *Australian Feminist Studies, 30*(83), 3–20.

Murphy, R. (2013). (De)constructing 'Body Love' Discourses in Young Women's Magazines. Unpublished Ph.D. thesis, University of Wellington, Victoria.

Rose, N. (1998). *Inventing Ourselves: Psychology, Power, and Personhood.* Cambridge: Cambridge University Press.

Rottenberg, C. (2014). The Rise of Neoliberal Feminism. *Cultural Studies, 28*(3), 418–437.

Scharff, C. (2012). *Repudiating Feminism: Young Women in a Neoliberal World.* Farnham: Ashgate.

Vernon, P. (2015). *Hot Feminist. Modern Feminism with Style Without Judgement.* London: Hodder & Stoughton.

17

'The Bottom Line Is That the Problem Is You': Aesthetic Labour, Postfeminism and Subjectivity in Russian Self-Help Literature

Maria Adamson and Suvi Salmenniemi

Introduction

This chapter explores the ways in which women are called upon to work on and manage their body, personality and sexuality in bestselling Russian self-help literature targeting a female audience. We argue that the aesthetic labour promoted in this literature needs to be understood as intrinsically embedded in the cultural and economic context where it is performed. Growing job insecurity, widespread gender discrimination,

M. Adamson (✉)
Department of Leadership Work and Organisation, Business School, Middlesex University, London, UK

S. Salmenniemi
Department of Social Research, University of Turku, Turku, Finland

A.S. Elias et al. (eds.), *Aesthetic Labour*,
DOI 10.1057/978-1-137-47765-1_17

insufficient social protection and decreasing employment quality characterise the everyday life of a great number of women in Russia (Adamson and Kispeter 2017; Kozina and Zhidkova 2006). At the same time, the rise of the service sector and the demand for 'aestheticised' forms of labour (Walker 2015) have been accompanied by a growing rhetoric concerning the importance of self-presentation and 'image' (Cohen 2013) and an increasing emphasis on beauty practices as a crucial part of successful femininity (Porteous 2013). As we show in this chapter, women are encouraged to invest time and energy in aesthetic labour in the hope that mastering 'the art of femininity' will allow them upward mobility in a context where channels for mobility are increasingly constrained. We suggest that aesthetic labour is mobilised as a form of tactical agency (de Certeau 1984) to combat social and economic precarity.[1] Through unpacking the elements of this labour we also suggest that this aesthetic makeover entails a profound transformation of subjectivity.

Our analysis draws on nine books by bestselling Russian authors explicitly addressing a female readership and dealing with relationships, love and sexuality. These authors were chosen because they are particularly popular: most of these books have been on the popular psychology bestseller lists (e.g. Kniga.ru, Ozon.ru, Bookberry.ru, Biblio-Globus.ru), and most early editions have been reprinted, indicating the books' continuing success We understand self-help books as a cultural technology that invites readers to shape their ways of being, feeling and acting in order to become particular types of gendered subjects. In this way, the books normalise certain understandings of gender, the self and social relations (for a more detailed discussion of data and methodology, see Salmenniemi and Adamson 2015).

In what follows we first discuss the concept of aesthetic labour in the context of our study, followed by a discussion of gender, (post)feminism and the therapeutic discourse in Soviet and post-Soviet Russia. We then analyse the different dimensions of aesthetic labour involved in mastering the 'art of femininity' as they appear in the self-help texts and continue

[1] de Certeau (1984) makes a distinction between strategy and tactic. Strategy refers to the grid of force relationships and rules of the game defined by dominant powers and within which tactical action can take place. Tactical action seeks to navigate this strategic grid by trying to make use of its frictions and turn them into opportunities, thereby seeking to subvert the grid.

with a discussion of this aesthetic labour as a variation of the spirit of 'cruel optimism' (Berlant 2011).

Aesthetic Labour

The crucial role of the body in the (re)production of gendered, classed and racialised inequalities has been persuasively highlighted in the literature. The body constitutes a pivotal site in and through which power relations operate and are lived. Although the monitoring and surveilling of one's bodily and psychic dispositions have long been part and parcel of the performance of successful femininity, what is new and distinctive in the present moment is the dramatically increased intensity and expansion of self-surveillance and regulation of the body (Gill 2007).

The concept of aesthetic labour, originally developed in work and employment studies, refers to the process of the mobilisation, development and commodification of one's embodied capacities and attributes at and for work (Witz et al. 2003, p. 37). The concept importantly captures the embodied nature of self-work. Entwistle and Wissinger (2006) suggest that the maintenance of embodied capacities and attributes as well as emotional investments is required to project a particular kind of self-presentation. The concept of aesthetic labour foregrounds how such embodied work is commodified and intentionally mobilised for commercial gain. Whilst a number of studies have explored how particular embodiments are valorised and 'converted into economic capital by and for organisations' (Witz et al. 2003, p. 41), Entwistle and Wissinger (2006) also highlight how aesthetic labour can be converted into personal economic gain by individuals who become skilful at managing the self as an 'aesthetic project'. For example, fashion models become enterprising in their efforts to shape their self-presentation according to fashion trends and clients' expectations, and they convert aesthetic labour into personal economic gain (Entwistle and Wissinger 2006, p. 91). The study also highlights the on-going nature of aesthetic labour because these models need to be 'always on' and 'cannot walk away from their product, which is their entire embodied self' (Entwistle and Wissinger 2006, p. 791).

In our analysis we argue that the concept of aesthetic labour may be helpful in making sense of the ways in which women are hailed to manage their bodies and minds in therapeutic self-help literature. Indeed, the self-help books in our data can be seen as 'how-to' manuals of aesthetic labour. They present the readers with a set of values, norms and tastes, which the 'new woman' of capitalist Russia is expected to command. As we will elucidate below, mastering the 'art of femininity' involves not only work on the surface of the body but also dramatic shaping of embodied desires and psychic dispositions. Women are encouraged to build on, mobilise and commodify their dispositions and capabilities and transform them into 'skills' (Witz et al. 2003, p. 37) geared towards gaining upward mobility.

Gender, Postfeminism and Self-Help in Russia

The body was in many ways a highly ideologically regulated and political issue in the Soviet Union. The Soviet state institutionalised collective care for the body with a programme of physical culture in order to develop its citizens' mental and physical capacities with the aim of cultivating a healthy and vital citizen-worker. The model Soviet citizen was imagined as strong, athletic and fit, and bodies deviating from this norm were targeted with moralising instruction (Vainshtein 1996, pp. 78–79).

The female body in the official Soviet discourse was predominantly conceived as a (re)productive body harnessed for the economic prosperity of the state and in the service of the nation. The body was not articulated as a source of pleasure and the official approach emphasised sexual restraint (Rotkirch 2000). Soviet ideology also rejected the emphasis on materialistic beauty. Fashion, jewellery and cosmetics were seen as 'bourgeois preoccupations which had no place in Soviet society' (Attwood 2001, p. 166). Western sexualised images of femininity were associated with exaggerated frivolity and prostitution (Rudova 2014). Instead, the Soviet ideology emphasised modesty, simplicity, 'naturalness' and moderate taste as key pillars of feminine appearance (Rudova 2011, 2014). Soviet women were nevertheless expected to look after their appearance, but they had few resources for that. Foreign beauty products were almost impossible to obtain and domestic ones were often of poor quality and had notorious effects; for example, according to Azhgikhina and Goscilo (1996, p. 105), the perfume 'Red Moscow' was 'potent enough to anesthetise a herd of buffalo'. As a corollary, women made use of 'natural' home expedients (butter, vinegar, honey, milk and so on) recommended by Soviet women's magazines.

The shift from state socialism to global consumer capitalism in Russia in the 1990s entailed an influx of new beauty products and services and a profound renegotiation of cultural understandings of femininity, beauty and the body. Reclaiming beauty, sexuality and 'true' femininity and the ability to consume shiny goods were seen as 'liberation' from the Soviet project of women's emancipation. Extensively promoted by the media, an emphasis on sexualised beauty and self-disciplining practices of diet, exercise and beauty treatments became an important aspect of the middle- and upper-class lifestyle and feminine subjectivity (Rudova 2011; Ratilainen 2012; Porteous 2013). The discourse of 'glamour' replaced 'bleak' discourses of moral collapse and survival of the late *perestroika* era, and glamour was presented as something that was 'achievable to anyone willing to try' (Rudova 2014, p. 389).

Popular media culture provides an illuminating lens for understanding the negotiation of and anxieties around the shifting gender and class orders in Russia. Women's magazines, chick lit, 'glamour fiction' and self-help literature constitute pivotal sites in which the symbolic production and contention of gender, sexuality and class take place. Popular psychology occupied a marginal position in Soviet society, but during late *perestroika* years the 'psy industry' grew dramatically (Griffin and Karepova 2011). Popular media culture has been the primary site through which the therapeutic discourse has been culturally appropriated and disseminated in Russia (Lerner 2015; Salmenniemi and Adamson 2015). Today, the self-help genre is an established and highly visible part of the Russian mediascape, consumed first and foremost by women, younger age groups and the middle class (Salmenniemi and Vorona 2014).

As pointed out by several commentators, popular media culture is also the key arena where postfeminist discourses are articulated (Gill and Herdieckerhoff 2006; Gill and Scharff 2011; Rudova 2014; Salmenniemi and Adamson 2015). Whilst in the West postfeminism has evolved partly as a response to second-wave feminism (Budgeon 2011), in Russia postfeminism is situated in a different context. It stands in a contentious relationship both with the state-sanctioned equality politics of the Soviet era and with feminism as a 'foreign' ideology. In contemporary Russia, feminism is simultaneously repudiated as Western and therefore unsuitable for Russia, and as a remnant of discredited Soviet equality politics, preventing women from 'fulfilling' and 'enjoying' femininity. However, whilst feminism remains unpopular, globally circulating postfeminist ideas have nevertheless been widely appropriated in Russian popular culture (see Salmenniemi and Adamson 2015 for a full discussion). The cultural landscape of gender discourses is highly conflicted: whilst the Orthodox Church and the Russian state have been actively propagating highly traditional ideas of gender and sexuality, popular media culture has circulated postfeminist images of women as autonomous and sexually empowered individuals. It is at this intersection that we can see a complex entanglement of therapeutic, neoliberal, conservative and postfeminist discourses (Salmenniemi and Adamson 2015).

Bodies Under Construction

We now move on to examine the forms of aesthetic labour articulated in the self-help books we have analysed. These books offer advice to women on how to become an optimising and entrepreneurial subject in order to get ahead in life and secure a position in the upper echelons of the class structure. Readers are presented with two closely connected tactics for achieving this: finding a lucrative career and 'capturing' a rich man. Both may be achieved by mastering the 'art of femininity', which requires meticulous aesthetic labour. Yet, in both cases, women's lives are portrayed as ultimately mediated and regulated by men.

One of the most prominent storylines in the analysed self-help books is the encouragement of continuous and relentless self-management and self-invention characteristic of the postfeminist sensibility (Gill 2007; McRobbie 2009). Women's subjectivity and bodies appear as sites that are permanently 'under construction'. Women are advised to learn to monitor and manage their emotions, attend to their body and become both sexually desiring subjects and sexually desired objects. The body is presented both as a resource and as unruly, requiring constant discipline (see Gill 2007). Caring for it is no longer perceived as a duty towards the state as during Soviet times, but a duty towards oneself and one's existing or potential partner. Aesthetic labour is portrayed as an ethical obligation and a key to success:

> Even when the pressure is high, a real woman always finds time to pull herself back together and look good [...] What kind of success [...] are we talking about if you were too lazy to wipe off the peeling nail varnish last night? (Sviyash 2012, np)

Most books contain detailed sections on appearance management, emphasising the importance of beauty treatments and giving advice on choosing the right clothes, the 'right' nail varnish colour, 'the right ways' of skin, facial and body care, doing make-up and hair 'properly' and even advice on how to wear glasses. There is also detailed advice about shopping and suggestions to invest in the most expensive products, because 'a real woman' must: 'always look top-notch. She will never let herself wear tatty old clothes, scruffy sports clothing or bland fake jewellery [...] Go to an expensive shop and buy only famous luxury labels' (Shatskaya 2007a, pp. 38–49). As this quotation indicates, mastering the 'art of femininity' is a thoroughly classed practice. Class is coded into the ways in which femininity is constructed through a symbolic association between 'good taste' and acquiring expensive items. In addition to beauty, controlling one's demeanour and embodied presence is also crucial; there are chapters dedicated to how to walk, how to conduct oneself during a meal, how to smoke a cigarette and so on. All these elements promise to increase the exchange value of the 'new improved self' (Skeggs 2004).

The books also suggest an intimate connection between appearance and subjectivity: appearance is taken to reflect moral character. As one book suggests, 'inner beauty always manifests itself in the appearance' (Pravdina 2002, p. 92). Sloppy appearance is seen as reflecting psychological pathologies. A slim and feminine figure, carefully polished nails and elegant clothes are, in turn, seen as signalling neoliberal and postfeminist virtues of responsibility, self-discipline and self-governance. By working on the body, women are assumed to remake their personality, and vice versa.

Reminiscent of the global postfeminist discourse (Gill 2007; Lazar 2009; McRobbie 2009), the Russian self-help texts repeatedly suggest that aesthetic labour is to be performed for women themselves. However, on closer inspection, this labour is presented as palatable mainly because it holds out the promise of the heterosexual relationship:

> For such a woman [who corresponds to men's fantasy] a man would do anything! He will be begging her to stay, he will never cheat, and he will break his back working hard to earn money to buy her a new pair of shoes [...] Isn't this worth getting up a bit earlier in order to put on some make-up and make him a coffee? (Shatskaya 2007c, np)

Femininity is time and again represented in the books only in relation to masculinity, and women's lives are described as ultimately mediated and regulated by men. Although women are encouraged to learn emotional detachment and not 'cling to men', a relationship is always posited as an unquestioned anchor of women's lives.

When Beauty Is Not Enough

Whilst aesthetic labour on the body is absolutely essential, the books also suggest that 'conquering a man with your beauty is only *the beginning*' (Shatskaya 2007a, our emphasis). Women are also urged to work on their psychic dispositions:

> Without an inner state of desire for radical change and a fundamental belief in yourself as well as meticulous work on your new image [...] all the expensive cosmetics, stylish clothes, refined manners and secrets of male seduction will be useless. (Shatskaya 2007c, np)

Through aesthetic labour, women are encouraged to cultivate specific psychic dispositions, such as attentiveness, self-confidence, self-love, self-reliance and motherliness directed towards men rather than children. Women are called to inhabit two contradictory subject-positions: an autonomous and self-sufficient woman and a maternal care-taker responsible for the emotional support of her male partner (see Salmenniemi and Adamson 2015). She is warned to downplay her independence, because becoming too independent 'is not healthy' (Pravdina 2002, p. 82) and also may 'scare men away', thus turning her into an undesirable commodity in the heterosexual marketplace.

Hence, similarly to the labouring on bodily dispositions, work on psychic dispositions is to be performed mainly for one's existing or potential partner: 'a real woman should nurture and cultivate her femininity so that she can bestow it on her man' (Sviyash 2012, np). The ideal postfeminist subjectivity is sketched in the books by drawing a contrast with 'other', abject femininities: that of a dull housewife, horrible feminist, pushy businesswoman, and a hysterical and clingy woman (Shatskaya 2007a, b, c; Robski and Sobchak 2007; Pravdina 2007a, b). Women are urged to understand and embrace that 'emancipated women puzzle men [...] a man needs to think that he is the boss and the master' (Shatskaya 2007b, np). Hence, the 'right looks' have to be aligned with the 'right' personality. The nature of this aesthetic labour is on-going and uncertain but is made attractive through the promise of a relationship:

> You will be loved if you [...] tailor yourself to your man [...] but the ideal [woman is able] to understand and bring to life the dream of a man [...] [she] is the one who feels what a man wants. (Shatskaya 2007b, np)

Always Work!

Aesthetic labour is also described as an essential part of achieving a successful career. The books advise women not to 'slave' day and night in tedious low-paid jobs but pursue a high-flying career in office jobs like journalism or business:

> Always work. Work allows you to have independence that men value so much [...] it disciplines you and doesn't let you leave the house without proper make-up, a proper hair-do or with peeling nail polish [...] it also allows you to meet a man [...] and there is a higher chance of meeting a Rockefeller's grandson if you work in a large top firm in a senior position. (Shatskaya 2007b)

Reminiscent of the Soviet ideology, paid work is seen a crucial ingredient of female subjectivity. But a stylishly dressed, sexually seductive business-woman has superseded the figure of a smiling female tractor-driver from Soviet cultural iconography. Moreover, although the rhetoric partly resonates with the postfeminist idea of a 'working girl' (McRobbie 2009), the quotation above suggests that work and economic independence are not necessarily seen as values in themselves, but are construed as a means of self-improvement in order to become more attractive in the eyes of prospective suitors. Whilst self-fulfilment in a career is important, many books place an even greater emphasis on finding a successful man as a source of a 'good life'. The books suggest that women should approach man-searching as a job and fastidiously study the science of 'menology' (Shatskaya 2007b) in order to find and exploit men's weaknesses (see also Gill 2009). A paradigmatic example of this is Oksana Robski's and Ksenia Sobchak's glamour slash self-help manual *How to Marry a Millionaire* (2007). On the cover, the authors pose in lingerie-like wedding dresses, armed with pistols, hand-cuffs and machine guns. With this heavy armour they aim to track down and capture a wealthy oligarch and scare away potential female competitors. The picture signals female sexual power being mobilised in order to seize the resources and power residing in the hands of men (Salmenniemi and Ratilainen 2014). This re-signifies the sexual terrain from being a sign of women's exploitation to that of women's empowerment (Lazar 2006, p. 512).

The texts do acknowledge at times the gendered forms of subordination and the restricted opportunities that women face in their lives. They give historical examples of how women have always had to 'sell' their embodied feminine capital in exchange for climbing the class ladder. The books suggest that this remains the case today and that women's lives are very much dependent on and regulated by men. They propose that women should mobilise femininity as a form of tactical agency in the pursuit of a better future:

> Manipulation is a typically feminine method. In the context of patriarchy [...] a woman had to find indirect routes to power, using men and her charm over them [...] [you should begin] to think like men, but nonetheless remain a woman [...] rather than have a bulldozer-like strategy and the

> pushiness of a bluestocking businesswoman, you can manipulate men without them knowing it. (Shatskaya 2007c, p. 59)

Most of the books portray aesthetic labour as an investment that helps to get hold of male-controlled resources. Getting into a relationship with a rich man is presented as worth the hassle as it will literally pay off: 'your darling husband will pay for treating your neurosis [that you get whilst searching for him] as well as for your Bentley, your yacht and a mansion in Belgravia' (Robski and Sobchak 2007, p. 3). However, the books warn about the precarity of such relationships:

> He can leave any minute. He can leave because of your constant nagging or because you refuse sex too often [...] he can leave because you go to bed wearing too much cream on your face, or stopped putting make-up on and stopped being a woman and began to turn into a comic-book housewife with curlers on her head [...] the bottom line is that the problem is you. (Shatskaya 2009, p. 10)

This precarity underscores the necessity of keeping up the aesthetic labour. As one of the books advise, 'any attempt to have a happy long-lasting family life with an oligarch is an illusion' (Robski and Sobchak 2007, p. 3). Thus, women should devote themselves to cultivating the 'art of femininity' as a way to postpone the inevitable break-up.

'Giving Oneself Without Asking Anything Back'

Finally, a crucial dimension of aesthetic labour is learning how to cultivate sexuality 'in the right way'. Sexuality is construed as an essential part of a healthy selfhood and a manifestation of women's empowerment. Women are expected to explore and work on their sexuality: 'A real woman sees sex as a healthy part of life. She allows herself not to feel guilty about having sex or wanting to have sex. She likes her body. She can enjoy herself' (Sviyash 2012, np). Despite the recurrent celebration of sexual empowerment, female sexuality does not appear as important in itself, but rather, once again, it is harnessed to serve the sexual pleasure of one's partner. The discussion of sexuality exclusively assumes heteronormativity and the ultimate motive for working on sexuality is to be able to fulfil the sexual needs of men:

> Let's be honest with ourselves: women don't just want to have sex for pleasure and this cannot be their main goal in life [...] sex is first and foremost a way to ensnare a man, to tie him; and wanting to please your man is a crucial element of a happy and balanced life [...] if you learn to do this you'll get love, admiration and the respect of your man [...] Giving oneself without asking for anything back should give the real woman the most pleasure and happiness. (Shatskaya 2009, np)

As this quotation indicates, women's sexuality is instrumentalised and conceived of as a way to preserve the relationship, a message which echoes the globally circulating postfeminist discourse of 'sexual entrepreneurship' (Harvey and Gill 2011) and 'compulsory sexual agency' (Gill 2008). These efforts are portrayed as an obligation; those women who refuse to engage in the labour of sexuality are proclaimed 'apathetic' and 'lazy' and thus rightly cheated on and abandoned by their partners (Shatskaya 2009). However, women are not only expected to embrace sexuality but also learn to derive pleasure from pleasing their partner's desires and leaving their own desires aside. This elucidates how the labour of sexuality involves a great deal of psychic and emotional labour and discipline. Women are urged to take care of their partners' sexual needs but also show genuine care, love and compassion. As one of the books explains: 'men are not only there to be used [...] you need to learn to love and learn to get pleasure from throwing yourself into a loving relationship' (Shatskaya 2009). Thus, although women's autonomy and independence are propagated in the books, they are also constantly destabilised by naturalising women's subordination and positioning women's lives as worthless without a man.

Conclusion

This chapter has explored the ways in which Russian self-help books encourage women to conceive of and shape their bodies and subjectivities. We have argued that aesthetic labour on the body, personality and sexuality is part and parcel of the 'art of femininity', which appears as a crucial tactic to navigate the social and economic precarity of contemporary Russia. In aesthetic labour, psychic and bodily surveillance and regulation are intimately enmeshed. Femininity appears in the books simultaneously as something natural and essential and as a complex performance accomplished through meticulous aesthetic practices.

The imperative of perpetual and arduous aesthetic labour is made attractive to the Russian female audience by portraying it as a form of self-enjoyment and a source of pleasure (Lazar 2009) and by holding out a promise of upward mobility for those who learn how to perform it successfully. We could think of this as a variant of a spirit of 'cruel optimism' (Berlant 2011): the books hail women to invest time and effort in the 'art of femininity' by holding out the promise of empowerment, success and a better future whilst simultaneously drawing women into forms of labour that are likely to wear them down, legitimise sexual hierarchies and reproduce women's subordination. Moreover, not only is this aesthetic labour never-ending and tedious, it is also difficult to 'walk away' from it (Entwistle and Wissinger 2006), as the cost of doing so is portrayed as being very high.

The feminine subject sketched in the books is a highly classed figure who has access to the material and symbolic resources of self-making and can invest in herself (see Skeggs 2004). However, this subject is also inherently fragile since much of her life is presented as ultimately regulated by and mediated through men. The books portray the commodification of personality, femininity and sexuality and their tactical deployment as a way to navigate gendered and classed constraints. In this way, they encourage the use of individual and commercial strategies to manipulate structural constraints rather than collective mobilisation to eradicate them.

References

Adamson, M., & Kispeter, E. (2017). Gender and Professional Work in Russia and Hungary. In C. Baker (Ed.), *Gender in the 20th Century Eastern Europe and the Soviet Union* (pp. 214–227). London: Routledge.

Attwood, L. (2001). Rationality Versus Romanticism: Representations of Women in the Stalinist Press. In L. Edmondson (Ed.), *Gender in Russian history and Culture*. London: Palgrave.

Azhgikhina, N., & Goscilo, H. (1996). Getting Under Their Skin. The Beauty Salon in Russian Women's Lives. In L. Edmondson (Ed.), *Russia-Women–Culture*. Bloomington, IN: Indiana University Press.

Berlant, L. (2011). *Cruel Optimism*. Duke University Press.

Budgeon, S. (2011). *Third Wave Feminism and the Politics of Gender in Late Modernity*. London: Palgrave-Macmillan.

Cohen, S. (2013). Image of a Secretary: A Metapragmatic Morality for Post-Soviet Capitalism. *Anthropological Quarterly, 86*(3), 725–758.

de Certeau, M. (1984). *The Practice of Everyday Life*. Berkeley: University of California Press.

Entwistle, J., & Wissinger, E. (2006). Keeping Up Appearances: Aesthetic Labour in the Fashion Modelling Industry. *The Sociological Review, 54*(4), 774–794.

Gill, R. (2007). Postfeminist Media Culture: Elements of Sensibility. *European Journal of Cultural Studies, 10*(2), 147–166.

Gill, R. (2008). Empowerment/Sexism: Figuring Female Sexual Agency in Contemporary Advertising. *Feminism and Psychology, 18*(1), 35–60.

Gill, R. (2009). Mediated Intimacy and Postfeminism: A Discourse Analytic Examination of Sex and Relationships Advice in a Women's Magazine. *Discourse & Communication, 3*(4), 345–369.

Gill, R., & Herdieckerhoff, E. (2006). Rewriting the Romance: New Femininities in Chick Lit? *Feminist Media Studies, 6*(4), 487–504.

Gill, R., & Scharff, C. (2011). *New Femininities: Postfeminism, Neoliberalism and Subjectivity*. London: Palgrave Macmillan.

Griffin, G., & Karepova, M. (2011). Psychological Counselling in Post-Soviet Russia: Gendered Perceptions in a Feminizing Profession. *European Journal of Women's Studies, 18*(3), 279–294.

Harvey, L., & Gill, R. (2011). Spicing It up: Sexual Entrepreneurs and the Sex Inspectors. In R. Gill & C. Scharff (Eds.), *New Femininities: Postfeminism, Neoliberalism and Subjectivity* (pp. 52–67). London: Palgrave Macmillan.

Kozina, I., & Zhidkova, E. (2006). Sex Segregation and Discrimination in the New Russian Labour Market. In S. Ashwin (Ed.), *Adapting to Russia's New Labour Market* (pp. 57–86). London: Routledge.

Lazar, M. (2006). Discover the Power of Femininity! *Feminist Media Studies, 6*(4), 505–517.

Lazar, M. (2009). Entitled to Consume: Postfeminist Femininity and a Culture of Post-critique. *Discourse & Communication, 3*(4), 371–400.

Lerner, J. (2015). The Chaging Meanings of Russian Love: Emotional Socialism and Therapeutic Culture on the Post-soviet Screen. *Sexuality & Culture, 19*(1).

McRobbie, A. (2009). *The Aftermath of Feminism: Gender, Culture and Social Change*. London: Sage.

Porteous, H. (2013). There Are No Ugly Women, Only Lazy Ones: The Duty of Beauty Labour in Contemporary Russian Women's Magazines. In H. Ehlers, G. Linke, N. Milewski, B. Rudlof and H. Trappe (Eds.), *Körper–Geschlecht–Wahrnehmung. Geistes–Und Sozialwissenschaftliche Beiträge Zur Genderforschung*. Lit Verlag.

Pravdina, N. (2002). *Ia privlekaiu uspekh [I Attract Success]*. Moskva: Astrel.

Pravdina, N. (2007a). *Chego khotiat zhenshchiny? [What Do Women Want?]*. Moskva: Astrel.

Pravdina, N. (2007b). *Ideal'nyi muzhchina dlia ideal'noi zhenshchiny [Perfect Man for a Perfect Woman]*. Moskva: Astrel.

Ratilainen, S. (2012). Business for Pleasure: Elite Women in the Russian Popular Media. In S. Salmenniemi (Ed.), *Rethinking Class in Russia*. Farnham: Ashgate.

Robski, O., & Sobchak, K. (2007). *Zamuzh za millionera ili Brak Vyshego Sorta. [How to Marry a Millionaire: A Marriage of the Highest Quality]*. Moscow: AST.

Rotkirch, A. (2000). *The Man Question. Loves and Lives in Late 20th Century Russia*. Helsinki: University of Helsinki, Department of Social Policy.

Rudova, L. (2011). Russian Glamour Culture and the Extraordinary World of Oksana Robski. *The Journal of Popular Culture., 44*(5), 1102–1119.

Rudova, L. (2014). 'Who's the Fairest of Them All?' Beauty and Femininity in Contemporary Russian Adolescent Girl Fiction. *The Russian Review, 73*(3), 389–403.

Salmenniemi, S., & Adamson, M. (2015). New Heroines of Labour: Domesticating Post-feminism and Neoliberal Capitalism in Russia. *Sociology, 49*(1), 88–105.

Salmenniemi, S., & Ratilainen, S. (2014). Kapitalismin uusi nainen [The New Woman of Capitalism]. *Idäntutkimus*, 3–14.

Salmenniemi, S., & Vorona, M. (2014). Reading Self-Help Literature in Russia: Governmentality, Psychology and Subjectivity. *The British Journal of Sociology, 65*, 43–62.

Shatskaya, E. (2007a). *Nachal'naya Shkola Stervy: Pervyi Shag k Sovershenstvu [The Primary School of a Bitch: First Steps Towards Success]*. Moscow: AST.

Shatskaya, E. (2007b). *Srednyaya Shkola Stervy: Muzhchiny: Posobie po Priobreteniu, Ekspluatatsii i uhodu [Middle School of a Bitch: Men—User Manual]*. Moscow: AST.

Shatskaya, E. (2007c). *Vyshaya Shkola Stervy: Upravlenie Liubov'u I Kar'eroi [Bitch High School: Controlling Love and Career]*. Moscow: AST.

Shatskaya, E. (2009). *Sterva V Postele… I Ne Tol'ko: Nauka Liubit' I Byt' Liubimoi [Bitch in bed: The Science of Loving and Being Loved]*. Moscow: AST.

Skeggs, B. (2004). *Class, Self, Culture*. London: Routledge.

Sviyash, Y. (2012). *10 Zapovedei Nastoyashei Zhenshchiny [10 Commandments of a Real Woman]*. Moscow: Tsentrpoligraph.

Vainshtein, O. (1996). Female Fashion, Soviet Style: Bodies of Ideology. In H. Goscilo & B. Holmgren (Eds.), *Women-Russia-Culture*. Bloomington: Indiana University Press.

Walker, C. (2015). 'I Don't Really Like Tedious, Monotonous Work': Working-Class Young Women, Service Sector Employment and Social Mobility in Contemporary Russia. *Sociology, 49*, 106–122.

Witz, A., Warhurst, C., & Nickson, D. (2003). The Labour of Aesthetics and the Aesthetic of Organization. *Organization, 10*, 33–54.

18

Look Good, Feel Good: Sexiness and Sexual Pleasure in Neoliberalism

Rachel Wood

Introduction

A lucrative and ubiquitous sex advice industry, pedalled by 'experts' in newspapers, magazines, on television and online, is built around telling us how to have 'good' sex. Good (hetero)sex requires that women become knowledgeable, consuming and using tips and products to make their sex lives more pleasurable, exciting and rewarding. Almost every list of sex tips will address the interrelated issues of 'feeling sexy', 'body confidence' or 'looking good'. The message of such advice is more than a little contradictory: first, women must undertake various forms of body work in order to look good, which will in turn allow them to feel good and enjoy sex; however, thinking 'too much', or too negatively, about looking good is the ultimate sin when it comes to 'good sex' and will certainly not

R. Wood (✉)
Department of Psychology, Sociology & Politics, Sheffield Hallam University, Sheffield, UK

A.S. Elias et al. (eds.), *Aesthetic Labour*,
DOI 10.1057/978-1-137-47765-1_18

lead to women (or their partners) feeling good. How can women expend considerable time and energy on making themselves 'look good' in the appropriate ways in order to enjoy sex, only to then almost simultaneously eradicate any thought or worry about how they look during sex? The answer is the 'mental makeover': the embodying of feelings of body confidence so that they are deeply felt and 'known', liberating women from anxiety and leaving them 'free' to enjoy sex.

The concept of the 'mental makeover' powerfully draws upon and reinforces neoliberal and postfeminist regimes of the self. Neoliberal governance perpetuates a rationality of selfhood in which citizenship, welfare and economic participation are understood as individual responsibilities (Brown 2003). Neoliberal subjects are expected to 'devise and implement' their own practices of consumer-driven self-improvement (Evans and Riley 2015, p. 6). A number of critics have pointed to the particular address of neoliberal individualism to the postfeminist female subject (Evans and Riley 2015; Gill 2007; McRobbie 2009). The ideal female neoliberal subject must continually work upon the self, becoming the best and most successful version of herself through a range of techniques including consumption. In the realm of sexual practice, this labour is primarily about gaining knowledge—not only technical knowledge regarding the best skills, positions and sex toys but about her sexual self, her desires, potential hang-ups or inhibitions in need of work and her body's ability to be sexually desirable and to have the appropriate quality and quantity of pleasure.

It is in this context that the idea of the body confidence 'mental makeover' makes sense. Gill points to the importance of the makeover paradigm within contemporary cultural texts with a 'postfeminist sensibility' (2007). She contends that postfeminist texts intensify and expand regimes of self-surveillance and discipline in such a way that women are expected to 'remodel' not only their exterior appearance but also their interior psychological selves (Gill 2007, p. 155). The self-work of making over the inner self can be understood as what Foucault calls a 'technology of the self' (2011). These technologies include ways of articulating, analysing, monitoring and understanding the self, often facilitated by 'experts', and encompassing the interrelated obligations of self-care and self-knowledge (Foucault 2011, p. 43). As Evans and Riley suggest, technologies of the self pervade contemporary neoliberal and postfeminist cultures, powerfully 'hailing' women to participate in a range of practices that will allow them to 'to take up a subject position and make it their own' and 'work on ourselves to make ourselves' (Evans and Riley 2015, p. 40). In the sex advice examined here it is not only the sexiness of the body that must be 'made over', but more crucially a range of technologies are taken up in order to facilitate the making over of one's entire way of thinking and feeling about the body. The prize for this mental makeover work is 'good sex'[1]; in postfeminist and neoliberal frameworks only those bodies who continue to undertake the appropriate self-work in both looking and being 'body confident' are able to access sexual pleasure.

This chapter begins by examining the discourses of sexiness and sexual pleasure in postfeminist sex advice,[2] identifying three key themes: the cycle of feeling/looking good, the importance of choice and individualism and the 'mental makeover'. In the second part of the chapter, I consider the ways in which neoliberal and postfeminist constructions of the sexual self and body are made meaningful in women's everyday lives. As scholarship on women's magazine readers suggests, this 'advice' can be interpreted in a variety of complex ways (Farvid and Braun 2006). With this in mind, I examine the accounts of heterosexual women drawn from an ethnography of sex shopping and point to some of the ways that women negotiate the technologies of 'looking good' and 'feeling good' within their sexual lives. Finally, I draw attention to instances in which women stubbornly fail, or refuse to take up such technologies, arguing

[1] It is beyond the scope of this chapter to explore the constructions of 'good sex' and sexual 'pleasure' in postfeminist sex advice in detail. However, it is worth noting that ideas of pleasure are narrow and prescriptive, with orgasm the primary indicator of 'successful' sex. As Hannah Frith (2013) notes, there is a powerful 'orgasm imperative' in contemporary constructions of heterosex. Women's magazines glorify orgasm as the 'sole source of female sexual pleasure', and at the same time portray female orgasm as 'hard work' to achieve, making female orgasm a subject of intense 'scrutiny and surveillance' (Frith 2013, p. 499). Much of the advice around body confidence reinforces this idea through the understanding that 'knowing' one looks good will allow for freedom from worry and increase the possibility of 'letting go' and achieving orgasm.

[2] Research was primarily undertaken in the print and online versions of *Cosmopolitan* magazine in early 2015. *Cosmo* is perhaps the women's magazine most well-known for a sexually candid approach, celebrating an 'active', 'emancipated', 'fun', 'fearless' version of sexuality (Farvid and Braun 2006). I also draw upon the print and website advice of the highly successful 'sexpert' Tracey Cox, who has built a lucrative career across books, magazine columns, websites, television appearances and sexual product ranges (Harvey and Gill 2011).

that these evidence the range of 'tactics' through which women 'make do' with neoliberal rationalities in mundane everyday sexual contexts (de Certeau 1998).

Sex Advice: Looking and Feeling Good

Sex advice for women has become big business over the last two decades. Gill provides a useful overview of the various forms of work, or 'intimate entrepreneurship' required in women's magazine sex advice (2009, p. 352). She finds that such advice presents 'finding a partner, maintaining a relationship and having satisfying sex' as '"goals" which require research, planning and strategy' (Gill 2009, p. 352). Sex advice draws on narratives of 'hard work' (Harvey and Gill 2011) and productivity from the realm of managerial techniques, business and bureaucracy (Tyler 2004), demonstrating that such advice is 'profoundly connected to neoliberalism' (Gill 2009, p. 362).

Much of the advice on 'body confidence' surrounds improving the sexiness and attractiveness of the body for sex. The 'body work' (Coffey 2012) required can appear onerous. Koenig (2010, np) suggests that women get 'fully groomed' by getting a manicure, pedicure, full bikini wax, buying new lingerie and even dying your 'down-there hair' a new colour or applying a pubic crystal tattoo. *Cosmopolitan* lists a range of preparation tasks including booking a pedicure and full wax, hitting the gym in order to 'tighten your muscles' and taking a long bath and applying luxurious moisturiser (Cosmo Team n.d.-a, np). Readers should dress for sex: *Cosmo* suggests a sexy slip to 'cover the bits you're concerned about', high heels to 'make your legs look longer and slimmer' and corsets to 'flatten your tummy and lift your boobs' (Cosmo Team n.d.-c, np). Tracey Cox recommends a low-cut vest to 'flatter your chest but cover the rest of you' (2010, np). Sexual activity is itself another component of the beauty/body work repertoire, as having sex will make you feel and look healthier, younger, slimmer and so on. Unlike sweet treats and online shopping, 'there's no such thing as too much of *this* good thing'; masturbation 'can burn as many as 150 calories in one session' (Green 2012, np). Orgasms will make the 'skin glow' (Cosmo Team 2013b, np), and frequent sex is 'the secret to looking younger' (Goddard 2013, np) and will help 'to make your hair shiny and your skin supple' (Cosmo Team 2013b, np).

Preparing a flattering environment is also suggested, for example, by placing candles on the floor to create a flattering light from below (Cox 2010, np), or using 'soft light' to 'make you look and feel amazing' (Cosmo Team n.d.-c, np). Also recommended is having sex at the 'time of the day you feel you do look your best' (Cox 2010, np), such as before dinner or in the morning when your 'skin still looks smooth as alabaster and your stomach taut and tiny' (Cosmo Team n.d.-d, np). When it comes to having sex, suggestions for monitoring and adjusting appearance in various positions can be found. Women are encouraged to lean back when on top to flatten the stomach (Cosmo Team 2013a, np), rest on their forearms in a 'rear entry' position as this 'makes your waist look tiny and your thighs slim and taut' (Cox 2010, np), or lying back in missionary such that 'the flab spreads out and we look extra thin' (Cox 1999, p. 62).

Lest this exhaustive list of tasks seem unreasonable, sex advice continually reinforces the message that such work is primarily 'for you' and not (only) 'for' a male sex partner. A range of postfeminist ideas around active, agentic and choice-full female sexuality are drawn upon here, with the monitoring and maintenance of the sexy body seen as evidence for, and a reinforcement of, feelings of inner 'sexiness', confidence and being 'in control'. Grooming is constructed as 'setting aside time to take care of yourself', enabling the reader to take 'ownership of your sexuality' (Koenig 2010, np); spending time on one's hair and makeup is not 'a tactic for attracting the opposite sex', rather it is about 'feeling confident' (Bond 2012, np). Of course, a male partner's enjoyment of the feminine sexy body is a fortuitous benefit of such labour—luckily those positions that flatter her body are also a 'visual treat' for him (Cox 2010, np), and taking nude photos will remind 'you *and* your guy of your sensuality' (Koenig 2010, np)—but it is rarely framed as the central objective.

Whilst men's preferences are not placed front and centre when it comes to the work of 'looking good', their perspectives are frequently mobilised to warn against the dangers of *not* being 'body confident' in the bedroom. 'Real men' are the voice of 'authority' in women's magazine sex advice, with men's desires represented inflexibly in the form of lists of 'dos and don'ts' that women must flexibly fulfil (Farvid and Braun 2006, p. 300). In *Cosmopolitan*, one such repeated 'don't' is the possibility of presenting any kind of self-consciousness or body insecurity: 'Hiding your body is not sexy' (Cosmo Team n.d.-b, np); 'If you wear a robe to bed and just reveal the necessary bits of you, you'll ruin your pleasure–and his' (Cosmo Team n.d.-c, np); 'Not having shaved … or thinking your bum looks big today are terrible reasons to deny yourself, and him, the pleasure of sex' (Cosmo Team 2006, np).

Whilst men's desires appear more foregrounded, these 'don'ts' also draw upon postfeminist ideas of individualism; to feel anxious about the body will only 'ruin' or 'deny' the possibility of *her* pleasure. Thinking too much about the body is positioned as an obstacle to enjoying sex: women should focus on what they are 'feeling', not how they are 'looking', because 'sex is about what's happening on the inside, not the outside' (Cox 2014, np). When women 'know' they 'look good' it helps them 'relax and enjoy sex' (Mullender 2012, np). If sex involves 'judging your body' it will be difficult to 'feel pleasure' and 'enjoy the experience' (Smith 2012, np); and sex that is 'all about trying to look good rather than feel good' will be 'disastrous' (Cox 2013, np). It is not a case of simply concealing body worries from a partner then; instead the advice is to *genuinely eradicate* any feelings of self-consciousness about appearance (despite the extensive labour that has gone into looking good in the first place) in order to be 'free' to feel sexual pleasure.

In order to achieve this, according to *Cosmo*: 'it just takes a mental makeover' (Cosmo Team n.d.-a, np). The 'mental makeover' involves techniques to help women 'love' their bodies, many of which involve a form of mental 'retraining' familiar from the neoliberal discourses circulating within populist versions of cognitive behavioural therapy (Teghtsoonian 2009). So readers are advised to replace negative 'body insults' with 'positive thoughts' by visualising a 'STOP' sign every time negative thoughts arise and to self-train themselves to look in the mirror nude without criticism (Smith 2012, np). *Cosmo* warns against 'trash talking your best friend (i.e. you)' and advises replacing bad thoughts about 'one part of your body' with 'a good thought about something you do like' (Cosmo Team n.d.-a, np). Similarly Tracey Cox advises nurturing positive feelings about non-problem areas such as 'your arms, shoulders, hands or feet' (Cox 2010, np).

Of course, this advice does not suggest that women stop caring about their appearance, or abandon spending time and money on improving it, as to do so would undermine the necessity of the consumer-oriented body work regimes promoted elsewhere in such advice. What must be achieved is the successful embodiment of 'body confidence'; looking good must not only be outwardly performed but inwardly *known* in order to feel good during sex. Potential contradictions are overcome by the representation of body work as proof positive of an authentically felt inner confidence; as the loved body will naturally be a pampered and beautiful body. As Cox states: 'thin people pay more attention to themselves—if you don't like your body and don't like paying attention to it, you're not going to want to shave, preen, fake tan etc.—yet all those things do make us feel more confident about showing it off to our partner' (2010, np). The advice comes full circle then: a 'mental makeover' will mean that women feel positive enough about their bodies to spend time working on them, which will in turn increase feelings of inner confidence, and so on. This continual cycle of inner/outer work opens the door to sexual pleasure—because only a body that looks good, and, more importantly, knows it, can feel good during sex.

Sexiness and Sexual Pleasure in Women's Sexual Lives

I turn now to the question of how technologies of body confidence are taken up in the sexual lives of primarily white, middle-class heterosexual women. The accounts examined below are drawn from my research on UK women's experiences of sex shopping, which involved twenty-two one-to-one semi-structured interviews (Wood 2015). Their accounts demonstrate the 'taking up' of some of the technologies on offer in sex advice. For the research participants, the idea that various forms of pre-sex body work are primarily done 'for me' was an important one. This was achieved in three key ways: through the interrelated narratives of relationship improvement or 'making the effort', increasing body confidence and achieving better sex. Whilst these strategies appear to echo the sex advice narratives examined above, I do not wish to present an overly deterministic account here. Indeed, the theoretical usefulness of technologies of the self lies in the potential to avoid simplistic ideas of 'internalisation'. Far from passively absorbing models of femininity, the focus here is on an active process of self-work through which technologies of sexiness are inhabited and made meaningful. This allows for a consideration of the ways in which individuals must 'draw on available discourses, and yet can act autonomously' (Attwood 2013, p. 211). By thinking of sex advice as a set of technologies that powerfully 'hails' the reader, and may be 'taken up' by her, we can see the potential for 'unpredictable subversions, slippages and resistances' within that active and ongoing 'taking up' process (Evans and Riley 2015, p. 39).

However, the question of precisely how and in what way such 'slippages' occur bears further theoretical attention. In the conclusion to the analysis, I examine how ideas around 'looking good' were negotiated by some participants in ways that do not neatly align with the presentation of such technologies in sex advice. Examining two examples of failure or refusal to 'look good' in sexual contexts, I offer some reflections on elements of contingency and 'slippage' in the process of taking up technologies of the self. These narratives are a key site at which the technologies of body confidence are challenged or negotiated in the context of women's everyday lives.

Looking Good 'for Me'

Preparing the body to look good for sex was described as an act of loving and caring for a partner and making time for the sexual side of that relationship. Claire believed she was doing something 'good for the relationship', and Agatha said: 'I think it's just making the effort isn't it? And it's just doing something for someone else'. Importantly, however, this 'gift' was framed as having important personal benefits for the giver. Claire asserted that she would get something in return: 'I mean you get kind of like a nice night out of it, and appreciation, and good sex'. Tallulah described a similar kind of exchange:

> Well I suppose you do it for both of you don't you … yeah it gives you confidence as a woman to be admired by your partner, which, you kind of think they would do anyway, but sometimes we all need reassuring don't we, and I guess it's just to give to both you, to make them excited and make you feel more confident.

For these women there is a promise of confidence, reassurance and appreciation that the body looks good. As Claire described, 'once you kind of get going it's alright because, you get a good reaction and sort of confirms what you've done is good, and it's nice and you feel sexy'. Similarly, Tallulah described her partner's gaze helping her to overcome feelings of self-consciousness during a striptease: 'We're all self-critical, but then you look at their face and they're like, "Yeah!", so you're like, ok, I'll keep doing this'. In both these accounts the validation provided by the desiring gaze promises a moment of forgetting, where 'hang-ups' and self-criticism melt away.

Looking good was described as enhancing positive feelings about the self and body, as Clara said: 'If you've got nice matching underwear on then you feel quite good, so that's what, yeah, I do that for myself'. Similarly, Shelly said: 'You want to look nice when you start to take your clothes off, I think it's partly about wanting to feel good about yourself as well'. Besides granting feelings of inner confidence, the physical sensation of wearing luxurious lingerie was seen as a pleasurable 'treat' in itself, as Beatrice described:

> I see it in the same way as you like put on nice clothes and perfume, it's that kind of little indulgences … I feel like I've got something physically lovely against my skin and that's a really nice feeling, so yeah.

Wearing lingerie for sex also promises a feeling of sexual excitement and anticipation, as Tallulah said: 'you know it's going to lead to something else and gets you both quite excited'. Alice too explained: 'It totally gets you going I think, like nice underwear gets you as well as your partner going'. Wearing lingerie could also enable women to shape both the timing and the pace of sexual activity. It could be used as a signal to initiate sex, as Beth described: 'If we're at home it's often like, he'll be downstairs working or doing something, and I'll put something sexy on and go and try and distract him [laughs]'. Beatrice spoke about her use of lingerie to prolong the 'foreplay' stage of sex, a stage that she suggested her male sex partners are inclined to rush:

> It kind of functions, it's almost like foreplay I think, that point of like I'm almost undressed but I'm not and that kind of teasing state, which is a sexy thing, is a nice thing, it's something a lot of people skip!

In these accounts, sexual pleasure is a relational terrain, involving intersecting levels of pleasure gained from feeling good about one's own body, feeling that the body is desirable and experiencing the appreciative gaze of a partner. The way that women have discursively framed these experiences points to the importance of positioning looking good for sex as something that is individually beneficial. This is achieved through the overlapping discourses of 'making the effort', body confidence and better sex. Looking good is understood as something personally fulfilling, rewarding and enabling of greater sexual control, confidence and pleasure. These accounts then show how women are hailed by and take up the technologies of the self in postfeminist sex advice, working on the sexiness of their bodies, and their feelings of body confidence, in order to have 'better', more pleasurable sex. These accounts point to the powerful ways in which such technologies are made meaningful as women take them up and use them to work upon and articulate themselves.

Failing and Refusing to 'Look Good'

The technologies of looking good and being body confident were not always taken up with such ease. Some accounts pointed to the contradictions and negotiations involved as women failed, or refused, to 'look good' and be 'body confident' in the appropriate ways.[3] In conclusion,

[3] I have written elsewhere of the narrative of 'discomfort' around wearing lingerie, contending that it suggests an ambivalent form of resistance to lingerie's visual imperatives (Wood 2016).

here I point to two instances of failure or refusal, in order to demonstrate that technologies of 'looking/feeling good' are not always smoothly taken up in the context of women's everyday sex lives. The first of these is Claire's description of 'wimping out' of wearing lingerie:

> I've wimped out before, y'know if I'm feeling particularly fat on a day or something I've wimped out. I've wimped out literally before we get in bed before, like, pulled it all off and hidden it under the bed … loads of times, I've done so many things where I've like, I'd say probably only about fifty percent of the time I decide to wear sexy underwear, it ends up being used with someone else, and I haven't just got nervous and pulled it off.

This is a narrative of failure in which Claire has been unable to embody the presentation of sexiness that she has prepared in terms of both her outer physical appearance and her inner feelings of confidence; she is both too 'fat' and too 'nervous' to pull off the performance. Bordo's theorisation of the feminine body understands feelings of failure to be a key consequence of continual disciplinary beauty work: 'we continue to memorise on our bodies the feel and conviction of lack, of insufficiency, of never being good enough' (Bordo 1993, p. 166). And yet, as Budgeon contends, such feelings of negativity towards one's appearance are often normalised in women's talk to the point that they are not positioned as problematic at all, thus undermining 'what cultural influences dictated as "normal" [and] counteracting the homogenizing and disciplinary capacity of these representations' (2003, p. 44). I am wary however of glorifying such anxious and unhappy bodily narratives as examples of women's resistance to postfeminist cultures of sexiness. Instead, I wish to suggest that Claire's account points to the problems of embodying the technologies of the self offered by such cultures. As Evans and Riley (2015) suggest, articulating the self by taking up technologies of sexiness is a form of work that is precarious, contingent and never complete. Claire's account then points to a moment of 'slippage' within the taking up of the technologies of 'body confidence', where Claire both fails and refuses to embody 'looking good'.

The second instance is a slightly more direct refusal to 'look good' in Karin's description of using a vibrator:

> Certainly usually with the vibes I'd prefer to be on my own if I'm honest. I find it a bit off-putting because you're expected to 'put a show on' if somebody's watching, but that's not really how it works. I don't do anything interesting. So if he's there then you feel like you have to, and that puts you off a bit … I prefer to know I'm not going to be interrupted, because I find it extremely off-putting if somebody puts his head round the door, even if it's my husband. I'll usually, I don't make a big production of it or anything I'll usually just sneak upstairs and get comfortable. Yes it would be extremely boring to watch cause I don't make any particular effort I just sort of get on with it. I like to have my favourite toy to do it with, saves me time! [laughs]

Karin's experience points to an understanding of her solo sexual practice as entirely unglamorous and functional; this is sexual time that is free from pressure to 'put a show on' and look appealing and 'interesting' to a partner's gaze. This mundane understanding of sexual pleasure is strikingly divergent from the sex advice imperatives of bodily preparation and confidence examined in the first half of this article. Indeed, it is the ordinary nature of Karin's sexual practice that I wish to draw attention to here. Michel de Certeau (1998) understands the everyday as a space of contradiction, negotiation and 'making do' with ready-made consumer capitalism. He refers to those ways of being/using that enter into a 'field that regulates them', whilst also 'introduce into it a way of turning it to their advantage that obeys other rules and constitutes something like a second level interwoven into the first' (de Certeau 1998, p. 30). These multiple 'transverse tactics' (de Certeau 1998, p. 29) operate within existing structures, adapting and exceeding them in ways that do not fully undermine or resist those structures. Karin's functional masturbation routine suggests a kind of 'tactic' by which she temporarily circumvents the imperative to 'look good' for sex, without straightforwardly challenging or changing it. This suggests that such tactics may intervene in the process by which women take up technologies of the self in neoliberalism. If the taking up of such technologies is understood as an active ongoing process, then everyday tactics of 'making do' might be seen as a kind of stubborn force exerting resistance upon that process, whilst not reversing or confronting it directly. Like Claire's narrative of 'wimping out' of performing sexiness, this points to the instability within the process of making the sexual self in ways that neatly align with the technologies of the self on offer in neoliberalism.

Conclusion

This chapter has examined the comprehensive programme of technologies for 'looking and feeling good' offered to sex advice readers. As the interview accounts have shown, these technologies of sexiness allow women to work upon and understand themselves as confident and choice-driven sexual agents who undertake the work of looking good 'for themselves'. However, by understanding women's enacting of 'looking/feeling good' not as deterministic internalisation, but as the active and ongoing taking up of technologies of the self, I have also been able to draw attention to those instances in which women fail and/or refuse to take up such technologies and so 'make do' with neoliberal technologies of the self.

Angela McRobbie has noted the potential for de Certeau's theorisation of 'making do' to serve a complacent 'cultural populist' agenda, asking: 'what need might there be for a feminist politics at all, if women could simply subvert the […] values of the dominant cultural world around them?' (2009, p. 3). It would indeed be wrong to overstate such practices and imply that they will throw off the constraints of postfeminist sexual culture either on an individual or collective level. Yet, I contend that a recognition of women's everyday 'tactics' is in fact an integral part of a feminist critique of postfeminist and neoliberal culture and not a placatory version of, or antithesis to, that critique. For practices of making do precisely demonstrate the contradictions within the technologies of the sexual self offered within postfeminist neoliberalism. That such technologies are vulnerable in the 'taking up' process—prone to refusal, stubbornness, slippage and failure suggests that they do not present a programme of self-work that is as cohesive and comprehensive as it might appear.

References

Attwood, F. (2013). Through the Looking Glass? Sexual Agency and Subjectification Online. In R. Gill & C. Scharff (Eds.), *New Femininities: Postfeminism, Neoliberalism and Subjectivity*. Palgrave Macmillan: Basingstoke.

Bond, A. (2012, April 22). The Way to a Woman's Heart? An Old-Fashioned Compliment Is Better than Sex, Shopping, or Chocolate. *Mail Online*. [Online] Retrieved from http://www.dailymail.co.uk/femail/article-2133505/The-way-womans-heart-An-old-fashioned-compliment-better-sex-shopping-chocolate.html

Bordo, S. (1993). *Unbearable Weight: Feminism, Western Culture, and the Body*. Berkeley: University of California Press.

Brown, W. (2003). Neo-Liberalism and the End of Liberal Democracy. *Theory & Event, 7*(1), 1–18.

Budgeon, S. (2003). Identity as an Embodied Event. *Body & Society, 9*(1), 37–57.

Coffey, J. (2012). Bodies, Body Work and Gender: Exploring a Deleuzian Approach. *Journal of Gender Studies, 22*(1), 3–16.

Cosmo Team. (2006). 5 Bedroom Blunders We All Make. *Cosmopolitan*. [Online] Retrieved from http://www.cosmopolitan.co.uk/love-sex/a432/5-bedroom-blunders-we-all-make-67230/

Cosmo Team. (2013a). 5 Common On-Top Mistakes that Are Holding You Back from Amazing Sex. *Cosmopolitan*. [Online] Retrieved from http://www.cosmopolitan.co.uk/love-sex/sex/tips/a20054/5-common-on-top-mistakes-67224/

Cosmo Team. (2013b). Health Benefits of Orgasms. *Cosmopolitan*. [Online] Retrieved from http://www.cosmopolitan.co.uk/love-sex/sex/tips/a21126/health-benefits-of-orgasms/

Cosmo Team. (n.d.-a). Body Confidence = Great Sex. *Cosmopolitan*. [Online] Retrieved from http://www.cosmopolitan.co.uk/love-sex/g2204/body-confidence-great-sex-73358/

Cosmo Team. (n.d.-b). His Top Ten Bedroom Bugbears. *Cosmopolitan*. [Online] Retrieved from http://www.cosmopolitan.co.uk/love-sex/relationships/g2020/his-top-10-bedroom-bugbears-110235/

Cosmo Team. (n.d.-c). How to Be Confident in Bed. *Cosmopolitan*. [Online] Retrieved from http://www.cosmopolitan.co.uk/love-sex/sex/tips/g1744/how-to-be-confident-in-bed-102377/

Cosmo Team. (n.d.-d). Make the Most of Orgasms. *Cosmopolitan.* [Online] Retrieved from http://www.cosmopolitan.co.uk/love-sex/sex/g290/Make-the-most-of-mornings/?slide=4

Cox, T. (1999). *Hot Sex: How to Do It.* London and Sydney: Corgi.

Cox, T. (2010, November 27). Ask Tracey Cox. *TraceyCox.com.* [Online] Retrieved from http://www.traceycox.com/blog/2010/11/27/ask-tracey-cox-27-november-2010/

Cox, T. (2013, July 24). Revealed: The Six Things You Hope He Will Do the First Time You have Sex. *MailOnline.* [Online] Retrieved from http://www.dailymail.co.uk/femail/article-2376698/REVEALED-The-things-hope-HE-time-sex.html

Cox, T. (2014, May 11). Ask Tracey Cox. *TraceyCox.com.* [Online] Retrieved from http://www.traceycox.com/blog/2014/11/06/ask-tracey-cox-how-do-i-have-great-sex-if-i-dont-like-my-body/

de Certeau, M. (1998). *The Practice of Everyday Life.* Berkeley: University of California Press.

Evans, A., & Riley, S. (2015). *Technologies of Sexiness: Sex, Identity and Consumer Culture.* Oxford: Oxford University Press.

Farvid, P., & Braun, V. (2006). 'Most of Us Guys Are Raring to Go Anytime, Anyplace, Anywhere': Male and Female Sexuality in Cleo and Cosmo. *Sex Roles, 55*, 295–310.

Foucault, M. (2011). *The Government of Self and Others: Lectures at the College de France, 1982–1983.* London: Macmillan.

Frith, H. (2013). Labouring on Orgasms: Embodiment, Efficiency, Entitlement and Obligations in Heterosex. *Culture, Health & Sexuality: An International Journal for Research, Intervention and Care, 15*(4), 494–510.

Gill, R. (2007). Postfeminist Media Culture: Elements of a Sensibility. *European Journal of Cultural Studies, 10*(2), 147–166.

Gill, R. (2009). Supersexualise Me!: Advertising and the 'Midriffs'. In F. Attwood (Ed.), *Mainstreaming Sex: The Sexualization of Western Culture.* London: I.B. Tauris.

Goddard, S. (2013, September 6). Would You Give up Sex to Look Younger? *Cosmopolitan.* [Online] Retrieved from http://www.cosmopolitan.co.uk/love-sex/a22513/would-you-give-up-sex-to-look-younger/

Green, S. (2012). Your A to Z of Orgasms. *Cosmopolitan* (UK), July, pp. 188–191.

Harvey, L., & Gill, R. (2011). The Sex Inspectors: Self-Help, Makeover and Mediated Sex. In K. Ross (Ed.), *Handbook on Gender, Sexualities and Media.* Oxford: Blackwell.

Koenig, R. (2010, July 1). 28 Hot Little Sex Life Ideas. *Redbook*, p. 72.
McRobbie, A. (2009). *The Aftermath of Feminism: Gender Culture and Social Change*. London: Sage.
Mullender, R. (2012). 50 Annoying Things Men (and Women) Do in Bed. *Cosmopolitan* (UK), November, pp. 88–90.
Smith, R. (2012, January 17). Feel Sexier Naked—Now! *Cosmopolitan*. [Online] Retrieved from http://www.cosmopolitan.com/sexlove/advice/a3773/feel-sexier-now/
Teghtsoonian, K. (2009). Depression and Mental Health in Neoliberal Times: A Critical Analysis of Policy and Discourse. *Social Science & Medicine, 69*(1), 28–35.
Tyler, M. (2004). Managing Between the Sheets: Lifestyle Magazines and the Management of Sexuality in Everyday Life. *Sexualities, 7*(1), 81–106.
Wood, R. (2015). *Consumer Sexualities: Women and Sex Shopping*. University of Sussex: Unpublished PhD Thesis.
Wood, R. (2016). 'You Do Act Differently When You're in It': Lingerie and Femininity. *Journal of Gender Studies, 25*(1), 10–23.

19

The Aesthetics of Sexual Discontent: Notes from the London 'Seduction Community'

Rachel O'Neill

Introduction

This chapter explores questions of sexual desire and gendered aesthetics through a discussion of research undertaken with and among men who participate in the London 'seduction community'. Recognising sexual desire as an affective and embodied dynamic that is nevertheless irrevocably social, I consider how the sexual desires of heterosexual men are shaped in and through normative feminine beauty ideals. I argue that the naturalisation of aesthetic labour as part of the cultural code of femininity has implications for the manner in which heterosexual men relate to women's bodies, both real and imagined.

The analysis proceeds in three parts. In the first section, I set out the context of my research in greater detail and put forward an understanding

R. O'Neill (✉)
Department of Sociology, University of York, York, UK

A.S. Elias et al. (eds.), *Aesthetic Labour*,
DOI 10.1057/978-1-137-47765-1_19

of the London seduction community as a site of mediated intimacy. In the second section, I discuss the sense of sexual discontent that frequently precipitates men's involvement in the London seduction community. Engaging Eva Illouz's insight that 'culturally induced desires … create ordinary forms of suffering, such as chronic dissatisfaction, disappointment, and perpetual longing' (2012, p. 207), I attempt to make sense of the pervasive dissatisfaction that characterised men's narratives about their past sexual and intimate relationships. I discuss how men I interviewed spoke about the bodies of their past sexual and intimate partners and illustrate how demands for women's aesthetic labour—whereby women are expected to actively shape and maintain their appearance through a range of disciplinary practices and procedures—figured within these narratives of sexual discontent. In the third section I go on to consider how participants described the kinds of partners they want to have sexual and intimate relationships with. I consider the tendency among participants to articulate sexual desire in numerical terms, with sexual partners ranked and accorded value through regimes of evaluation and quantification.

Placing these discussions in relation to broader social and cultural developments, I consider how the demand for women's aesthetic labour in the context of sexual and intimate relationships is caught up with the neoliberal extension of market logics to previously non-economic domains (Brown 2005). In examining how narrowly defined beauty ideals shape the embodied experience of sexual desire among heterosexual men and produce circumscribed patterns of eros and eroticism, this chapter attempts to open up a subject that has been largely overlooked in feminist media and cultural studies scholarship to date.

Seduction as Mediated Intimacy

The London seduction community is a central locus within a transnational community-industry, the express purpose of which is to enable heterosexual men to achieve greater control and choice in their relationships with women through various forms of skills training and personal development. An import from the USA, the seduction community has had a commercial presence in London for at least ten years, with the first

UK-based seduction training company, PUA Training, established in 2007 (La Ruina 2007). Today, a panoply of private companies as well as independent trainers offer fee-based seduction training services including one-to-one coaching, weekend 'bootcamp' courses and live-in 'residential' programmes. Free and ostensibly non-commercial events also regularly take place in the city, while online forums provide platforms for men involved in this setting to document their activities, discuss concepts and techniques, solicit advice and provide feedback to one another. Those with established profiles as trainers within the London industry host channels on social media sites such as YouTube, where the instructional videos they produce routinely garner tens or even hundreds of thousands of views.

Although those involved in the London seduction community are often referred to and refer to themselves as 'pickup artists' or 'PUAs', there is a good deal of ambivalence around these terms such that it has become common for those who have made careers in this industry to at least nominally distance themselves from such appellations. The term 'community' is also something of a misnomer, concealing the machinations of what is in fact a lucrative but highly precarious industry, while also promoting a sense of authentic collectivity that is readily exploited for commercial gain. Because the term 'community' remains the most common appellation used to describe this cultural formation, I use it alongside and in conjunction with the hybridised term 'community-industry', which I have formulated in order to signal the commercial interests at stake in this setting.

My research within the London seduction community is ethnographic in character, encompassing media analysis, observational fieldwork and in-depth interviews. For this project I have examined popular seduction books and blogs, promotional materials from seduction training companies, as well as instructional seduction videos posted online. During my fieldwork I attended a variety of seduction training events and also observed private coaching sessions. Interviews with 32 research participants provide the central axis around which much of my analysis in this chapter turns. Interview participants—all of whom have been attributed pseudonyms—represent a broad cross-section of those involved in the London seduction community, including trainers at different levels of the industry hierarchy and students attending free and paid events.

While researchers elsewhere have characterised the seduction community as a subculture (Baker 2013; Schuurmans and Monaghan 2015) or self-help movement (Hendriks 2012; Almog and Kaplan 2015), I approach the London seduction community as a site of mediated intimacy (see also O'Neill 2015a). This analysis is located within a wider body of literature concerned to examine how contemporary formations of intimate and sexual subjectivity are configured through broader social and cultural rationalities, most particularly those of postfeminism and neoliberalism (Gill 2009a).

The discursive patterning of sex and relationships as sites of management and entrepreneurship has been analysed across a broad range of media, including self-help texts, makeover television and lifestyle magazines (Farvid and Braun 2013a; Farvid and Braun 2013b; Gill 2014; Harvey and Gill 2011; Tyler 2004). While both men and women are enjoined to become enterprising sexual subjects, these discourses are deeply gendered, with masculine repertoires frequently organised around themes of scientific rationality and efficiency (Harvey and Gill 2011) as well as planning and strategy (Farvid and Braun 2013b). These discourses are also highly contradictory, as gendered performances are 'presented simultaneously as moments of freedom, choice, empowerment and pleasure, yet also as hard work that is normatively demanded and essential to the success of heterosexual relationships' (Harvey and Gill 2011, p. 488).

Surveying this cultural landscape, Melissa Tyler argues that 'through the incorporation of managerial imperatives, discourses and techniques into those cultural resources that in part guide us through everyday life, sexuality has also become yet another aspect of the lifeworld in which the work ethic seemingly reigns supreme' (2004, p. 100). Tyler's research suggests that the exhortation to manage sex inculcates a performance imperative that has the potential to fundamentally alter the character of sexual encounters and intimate relationships. She contends: 'with this incitement to sexual and managerial discourse, has come a corresponding performance imperative that does not simply repress sex, but suppresses (or rather arrests) the inter-subjectivity of eroticism' (Tyler 2004, p. 101; see also Fahs 2011).

In approaching this community-industry as a site of mediated intimacy my research draws attention to the continuities between this and 'mainstream' sites of sex and relationship advice. To this end, it is important to point out that the seduction community is heavily imbricated with more conventional sites of mediated intimacy. Established figures from the seduction industry both within and outside the UK routinely contribute sex advice to magazine titles such as *FHM* and *Men's Health* as well as popular online sites such as *AskMen,* where they rebrand themselves as 'dating coaches' or 'lifestyle experts'. The seduction urtext and popular best-seller *The Game* (2005), in which journalist Neil Strauss chronicles his rise within the then-burgeoning seduction community in the USA while also providing instructional guidelines teaching readers how to 'seduce' women, is one of the most widely read pieces of sex advice literature ever produced (Farvid and Braun 2013b). Popular programming such as VH1's *The Pickup Artist* and ITV's *Dapper Laughs: On The Pull*—both of which proffer to transform 'losers' and 'chumps' into 'players' and 'pickup artists'—are also part of this cultural trajectory. Tactics and techniques elaborated in the seduction community frequently manifest elsewhere. Exemplifying this, a seduction technique known as 'negging'—whereby a man gives a woman a compliment that contains a negative element in an effort to undermine her status in a given interaction—has entered the wider cultural lexicon and indeed been inaugurated by journalists in the UK as a 'dating trend' (Bradshaw 2012; Woolf 2012).

The London seduction community is thus not a *deviation* or *departure* from current social conventions, but instead an *extension* and *acceleration* of existing cultural norms. That is to say, the underpinning logics of the London seduction community are *consistent with* broader configurations of intimacy and subjectivity in the contemporary British context. Thus, while the perspectives and experiences of men who participate in this setting are not necessarily representative of those of heterosexual men in any general sense, the patterns I discuss here are nevertheless symptomatic of much broader social and cultural problematics.

Desire and Discontent

When talking about how and why they became involved in the London seduction community, men I interviewed routinely made reference to their past sexual encounters and intimate relationships, or described a relative lack thereof. For some, this was a topic they arrived at after some time and were evidently hesitant to discuss in any detail; for others, this was a central motif of their self-narrative and a recurrent topic of discussion. While the kinds of relationships participants described varied widely—including live-in relationships and long-distance partnerships; marriages accompanied by separation or divorce; one night stands and casual affairs; 'no strings attached' and 'friends with benefits' arrangements—they were, without exception, *dissatisfied* with their sexual and intimate lives. On the one hand, this is hardly surprising: the London seduction community is, after all, a community-industry which promises men greater control and choice in their relationships with women and is, as such, likely to be populated by those who feel they lack this. Yet these narratives also seem to point towards a broader problematic, wherein sexual and intimate relationships have become the sites of more persistent forms of disaffection (Hochschild 2012; Illouz 2012). Discussing this issue, Illouz notes that: 'Disappointment [...] is either the inability to find the anticipated (aesthetic) form in the actual experience, or the difficulty to sustain it in real life' (2012, p. 218).

Discussing their past sexual and intimate relationships, a number of participants described being unhappy in previous relationships because they felt their partners were not attractive or not attractive *enough*. Introducing himself to trainers and students at a weekend training event, a business consultant in his early twenties named Moe described having taken two previous training courses with other companies, but still found himself unable to date the kinds of women he really wants to be with. Nodding with recognition, the trainer leading the event said:

> If you're getting with girls who are not at the level you want, you're settling. And settling is the worst thing you can do, because every time you see a guy with a hotter girl, you think, 'I wish I was him'.

When I later interviewed Moe, he described having first sought out seduction-related advice following the demise of a two-year relationship. When I asked him to describe what the relationship had been like, he somewhat hesitantly began by saying: 'Ahm ... well ... she was not that attractive'.

Moe went on to explain that although at first he was 'just happy I had a girlfriend', his feelings about the relationship soon changed and he became increasingly unhappy. Accounting for why the relationship lasted for almost two years despite his unhappiness—much of which he attributed to his girlfriend being 'big'—Moe admitted that: 'At the time I … that was, in my mind, it was the best I could get, if I could get any at all'. The disgust that permeated Moe's memory of this relationship was palpable, as he asserted:

> I will never, *never*, go back to that again, *never*. I will even do whatever. I mean, I will even be single to … to … never go back to that … And that's-that's what motivated me to get into all this, really.

Elsewhere, a university student in his early twenties named Jay described his ex-girlfriend, with whom he had been in a relationship with for more than four years, as 'quite attractive, but not like … my ideal'. He went on to explain:

> I mean, when she woke up in the morning, without makeup it wasn't … ahm … it wasn't … I didn't … I liked her better with makeup on, so … so yeah. More than … more than other people, like you know. I think she needed a little bit of makeup on, at least. But yeah, I think that should be a problem for you, if you're gonna be ahm like waking up next to … if I'm going to be waking up next to her like everyday, that would be a problem in the long term.

Contending that his ex-girlfriend 'needed a little bit of makeup on, at least', Jay reproduces a commonplace logic through which women's bodies are figured as lacking and incomplete. He describes his ex-girlfriend's cosmetically unadorned appearance as something that would be a 'problem' in sustaining a sexual and intimate relationship 'in the long term', and ultimately cites this as one of the reasons he ended the relationship. There is no question here for Jay of whether the aesthetic standards he expects his intimate partners to maintain at all times are perhaps unreasonable or unrealistic, much less the manner in which unequal power relations between women and men generally enable him to hold such expectations.

The readiness with which men I interviewed criticised the bodies of their sexual and intimate partners stands in stark contrast to the innocuous male gaze imagined in some spaces of postfeminist media culture. Discussing this in her work on 'postfeminist sisterhood', Alison Winch explains that 'girlfriend culture revolves around homosocial forms of control where women bond through the bodies of other women … the male gaze is veiled as benign, and instead it is women who are represented as looking at other women's bodies' (2014, p. 5). Elsewhere, research undertaken by Avelie Stuart and Ngaire Donaghue (2011) demonstrates a commonly held conviction among women that it is only or primarily women who police and enforce feminine beauty ideals. Women interviewed by Stuart and Donaghue routinely positioned other women as being 'catty, judgmental, back-stabbing and insecure' (2011, p. 104), while claiming that men '[see] through media portrayals of women' and are generally 'unconcerned whether women looked like models and celebrities' (2011, p. 105). By contrast, among the men I spoke with and interviewed women's bodies were routinely held up for scrutiny, critically appraised and found wanting. This was vividly demonstrated by an exchange between two trainers I observed during a training event in central London. As we stood outside the flagship Topshop store at Oxford Circus, a junior trainer pointed to the billboard adorning the multi-story shop front. With a contrived casualness, he told another more senior trainer that he had approached the model from the billboard in person a week before. Looking up from his phone briefly, the senior trainer cast an eye over the billboard before pronouncing: 'She's not that hot'. Apparently trying to impress his colleague, a much more experienced 'seducer' than himself, the junior trainer quickly agreed, saying: 'She's not great, and definitely not as good in real life'. Far from being unconcerned with whether or not women look like models, it seems that even models—women who supposedly embody normative ideals of feminine beauty—are subject to criticism by men for their apparently flawed and inadequate appearance. A key issue here is the manner in which women's bodies are made available as objects of *sexual scrutiny* as well as sexual desire in contemporary culture.

The particular form of sexual discontent described by research participants raises questions about the ways in which the psychic and embodied dynamics of heterosexual desire are trained by a visual culture that exalts an exceedingly narrow definition of feminine beauty. While this issue would seem to be of obvious concern to feminist media and cultural studies scholars, it remains sorely under researched. Although it is virtually taken for granted that images of ideal feminine beauty frequently shape women's relationship with their own bodies in negative ways—to the extent that this has become a kind of 'sociological banality' (McRobbie 2009, p. 96)—there seems to be a general reluctance to discuss how these same images might also inform how heterosexual men perceive and relate to women's bodies, most especially the bodies of women with whom they share sexual encounters and intimate relationships.[1] Yet if it is recognised that media imagery of feminine perfection—extending not only from billboards, magazines and television screens, but also circulating via highly orchestrated displays on social media—has decisive implications for the manner in which women relate to their own bodies, then it would seem to follow that this same imagery may also shape the kinds of relationships men have to and with women's bodies. Putting this another way, we might ask: given that the manner in which women relate to their own bodies is frequently characterised by 'normative discontent' (McRobbie 2009, pp. 94–98), is it any surprise that this sense of discontent can and does manifest in men's relationships with women's bodies?

In taking up questions such as these, it is crucial to avoid resorting to crude and simplistic assumptions about media 'effects'. What is needed instead are more nuanced analyses of the relationship between culture and subjectivity. Rebecca Coleman provides a model for this kind of enquiry by taking a relational approach to the study of girls' body image, examining 'the ways in which bodies are known, understood and experienced *through* images, that is, the ways in which bodies *become* through their relations with images' (2008, p. 163). Without necessarily adopting the Deleuzian perspective that informs Coleman's analysis, I find the discussion she develops immensely useful for thinking about how sexual desire comes to be constituted—known, understood and experienced—in relation to and through relations with media imagery. In the context

[1] An important exception here is Susan Bordo's *The Male Body*, where she describes how images of feminine perfection in the media shape the desires of heterosexual men, such that 'straight male sexuality is honed on the images, even fixated on them' (1999, p. 287).

of my own research within the London seduction community—a project that did not deliberately set out to examine such issues, but in which bodies and desires were discussed extensively—women's bodies were routinely figured as deficient and defective, in a manner closely approximating the cultural pathologisation of women's bodies encapsulated by the postfeminist 'makeover paradigm' (Gill 2007; Tincknell 2011). The aesthetic inadequacy of women's bodies was indexed as a significant problem for men, not only in the context of their own sexual and intimate relationships but also at a broader cultural level. Exemplifying this latter tendency, a trainer named Danny problematised what he termed the culture of 'fat acceptance' in the UK. Referencing the Dove 'Real Beauty' advertising campaign as an example of this cultural tendency, he explained: 'The more fat women you have, the less choice you have [...] It's bad for men because there's more competition'. These kinds of statements by men point to the need for feminist scholars to attend to questions of how men negotiate postfeminist discourses, representations and practices (see also O'Neill 2015b).

Aspirational Bodies

Participation in the London seduction community among heterosexual men is generally motivated by a desire for greater control and choice in their relationships with women. Of particular concern among those I interviewed was a desire to access a better 'quality' and 'calibre' of sexual partner, based largely if not exclusively on aesthetic criteria. Participants regularly assumed that it is only 'natural' for men to give primary importance to women's physical appearance and sexual attractiveness—while at the same time claiming that women generally place far less emphasis on men's appearance. James, in his late twenties, explained in our interview: 'Men respond to like the visual ... like, we see attractive women. Whereas women respond to different things'. Gavin, also in his late twenties, similarly contended that: 'Women are more emotional rather than visual like we are'. In a more assertive tone, a university student in his early twenties named Brent posited: 'We are like visual one hundred percent of the way. People- guys will talk about mentality, that might be in the second phase, but in the beginning it's all about the body. If they say [otherwise] they're total liars'.

Ralph, in his late forties, commended women for being able to look beyond physical appearance, saying: 'I genuinely do feel that women care less about looks than guys do. And, you know, I'd big women up for that [...] I think they do care more about what a person's like inside'. He went on to elaborate that, as an older man, this made him feel better about his own appearance: 'It's just good to know that women are deep enough to see more in you than just the ... just the sort of ... the exterior'. While some men were not entirely comfortable with the emphasis they themselves placed on women's physical appearance, this was nevertheless presented as somehow unavoidable, an inextricable fact of male sexuality. Exemplifying this, a business owner in his late thirties named Anwar professed: 'I know I sound shallow, and I *hate* myself for saying it [...] but then ... sexually, at a sexual level, it matters'. Others, however, seemed to attach a certain pride to being 'picky' and 'fussy' about women, as though this were a mark of discernment. Ralph pronounced: 'I am incredibly fussy about women', while Brent stated: 'I'm really picky. I mean, there's no other word for it. I really am'.

In interviews, participants routinely offered detailed specifications about the physical characteristics their desired partners should embody, including age, weight and height; skin, hair and eye colour; and 'race', ethnicity and nationality. While many men framed their preferences as unique and idiosyncratic, the overall *uniformity* of these descriptions was striking, as participants almost invariably described a feminine ideal that closely resembles that which is celebrated in contemporary advertising and celebrity culture: young, slim and able-bodied, normatively white or an exoticised 'Other', and with conventionally attractive physical features such as large breasts, long hair and a slim waist (Gill 2008; Gill 2009b). Harry, a university student in his early twenties, provided an illustrative example of this when he described:

> I like long legs, toned. Petite, short petite body. I don't really like girls that are a lot taller than me, so if she's the same height as me or shorter, that's what I like. I like a nice flat stomach [...] to me that is really really sexy. And, you know, healthy soft good looks. Long hair I find really attractive.

> And like I said before, I'm kind of veering towards more of like these … the Scandinavian look these days.

Notably, Harry's description of the physical characteristics his sexual partners should embody—alongside those given by many of the other men I interviewed—fails to reproduce the postfeminist logic found in contemporary 'lad lit', wherein the objectification of women's bodies is routinely accompanied by a kind of ersatz sense of contrition or self-consciousness (Gill 2014). Rather, objectifying descriptions of women's bodies were for the most part offered freely and without any apparent unease, and participants generally appeared comfortable dictating the aesthetic standards they expect their sexual and intimate partners to conform to. For many men it was imperative that their sexual and intimate partners be 'fit', with participants regularly describing a preference for women who 'work out' and are 'in shape'. Harry described: 'Something I'm really into is girls that take care of themselves and are quite fit, that's something I'm definitely attracted to'. Gavin similarly related his ideal as: 'Someone who has a figure like a fitness model'. Elsewhere, Jay stated that he wants women he dates to have an interest in fitness, readily acknowledging: 'That's a superficial thing—it translates to a superficial thing'.

The exhaustive aesthetic criteria participants described expecting their sexual and intimate partners to conform to—with little substantive consideration given to the interpersonal and affective dynamics that might animate these relationships—appear consonant with the view that 'it is often not women per se that men desire, but women's bodies' (Burkett and Hamilton 2012, p. 827). Yet what was perhaps most notable about how participants described their desired sexual and intimate partners was the relentlessly *aspirational* ethos which permeated these descriptions. Across interviews, men appeared thoroughly preoccupied with attaining a higher 'quality' of sexual and intimate partner. Indeed, within the London seduction community, women's 'value' is seen to be of more or less calculable, such that it is *de rigueur* for men involved in this community-industry to talk about women in numerical terms. In our interview, trainer Danny explained:

> The reason why some guys- why a lot of guys want to do game, is so that they can attract higher value women. So they might be dating say fives and

sixes, and they actually want to have a girl who's a ten in terms of looks. And so in order to attract her and possibly try to keep her there, they have to work on themselves and learn game.

The marketised logic that organises this mentality was not lost on Danny, who himself acknowledged: 'It's an exchange of values, "What can I get for what I'm offering?" […] It becomes very economical'. This overwhelming concern with attaining access to high 'value' women—a value that is apparently calculated largely in aesthetic terms—is testament to the relentless economisation of social and cultural life that neoliberalism entails. As Wendy Brown argues, 'neoliberal rationality disseminates the *model of the market* to all domains and activities—even where money is not at issue—and configures human beings exhaustively as market actors, always, only, and everywhere as *homo oeconomicus*' (2005, p. 31). In a society in thrall of market metrics, and where women's bodies are constantly held up for sexual scrutiny, it is at once entirely lamentable and thoroughly predictable that a logic of value exchange so completely pervades the way in which some men relate to women—real and imagined—as sexual and intimate partners.

While these kinds of marketised logics have become embedded within contemporary intimate and sexual life—exemplifying a cultural logic predicated upon 'taking as much as you can get' (Gavey et al. 1999, p. 54)—it seems fair to suggest that engagement with the London seduction community is likely to bolster men's sense of sexual entitlement. Specifically, this is because the knowledge-practices elaborated in this setting frame sexual and intimate relationality as a competency that can be achieved through skills training and self-development, thereby inscribing sexual encounters and intimate relationships within a logic of investment and return, opportunity and outcome. To this end, it is worth noting that a number of men I interviewed claimed that involvement in this community-industry had made them more 'picky' and 'fussy'. Having already stated that he is 'really picky' about women, Brent further related:

Actually, through pickup it became even worse. Sometimes I can see a really like nice girl, but if I don't think that I should go, my head just … that's why I say that it made me more picky—I just don't settle for less, I would say.

Elijah, in his late twenties, explained that his 'standards' have become so exacting that: 'Every time I go out with a woman I kind of get bored of them. Because I think I can do better'. These kinds of statements demonstrate that far from ameliorating or resolving the sense of dissatisfaction which leads men to seek out the forms of expertise made available within the London seduction community, participation in this community-industry may actually *exacerbate* this sense of disaffection by inflating men's sense of sexual entitlement. As such, the knowledge-practices on offer here may well *contribute to* the chronic sense of dissatisfaction and disappointment that have become the unhappy hallmarks of contemporary sexual and intimate relations.

Conclusion

In this chapter I have examined the aesthetics of sexual discontent through a discussion of the ways in which men who participate in the London seduction community talk about their actual and ideal sexual partners. While acknowledging that those who become involved in the London seduction community do so precisely because they are unhappy with their sexual and intimate lives, this analysis provides evidence to support the view—unpopular within much sociological work on intimacy—that contemporary sexual and intimate relationships are marked by persistent forms of discontent and disaffection and that this has something to do with the political-economic structures of neoliberal capitalism (Gregg 2013; Hochschild 2012; Illouz 2012). Far from the celebrated 'democratisation of desire' (McNair 1996), wherein desire becomes radically pluralised and de-hierarchised, the narratives these men present suggest that the affective rhythms and embodied impulses of desire are being colonised by a visual cultural that celebrates an exceedingly narrow definition of feminine desirability, alongside the machinations of an economic system that privileges enterprise and capital acquisition over all else. In this context, the 'specific feelings, specific rhythms' (Williams 1977, p. 133) which constitute wider structures of sexual desire become overdetermined by market logics, producing a kind of circumscribed libidinousness that is entirely generic in its aims and ambitions. As in neoliberal culture more broadly, there is an emptying out of the subjective and the interpersonal, as a capitalist logic of value comes to undermine and obscure a more expansive appreciation of human *values* (Skeggs 2014).

References

Almog, R., & Kaplan D. (2015). The Nerd and His Discontent: The Seduction Community and the Logic of the Game as a Geeky Solution to the Challenges of Young Masculinity. *Men and Masculinities*, online first: 1–22.

Baker, K. (2013). Cockblocked by Redistribution: A Pick-up Artist in Denmark. *Dissent, 60*, 8–11.

Bordo, S. (1999). *The Male Body: A New Look at Men in Public and in Private.* New York: Farrar, Straus, and Giroux.

Bradshaw, P. (2012). A Brief History of Pozzing and Negging. *The Guardian.* [Online] Retrieved October 6, 2015 from http://www.theguardian.com/commentisfree/2015/jan/21/negging-loathsome-trend

Brown, W. (2005). Neoliberalism and the End of Liberal Democracy. In *Edgework: Critical Essays on Knowledge and Politics* (pp. 7–59). Woodstock, Oxfordshire: Princeton University Press.

Burkett, M., & Hamilton, K. (2012). Postfeminist Sexual Agency: Young Women's Negotiations of Sexual Consent. *Sexualities, 15*, 815–833.

Coleman, R. (2008). The Becoming of Bodies. *Feminist Media Studies, 8*(2), 163–179.

Fahs, B. (2011). *Performing Sex: The Making and Unmaking of Women's Erotic Lives.* Albany, NY: State University of New York Press.

Farvid, P., & Braun, V. (2013a). Casual Sex as 'Not a Natural Act' and Other Regimes of Truth About Heterosexuality. *Feminism & Psychology, 23*(3), 359–378.

Farvid, P., & Braun, V. (2013b). The 'Sassy Woman' and the 'Performing Man': Heterosexual Casual Sex Advice and the (Re)constitution of Gendered Subjectivities. *Feminist Media Studies, 14*(1), 118–134.

Gavey, N., McPhillips, K., & Braun, V. (1999). Interruptus Coitus: Heterosexuals Accounting for Intercourse. *Sexualities, 2*(1), 35–68.

Gill, R. (2007). *Gender and the Media.* Cambridge: Polity.

Gill, R. (2008). Empowerment/Sexism: Figuring Female Sexual Agency in Contemporary Advertising. *Feminism & Psychology, 18*(1), 35–60.

Gill, R. (2009a). Mediated Intimacy and Postfeminism: A Discourse Analytic Examination of Sex and Relationships Advice in a Women's Magazine. *Discourse & Communication, 3*(4), 345–369.

Gill, R. (2009b). Beyond the 'Sexualization of Culture' Thesis: An Intersectional Analysis of 'Sixpacks', 'Midriffs' and 'Hot Lesbians' in Advertising. *Sexualities, 12*(2), 137–160.

Gill, R. (2014). Powerful Women, Vulnerable Men and Postfeminist Masculinity in Men's Popular Fiction. *Gender and Language, 8*, 185–204.

Gregg, M. (2013). Spousebusting: Intimacy, Adultery and Surveillance Technology. *Surveillance & Society, 11*(3), 301–310.

Harvey, L., & Gill, R. (2011). The Sex Inspectors: Self-Help, Makeover and Mediated Sex. In *Handbook of Gender, Sexualities and Media* (pp. 487–501). Oxford: Blackwell.

Hendriks, E. C. (2012). Ascetic Hedonism: Self and Sexual Conquest in the Seduction Community. *Cultural Analysis, 11*, 1–16.

Hochschild, A. R. (2012). *The Outsourced Self: Intimate Life in Market Times*. New York: Metropolitan Books.

Illouz, E. (2012). *Why Love Hurts: A Sociological Explanation*. Cambridge: Polity.

La Ruina, R. (2007). *The Natural Art of Seduction*. London: Pennant Books.

McNair, B. (1996). *Mediated Sex: Pornography and Postmodern Culture*. London: Arnold.

McRobbie, A. (2009). *The Aftermath of Feminism: Gender, Culture and Social Change*. London: Sage.

O'Neill, R. (2015a). The Work of Seduction: Intimacy and Subjectivity in the London 'Seduction Community'. *Sociological Research Online, 20*(4), 5.

O'Neill, R. (2015b). Whither Critical Masculinity Studies? Notes on Inclusive Masculinity Theory, Postfeminism, and Sexual Politics. *Men and Masculinities, 18*, 100–120.

Schuurmans, J., & Monaghan, L. F. (2015). The Casanova-Myth: Legend and Anxiety in the Seduction Community. *Sociological Research Online, 20*(1), 1.

Skeggs, B. (2014). Values Beyond Value? Is Anything Beyond the Logic of Capital? *British Journal Sociology, 65*(1), 1–20.

Strauss, N. (2005). *The Game: Penetrating the Secret Society of Pickup Artists*. Edinburgh: Canongate.

Stuart, A., & Donaghue, N. (2011). Choosing to Conform: The Discursive Complexities of Choice in Relation to Feminine Beauty Practices. *Feminism & Psychology, 22*(1), 98–121.

Tincknell, E. (2011). Scourging the Abject Body: Ten Years Younger and Fragmented Femininity under Neoliberalism. In R. Gill & C. Scharff (Eds.), *New Femininities: Postfeminism, Neoliberalism and Subjectivity* (pp. 83–95). Palgrave: Basingstoke.

Tyler, M. (2004). Managing Between the Sheets: Lifestyle Magazines and the Management of Sexuality in Everyday Life. *Sexualities, 7*(1), 81–106.

Williams, R. (1977). *Structures of Feeling. Marxism and Literature* (pp. 128–135). Oxford: Oxford University Press.

Winch, A. (2014). *Girlfriends and Postfeminist Sisterhood.* Basingstoke: Palgrave Macmillan.

Woolf, N. (2012). 'Negging': The Anatomy of a Dating Trend. *New Statesman.* [Online] Retrieved October 6, 2015 from http://www.newstatesman.com/blogs/voices/2012/05/negging-latest-dating-trend

20

Invisible Labour? Tensions and Ambiguities of Modifying the 'Private' Body: The Case of Female Genital Cosmetic Surgery

Amy Shields Dobson, Karalyn McDonald, Maggie Kirkman, Kay Souter, and Jane Fisher

Introduction

The 'designer vagina' is a relatively new phenomenon, becoming part of public discourse only in the late 1990s. Although female genital surgery has a history longer than 150 years, modification has not usually

A.S. Dobson (✉)
Institute for Advanced Studies in the Humanities, University of Queensland, Brisbane, QLD, Australia

K. McDonald • M. Kirkman • J. Fisher
The Jean Hailes Research Unit, School of Public Health and Preventive Medicine, Monash University, Melbourne, VIC, Australia

K. Souter
Faculty of Law and Business Australian Catholic University, Melbourn, VIC, Australia

A.S. Elias et al. (eds.), *Aesthetic Labour*,
DOI 10.1057/978-1-137-47765-1_20

been for aesthetic reasons (Green 2005). Nowadays, cosmetic surgeons promising 'designer vaginas' offer to modify all parts of women's genitals, often to render them more attractive: the labia minora are minimised and made symmetrical (labiaplasty), the clitoral hood is made less prominent (clitoral hood reduction), the labia majora are plumped to make them look more 'youthful', and liposuction is available for a 'fat' mons pubis (Michala et al. 2012). Normal genital variation among women has been pathologised by describing visible labia minora as 'hypertrophic' (Miklos and Moore 2008). Simone Weil Davis (2002, p. 15) quotes a cosmetic surgeon as telling her that 'the ideal look for labia minora was not only minimal and not extended but also symmetrical, "homogeneously pink," and "not wavy".'

This genital pathology discourse blurs the distinction between aesthetics and function, where 'vaginal rejuvenation' to improve sexual pleasure may be sought in conjunction with procedures to alter appearance. Whose sexual pleasure is being improved? It can be argued that it is not the woman's, because genital surgery may entail nerve damage and reduced sensation. Nevertheless, Virginia Braun's (2005) analysis of magazine articles and interviews with surgeons found that female genital cosmetic surgery (FGCS) was framed as enhancing female sexual pleasure, specifically orgasm. Further reasons given for female genital cosmetic surgery include 'discomfort', where larger labia are claimed to be problematic in tight clothing, when cycling, or during sexual activity (Miklos and Moore 2008), and cleanliness, with the unsupported assertion that larger labia limit good hygiene (Bramwell et al. 2007).

Australia has a taxpayer-funded universal health care system known as Medicare. It is not straightforward to interpret the threefold increase in Medicare claims for labiaplasty between 2001 and 2011 (Medicare Benefits Schedule 2012) because of the exclusion of all cosmetic procedures except those that have been presented as having clinical indications. The most prominent category of women claiming for labiaplasty in Australia from January–April 2012 were those aged 15 to 24. There is no national register of the vast majority of cosmetic procedures that are privately funded. The as-yet-unanswered question is why girls and women in Australia and elsewhere appear to be seeking cosmetic surgery on their genitals.

The modification and disciplining of women's bodies through cosmetic surgery has long been critiqued by feminist scholars (Blum 2003; Davis 1995). They have reflected on the ways in which cosmetic surgery is normalised, for example, through reality television shows (Markey and Markey 2010; Sperry et al. 2009) as well the neoliberal rhetoric of choice and agency (Banet-Weiser and Portwood Stacer 2006; Fraser 2003). Shame about their inadequate bodies appears to underpin the decision made by some women to have cosmetic surgery (Northrop 2012). In accepting the need to attempt to perfect their bodies, women have been positioned as victims of a patriarchal construction of femininity and beauty (Taylor 2012).

The instance of FGCS is, like cosmetic surgery in general, positioned as both a surgical and a cultural practice (Fraser 2003). Lih-Mei Liao et al. (2010) reviewed the literature on labial surgery for 'well women' and concluded that medically unjustified surgery to the labia minora was being promoted as beneficial to women (claiming high levels of patient satisfaction based on methodologically unsound data) in the absence of any data on clinical effectiveness. In online advertising by surgical providers, FGCS was found to be presented as an effective treatment for concerns about genital appearance, with little reference to genital diversity, clinical outcomes, risks, or other potential ways of managing concerns about appearance (Liao et al. 2012). Braun (2010, this volume) has identified the limited scholarship on FGCS and called for the deficiency to be remedied. Building on what is already known, this chapter arises from a project that seeks to map the gendered cultural and psychosocial factors leading women to seek FGCS, and to explore broader public discourses about 'normal' female genital appearance among women and men in Australia, health care professionals, beauty therapists, and in social media communications. At the outset of this project, we first see a need to try to ascertain where and how FGCS currently fits within neoliberal and post-feminist discursive frameworks of 'body work' and 'self' transformation and reinvention. Our views are shaped by our interviews with women about genital modification.[1]

[1] These interviews are part of a research project, *Elucidating the Increasing Demand for Genital Cosmetic Surgery among Girls and Women in Australia* (2014–2017), funded by the Australian

The purpose of this chapter is to consider how labour on the private body should be understood differently from labour on the publicly visible body. Thinking through the ways in which genital cosmetic surgery fits within 'inner' and 'outer' body work projects is vital for understanding contemporary attitudes in Australia and the Anglophone West towards FGCS, as well as women's own complex positionings and experiences of genital modification. We explore some possible differences between cosmetic surgery on women's genitals and other, more publicly visible, parts of the female body that are commonly modified through surgery. The excerpts are taken from our interviews with women who have undergone or thought about FGCS or modified their genitals in others ways. They distinctively offer examples of women's reflections and comments that have prompted us to think through tensions and contradictions arising around projects of modifying the private body in a postfeminist and neoliberal social, cultural, and economic context.[2] FGCS, we contend, confuses and begs questions about neat divides between the labour of aesthetics and the labour of intimacy and relationality. More specifically, tensions arise in relation to three concepts that are theorised as central to understanding cosmetic surgery practices more broadly. These are: (1) tensions between 'body' and 'self' work; (2) cosmetic surgery as driven by neoliberal, individualist competitive culture; and (3) autonomous versus relational understandings of the self in society. We suggest that a more open analytical framework than is currently available is needed in order to start a public conversation about FGCS that can move beyond simple logics of choice and agency versus cultural determination, as well as beyond the logic of neoliberal, postfeminist individualism as an all-pervasive internalised ideology that has 'colonised' across divides of class, gender, sexuality, and race in the West (Skeggs 2014). Relationality and intimacy are areas that are sometimes overlooked in analyses of discourses

---

Research Council and partners Jean Hailes for Women's Health, Monash Health, Women's Health Victoria, Family Planning Victoria, and the Australian Federation of Medical Women. The four components are in-depth interviews with women; semi-structured interviews with medical practitioners and beauty therapists; a national online survey; and analysis of social media.

[2] We do not have space to map this context here and point the reader to the work of Gill and Scharff 2011; Scharff 2012; Evans and Riley 2015; and Dobson 2015 for fuller discussions of postfeminism and neoliberalism in feminist cultural studies.

about cosmetic surgery and FGCS in the postfeminist neoliberal context. We argue these aspects of discourse should be further considered as potential sites of rupture or contradiction of neoliberal individualism in relation to cosmetic surgery practices; but also so as not to miss the ways in which power may operate via deeply intimate encounters and relations as well as via more 'public' cultural discourses of individualised aesthetic competition and the body beautiful.

The 'Private' Body and Aesthetic Modification

Sociological and cultural studies literature helps to place the rise of cosmetic surgical practices and industries within a historical, social, and cultural context. It does so by broadly locating cosmetic surgery and other kinds of body modification practices within post-Enlightenment projects of individualisation, self-transformation, and self-improvement for the betterment of both the individual and, in turn, society (Featherstone 2010; Gilman 1999; Tanner et al. 2014). Extending notions of Enlightenment self-making into contemporary culture, cosmetic surgery culture has been theorised as part of self-reinvention projects necessitated in globalised 'new economies' (Elliott 2008) and part of a broader 'makeover culture' (Jones 2008) that authorises and encourages 'new good vanities of the self' (Tanner et al. 2014). Contemporary cosmetic surgery is conventionally understood to make body parts visibly different: bellies are made noticeably smaller, buttocks are 'lifted' or tightened to appear more prominent, and breasts are increased or reduced. But even external parts of the female genitals, such as the mons pubis and the labia, are not visible in everyday public contexts where bodies are conventionally clothed. For this reason, the 'aesthetic' and 'cosmetic' categorisation of FGCS is perhaps more complex than it is for surgeries performed on more visible and protrusive parts of the body, covered or uncovered.

It is unclear whether FGCS fits into the existing theoretical frameworks of contemporary cosmetic surgery as 'body work' and surgical 'self-reinvention' (Elliott 2008; Featherstone 2010). Some cosmetic surgeons have claimed that there is 'no difference between nose jobs and surgery on the vagina' (quoted in Braun 2009, p. 237). Some of our interviewees agree with this sentiment. Other interviewees feel differently. They differentiate labiaplasty and other FGCS procedures from more common cosmetic surgical procedures performed on women because genitals are not conventionally publicly visible but are usually seen only by the self and intimate others. Both positive and negative distinctions between FGCS and surgical modification of more visible parts of the female body are made by our interviewees. One interviewee who was satisfied with the results of her labiaplasty told us that, in relation to other kinds of cosmetic surgery, labiaplasty is:

> very different, because it's a very personal, very private area that is only going to be seen by a sexual partner, most likely. You know, if you're having a nose job, it's a thing that everybody sees, or if you're having breast implants, you know, that's enhancing your look from the outside to anyone that can see it. I think labiaplasty is a little bit different in that sense. (Alicia B, 21 years of age)

Another young woman, Rachel, echoed this view, and then positioned herself as against the practice of labiaplasty, stating:

> I think if you're changing something, if you're changing yourself just for you and your intimate partner, I think that should be something that you and your intimate partner should be able to overlook or deal with without having to get surgery about it. I know it's like, with boob jobs or whatever, everybody's going to judge, whatever, but I think you and your intimate partner—well, you should be sleeping with partners that accept you the way you are, maybe. (Rachel, 21 years of age)

Rachel, along with many of the women we have interviewed, frequently removes all of her pubic hair, known as 'Brazilian' waxing and states that she does this for her partner. Most of the women who responded to our call for participants who modify their genitals do so by full waxing or shaving, and most also position themselves as subjects who have not and would not consider surgical modification of their genitals. Most women seem reluctant to vilify other women who undergo FGCS, but would not go 'that far' themselves, positioning FGCS as unnecessary for them, and/or as a problem of the psyche or self-esteem, that requires not a surgical fix but self-help or therapy of some kind. In short, it would seem Brazilians are part of accepted and routine feminine 'body work' while surgery on the genitals is not.

These quotations allow us to see some of the tensions and distinctions made in understanding cosmetic surgery, and FGCS in particular, between 'productive' and vain or 'wasteful' body work. There are differences, perhaps, in the perceived necessity and value of work on the public and private body. Cosmetic surgery on genitals can be positioned as both morally 'better' and 'worse' than other kinds of popular cosmetic surgery because of the assumed centrality of intimate others to this practice. Surgery on parts of the body only seen by the self and intimate others can be positioned as more intrinsically motivated, authentic, and morally legitimate in a neoliberal context where notions of individual agency are strongly valued. However, within this same ideological framework of value, the judgements of intimate others and self-judgements are seen as 'easier' and more important to overcome psychologically, without resort to surgery, than are general social expectations and judgements. The way in which social expectations and intimate encounters are complexly intertwined sometimes becomes obscured here.

'Body' and 'Self' Work: Conflicting Discourses?

Feminist literature on the subject of cosmetic surgery and FGCS to date has complicated notions of 'agency' and 'free choice' in the postfeminist cultural context of intense visual and cultural objectification of women's bodies (Braun 2009; Fraser 2003; Jones 2008; Wolf 1991). Feminists, following Foucault, have also identified the processes by which sociocultural norms around beauty, body work, and aesthetic labour are reconfigured as 'empowering' projects of self-care and 'pampering' of the self, so that gendered forms of power are internalised and work *through* the self, rather than via external authorities (Bartky 1988; Gill 2007; McRobbie 2009; Gill and Scharff 2011). Cosmetic surgery is frequently explained in feminist accounts as stemming from strong cultural imperatives towards 'the display of the never-ending renovation of the self' (Jones 2008, p. 12). Bordo concludes that, while women can 'choose' not to have cosmetic surgery—and many, she notes, will never be able to afford it—those who do not 'are at an increasingly significant professional and personal disadvantage' (Bordo 2009, p. 25). In relation to FGCS, Braun argues: 'Work on both the interior and exterior of the self has become not only possible but obligatory for the idealised Western subject' (2009, p. 239). We agree with these feminist scholars who point to the complexity of power in this cultural context and identify potent cultural imperatives towards both physical 'body work' projects and more holistic 'self-work'. What is perhaps less well accounted for in feminist work to date are the contradictory cultural discourses prominent in public and media commentary about cosmetic surgery as 'vain', unnecessary, narcissistic, and even immoral, and the way women negotiate this *contradictory* discursive landscape (Tanner et al. 2014).

Eva Illouz's work helps identify what we suggest is another centrally important cultural discourse, related to but in tension with the 'body work imperative', that perhaps helps us better understand the stated positions of women who disavow desires for cosmetic surgery, and especially desires to appeal to male partners' ideals, as desires that 'should' be overcome, implying a moral hierarchy. Illouz (2007) maps the rise of 'therapy culture', whereby psychology as a discipline and psychologised understandings of the self as internally located have become so prevalent as to seem natural. An ethic of difficult and ongoing psychological work on the self is central to the discursive and ideological terrain of neoliberalism in a way that contradicts imperatives towards surgical 'body work' and positions cosmetic surgery as faster, easier, and less 'real' than psychological self-work and lifestyle change. Within dominant discourses of, and imperatives towards, psychological interior complexity and 'hard' *internal work* on the self, surgical body modification, perhaps especially on the private body, can normatively be framed as vain and superficial, even indicative of a pathologised lack of 'self-esteem', a quality that is central to postfeminist feminine subjectivity (Dobson 2015). Understanding the subtle distinctions and tensions around prominent cultural discourses and imperatives towards different forms of 'body' and 'self' work, and the high cultural value currently placed on self-esteem and self-acceptance for girls and women, helps to make sense of the fact that various cosmetic surgery practices are *not consistently accepted in Anglophone culture*. Rather, they are frequently critiqued by women who routinely engage in other painful and laborious kinds of body work. The rhetoric of some feminist accounts makes it sound as if cosmetic surgery culture and normative beauty culture are un-ambivalently accepted and endorsed in the West across divisions of gender, race, sexuality, and social class. We would suggest that cosmetic surgery practices are in tension with other strong cultural narratives addressed to women about the ethics of 'body' and 'self' work.

Market Logics and the 'Value' of Work on the Private Body

Several scholars have noted the connection between labour markets, careers, and visible self-transformation (Bordo 2009; Elliott 2008; Fraser 2003; Jones 2008). More visible kinds of cosmetic surgery are often tied in media stories and among women themselves to career enhancement. Investment in the beautification of the body is seen to lead to potentially more economic value creation for the individual through career and social competitive advantage tied to youth and attractiveness. Elliott argues that the rise of cosmetic surgery culture is linked broadly to the economic uncertainties brought by globalisation and neoliberalism. He suggests that 'people's sense of identity, life and work' are profoundly affected by 'new' standards of risk and uncertainty brought by routine downsizing and lay-offs (Elliott 2008, p. 9). He argues that people turn to cosmetic 'self-reinvention' in such a climate as a kind of proactive response. This argument is insufficient in light of the fact that women, and increasingly *young women,* are by far the biggest consumers of cosmetic surgery (Bordo 2009; Davis 1995; Gilman 1999; Wolf 1991). As Walkerdine et al. (2001) argue, women have long had to face the task of self-reinvention throughout the life course as they transition in and out of marriage and motherhood. For many women, especially those marginalised along intersections of class and race, the job insecurity Elliott describes is not 'new': women have seldom had 'jobs for life', besides underpaid and undervalued ones, and have long faced the necessity of continual self-reinvention (Walkerdine et al. 2001, p. 9).

The rise of FGCS raises important questions about what is missing from accounts of cosmetic surgery as driven primarily by economic and social rationales. It is difficult to position FGCS as obviously tied to increased social value, and the competitive edge a beautiful and youthful appearance is theorised as providing. This lack of obvious economic and social imperative for FGCS potentially adds an extra layer of pathologisation around this practice in a neoliberal context. Via logics of capitalist value, the desire for FGCS can be disavowed as something women should 'just get over' rather than invest time or money in. At the same time, FGCS might also be understood through prominent cultural logics and by women themselves as more about 'intimacy' and less about material 'value' because it involves labour on the private rather than publicly visible body. The lack of any obvious social or material reward for engaging in FGCS opens it to complex discourses of 'authentic' desire. Our female participants' comments suggest that both of these contradictory frameworks exist, in some tension with each other. Rachel expresses this kind of ambivalence when she compares surgical modification on the public and the private body: 'I guess if you're showing it to the whole world, you're changing your entire appearance, but if you're changing your appearance just for someone else, I don't know if that makes it more special or less special. I don't know'.

In the individualised, competitive world outlined by sociologists such as Elliott, there is more socio-cultural validity and legitimation for individual subjects who position their desires for and practices of cosmetic surgery in terms of giving the self a competitive edge in globalised, neoliberal labour markets. In a circular fashion, this is how Elliott theorises the rise of cosmetic surgery broadly: as part of projects of individualised and economically-driven self-reinvention. The frameworks of neoliberalism and individualism being critiqued here are perhaps reinforced. As Beverley Skeggs (2014, p. 2) writes:

> Many sociologists, among others, have proposed that our subjectivity changes to fit capital's logic; we become the living embodiment of capital. The naturalizing and normalizing of capitalism via market populism reduces ideas about what constitutes a person to the imperatives of the market and humanity is reduced to rational action and self-interested calculation through the figure of Mr Homo Economicus.

Skeggs suggests that her empirical studies of women's lives 'question the internalisation of the logic of capital because what really matters to us is other people' (Skeggs 2014, p. 14). Questions of relationality, of the desire to please or be desirable to intimate others, can be left out of both sociological *and* feminist analysis, albeit for different reasons. Qualitative feminist research on gender and cosmetic surgery demonstrates the pervasiveness of the 'doing it for myself rather than for others' discourse, and productively seeks to complicate the rationality and simplicity of such accounts (Braun 2009; Davis 1995; Fraser 2003; Jones 2008). In the socio-cultural conditions of postfeminism, where self-confidence, independence, and invulnerability are among the most highly valued traits for girls and women, the places of both intimate and social 'others' are particularly ambiguous, and frequently disavowed in popular culture addressed to women and girls (Dobson 2015; Harris and Dobson 2015). It is unsurprising that girls and women may seek to position themselves as fiercely autonomous and independent, and this has been convincingly argued in feminist scholarship. What remains less well explored is where and how social and intimate others *do make appearances* in the accounts women provide. Preliminary analysis of our interview data suggests that the place of the other is something here that is difficult for women to articulate, and cannot be clearly and unambiguously accounted for by women in relation to FGCS. But an imagined intimate other is clearly there.

Locating, and Making Space for, Relationality

Earlier we quoted Rachel, who suggests that she would try to talk women out of surgical genital modification, especially if it were for an intimate other, stating 'you should be sleeping with partners that accept you the way you are, maybe'. Rachel modifies her own genitals by regularly shaving all of her pubic hair. One of the reasons she gives for continuing this practice over several years is the preference of her sexual partner. She states: 'I've also got a boyfriend, and he prefers no hair, so I do that for him'. In her statement about pubic hair modification, along with several other similar statements, we can see how the self *is* understood as relational: the self is affected and affecting the other, doing things 'for' the other, but also for the self in a way that becomes difficult to untangle. Rachel's quotations, along with those of several other women we interviewed, allow us to see how borders are erected between aesthetic labour on the private body that is legitimately or acceptably practised for another, and aesthetic labour on the private body that is seen as illegitimate, or labour that must be practised 'only' for the self. Surgical genital modification becomes a constitutive limit in some of these interviews, marking a boundary between accounts of the self as inherently, acceptably and legitimately relational, and the self as a closed, rational, and necessarily autonomous subject of neoliberal capitalism.

When asked if there was anything she wanted to add at the end of the interview, Lynda, who had recently undergone FGCS, said:

> I just wanted to say … it's not for a sexual partner; it's not to please a man. I just want you to sort of know that. It's all about how I feel about myself. I feel purer and I feel cleaner. But as I said before, I felt uncomfortable about oral sex … No-one's ever commented; it was just about how I felt. So it just was nothing that anyone said to me or—I didn't do it to please a man. It was all for my benefit. (Lynda, 45 years of age)

This statement is strongly couched in the language of autonomous choice and 'self-benefit above all else', but it is steeped in relationality too. The feelings about the individual self and body as 'clean' and 'pure' are inextricably tied here to practices that involve others, and perhaps their imagined judgements. Lynda adamantly justifies her surgery as purely autonomous in the account she provides to the interviewer. It is possible that Lynda is positioning herself in relation to someone she identifies as 'feminist researcher'. But we suggest that this justification is also performed in response to broader postfeminist and neoliberal discourses of femininity, whereby relationships with others, care, and intimacy beyond the scope of material value are continually discredited and devalued (Skeggs 2014). It then becomes important for feminist scholars to remain conscious not to repeat such disavowals by seeing and explaining only the prevalence of 'autonomous choice' in women's accounts. To pay attention to the complex and sometimes unspoken place of intimate others here is important in unpacking what *cannot* be said in neoliberal conditions, as well as how power works intimately and relationally. Even when logics of pure self-benefit and autonomy are pervasive in women's own accounts we must remember to ask what is ambiguous and contradictory rather than clearly and 'rationally' accounted for in women's accounts of cosmetic surgery and FGCS.

We suggest the need to make more material-discursive space for the imagining of projects of self and body modification as relational projects (Tanner et al. 2014), so as to be able to see further beyond the logic of capital as well as to see where power enters deeply intimate spheres. Future analysis must go beyond pointing to the limitations of 'choice' and 'agency' as frameworks for understanding women's actions, to ask: Where does space currently exist for women to feel, claim, articulate, or experience their actions as not just for their own personal benefit, satisfaction, career advancement, or sense of self, but also for social and intimate others to whom the self is inherently connected? If there is not currently much space for identifications with and articulations of agentic actions outside the closed-off 'autonomous' individual, what is the psychic cost of constantly discounting the other in one's accounts of one's choices? What is omitted when labour on the self and body is framed by both scholars and women primarily in the language of 'autonomy'? We suggest it is important for feminists to question and explain not only *why* women largely claim independence and autonomy, but where and how women's actions *are* articulated as relational, sometimes ambivalently or ambiguously so.

Conclusion

In this chapter we have argued for the need to account for prevalent cultural discourses of 'self-acceptance' and 'self-esteem' that pathologise cosmetic surgery, and cosmetic surgery on the invisible private body in particular, as indicative of psychological rather than physical 'problems'. Foucauldian accounts of bodily discipline and self-governmentality as explanations of intense and extreme new forms of aesthetic labour cannot fully account for the *rejection* of surgical bodily modification practices by many women as something to be psychologically 'gotten over' rather than surgically pursued. Cultural discourses of self-esteem and self-acceptance that emerge from 'therapy culture' (Illouz 2007) perhaps act as powerful contradictory imperatives here. We have thus suggested the need for investigations into how women negotiate what is a contradictory cultural landscape; one where the body beautiful is lauded, and self-reinvention strongly encouraged, at the same time as a psychologised model of the self as internally located prevails, a self that is ideally 'complex' and 'esteemed' rather than superficial and vain.

Further, we have argued, FGCS as a growing cosmetic surgical practice raises vital questions about the guiding logics of self-interest, individualised choice, and material value that some scholarly accounts suggest have been internalised by women. We have suggested the need to be mindful of not flattening accounts of self and body work under a rhetoric of choice and clear 'autonomous' motivation, even when discourses of such appear prevalently in the words of women themselves. We have argued that it is important to pay attention to where relationality and others make appearances. This is not because we wish to validate FGCS surgery as a cultural practice, nor to suggest in any straightforward way that intimate relations with others constitute a solid justification for FGCS. To the contrary, it is a practice that we find problematic for a range of reasons documented in the available medical and feminist literature. Rather, we see it as vitally important to be able to contribute to a public conversation about this gendered cultural practice that moves beyond dominant binary logics of autonomy, choice, and rational self-benefit, or victimhood and cultural determination. In order to do this it is vital to approach FGCS via a more open and inclusive framework than is currently available, one that perhaps needs to start by acknowledging the place of both social and intimate others, and the deep relationality of the self in ways that currently seem difficult or less possible for women themselves and in feminist scholarship. To miss relationality in cosmetic surgery and FGCS practices is to miss potential challenges to the pervasive discourse of neoliberal individualism, as well as vital questions about the intimacy of power.

References

Banet-Weiser, S., & Portwood Stacer, L. (2006). 'I Just Want to Be Me Again!': Beauty Pageants, Reality Television and Post-Feminism. *Feminist Theory, 7*(2), 255–277.

Bartky, S. L. (1988). Foucault, Femininity, and the Modernization of Patriarchal Power. In I. Diamond & L. Quinby (Eds.), *Feminism & Foucault: Reflections on Resistance* (pp. 61–86). Boston: Northeastern University Press.

Blum, V. (2003). *Flesh Wounds: The Culture of Cosmetic Surgery*. Berkeley, CA: University of California Press.

Bordo, S. (2009). Twenty Years in the Twilight Zone. In C. Heyes & M. Jones (Eds.), *Cosmetic Surgery: A Feminist Primer* (pp. 21–33). Surrey, England: Ashgate.

Bramwell, R., Morland, C., & Garden, A. S. (2007). Expectations and Experience of Labial Reduction: A Qualitative Study. *BJOG: An International Journal of Obstetrics and Gynaecology, 114*(12), 1493–1499.

Braun, V. (2005). In Search of (Better) Sexual Pleasure: Female Genital 'Cosmetic' Surgery. *Sexualities, 8*(4), 407–424.

Braun, V. (2009). The Women Are Doing It for Themselves': The Rhetoric of Choice and Agency Around Female Genital 'Cosmetic Surgery. *Australian Feminist Studies, 24*(60), 233–249.

Braun, V. (2010). Female Genital Cosmetic Surgery: A Critical Review of Current Knowledge and Contemporary Debates. *Journal of Women's Health, 19*(7), 1393–1407.

Davis, K. (1995). *Reshaping the Female Body: The Dilemma of Cosmetic Surgery*. New York: Routledge.

Davis, S. W. (2002). Loose Lips Sink Ships. *Feminist Studies, 28*(1), 7–35.

Dobson, A. S. (2015). *Postfeminist Digital Cultures: Femininity, Social Media, and Self-Representation*. New York: Palgrave Macmillan.

Elliott, A. (2008). *Making the Cut: How Cosmetic Surgery Is Transforming Our Lives*. London: Reaktion Books.

Evans, A., & Riley, S. (2015). *Technologies of Sexiness: Sex, Identity, and Consumer Culture*. Oxford: Oxford University Press.

Featherstone, M. (2010). Body, Image and Affect in Consumer Culture. *Body & Society, 16*(1), 193–221.

Fraser, S. (2003). *Cosmetic Surgery, Gender and Culture*. New York: Palgrave Macmillan.

Gill, R. (2007). Critical Respect: The Difficulties and Dilemmas of Agency and 'Choice' for Feminism. A Reply to Duits and van Zoonen. *European Journal of Women's Studies, 14*(1), 69–80.

Gill, R., & Scharff, C. (Eds.). (2011). *New Femininities: Postfeminism, Neoliberalism, and Subjectivity*. New York: Palgrave Macmillan.

Gilman, S. (1999). *Making the Body Beautiful*. New Jersey: Princeton University Press.

Green, F. J. (2005). From Clitoridectomies to 'Designer Vaginas': The Medical Construction of Heteronormative Female Bodies and Sexuality Through Female Genital Cutting. *Sexualities, Evolution & Gender, 7*(2), 153–187.

Harris, A., & Dobson, A. S. (2015). Theorizing Agency in Post-Girlpower Times. *Continuum: Journal of Media and Cultural Studies, 29*(2), 145–156.

Illouz, E. (2007). *Cold Intimacies: The Making of Emotional Capitalism*. Oxford: Polity.

Jones, M. (2008). *Skintight: An Anatomy of Cosmetic Surgery*. Oxford, New York: Berg.

Liao, L. M., Michala, L., & Creighton, S. M. (2010). Labial Surgery for Well Women: A Review of the Literature. *BJOG: An International Journal of Obstetrics & Gynaecology, 117*(1), 20–25.

Liao, L. M., Taghinejadi, N., & Creighton, S. M. (2012). An Analysis of the Content and Clinical Implications of Online Advertisements for Female Genital Cosmetic Surgery. *BMJ Open*, 2(6), online.

Markey, C. N., & Markey, P. M. (2010). A Correlational and Experimental Examination of Reality Television Viewing and Interest in Cosmetic Surgery. *Body Image, 7*(2), 165–171.

McRobbie, A. (2009). *The Aftermath of Feminism: Gender, Culture and Social Change*. London: Sage.

Medicare Benefits Schedule. (2012). Item Numbers 35533 and 35569. www.medicareaustralia.gov.au

Michala, L., Liao, L. M., & Creighton, S. M. (2012). Female Genital Cosmetic Surgery: How Can Clinicians Act in Women's Best Interests? *The Obstetrician & Gynaecologist, 14*(3), 203–206.

Miklos, J. R., & Moore, R. D. (2008). Labiaplasty of the Labia Minora: Patients' Indications for Pursuing Surgery. *The Journal of Sexual Medicine, 5*(6), 1492–1495.

Northrop, J. M. (2012). *Reflecting on Cosmetic Surgery: Body Image, Shame and Narcissism*. New York: Routledge.

Scharff, C. (2012). *Repudiating Feminism: Young Women in a Neoliberal World.* Farnham: Ashgate.

Skeggs, B. (2014). Values Beyond Value? Is Anything Beyond the Logic of Capital? *The British Journal of Sociology, 65*(1), 1–20.

Sperry, S., Thompson, J. K., Sarwer, D. B., & Cash, T. F. (2009). Cosmetic Surgery Reality V Viewership: Relations with Cosmetic Surgery Attitudes, Body Image, and Disordered eating. *Annals of Plastic Surgery, 62*(1), 7–11.

Tanner, C., Maher, J. M., & Fraser, S. (2014). *Vanity: 21st Century Selves.* New York, NY: Palgrave Macmillan.

Taylor, S. J. (2012). Buying and Selling Breasts: Cosmetic Surgery, Beauty Treatments and Risk. *The Sociological Review, 60*(4), 635–653.

Walkerdine, V., Lucey, H., & Melody, J. (2001). *Growing up Girl: Psychosocial Explorations of Gender and Class.* New York: New York University Press.

Wolf, N. (1991). *The Beauty Myth: How Images of Beauty are Used Against Women.* London: Vintage.

21

Beautiful Israeli Girls: Between Being in the Present and Future Unpredictability

Dana Kaplan

Introduction

In this chapter I treat women's beauty as a form of aesthetic labour and ask how it is represented in popular culture. Specifically, and using popular culture's images and representations of Israeli girls and young women, this chapter identifies a tension between two temporal logics that characterise neoliberal outlooks. On the one hand, entrepreneurial and aspirational neoliberal subjects must be reflexive and always changing and in the process of subjectification or 'becoming'. On the other hand, they must also act responsibly and render a self-assured personhood and 'being'. This raises the following question: if projecting beauty, self-aestheticising and excitable self-presentation have become prerequisites for employability,

D. Kaplan (✉)
Department of Sociology, Political Science and Communication, The Open University of Israel, Raanana, Israel

A.S. Elias et al. (eds.), *Aesthetic Labour*,
DOI 10.1057/978-1-137-47765-1_21

as critical theorists of neoliberalism suggest (see below), how does beauty make visible a person's inner capacities for simultaneous 'being' and 'becoming'? I will address the tension between personhood (being) and subjectification (becoming) through a brief examination of a 2014 coffee table fashion/art/erotic book entitled *Israeli Girls* that has provoked an interest in Israeli media. As the Israeli-born photographer Dafy Hagai explained in several newspaper interviews, she hand-picked her subjects according to whether she 'felt connected to what they projected and to how they look'. Hagai also said: 'If someone sparked an interest in me and we had a good vibe between the two of us then I took her picture. The outcome is diverse' (Hagai, quoted in Shalev 2014, np). The photographer thus presents her work as a form of curation of individual singularities. As she describes it, it was through the supposedly authentic 'appeal', 'beauty', 'connection', 'vibe' or 'attention'—the aesthetic labour of being herself that each of the models performed in real life even before she was actually photographed—that the book receives its value as a 'diverse' work of art. Specifically, this chapter argues that as a representative of contemporary popular cultural artefacts, *Israeli Girls* utilises an imaginary space between being and becoming, between local and cosmopolitan Israeliness (a point I shall return to below), and, ultimately, between art and commodified life. In this, *Israeli Girls* represents the logic of current capitalism, whereby non-work activities are deemed empowering, liberating and non-exploitive and lifeworlds become exchangeable assets for employment.

The dealings of popular culture with beauty and appearance are fascinating for two main reasons. First, as will be explained below, physical attractiveness and presentable, aesthetic appearance have gained a considerable weight in current working life. While standards of beauty are historically and culturally constructed, beauty is both and at the same time inborn, achieved and can even be technologically modified. Perhaps more than any other visible corporeal features, beauty is not simply performed but is 'a double embodiment' (Kuipers 2015) inscribed as we tend to conceive appearance (beautiful or not) as a property of a particular self that bears it and, hence at times we conflate it with the bearer, and at other times we separate it from that person's being. This indeterminacy between the self's true essence and the face-surface is further complicated by the ability to transform faces technologically. Beauty and its surrounding cultural narratives are thus one site to probe the relationships between what one *is* by birth and breed, namely, one's personhood or 'being'—and what one aspires to be or, more precisely, one's ability to constantly change. Here I follow media scholar Zizi Papacharissi who addressed this 'becoming' capacity, by foregrounding what she terms 'accelerated reflexivity' as a contemporary temporality which invites us 'not only to constantly readjust, but also to expect to have to readjust' (Papacharissi et al. 2013, p. 603; also Scharff 2015).

Secondly, I probe entrepreneurialism, a main ideological tenet of neoliberalism through the ways it is being imagined, represented and transmitted in popular culture. Popular culture is one of the key vectors of neoliberal capitalism. It is not only a major business but also where identities, experiences and subjectivities are moulded. Popular artefacts therefore make of a good way to identify how neoliberalism works (Gilbert 2013; Gill and Scharff 2011). Unlike most critical popular culture analyses, I am less interested here in the 'pedagogical' effects of mediated neoliberal narratives, whether they are empowering or not. Rather, my aim is to look at individualised self-identities and human capital and how they are constructed as labour power (Feher 2009; Flisfeder 2015; Hearn 2008). My focus on contemporary Israeli culture is fitting since it exemplifies aesthetic labour in a hyper-neoliberal yet non-American/European context. Significantly, and as I explain below, while *Israeli Girls* depicts the cosmopolitan, 'model' neoliberal subject—the white middle class, 'can do', 'alpha girls' (Duffy 2015b; Hey 2009)—it is nevertheless embedded within a local matrix of gender/class/ethnicity relations, with its own distinctive trajectory.

The chapter is organised as follows: I first discuss briefly the theoretical perspectives that inform my research. Specifically, scholarship on immaterial as well as literature on gendered aesthetic labour shed light on the role of beauty in neoliberal capitalism, whereby workers must constantly produce themselves as belonging to the class of the potential 'employables' and 'winners' (Dean 2008). I then proceed to analyse the *Israeli Girls* project as a form of aesthetic labour that amalgamates 'becoming' and 'being' within Israeli neoliberalism.

Beauty as Aspirational Labour Power

Women's aesthetic labour, self- or other-directed, is commonly perceived long-term processes of socialising others by instilling *durable* aesthetic dispositions and embodied cultural capital. As such, it is deemed reproductive, affective and communicative rather than productive, economic and instrumental (Rioux 2015). However, recent theorisations have challenged the notion that 'gender capital' necessarily affixes women to the reproduction sphere. Rather, some emotional, communicative and aesthetic skills, traditionally associated with the social roles of women in the reproductive sphere, have become desirable in the productive sphere as well (Adkins 2005). This chapter addresses women's self-aestheticisation and perceives it as signalling an entrepreneurial self-identity. Especially, I refer to those aesthetic skills such as self-styling and branding that, furthermore, manifest an aspirational entrepreneurial subjectivity geared towards an unpredictable future.

My point of departure is that while the bodies, demeanour and appearance of young women and girls have always been a 'social problem', they are increasingly considered the model aspirational, self-branding middle-class subjects of neoliberal capitalism (Banet-Weiser 2012, p. 56; Gonick 2006; Hey 2009; Landén 2012). Sociological works on the neoliberal subjectification of young women focus on consumption practices and on gender ideologies proffered by the beauty, fashion, glamour and media industries. Another major strand of research focuses on the aesthetic labour now demanded in the production sphere, particularly in the cultural and interactive service sectors (Entwistle and Wissinger 2006; Haynes 2012; Mears 2014; Pettinger 2008; Warhurst and Nickson 2007). In explicating beauty and appearance as a labour power commodity, this chapter is informed by a growing body of work on gendered social media entrepreneurship ('instafamous' beauty/fashion vloggers, etc.) that is premised on 'contemporary logics of individual self-branding, consumer empowerment, and worker autonomy' (Duffy 2015b, p. 711). Similarly, I see neoliberal subjects not just as consumers, but, primarily as the producers of their self-brands (Feher 2009). In the neoliberal attention economy beauty is a central branding resource that has exchange value in employment *at large* and not just in those sectors that *directly commodify* workers' good looks and presentability.

In order to theorise beauty as an essentially neoliberal labour power I use insights from both *social reproduction theorists* (SRTs) such as Bakker (2003) or Ferguson (2008) and *immaterial labour* theorists. SRTs have noted how social identities, such as gender or sexuality that are forged outside the sphere of production, become productive labour power through the social marking of bodies. According to this perspective, *collective* identities are inscribed onto *specific* bodies. The body thus becomes valuable (or not) 'according to whether it expresses its capacity to generate a surplus in production or the reality of its differentiated valuation' in culture and society at large (Rioux 2015, p. 200). The economic value of labour power is already historically determined as collective social identities but experienced as a *subjective*, personal and embodied set of differences. SRTs aim to explain the continuous material and social marginality of women and their bodies. Yet, and more relevant to my argument, in proposing that the marginality of collective identities is always inscribed on particular bodies SRTs also acknowledges that singularities of 'embodied subjectivities' (Sekimoto 2012) are part of capitalist production.

Other theorists have recently noted that non-marginal, individualised bodies and subjectivities are being exploited, too. This, however, takes the shape of voluntary practices of self-inscription and self-branding. According to Teresa L. Ebert, a prevalent contemporary belief is that 'the only way out of capitalism is the way back into it, namely, setting up your own 'free' enterprise' (Ebert 2009, p. 5). Ebert further argues that 'delectable materialism'—everyday experiences that generate inner feelings of choice, pleasure, entrepreneurialism, critique, transgression and freedom—becomes part of capitalist production (Ebert 2009, pp. 46–47). Individualised non-work practices of 'delectable materialism' such as shopping, sports, going to therapy or having sex, all contribute to performing a singular, 'embodied subjectivity' (Sekimoto 2012).

The immaterial labour scholarship provides structural explanations for this shift, whereby middle class embodied subjectivities are put to work. It is argued that in the last 25 years sociality 'has become interiorised into the logic of economy to a historically unprecedented extent' (Konings 2015, p. 13), making affects, communicative and aesthetic skills a dominant part of working life (Adkins 2005; Lazzarato 2004; Morini and Fumagalli 2010; Virtanen 2004). In this view, we are witness to a simultaneous increase in the exploitation of labour power *and* the social power of labour. Under these circumstances, capitalism tends to take 'back into value relations what had been 'outside of capitalism' (Kennedy 2010, p. 829). Employment 'hinges on a more intensive utilisation of labour power' including 'workers' tacit knowledge and skills… as well as mobilising new sources of emotional and aesthetic labour' (Thompson 2010, p. 10). Indeed, 'compared to 'old work', where personality was a handicap, which the division of work and organisations tries to demolish, today's work is rather a subjective attitude, the workers' skills are indistinguishable from his or her personality and habits, aptitudes and experiences' (Virtanen 2004, p. 225). It is also not separated from how they look. Thus, workers' singularity—their self-identities, embodied cultural capital and appearances have all become prerequisites for being hired *and* for doing your job. Workers must use their (supposedly) non-work time and activities to cultivating, designing and performing an embodied subjectivity that is entirely adapted to the employment imperative, and, furthermore, must 'always be on' (Entwistle and Wissinger 2006, p. 788). This requires workers to not only *have* experiences and develop distinct self-identities around them but also to employ new sets of skills for styling and externalising these singular, embodied subjectivities.

However, because the immaterial scholarship sustains a theoretical, macro perspective, it eludes the intricate ways middle-class subjects turn their embodied subjectivities and singularities into labour power. The following analysis of beauty in popular culture aims to illuminate the ways embodied subjectivities are simultaneously selved *and* branded, being at once the whole person and its potential labour power. This matrix shall be addressed by focusing on the temporal dimensions or logics within which these beautiful *Israeli Girls* are situated. Temporality is 'the experience of being in time' and it is inseparable from subjectivity and embodiment (Sekimoto 2012, p. 237). The following analysis shows that beauty simultaneously retains two temporal logics: that of an accomplished and responsible 'being' *and* of an experiencing and aspirational 'becoming' that reflexively adapts to the unpredictable futures of neoliberalism.

Hagai's *Israeli Girls*

In a *TimeOut Israel* interview (Gonshorovitch 2014) with Hagai the year 2014 was deemed as 'the year of the girl', where a new feminist 'genre' enables women artists to tackle the 'ambivalent space between girlhood and adulthood, via references to body image, personal expression, success and beauty'. As *a Dazed* interviewer commented, 'essentially, Hagai, who is often surprised to hear that people expect these girls to be covered up and conservative, is championing a generation of females exploring their sexuality, body ownership and the beauty of girl power amongst an uncertain political and social climate' (Kane 2014). Apparently and as Berick-Aharony (2013) argues in her study on national and international representations of Israeli femininity within American and Israeli magazines, hyper-sexual, porno-chic media images of Israeli women are geopolitical texts, symbolising Western belonging, and hence also contributing to the Othering of veiled Muslim women. Indeed, the models Hagai chose to represent Israeliness (as suggested by the book's title), the way she photographed them and the overall atmosphere of the photos, are anything but stereotypically middle-eastern.

As talk-backers repeatedly commented on-line, Hagai's girls were all Jewish, secular and white (*Ashkenazi*). While most Israelis are more brown-skinned than white, the whiter *Ashkenazim*—Israelis who are descendants of immigrants from European countries, generally belong to the upper class and hence embody what is normatively considered beautiful (Mizrachi 2013, pp. 61–63). Similarly, although Hagai argued that she wanted to set her locations in 'villages and places that are remote from Tel Aviv', as if to indicate that her book captures the cultural diversity of Israel, in reality most pictures were taken in upscale suburbs around Tel Aviv, where Hagai herself grew up. As Berick-Aharony (2013), p. 12–13) found in her study, 'by adhering to the western model of femininity, and at the same time defying fundamental (Muslim and Jewish) models of femininity, mainstream Israeli identity is redefined as western, modern and free'. In this respect, the 'Western' look and the hyper-sexualised feel of the images (which I discuss below) cannot be separated from the local setting that renders it meaningful. While neoliberalism is a global political rationality, and although it has permeated Israeli society at large, it is the secular middle class that claims ownership over it.

Another way in which *Israeli Girls* is linked to the global culture is through artistic practices and affiliations of Hagai herself, who identifies with a group of international artists interested in the 'female gaze' (Tamir 2014). This artistic movement is premised on a postfeminist sensibility 'which celebrates individual choice, independence and modes of self-expression rooted in the consumer marketplace' (Duffy 2015a, p. 3; see also Gill 2007; Smaill 2013). It 'embraces femininity and sexuality' (Murray 2015, p. 495) and packages it into popular media commodities for similarly self-confident, (post)feminist and creative women. In other words, it is created by and for young, white and privileged women producers of self via consumption (Murray 2015). The main subject-matter of works such as Hagai's (or other artistic female iconic photographers she names as her sources of inspiration, including Petra Collins, Valerie Phillips or Gia Coppola) is young women and girls and their lifeworlds. Moreover, these works share what some have described as the *selfie* or *Instagram* aesthetics and thematic. Murray (2015, p. 495) associates this with 'young girls in the blogosphere' who construct 'an image of themselves as a sexual fantasy, to be consumed online, and in the public domain'. Arguably, the trickling up of amateur selfie photography to an art form is part of a broader technological and organisational transformation within the artistic field that dismantled some of the traditional barriers women artists used to face. As Hagai explains, social media platforms have opened up more opportunities for creative women by enabling women-to-women networking. Another significant feature of the selfie amateur-looking 'female gaze' photography is how it blurs 'the lines between documentary, fine art, and fashion' (Murray 2015, p. 504). A good example in this respect is the *American Apparel* phenomenon, an American young fashion retailer best known for its 'anti-marketing', countercultural and hipster branding techniques that foreground 'raw sexuality, anti-establishment and progressive' sentiments (Manlow 2011, p. 89; see also Moor and Littler 2008; Murray 2015).

Hagai's 'female gaze' is directed towards very young women in their early twenties, wearing cool 1980s-looking apparel and located in semi-suburban settings, that 'could have actually been photographed in a Michigan suburb' (Tamir 2014). This is in direct reference to Sofia Coppola's movie *The Virgin Suicides*, located in a Detroit suburb. As Hagai explains: 'I was looking for girls who reminded me of what I used to look like when I was growing up. I shot all over the suburban parts of Tel Aviv and the centre of Israel, looking for places that didn't have a distinct cultural outlook and reminded me more of those American teen films that I had seen growing up' (Kane 2014). While the girls and locations are Israeli indeed, as explained above, there is nothing distinctively local about their looks or the contents of the photos more broadly. Thus while a *Dazed* reader commented: 'Very cool. Though, would love to see a mix of Palestinian and Israeli women in a project' and another sarcastically wrote 'wow, more photos of hot girls not smiling and doing "cool" things like smoking—what a game changer because they've been chosen from a specific region of the earth. Give me a break', it could also be argued that the potential value of these works lies in showing that Israel, too, is home to the 'universal' tall, fresh-looking white middle-class girl.

Beauty as Immanence: Being and Becoming

The photographs depict beauty as a nonchalant, *immanent presence* of individualised, singular and entrepreneurial selves, thus mixing 'being' and 'becoming'. This is manifest in the styling of the photos that denotes a nonchalant fashionability, and through their Instagram, 'selfie' and 'American Apparel' aesthetic quality. While the images are not strictly pornographic, they are erotically suggestive and show skin and see-through clothing. The photographed women look almost like models yet in a rather natural way. Most of the photos are shot from a middle range angle, showing bodies and surroundings and not just faces. The camera lingers on the beauty of the young women, who are portrayed as doing almost nothing: just sitting, gazing or smoking. The more active girls would be reading a book or just standing in a tennis court or lying on a gymnasium floor. But it would be inaccurate to see these photos as representations of the everyday lives of girls. Not only are these girls not shown as working, at least not in the traditional sense of the word, they are also not shown as involved in any sports, leisure or consumption activities. The girls are not misplaced, yet they are also neither shown in their rooms (as many selfies are), nor communicating or socialising with friends. Unlike the well-known 1990s 'JenniCam', Hagai's *Israeli Girls* do not form a 'catalog of a young woman's life' (Banet-Weiser 2012, p. 51). Rather than *doing*, the girls, partly isolated from their social environments, are being photographed as present, as 'themselves'. They just *are*, in a zone of *being*. Hagai's photos thus treat beauty as a *surface* of *immanent presence*, and one that denotes nothing but the aura of a self-appreciating being. 'She' is deemed successful—self-assured, fashionably-dressed and good-looking—because she 'is'.

In this regard, Belinda Smaill (2013) disagrees with feminist critiques of many 'dreamy looking' popular culture artefacts that link girls with disempowerment, ennui and isolation. Instead, she argues that Sofia Coppola's women, a paradigmatic example for this kind of aesthetic, 'offer an image that is both entrenched in and critiques the sensibility of post-feminism', in being on the one hand purposeful and aspirational but at the same time inflicted with 'moral and existential uncertainty that manifests as boredom' (Smaill 2013, p. 158). While I agree that Hagai's neoliberal girls are not exactly disempowered, I also do not subscribe to Smaill's view that they are bored, or that their boredom is a critique of neoliberalism. If at all, such embodied gestures add a touch of singularity and personality, which, in the neoliberal condition, ultimately enhances one's employability potential. In this respect, Hagai's photos do not just show very young women as being themselves. They also present the 'becoming' capacity of these rather generic women, their talent for 'accelerated reflexivity' (Papacharissi et al. 2013). Hagai's 'female gaze' places these twenty-something accidental models in 'girl' settings such as a schoolyard, after-school tennis class, swimming pool, playground or what looks like their parent's villas. The photographed women thus re-enact in front of the camera their previous, albeit not-too-long-ago, girly selfhood. The photos thus simultaneously exhibit the strong *being* of young women through the actual grown up models *and* the undetermined *becoming* through locations and settings that cast the seen images as girls, still.

To be sure, neoliberal aesthetic labour is very much about presenting a coherent self-identity. The aesthetics of aspiration is thus grounded in *presenting* and in being in the present. I argue that the 'being' mode of Hagai's works does render the girls agentic and self-assured in their individualised singularity. This is expressed in their slightly bored and effortless sexed-up looks. At the same time, however, the beauty of the girls also foregrounds *becoming*, a process, or continuous transformation. This is expressed in the arrangement of the photos as depicting girls' bodies that are not-yet women. What we supposedly see (and feel—see Coleman 2011) is an unfinished body. At this point it should be noted that while the being/becoming terminology is much indebted to Deleuzian thought, I am less inclined to perceive 'becoming' in terms of 'multiplicity and difference' that are the outside of capitalism and unlike the fixedness of 'being' (Coleman 2011, p. 152). Rather, it is my contention that beauty and the gendered aesthetic labour around it do not either stabilise capitalism (being in the present) or subvert it (becoming for future unpredictability). Obviously, and as ample feminist theory has argued, the empowered, ambitious woman, endowed with high self-esteem, determination, strong sense of self and the body to show for it, does not disrupt capitalism. But modes of *becoming*—of fractured self-identities, of transformation under uncertain socio-economic conditions—are also productive to capitalism. The *aesthetic labour of both being* and *becoming* is productive because it signals subjects' never-ending ability to produce an inner sense of singularity. This capacity to be always changing and becoming singular in new ways is, I would argue, the neoliberal labour power.

Beauty as Human Capital

This chapter sought to characterise the aesthetic labour in and around beauty as it transpires in popular culture. Ashley Mears delineates the contours of the sociological discussion on beauty 'and its privileges: is beauty achieved or ascribed? Can beauty be earned meritocratically, or is it unequally available to persons with other forms of privilege, thus perpetuating durable inequalities...?' (Mears 2014, p. 1331). Notably, at first sight beauty in Israeli Girls is presented as ascribed, a quality that is 'there' and needs neither cultivation nor realisation. By a closer look, choosing girls as its bearers gives this beauty a 'becoming' quality of future unpredictability. In both cases *Israeli Girls* does not show beauty as directly exploited by capital: the women are neither working nor consuming. Nevertheless, Hagai's work can help us think of ascribed and achieved aesthetic qualities as human capital (Feher 2009). The human capital approach suggests that in neoliberalism the *whole* self, and not just her physical strength or intellectual skills becomes labour power. Neoliberalism redefines production and reproduction, and as Lazzarato (2004, p. 192) puts it, 'invention, as the creation of the possible and its process of actualisation in the souls (of consumers as well as workers) is the real production, whilst what Marx and the economists call production is, in reality, reproduction (or a manufacture of a product or a management of a service…)'. Thus, the ideal aspirational, forward-thinking neoliberal subject constantly produces herself and works to enlarge her human capital (Dean 2008; Feher 2009; Hearn 2008).

For Dean neoliberal ideology foregrounds what she calls after Lacan 'imaginary identities'. Not only are these identities not collective, but even as self-identities they are extremely vulnerable and unstable since 'the frames of reference that give it meaning and value are forever shifting; the others who might challenge it… can appear at any moment. Their successes, their achievements, their capacities to enjoy can all too easily call mine into question (Dean 2008, p. 61). In this respect, neoliberalism

> offers its subjects imaginary injunctions to develop our creative potential and cultivate our individuality, injunctions supported by capitalism's provision of the ever new experiences and accessories we use to perform this self-fashioning—I must be fit; I must be stylish; I must realise my dreams. I must because I can—everyone wins. If I don't, not only am I a loser, but I am not a person at all'. (Dean 2008, pp. 61–62)

Entrepreneurial subjects must constantly turn future unpredictability into a more or less stable form of being, even if only momentarily. From this perspective, aesthetic labour emerges as the work we put, through everything that we do, not only in finding 'who we really are' (being) but in continuously updating our status (becoming).

As noted above, the girls are doing nothing but being themselves, at the same time that they become. White, blonde, sexy and perfect in a fairly generic kind of way, they are neither happy nor sad, not active but also not passive. They do not show strong emotions and are not too aesthetically made up. Thus, while the explicit theme of the photos is post-feminist entrepreneurial tenets—such as girl power, self-improvement, self-determination and empowered sexuality—implicitly they depict human capital as labour power. I would therefore propose that neoliberal aesthetic labour balances between being in the present and accelerated reflexivity. Arguably, it is this new structural ability to project both the being and becoming potentiality that recuperates the prospects of a precarious middle class. At least for now.

References

Adkins, L. (2005). Social Capital: The Anatomy of a Troubled Concept. *Feminist Theory, 6*(2), 195–211.

Bakker, I. (2003). Neoliberal Governance and the Reprivatization of Social Reproduction: Social Provisioning and Shifting Gender Orders. *Power, Production and Social Reproduction,* (pp. 66–82).

Banet-Weiser, S. (2012). *Authentic™: The Politics of Ambivalence in a Brand Culture*. New York and London: NYU Press.

Berick-Aharony, O. (2013). The Bare Truth: Porno-Chic Models of Femininity as a National Narrative. *European Journal of Women's Studies, 20*(4), 390–407.

Coleman, R. (2011). Be(come) Yourself Only Better: Self-Transformation and the Materialisation of Images. In L. Guillaume & J. Hughes (Eds.), *Deleuze and the Body* (pp. 144–164). Edinburgh: Edinburgh University Press.

Dean, J. (2008). Enjoying Neoliberalism. *Cultural Politics, 4*(1), 47–72.

Duffy, B. E. (2015a). The Romance of Work: Gender and Aspirational Labour in the Digital Culture Industries. *International Journal of Cultural Studies,* online first, 1–17.

Duffy, B. E. (2015b). Gendering the Labor of Social Media Production. *Feminist Media Studies, 15*(4), 710–714.

Ebert, T. L. (2009). *The Task of Cultural Critique*. Urbana and Chicago: University of Illinois Press.

Entwistle, J., & Wissinger, E. (2006). Keeping up Appearances: Aesthetic Labour in the Fashion Modelling Industries of London and New York. *The Sociological Review, 54*(4), 774–794.

Feher, M. (2009). Self-Appreciation; or, the Aspirations of Human Capital. *Public Culture, 21*(1), 21–41.

Ferguson, S. (2008). Canadian Contributions to Social Reproduction Feminism, Race and Embodied Labor. *Race, Gender & Class, 15*(1/2), 42–57.

Flisfeder, M. (2015). The Entrepreneurial Subject and the Objectivization of the Self in Social Media. *South Atlantic Quarterly, 114*(3), 553–570.

Gilbert, J. (2013). What Kind of Thing Is 'Neoliberalism'? *New Formations, 80*(81), 7–22.

Gill, R. (2007). Postfeminist Media Culture Elements of a Sensibility. *European Journal of Cultural Studies, 10*(2), 147–166.

Gill, R., & Scharff, C. (Eds.). (2011). *New Femininities: Postfeminism, Neoliberalism, and Subjectivity*. Basingstoke: Palgrave Macmillan.

Gonick, M. (2006). Between Girl Power and Reviving Ophelia: Constituting the Neoliberal Girl Subject. *NWSA Journal, 18*(2), 1–23.

Gonshorovitch, B. (2014). Hello Youth, High There Camera: Tel Aviv Femininity in Photos. TimeOut Israel. [Online] Retrieved from http://bit.ly/1D3qumR

Hagai, D. (2014). Israeli Girls with a Western Feel. [Online] Retrieved from http://thisispaper.com/dafy-hagai-israeli-girls/

Haynes, K. (2012). Body Beautiful? Gender, Identity and the Body in Professional Services Firms. *Gender, Work & Organization, 19*(5), 489–507.

Hearn, A. (2008). Meat, Mask, Burden: Probing the Contours of the Branded Self. *Journal of Consumer Culture, 8*(2), 197–217.

Hey, V. (2009). The Girl in the Mirror: The Psychic Economy of Class in the Discourse of Girlhood Studies. *Girlhood Studies, 2*(2), 10–32.

Kane, A. (2014). Israeli Girls: A New Coming-of-Age Photography Book Is Shattering the Perception of Israeli Girls with Its Gang of 'Cool' Teens. *Dazed*. [Online] Retrieved from http://www.dazeddigital.com/photography/article/22024/1/israeli-girls

Kennedy, P. (2010). The Knowledge Economy and Labour Power in Late Capitalism. *Critical Sociology, 36*(6), 821–837.

Konings, M. (2015). *The Emotional Logic of Capitalism: What Progressives Have Missed*. Stanford: Stanford University Press.

Kuipers, G. (2015). Beauty and Distinction? The Evaluation of Appearance and Cultural Capital in five European Countries. *Poetics, 53*, 38–51.

Landén, A. S. (2012). A Fantasy of the Ambitious Young Girl as Flexible Knowledge-Worker Subject. *NORA, 20*(4), 249–265.

Lazzarato, M. (2004). From Capital-Labour to Capital-Life. *Ephemera, 4*(3), 187–208.

Manlow, V. (2011). Creating an American Mythology: A Comparison of Branding Strategies in Three Fashion Firms. *Fashion Practice, 3*(1), 85–109.

Mears, A. (2014). Aesthetic Labor for the Sociologies of Work, Gender, and Beauty. *Sociology Compass, 8*(12), 1330–1343.

Mizrachi, B. (2013). *Paths to Middle-Class Mobility Among Second-Generation Moroccan Immigrant Women in Israel.* Detroit: Wayne State University Press.

Moor, L., & Littler, J. (2008). Fourth Worlds and Neo-Fordism: American Apparel and the Cultural Economy of Consumer Anxiety. *Cultural Studies, 22*(5), 700–723.

Morini, C., & Fumagalli, A. (2010). Life Put to Work: Towards a Life Theory of Value. *Ephemera, 10*(3), 234–252.

Murray, D. C. (2015). Notes to Self: The Visual Culture of Selfies in the Age of Social Media. *Consumption Markets & Culture, 18*(6), 490–516.

Papacharissi, Z., Streeter, T., & Gillespie, T. (2013). Culture Digitally: Habitus of the New. *Journal of Broadcasting & Electronic Media, 57*(4), 596–607.

Pettinger, L. (2008). Developing Aesthetic Labour: The Importance of Consumption. *International Journal of Work Organisation and Emotion, 2*(4), 327–343.

Rioux, S. (2015). Embodied Contradictions: Capitalism, Social Reproduction and Body Formation. *Women's Studies International Forum*, 48.

Scharff, C. (2015). The Psychic Life of Neoliberalism: Mapping the Contours of Entrepreneurial Subjectivity. *Theory, Culture & Society*, online first, 1–16.

Sekimoto, S. (2012). A Multimodal Approach to Identity: Theorizing the Self Through Embodiment, Spatiality, and Temporality. *Journal of International and Intercultural Communication, 5*(3), 226–243.

Shalev, S. (2014). How Would You Describe Yourself as Israeli? *Haaretz.* [Online] Retrieved from http://www.haaretz.co.il/gallery/fashion/.premium-1.2524588

Smaill, B. (2013). Sofia Coppola: Reading the Director. *Feminist Media Studies, 13*(1), 148–162.

Tamir, S. (2014). There Is Something About Israeli Girls Beyond Beauty. *Fashion Forward.* [Online] Retrieved from http://fashionforward.mako.co.il/news/86781/

Thompson, P. (2010). The Capitalist Labour Process: Concepts and Connections. *Capital & Class, 34*(1), 7–14.
Virtanen, A. (2004). General Economy: The Entrance of Multitude into Production. *Ephemera: Theory & Politics in Organization, 4*(3), 209–232.
Warhurst, C., & Nickson, D. (2007). Employee Experience of Aesthetic Labour in Retail And Hospitality. *Work, Employment and Society, 21*(1), 103–120.

Index

Note: Page numbers with "n" denote footnotes.

A.S. Elias et al. (eds.), *Aesthetic Labour*,
DOI 10.1057/978-1-137-47765-1

G

H

104830

Lightning Source UK Ltd.
Milton Keynes UK
UKHW02f0639090518
322322UK00019B/767/P

9 781349 693313